ADVANCED PROGRAMMER'S GUIDE TO UNIX SYSTEM V

Rebecca Thomas, PhD

Lawrence R. Rogers

Jean L. Yates

Osborne **McGraw-Hill**
Berkeley, California

Published by
Osborne McGraw-Hill
2600 Tenth Street
Berkeley, California 94710
U.S.A.

For information on translations and book distributors
outside of the U.S.A., please write to Osborne/McGraw-Hill
at the above address.

UNIX is a trademark of Bell Laboratories

Advanced Programmers Guide to UNIX™ System V

123456789 DODO 898765

ISBN 0-07-881211-9

Cindy Hudson, Aquisitions Editor

CONTENTS

PREFACE

UNIX System V marks the beginning of an aggressive and comprehensive approach to the UNIX Operating System by AT&T. AT&T now sells, supports, and trains users on UNIX System V and on their 3B line of computers. UNIX System V has been endorsed by four major silicon vendors in the United States, namely Motorola, Intel, Zilog, and National Semiconductor, as well as several other vendors who build hardware that uses the UNIX Operating System. Clearly, UNIX System V is the standard version of the UNIX Operating System for applications and their development.

A Programmer's Guide to UNIX System V addresses the needs of programmers who must use UNIX System V to build software. It explains and gives examples that show how to use the Bourne and C Shells, the **vi** and **ex** text editors, the C compiler, library archives, the **make** utility, subroutines, and system calls. More importantly, **A Programmer's Guide to UNIX System V** also teaches the UNIX System programming philosophy which concentrates on the content of programs and their user interface. To learn to use all features explained in **A Programmer's Guide to UNIX System V**, you must know the C language and have access to a computer running UNIX System V.

A Programmer's Guide to UNIX System V also presents a concise and complete explanation of the new interprocess communication features available in UNIX System V. These features are essential to building reliable distributed systems with performance characteristics required by commercial applications software.

A book of this size requires much help in its production. I would like to thank several people for their assistance in various aspects of this book.

First, I would like to thank Ms. Jean Yates for allowing me to work on this project. As an unproven writer, I appreciate her confidence in letting me contribute to **A Programmer's Guide to UNIX System V**.

Second, I thank my wife, JoAnn, and Roberta C. Schott for their comments on the grammar, punctuation, and clarity of the sections of the book that they reviewed.

Next, I want to thank Clarice Belusar, David Chodorow, Beth Hemmelgarn, and Michael Rissman, who read the book and made valuable comments on its content.

I would also like to thank Dr. Karl Zaininger and Mr. Thomas Murphy of Siemens Corporate Research and Support, Inc., Research and Technology

Laboratories in Princeton, NJ. They let me take time away from my assigned duties with the Systems Software Group to devote my efforts to finishing this book.

Finally, I would like to thank my 2 year old son Benjamin who couldn't spend time playing downstairs because his Daddy had to write, rewrite, and edit a large stack of paper that looked fun to play with. Some day, Benjamin, you'll understand.

Lawrence R. Rogers

CHAPTER 1

INTRODUCTION TO UNIX PROGRAMMING

A. INTRODUCTION

Programming. The UNIX system was developed to increase your productivity and to reduce the effort you spend writing programs. The UNIX system is built around several utilities, a hierarchal file structure, powerful command languages, and a structured software tool design philosophy that is essential to producing reliable, maintainable, portable, and practical programs. These characteristics make the UNIX system one of the most popular software development systems available today.

This book is a guide to the software tools in the UNIX system that help you write better programs quickly and easily. You probably should not read it from cover to cover relaxed in an armchair by a roaring fire some evening after dinner. Instead, **A Programmer's Guide to UNIX System V** is meant to be a practical book that guides you through the programming parts of the UNIX system at your terminal's side. It shares the combined experience of several professional programmers with:

- the applications and systems programmer who must develop commercial software using the UNIX system,

- the student who is learning to program using the UNIX system, and

- the hobbyist who wants to write programs for home use.

A Programmer's Guide to UNIX System V complements the existing the UNIX system reference manuals, tutorials, and utility documents. It requires some familiarity with the C language and experience using the UNIX system.

A Programmer's Guide to UNIX System V should not be the first book you read when you are beginning to learn the UNIX system. It doesn't tell you how to login to the UNIX system, how to use the text editor, or how to use programs like **ls**, **rm**, and **cd**. To learn these parts of the UNIX system, refer to the **UNIX System V - Release 2.0 User Reference Manual** distributed with the UNIX system and **A User's Guide to the UNIX System**, by Rebecca Thomas, PhD, and Jean Yates, published by Osborne/McGraw-Hill.

This book contains opinions and recommendations on those features of the UNIX system that you should use and those features that you should avoid. It shows how to combine features to solve typical programming problems encountered in problem solving. In almost all cases, the programming examples shown in succeeding chapters are more than just academic exercises that show a feature of the UNIX system. These examples are instructional and they provide a foundation for building more elaborate problem solutions. As a programmer, you are encouraged to use the techniques, philosophies, and code shown in this book.

B. THE SOFTWARE TOOL DESIGN PHILOSOPHY

A Programmer's Guide to UNIX System V shows you how to use and write a specific class of programs called software tools. A *SOFTWARE TOOL*, as defined by Kernighan and Plauger in **Software Tools**, is a program that:

- "solves a general problem, not a special case,

- and is so easy to use that people will use it instead of building their own."

The concepts of versatile and convenient software are the basis of a programming philosophy that focuses on software tools. This book emphasizes the software tools philosophy, and we have used it in writing the programs shown as examples.

The UNIX system contains several programs that comply with the definition of a software tool. Among them are programs that create and manipulate text, programs that analyze text files, and programs that format text files to produce high-quality hard copy suitable for publication. One characteristic of these tools is that they operate on ordinary text files, which means that you can read the input and output files by simply listing them on a terminal.

You should know what software tools are available in the UNIX system before you begin to design and write your own software tools. The **UNIX System V - Release 2.0 User Reference Manual** and **UNIX System V - Release 2.0 Programmer Reference Manual** tell you what software tools your system provides. In many instances, the right tool is already available to solve your problem.

When you must write a software tool to solve a problem, design it to solve only that problem. Avoid overloading a tool with excess functionality that clutters its interface and makes it difficult to use. If you need to solve another problem, build a different tool. For example, the C compiler solves the general problem of compiling C language programs. It does not list a C language program nor does it intersperse error messages into C language program.

Make sure you understand the problem you're trying to solve before you begin an in-depth design of a software tool. A well-written tool that doesn't solve the problem at hand is of little use.

Design your new software tool so that you can begin to test it early in the design phase. Ideally, you should begin testing after a few weeks of designing. This technique lets you try your tool to see if works as expected. If it doesn't work properly, don't hesitate to throw it away. All too often, a problem statement is changed to match the programmed solution because testing started late in the development cycle after much time, effort, and money had already been spent.

The tools you design should be filters wherever possible. A *FILTER* is a software tool that reads its input from the standard input file – typically your terminal's keyboard – and writes its output on the standard output file – typically your terminal's screen. The command languages available with the UNIX system let you replace these standard input and standard output files with arbitrary files when necessary.

The tools you design should also be portable, meaning that they only need to be recompiled on other the UNIX system systems to make them usable. To help achieve this, use the subroutines defined in Section 3 of the **UNIX System V - Release 2.0 Programmer Reference Manual** and explained in Chapter 6 of this book. However, if you must use the system calls found in Section 2 and Chapter 7, localize them in a small subset of the subroutines that make up your software tool, and then call only those subroutines.

Finally, when you write the code for a software tool, use the following guidelines:

- Write code that is as clear and as simple as possible. The C language can be difficult to read if you combine all syntactic features in a single statement. Break complicated constructions into several easy to understand statements for the sake of readability. **A Programmer's Guide to UNIX System V** shows by example a proven coding style for C language programs and Bourne and C Shell procedures. This style helps to make your programs more readable and error-free.

- Use the flow control structures provided by the C language to make your programs readily understandable and easy to follow. Avoid using the goto statement except where necessary.

- Limit the size of subroutines to 100 lines or less. This makes your subroutines easier to comprehend.

- Wherever possible, allow only one entrance into and one exit out of a subroutine. This minimizes a subroutine's interfaces to the outside world.

- Design a subroutine to have well-defined inputs and outputs, and to do a single job. This allows a subroutine to be rewritten and improved, if necessary, without disturbing the rest of a program, as long as the new version conforms to the subroutine's original definition.

- Store closely related subroutines in a single file.

● Design tools to work with other tools. This makes your tools more widely applicable and therefore more usable.

C. USING THIS BOOK WITH OTHER DOCUMENTATION

This book is not the final word on the syntax of programs, subroutines, and system calls in the UNIX system. The precise syntax of all programs, system calls, subroutines, and other constructs can be found in the **UNIX System V - Release 2.0 User Reference Manual** and **UNIX System V - Release 2.0 Programmer Reference Manual**. The user reference manual has two sections and the programmer reference manual has seven sections. These sections are highlighted below.

User Reference Manual - Section 1 - Programs
This section describes, albeit briefly, most of the programs and utilities in the UNIX system you will need. Programs and utilities for the system administrator are explained in the **UNIX System V - Release 2.0 Administrator Reference Manual**.

User Reference Manual - Section 6 - Games
This section describes the games available with the UNIX system.

Programmer Reference Manual - Section 2 - System Calls
This section describes the UNIX system kernel level interface as a set of subroutine calls. System calls are easy to make from a C program, and system calls let you access the resources of your computer.

Programmer Reference Manual - Section 3C and 3S - Subroutines
This section describes the C language library of subroutines and the Standard I/O subroutines available in the UNIX system. Among those described are subroutines for buffered input and output, and process control.

Programmer Reference Manual - Section 3M - Math Subroutines
This section describes the subroutines in the math library.

Programmer Reference Manual - Section 3X - Specialized Subroutines
This section describes the curses and terminfo subroutines, the common object file format subroutines, memory allocation subroutines, and regular expression handling subroutines.

Programmer Reference Manual - Section 3F - FORTRAN Subroutines
This section describes the subroutines in the FORTRAN library.

Programmer Reference Manual - Section 4 - Formats
This section specifies the formats of certain files in the file system, such as the password file, /etc/passwd. System administrators and system programmers should find this section useful.

Programmer Reference Manual - Section 5 - Miscellaneous Facilities
This section describes macro packages, character sets, and the format of commonly used files.

Manual pages are organized in alphabetical order within a section, and each page has the following format:

NAME   The **NAME** section identifies the program, system call, subroutine, file, or convention that the page describes. A single page may show several items. For example, the **printf** page also shows the **fprintf**() and **sprintf**() subroutines. To find these additional items, use the permuted index located at the beginning of the **UNIX System V - Release 2.0 User Reference Manual** or **UNIX System V - Release 2.0 Programmer Reference Manual** just after the table of contents.

SYNOPSIS   The **SYNOPSIS** section describes the syntax of the item. If the page describes a program, the synopsis shows all options and arguments that may be used when running the program. If the page describes a subroutine or a system call, then the synopsis shows the parameters, the parameter types, and the type of the value returned by the system call or subroutine. If no return type is shown, the integer type should be assumed.

DESCRIPTION   The **DESCRIPTION** section gives a brief explanation of the program, subroutine, or system call and describes how to use it.

FILES   The **FILES** section lists all files that the program, subroutine, or system call uses to do its job.

SEE ALSO   The **SEE ALSO** section lists other pages related to the page you are reading.

DIAGNOSTICS   The **DIAGNOSTICS** section defines the return values and lists the error messages that the program, system call, or subroutine can produce. Unfortunately, this section is incomplete for most manual pages.

BUGS   The **BUGS** section defines the set of conditions that the item should handle but cannot.

All other documentation provided with the UNIX system is contained in the following guides and manuals.

● **UNIX System V - Release 2.0 User Reference Manual**

- UNIX System V - Release 2.0 Programmer Reference Manual
- UNIX System V - Release 2.0 Administrator Reference Manual
- UNIX System V System Release Description 2.0
- UNIX System V - Release 2.0 Error Message Reference Manual
- UNIX System V - Release 2.0 Administrator Guide
- UNIX System V - Release 2.0 Operator Guide
- UNIX System V User Guide
- UNIX System V - Release 2.0 Support Tools Guide
- UNIX System V - Release 2.0 Programming Guide
- UNIX System V - Release 2.0 Graphics Guide

D. COMING ATTRACTIONS

The remaining eight chapters of this book describe and show examples of the programming features of the UNIX system. They move from an overview of the UNIX system, through the Bourne Shell, programming philosophies, tools, and the kernel interface, to shell programming using the Bourne Shell and the C Shell. The emphasis throughout these chapters is on problem solving using the software tools design philosophy.

The following paragraphs give a brief synopsis of the remaining chapters.

Chapter 2: An Overview of the UNIX System
This chapter briefly explains the UNIX system. It explains how the UNIX system is structured, the file structure, and the kernel. Chapter 2 provides a base that Chapters 3 through 9 build on to help you better understand the UNIX system philosophy and its capabilities.

Chapter 3: Using the Bourne Shell Interactively
The Bourne Shell is an appropriately named program because it surrounds the UNIX system kernel. Though it is only one of several programs available in the UNIX system, the Bourne Shell plays an essential role in your use of the UNIX system because it provides access to all other features in the UNIX system. The Bourne Shell is a sophisticated command interpreter that handles much of the input and output requirements of your programs.

Chapter 4: Basic C Language Development Tools
This chapter focuses on the C language development tools available in the UNIX system. It explains those features of the **ex** and **vi** text editors that help you enter and edit C language source files, the C compiler system, library archives, and the **make** program. This chapter is essential to writing programs in the C language.

Chapter 5: Forging a Software Tool

Once you know how to use the C language program development tools described in Chapter 4, you can design your own software tools. Chapter 5 describes the characteristics of good UNIX system software tools and lists seven guidelines for writing programs. The most important of these is the way that a program interprets its arguments. Chapter 5 shows the **scf**() subroutine that was designed to encourage a standard format for options, option arguments, and file names. **scf**() is used throughout this book to interpret arguments in C language programs and in shell procedures.

Chapter 6: The Standard UNIX Subroutine Library

The UNIX system provides several portable subroutines that do important jobs. Chapter 6 describes 62 of the more useful subroutines available in the UNIX system and shows examples of how to use them.

Chapter 7: Introduction to UNIX System Calls

This chapter describes part of the system call interface to the UNIX system. It is especially useful to systems programmers who need access to the lower level functions available in the UNIX system. Just as a shell is the user interface to the UNIX system, system calls are the C programmer interface.

Chapter 8: Programming the Bourne Shell

The Bourne Shell also provides a programming interface that you can use to coordinate software tools to build a problem solution. Although a Bourne Shell procedure cannot directly access the kernel nor execute as quickly as a program written in the C language, it can interactively manipulate files, processes, and other operating system resources. The Bourne Shell interprets a shell procedure, which lets you build software tools to solve a problem faster than you can with the C language. Shell programming is the recommended way to build prototype problem solutions to more fully understand a problem's scope.

Chapter 9: The Berkeley C Shell

This chapter describes the interactive and programming use of the Berkeley C Shell. It includes revisions of examples from Chapters 3 and 8 to let you compare the two shells to decide which is more suited to the problem you are solving.

A Programmer's Guide to UNIX System V uses the following conventions for showing various items:

- All program names are shown in boldface. For example, **grep**.

- All subroutine and system call names are shown boldface, followed by a set of parenthesis. For example, **fprintf**().

- All file names are shown in italics. For example, *letc/passwd*.

- All keywords are shown in upper case italics and are defined in Appendix A. For example, *PROCESS*.

- All definitions are enclosed in a double box. Definitions are summarized in Appendix B. For example,

Sample Definition

DEFINITION 0. Sample Definition

Finally, all programs and shell procedures are listed with the **number** program. **number** is not a distributed program, but was written specifically for **A Programmer's Guide to UNIX System V**. Its source is shown in figure 1.D.1.

```
$ number number.c
 1      /*
 2       *          number
 3       *                  number a file
 4       */
 5
 6      #include <stdio.h>
 7
 8      main(argc, argv)
 9      int argc;
10      char *argv[];
11      {
12              FILE *fp;
13              char buf[BUFSIZ];
14              int rc = 1, n, x;
15
16              if (argc != 2) {
17                      fprintf(stderr, "usage: %s file\n", argv[0]);
18              } else if ((fp = fopen(argv[1], "r")) == (FILE *) NULL) {
19                      perror(argv[1]);
20              } else {
21                      for (x = 0; fgets(buf, sizeof(buf), fp) != (char *) NULL; x++);
22                      fseek(fp, 0L, 0);
23                      if (x < 10) {
24                              x = 1;
25                      } else if (x < 100) {
26                              x = 2;
27                      } else {
28                              x = 3;
29                      }
30                      for (n = 1; fgets(buf, sizeof(buf), fp) != (char *) NULL; n++) {
31                              fprintf(stdout, "%*d\t", x, n);
32                              fputs(buf, stdout);
33                      }
34                      fclose(fp);
35                      rc = 0;
36              }
37              exit(rc);
38      }
$ []
```

Figure 1.D.1

number first counts the lines in the file given as the first argument. **number** then rereads the file and prints each line prefaced with a line number followed by a tab character. Line numbers are printed so that the line number of the last line in the file is left justified.

When you finish this book, you should be well-versed in both the programming philosophy of the UNIX system and the techniques available to put it into practice.

CHAPTER 2

AN OVERVIEW OF THE UNIX SYSTEM

A. INTRODUCTION

The UNIX system is a time-sharing, multi-tasking system. It is a modular, integrated set of software that resides on and coordinates a computer system's resources. The UNIX system serves as the interactive interface between you and a computer system.

The UNIX system is not a real-time system nor was it designed to be real-time. It does not guarantee that a program will be able to respond to an event (e.g. typing a character on a keyboard) within a certain amount of time. While some vendors have made real-time extensions to UNIX, the standard versions of the UNIX system do not contain these extensions.

The UNIX system is not structured as a single operating system program. Instead, it is a team of programs that work with the operating system program to do certain jobs. Since most people who use the UNIX system don't use all its features, they only learn it through a few programs. These users develop a model of the UNIX system based on the programs they use. For those interested in running only a few applications, an in-depth knowledge of how the UNIX system works is not essential. However, for those who must develop software systems that are in resonance with the UNIX system and all it has to offer, detailed knowledge of it is essential.

This chapter explains the major elements of the UNIX system. Even if you know the UNIX system and other operating systems, you should read this chapter. It gives a general view and provides information that lets you use the UNIX system more effectively.

B. THE STRUCTURE OF THE UNIX SYSTEM

Most operating systems consist of:

- a central operating system program,
- an assortment of utilities and applications software, and
- a file structure.

The central operating system program supports and coordinates all programs and controls all physical resources. It runs programs that use the CPU, memory, disks, tapes, printers, terminals, and any other hardware so that these programs use resources efficiently and do not interfere with each other.

There are two basic types of programs. The first type is called a *UTILITY*. A utility is a program that does an auxiliary job such as linking programs, converting files from one format to another, and editing files. The second type is called an *APPLICATION*. An application is a program that helps you solve problems that are not directly computer related. Examples are accounting systems, personal calendar management, and games. Applications are either bundled with the central operating system program and its utilities, or sold as accessories.

The UNIX system has the elements listed above, except they are structured differently. The UNIX system consists of a *KERNEL* – the operating system program – that is only a skeleton of the traditional operating system program. The UNIX system kernel does only the low level jobs necessary to schedule processes, keep track of files, and control hardware devices. All other typical operating system functions are done by utility programs written as software tools. The use of software tools instead of a single large operating system program distinguishes the UNIX system from other systems.

What makes the kernel/utility structure of the UNIX system work is the interface to the kernel, called the *SYSTEM CALL INTERFACE* and described in Chapter 7, and the interface to hardware devices, available through a type of file called a *SPECIAL FILE*. The table below describes some of the utilities that play a prominent role in the operation of the UNIX system.

UTILITY	DESCRIPTION
init	Initializes the process creation mechanism
getty	Conditions a terminal for a login session
login	Allows a login to the UNIX system
stty	Changes a terminal's characteristics
mkfs	Builds a file system
mknod	Builds a special file
fsck, fsdb	Repairs a file system
clri	Removes a file forcefully
mount, umount	Mounts and unmounts a file system
sync	Writes disk block images from memory to disk
nice	Controls a process' priority
ps	Monitors processes

The most important of these utilities are **init**, **getty**, and **login** because they allow you to login to the UNIX system. Figure 2.B.1 shows how **init**, **getty**, and **login** fit into the UNIX system as an example of how it is structured.

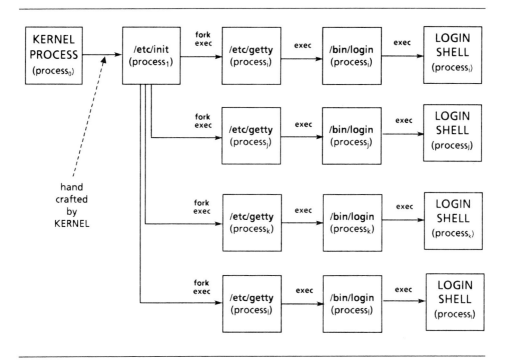

Figure 2.B.1

The UNIX system starts when a combination of firmware and software reads the kernel from a disk file named */unix* into the computer's memory and executes it. The UNIX system kernel first initializes various data structures and then creates the processes necessary to allow you to login. A *PROCESS* in the UNIX system is a running program.

One data structure initialized and maintained by the UNIX system kernel is called the *PROCESS TABLE*. The process table describes every running program. When a process begins, the UNIX system kernel builds a process table entry for that process. When a process ends, the kernel destroys its process table entry and marks that entry available for another new process. The number of entries in the process table defines the maximum number of processes that can be running at any time.

The UNIX system kernel is also a process. It starts when read from disk and executed, and ends when the processor is halted. Because the kernel is a process, it must have a process table entry, and because it is the first process created, it is assigned process ID 0.

To allow you to login to the UNIX system, the kernel must first create the one process that oversees the creation of all other processes in the login sequence. Called the *INIT PROCESS*, it is a program stored in a file named */etc/init*. The kernel reads and executes */etc/init*, and because it is the second process created, the kernel assigns it process ID 1. **init** runs from the time the kernel creates it until the kernel process ends, when the processor is halted.

Although the kernel and **init** are both processes, they differ in one significant aspect: **init** runs just like any other utility or application, but the kernel process does not. Instead, the kernel process runs in a mode that lets it access all special CPU features and all devices directly. Access to these machine specific elements is unavailable to utilities and applications except through the kernel. Because the kernel process has access to all CPU features and devices, it can arbitrate access to the CPU and to devices. All processes therefore rely on the kernel to allow them to use the CPU and devices.

init is in charge of creating the processes necessary to allow you to login to the UNIX system. In a conventional operating system, this responsibility usually lies with the operating system program. Because **init** is a conventional process that decides which terminals can be used to login to the UNIX system, it is easier to change which terminals are used for logins.

init is driven by the */etc/inittab* file that tells **init** what to do, including which terminals can be used as login terminals. For each terminal where a login is allowed, the */etc/inittab* file tells **init** to create a process that prints the login: message. To do this, **init** uses the **fork**() and **exec**() system calls, explained in Chapter 7, to start the program stored in the */etc/getty* file. This resulting **getty** process "conditions" the connection to the terminal so that the terminal can communicate with the computer, and then prints the login: message.

getty is driven by a file named */etc/gettydefs*. */etc/gettydefs* tells **getty** how to condition the terminal connection and the order of speed changes for connections that allow changes in speed, for example dial-up lines.

When you respond to the login: prompt, the **login** program replaces **getty**. A new process is not created for the **login** program.

If your account has a password, **login** prints the Password: message and turns off character echoing so that the password you enter won't be displayed on the terminal. When you respond to the Password: prompt, **login** checks to see that the password entered is correct. If it is correct, the program named in the password file replaces **login**. Again a new process is not created. The program named is usually either the Bourne Shell or the C Shell, and is called the *LOGIN SHELL*. You are now successfully logged into the UNIX system.

When you finish the session and log out, the login shell ends. The kernel tells the process that started the login shell process that the login shell process has ended. Recall that the process that started the login shell process is **init**, and that the process that caused the login shell to be executed was created first as **getty**, then **login**, and finally the login shell. When informed that the login shell process has ended, **init** begins the **getty**/**login**/login shell sequence again, if directed by the */etc/inittab* file.

This explanation of the **init**, **getty**, and **login** utilities is an example of the structure of the UNIX system. Each of these utilities runs as a user process and is not part of the operating system program.

C. THE FILE STRUCTURE

All utilities, applications, and data in the UNIX system are stored as files in the file structure. The UNIX system file structure is a device-independent structure that resembles an upside down rooted tree made from the following types of files:

- ordinary files,
- directory files,
- fifo files, and
- special files.

This file structure architecture provides a convenient and useful method for partitioning utilities, applications, and data into distinct units. Units can be shared among some users while at the same time restricting access of those units to other users.

ORDINARY FILES contain information stored in some format, and they can be thought of as leaves in the tree. The UNIX system does not impose any format on ordinary files. Examples of ordinary files are binary programs, source code files, and document files.

DIRECTORY FILES are nodes that tie the file structure together. They can be thought of as branches in the tree. A directory file has a predefined format explained in Chapter 7 and can only be written by the kernel.

FIFO FILES are files that allow unrelated processes to communicate with each other. They can also be thought of as leaves in the tree. Fifo files are typically used in applications where the communication path is in only one direction, and where several processes need to communicate with a single process, often called a *DAEMON PROCESS*. Each process writes a message to the fifo file, and the UNIX system guarantees that each individual message will not be overwritten by messages from other processes. The daemon process then reads from the fifo file. The UNIX system puts the daemon process to sleep until there is something for it to read.

Finally, special files are files that represent physical devices. They too can be thought of as leaves in the tree. When a process writes to a special file, the data written is sent to the associated physical device. Likewise, when a process reads from a special file, the data is read from the associated device and returned to the process. Special files are not really files, but instead they are pointers to device drivers located in the kernel that handle the data flow.

By integrating devices into the UNIX system through extensions to the file structure, the method for addressing a device is identical to the method for addressing a file. File names and device names may be used interchangeably. Finally, because devices are represented as files, file protections also apply to devices.

Figure 2.C.1 shows a typical file structure.

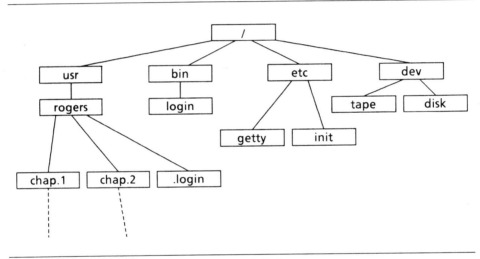

Figure 2.C.1

The root of the file structure is a directory file named /. Figure 2.C.1 shows that / contains the files *usr*, *bin*, *etc*, and *dev*, and that each of these files is also a directory file. In these directory files are more directory files (*rogers*, *chap.1*, and *chap.2*), ordinary files (*.login*, *getty*, and *init*), and special files (*tape* and *disk*).

No two files in a given directory can have the same name. Nonetheless, files in different directories can have identical names and remain distinct because the absolute path names (see below) for these two files are distinct. This means that files with similar functions can have identical names when stored in different directories. In file structures that do not provide a tree-structured or similar file partitioning, all file names must be distinct, meaning that files with similar functions cannot have identical names.

Files are addressed in two ways. Both addressing methods use the / character to separate directory names from other directory file names, ordinary file names, fifo file names, and special file names.

The first type of reference uses an *ABSOLUTE PATH NAME*, which is a file name that begins with the root directory of the file structure. For example, the absolute path name of the *.login* file in the *rogers* directory is */usr/rogers/.login*.

The second type of reference uses a *RELATIVE PATH NAME* that makes use of a property of every process in the UNIX system called the *CURRENT WORKING DIRECTORY*. The current working directory is the name of the directory in the file structure where a process is working. All file references that do not begin with the / directory name are path names relative to the current working directory.

Relative path names typically make use of two alternate names for directories. The first is .. (pronounced **dotdot**) which refers to the parent directory of the current working directory. For example, the parent directory of */usr/rogers* is */usr*. The second alternate name is . (pronounced **dot**) which is another name for the current directory. For example, if the current working directory is */usr/rogers*, then another name for the *.login* file is *./.login*.

Recall that the root of the file structure starts at the / directory. Below this directory are several other directory files that are distributed with the UNIX system. These directories are highlighted in the table below.

DIRECTORY	CONTENTS
bin	The *bin* directory contains the executable versions of the programs distributed with the UNIX system. These programs are essential to running and using the UNIX system.
dev	The *dev* directory is the repository for all special files.
etc	The *etc* directory contains programs and data files that are essential to running the UNIX system, and are usually used by the system administrator.
lib	The *lib* directory contains the *libc.a* archive that contains the subroutines and system calls described in Chapters 6 and 7 of this book.
stand	The *stand* directory contains several programs that run in a stand alone mode, that is, they run on a bare machine and do not rely on the UNIX system kernel.
tmp	The *tmp* directory is the place in the file structure where temporary files are created. The software tools you write should use */tmp* for temporary files built while a tool runs and not needed afterwards.
usr	The *usr* directory contains the files for each user.

From the perspective of a UNIX system user, the file structure resembles a rooted tree with branches and leaves. The tree can be traversed in both directions, and any point in the tree is directly accessible from any other point in the tree. Each process in the UNIX system is always located somewhere in the tree and has available to it all files in the tree, subject to each file's permissions. File permissions are discussed in Chapter 7, section B.7, on Access Control.

The kernel's view of the file structure is more detailed than that of a user. Within the kernel, the file structure is a collection of one or more *FILE SYSTEMS*. A file system is also a tree that contains a root, branches, and leaves. File systems are grafted together by attaching the root of one file system onto a directory of another file system with the **mount** utility. Figure 2.C.2 shows an example of a file system containing all user files grafted onto the */usr* directory.

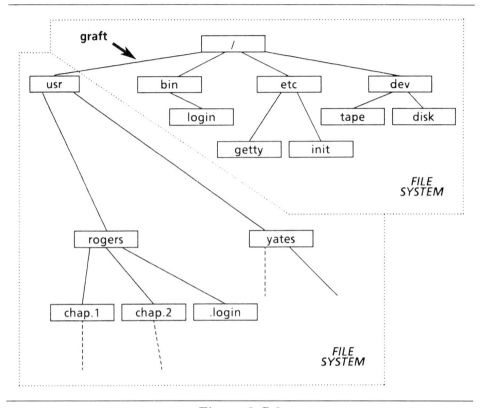

Figure 2.C.2

When the file structure tree is traversed from the root to the *chap.1* directory and back again, the UNIX system kernel moves from file system to file system in a way that is invisible to you. The **umount** utility severs the graft made by the **mount** utility and makes the files in the unmounted file system inaccessible until the file system is mounted again with **mount**.

When a file system resides on a disk that can be removed from a disk drive, the **mount** and **umount** utilities become even more powerful and useful. For example, sets of infrequently used information could be stored on separate disks. When the information on the disk must be accessed, the appropriate disk can be loaded into a disk drive. The file system stored on that disk can be made accessible with the **mount** utility. When the information is no longer needed, the file system can be made inaccessible with **umount** and the disk can be removed from the disk drive.

Each file system in the UNIX system has the same format that contains, in order, the following four sections.

- The *BOOT BLOCK*. The boot block usually contains a program that reads a file (e.g. */unix*) into the computer's memory and executes it.

- The *SUPER BLOCK*. The super block contains all information that describes the file system, such as:

  — The size of the file system.

  — The size of the i-list section of the file system which follows the super block.

  — The number of unallocated blocks in the data portion of the file system which follows the i-list.

  — The block numbers of some of the unallocated blocks in the data portion.

  — The last time that the super block was written to disk.

  — The file system type that tells the size of a logical block in the file system. UNIX System V supports file systems with 512-byte blocks and 1K-byte blocks.

- The *I-LIST*. The i-list is an array of *I-NODES*, where each i-node defines the properties of a file. Section B.5 in Chapter 7 describes the contents of an i-node.

- The *DATA BLOCKS*. The data blocks contain the data for all files in the file system and all blocks not yet allocated to files.

The structural information maintained in the file system by the UNIX system kernel is independent of the architecture and the properties of the media where the file system is stored. A file system is a logical structure that is bound to the physical structure of the media by a device driver. Therefore, a file system can be transferred easily to another storage medium without changing its contents.

In summary, the UNIX system file structure provides the means to organize all utilities, applications, and data. Furthermore, the UNIX system file structure also provides a straightforward way to transfer data between processes and hardware devices through special files. From the user's perspective, the UNIX system file structure resembles a rooted tree with branches (directory files) and leaves (ordinary, fifo, and special files). From the kernel's perspective, the UNIX system file structure is made up of file systems that are themselves rooted trees with branches and leaves that are grafted together to make a complete file structure. One important property of a file system, and therefore the file structure, is that it does not contain any information that depends on the medium where the file system is stored. This property adds to the portability of the UNIX system.

D. THE KERNEL

The UNIX system kernel is the core of the UNIX system. Every process interacts with the kernel in some way, either directly, by making a system call, or indirectly, by being allowed to run.

The kernel's main task is to arbitrate competition among all processes for the CPU. It selects a process with the highest priority that is ready to run and allocates the CPU to that process. *PRIORITY* is a measure of the importance of a process and is typically used for scheduling processes. The UNIX system dynamically changes a process' priority so that the priority of a computationally oriented processes will be lowered and the priority of a process not allocated the CPU in a while will be raised.

The process selected by the kernel then runs until one of the following happens:

- The process exhausts its interval. An interval is a small amount of time that the kernel gives to each process to allow all processes the chance to run.

- The process can go no further until some event happens. For example, when a process reads or writes a file, the process must wait until the information has been transferred.

- A process with a higher priority becomes a candidate to run because the event it was waiting for has happened. The process that was running is preempted by the process whose event happened.

When one of the above conditions happens to a process, the kernel stops that process and allocates the CPU to another process.

The total size of all processes typically exceeds the amount of main memory available. The kernel responds to this problem by moving processes between main memory and a secondary storage device, a technique called *SWAPPING*. Before a process can be allocated the CPU by the kernel, all parts of a process must be in main memory. To make room for a process, the kernel may be forced to swap other processes from main memory to secondary storage. The kernel's CPU allocation algorithms do not let processes atrophy on secondary storage. Every process is considered, even the swapped processes.

Another of the kernel's tasks is to service requests made by processes making system calls. Chapter 7 describes some of the system calls available with the UNIX system. A process makes a system call by executing a special machine instruction that causes the CPU to change its *CONTEXT* from a restricted mode, called *USER MODE*, to an unrestricted mode, called *KERNEL MODE*. Figure 2.D.1 shows the sequence of change in context, called a *CONTEXT SWITCH*.

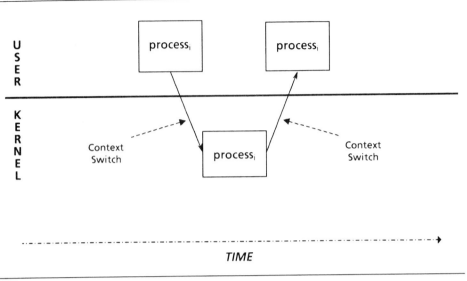

Figure 2.D.1

In the figure, process$_i$, executing in user mode, makes a system call that causes a context switch from user mode to kernel mode. Even though the CPU changes contexts, the UNIX system does not change processes. process$_i$ executes in kernel mode to service the system call.

When process$_i$, executing in kernel mode, finishes servicing the system call, the kernel causes another context switch back to process$_i$, executing in user mode. The kernel process, process$_0$, played no part in servicing the system call.

In contrast, figure 2.D.2 shows process$_i$ making a system call that causes a context switch that results in a *PROCESS SWITCH* to process$_0$, the kernel process. This usually happens when a process makes a system call that causes it to wait for an event.

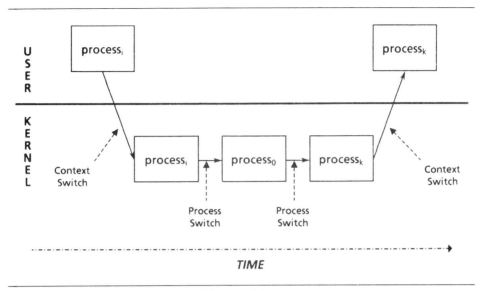

Figure 2.D.2

$process_i$, executing in kernel mode, switches to $process_0$. $process_0$ selects a process that is ready to run, swapping processes between main memory and secondary storage if necessary. $process_0$ changes to $process_k$, executing in kernel mode. $process_k$, executing in kernel mode, then changes context to $process_k$, executing in user mode.

The last major task of the kernel is accessing files in file systems in the file structure. The kernel accesses files when processes make file system related system calls, such as **open**(), **close**(), **read**(), **write**(), and **chdir**(), and process related calls, such as **exec**(). The kernel allows processes to view files from the user's perspective, where files are stored in directories in the file structure, and from the kernel's perspective, where files are accessed by reading and interpreting the file system's structural information that defines where files are stored.

In summary, the UNIX system kernel is a single program whose jobs are to allocate the CPU among competing processes, service requests from those processes, and access files. Processes are allocated the CPU in a time-sharing fashion that provides for preemption by processes with higher priorities. Process system calls are serviced by the process executing in kernel mode. The kernel process, $process_0$, only runs when a the CPU must be allocated to a different process. Finally, processes access the file system in response to various system calls.

23

The UNIX system is a combination of an operating system program, utilities, and specialized applications that work together to provide a time-sharing system that allows multi-tasking. It differs from other systems because it has a smaller kernel that relies on utilities to do most of the work necessary to let you login and do work. Because it relies on utilities instead of the operating system program, the UNIX system can be changed as required to support the applications that must run on it.

CHAPTER 3

USING THE BOURNE SHELL INTERACTIVELY

A. INTRODUCTION

A *SHELL* is a user program much like any other program in the UNIX system. It interprets the commands you type at the terminal and executes the programs you specify. Although not part of the UNIX system kernel, a shell uses much of the UNIX system kernel to execute programs, create files, and coordinate programs running in parallel.

Several shells currently exist, including the C Shell, written at the University of California at Berkeley and explained in Chapter 9; and the Bourne Shell, written by S.R. Bourne formerly of Bell Laboratories, Murray Hill, New Jersey. Each shell does the same job of interfacing between its user and the operating system, but each understands a different command syntax and provides different built-in functions.

This chapter describes the Bourne Shell, the interface program found on most UNIX systems. The Bourne Shell is explained at this point because you need to use a shell for the programs described in Chapters 4 and 5. While this chapter explains the Bourne Shell in particular, many of the concepts described here also apply to shells in general. Even if you intend to use the Berkeley C Shell as your standard shell, you should understand the ideas explained in this chapter before going on to Chapters 4 and 5.

B. INVOKING THE BOURNE SHELL

Recall from Chapter 2 that the UNIX system starts a shell for you when you login. Called the login shell, it operates interactively and uses $ to prompt you for commands. Recall also from Chapter 2 that ending the login shell logs you off the system.

Although the shell can act like an interactive interpreter by prompting for commands and processing them, it doesn't always have to be interactive. If you use a sequence of commands repeatedly, you can store them in a file and tell the shell to execute this *COMMAND FILE* instead of entering the commands individually. A file of commands is called a *SHELL PROCEDURE*; when you execute a shell procedure, a new shell is started to read the commands in the command file and execute them. Chapter 8 explains how to write Bourne Shell procedures.

C. CREATING BOURNE SHELL COMMANDS

Once you've logged into the UNIX system, you must issue commands to do your work. This section defines the term "command," describes how the shell locates programs named in commands, defines the structure of shell commands, and explains how to run commands in the background.

C.1 What is a Command?

A *COMMAND* is the unit of conversation between you and the shell. Syntactically, a command is a string of one or more characters that ends with a NEWLINE character. The shell breaks such a command into its constituent parts, called *WORDS*. For example, in the command:

$ ls -l /bin <NEWLINE>

Figure 3.C.1

the shell discovers three words: ls, -l, and /bin.

The first word of a command is a command built into the shell, the name of a function defined to the shell, or the name of a program that the shell must start to execute the command. If the word is a program name, then it must be the name of a file in a directory in the file structure. The file must have at least execute permission, and can be either a binary file, created by the loader **ld** as the last step in compiling and assembling a file containing a program written in a programming language, or a shell procedure.

But there is more to most commands than just a program name. A command may include options, file names, and other special shell operators such as redirection. The **UNIX System V - Release 2.0 User Reference Manual** shows which options and file names are recognized by each program distributed with the UNIX system. This chapter concentrates on redirection and other special shell operators that apply to all programs.

C.2 How the Shell Locates a Program

Once the shell has identified the program name selected by a command, it must then locate a file with that name in a directory. The shell searches the directories named in the PATH shell variable, in the order specified, for the file named in a command.

Figure 3.C.2 shows how to set the PATH variable to a string that names five directories.

$ PATH= / bin: / usr / bin: / usr / local / bin: / usr / rogers / bin:.

Figure 3.C.2

Directory names are separated by colons and the current directory is named by either dot (.) or a null directory name.

The assignment statement in figure 3.C.2 names, in order, the following directories:

/ bin
/ usr / bin
/ usr / local / bin
/ usr / rogers / bin
. (the current working directory)

Order is important because the shell searches the directories named in the PATH variable until it locates the program named in the command. If most of the commands you execute reside in one or two directories, those directories should appear first in your PATH variable. Less frequently used command directories should appear last.

When the shell finds a file in a named directory that matches the selected program name, the shell then checks the file's permissions for execution privileges. If the file lacks execution privileges, the shell continues the search in the remaining named directories. Once the shell finds a file that does have execute permission, the shell executes it. If the shell cannot find the appropriate file, it responds with:

program: **not found**

In UNIX System V Release 2.0, once the shell finds the location of a program in the file system, it remembers that location. For subsequent invocations of the same program, the shell uses this information instead of searching the file system.

If a program name contains a /, the shell assumes that you know where the program file is located. The shell does no directory searching, but does check to see that the file exists and that the file's permissions allow you to execute it.

C.3 Basic Shell Grammar

This section covers the basic structure of shell commands, including command line syntax, command grouping, and argument lists.

C.3.a Command line syntax Recall that a command is a string of one more characters that ends with a NEWLINE character, and that the shell breaks a command into words. Words of a command are usually separated by *WHITE*

SPACE, typically any number of spaces and tabs. Exceptions to this are white space in quoted strings, using either single (') or double (") quotes, and white space prefaced with the \ character. Recall also that the first word in a command is the program name.

Arguments for the program follow the program name. Arguments consist of options, option arguments, and file names; and the meaning of the arguments differs from program to program. Chapter 5 describes the *STANDARD COMMAND FORMAT* as the recommended way to define arguments for a program. Sadly, not all programs conform to the standard command format. Nonetheless, programs you write should adhere to the standard, and Chapter 5 provides a C language skeleton that you can customize to meet your program's requirements.

In general, commands follow the syntax shown below.

program__name -options file__names

options are prefaced by a dash (–) and appear before any file name arguments. Both *options* and *file__names* are optional.

C.3.b Command grouping A command usually ends with the **NEWLINE** character at the end of the command. However, several commands can also be grouped on one line by using a semi-colon as a command separator. The semi-colon is a directive to the shell that defines the end of a command and is not passed as an argument to the program selected by the command. For example:

```
$ who; date; ls
smith    ttya    Jun  1  08:19
jones    tty11   May 31  19:09
reagan   ttyR    Jun  1  08:49
rogers   tty12   Jun  1  07:46
Wed Jun  1 12:14:13 EDT  1983
Print
macros
part.A
part.B
part.C
$ □
```

Figure 3.C.3

produces the same output as:

```
$ who
smith    ttya    Jun  1  08:19
jones    tty11   May 31  19:09
reagan   ttyR    Jun  1  08:49
rogers   tty12   Jun  1  07:46
$ date
Wed Jun  1 12:14:13 EDT 1983
$ ls
Print
macros
part.A
part.B
part.C
$ ▢
```

Figure 3.C.4

The shell executes each command on a line before starting the next command on the line.

C.3.c Argument lists All words in a command, except those words that are special to the shell, are called *ARGUMENTS* and are passed to the program selected by the first word of the command. The shell provides a straightforward *short-hand* for specifying arguments, typically file names, that reduces the number of characters entered at the keyboard.

C.3.c.i File name generation File names can be as long as required, but only the first 14 characters are saved as the name of a file. File names can be built with alphabetic, numeric, and special characters, including non-printing characters such as the ASCII bell character. We recommend that file names contain only alphabetic and numeric characters and printable special characters that do not have special meaning to the shell.

C.3.c.ii Metacharacters When a command has been broken into words, the shell scans each word for special characters called *METACHARACTERS*. If a word contains metacharacters, the word is replaced by an alphabetically sorted list of the file names that match the word. If no file names match the word, the word remains unchanged.

The metacharacters that the shell recognizes are:

- The asterisk (*) which matches any string, including the null string. For example:

```
$ ls
a.out
count.c
datafilea
datafileq
program6.c
programa.c
programb.c
$ ls *
a.out
count.c
datafilea
datafileq
program6.c
programa.c
programb.c
$ ls data*
datafilea
datafileq
$ ls *.c
count.c
program6.c
programa.c
programb.c
$ ls count*.c
count.c
$ ls *file*
datafilea
datafileq
$ □
```

Figure 3.C.5

- The question mark (?) which matches any string that is one character long. For example:

```
$ ls
a.out
count.c
datafilea
datafileq
program6.c
programa.c
programb.c
$ ls program?.c
program6.c
programa.c
programb.c
$ ls ?????
a.out
$ ☐
```

Figure 3.C.6

- Brackets ([...]) which match a single character drawn from the enclosed character set. A pair of characters separated by a dash (-) means that all characters between the pair, inclusive, are in the character set, e.g. [a–f] is the same as [abcdef]. For example:

```
$ ls
1intro
2body
3conclusion
programa.c
programd.c
programe.c
$ ls program[a-f].c
programa.c
programd.c
programe.c
$ ls [1-3]*
1intro
2body
3conclusion
$ ☐
```

Figure 3.C.7

Furthermore, if the first character after the left bracket is an exclamation mark (!) then the characters in the character set are all characters not specified by the remaining characters. For example:

```
$ ls
1intro
2body
3conclusion
programa.c
programd.c
programe.c
$ ls [!1-3]*
programa.c
programd.c
programe.c
$ ▢
```

Figure 3.C.8

The shell accepts any combination of metacharacters to specify file names. For example:

```
$ ls
1intro
2body
3conclusion
Ab123.c1
Bz456.c4
programa.c
programd.c
programe.c
$ ls [A-Z][a-z]*.c?
Ab123.c1
Bz456.c4
$ ▢
```

Figure 3.C.9

Metacharacters are useful in selecting files for arguments to a program. However, you can easily select more files than you intend if you do not sufficiently restrict words with metacharacters. To discover which files match a word containing metacharacters, code the word as the argument to the **echo** program. **echo** will display its arguments as expanded by the shell without affecting any files. This can, for example, save you the trouble of restoring files mistakenly deleted by an unrestricted use of metacharacters. Figure 3.C.10 shows an example.

```
$ ls
1intro
2body
3conclusion
Ab123.c1
Bz456.c4
programa.c
programd.c
programe.c
$ echo [A-Z][a-z]*.c?
Ab123.c1 Bz456.c4
$ ☐
```

Figure 3.C.10

C.3.c.iii Escaping metacharacters At times, you may want the shell to treat metacharacters as regular characters and not replace words using them by a list of matching file names. One example occurs when using the **grep** program. **grep** selects lines from files that match a pattern, and the pattern can contain metacharacters. For example, if you wanted all words in the UNIX system dictionary that contain the vowels i and e in that order, you might code:

```
$ grep *i*e* /usr/lib/w2006
```

Figure 3.C.11

The shell breaks this command into three words and then replaces all words containing metacharacters by their corresponding expanded file names. If the current directory contains:

```
$ ls
fried
lied
tried
$ ▯
```

Figure 3.C.12

then **grep** is invoked as:

$ grep fried lied tried /usr/lib/w2006

Figure 3.C.13

and it searches for all lines with the pattern fried in the files *lied*, *tried*, and */usr/lib/w2006*. That is not what you wanted to do!

To force the shell to pass a word containing metacharacters to a program without replacement, use any of the following forms:

```
$ grep \*i\*e\* / usr / lib / w2006
$ grep "*i*e*" / usr / lib / w2006
$ grep '*i*e*' / usr / lib / w2006
```

Figure 3.C.14

The shell bypasses the replacement operation and passes the word *i*e* to **grep**. **grep** then looks in the file */usr/lib/w2006* for this string.

C.4 Running Commands in the Background

Now that you know the correct syntax for building shell commands, you should start doing some work by issuing some commands. You will soon discover that some commands that you enter in the UNIX system take a long time to execute. While these long-running commands execute, you could be doing something else, so the time you spend waiting at your terminal is wasted.

You can run a command in the BACKGROUND by ending the command with an ampersand (&). The ampersand is a directive to the shell and is not passed to a program as an argument.

A command that ends with an ampersand is started as usual, but the shell does not wait for the command to finish before prompting you for another command. You can run several commands concurrently when you end each command with an ampersand.

For example, you can force a compilation run in the background as figure 3.C.15 shows.

```
$ cc test4.c &
602
$ □
```

Figure 3.C.15

The shell displays the process ID of the command just started, and then prompts you for another command. A *PROCESS ID* is a positive integer that uniquely identifies each process.

Programs that run in the background still use the terminal as the standard output and standard error files, unless otherwise redirected. The standard input file is automatically redirected from the terminal to the empty file named */dev/null*. If the shell did not redirect standard input, then both the shell and the background process could be reading from the terminal at the same time. Any characters you type would be sent to one process or the other, but it is impossible to predict which process would get which characters. Since the standard input for all commands run in the background is redirected, all characters entered at the terminal go to the shell.

You can check the progress of a background process with **ps**, the process status command. **ps** displays a list of all processes you own that are currently in progress. For example, in figure 3.C.16:

```
$ cc test4.c &
602
$ ps -f
    UID  PID PPID C    STIME TTY      TIME COMMAND
  rogers   65   1 0 17:16:22 tty12   0:06 -sh
  rogers  602  65 0 18:49:39 tty12   0:00 cc test4.c
  rogers  605  65 0 18:49:40 tty12   0:03 ps -f
$ □
```

Figure 3.C.16

ps shows three processes: the login shell, the compilation, and the **ps** command. The TTY column names the terminal where the command was started and the TIME column shows the amount of CPU time used by the command. So far, process 602 hasn't done much, but process 605, the **ps** command, has used 3 CPU seconds to print the status of all the processes you own.

When you must wait for all background processes to end before going on, you should use the **wait** built-in shell command. **wait** is described in Chapter 8; but simply stated, **wait** suspends operation of your terminal until all background processes finish. As an example:

```
$ cc test4.c &
602
$ wait
```

Figure 3.C.17

is identical to:

```
$ cc test4.c
```

Figure 3.C.18

except that the background process' standard input is redirected from */dev/null.*

Finally, the **kill** program lets you end a background process before it finishes of its own accord. The first argument to **kill** is a signal number, and signal numbers are listed and explained in Chapter 8. All remaining arguments to **kill** are process IDs. **kill** sends each process the specified signal. If no signal is specified, the software termination signal (15) is sent. Signal 9 is a *sure kill* and will always end a process immediately. For example, in:

```
$ cc test4.c &
602
$ kill -9 602
602 Killed
$ □
```

Figure 3.C.19

kill ends the compilation program.

D. SHELL VARIABLES

Words in a command can also contain references to *SHELL VARIABLES*. The shell replaces a variable's reference with the variable's value. Shell variables provide a way to parameterize the commands you enter at the terminal.

The Bourne Shell offers five types of shell variables: user-definable, predefined, positional parameters, command substitution, and parameter substitution. While all five types are often used in shell procedures as Chapter 8 explains, only the first three are commonly used with an interactive Bourne Shell. This section defines the user-definable and predefined shell variables and shows examples of their use.   Section F defines the positional parameter shell variables which are used with shell functions in an interactive Bourne Shell.

D.1 User-Definable Shell Variables

A user-definable shell variable is simply a name to which a string value can be assigned. The name may contain only alphabetic and numeric characters and the underscore character (_). The string value can be a file name, a path name, a list of file names, or even an entire file's contents.

You can assign a string to a user-definable shell variable with an assignment statement in the form of:

name = value

Notice that there are no spaces between the variable name and the assignment operator (=) and between the assignment operator and the string value. Furthermore, a string value ends when the shell encounters any white space not prefaced with a \ or enclosed in quotes. The example below shows three assignment statements, assigning identical values.

```
$ A=this\ is\ a\ test
$ B="this is a test"
$ C='this is a test'
$ ▢
```

Figure 3.D.1

The value of a shell variable can be obtained by prefacing the shell variable's name with a $. In figure 3.D.2:

```
$ FILE=help
$ ls -l $FILE
-rw-r--r--  1 rogers   writers      72 Feb 27 09:55 help
$ cat $FILE
This file contains very little useful information, as you
might expect.
$ rm $FILE
$ ls -l $FILE
help not found
$ ▢
```

Figure 3.D.2

the shell variable FILE is first assigned a file name. The file's permissions, owner, and size are listed with **ls** and then the file's contents are displayed with **cat**. **rm** is used to remove the file, and **ls** is run again to verify the file's removal.

Shell variables may be undefined; that is, the shell may not have an assignment on record before a reference, or may be defined as the null string. In both cases, the value of the variable is the null string. The **echo** program can be used to display the value of a shell variable the same way that it was used to show expanded file names containing metacharacters. The figure below shows an invocation of the **echo** program; and although two shell variable values are to be substituted, no arguments are passed to **echo** because one string is undefined and the other is null.

```
$ B=
$ echo $A $B

$ ▢
```

Figure 3.D.3

Unless it finds a \c character sequence somewhere in its arguments, **echo** displays a newline after all arguments have been printed.

Sometimes it is necessary to append a string onto a variable's name. For example, you might think that in:

```
$ VERB = can
$ echo $VERBnot

$ ▯
```

Figure 3.D.4

echo would display:

cannot

but instead, **echo** displays only a newline. The variable name recognized by
the shell is VERBnot, so the shell replaces the reference with VERBnot's value;
here, the null string. To force the shell to separate the variable's name from
an appended string, enclose the name in braces as figure 3.D.5 shows.

```
$ VERB = can
$ echo ${VERB}not
cannot
$ ▯
```

Figure 3.D.5

A shell variable's value always replaces its reference except when the $ operator
is prefaced with a \ or when the reference is enclosed in single quotes. For
example:

```
$ A = testing
$ echo \$A
$A
$ echo '$A'
$A
$ echo "$A"
testing
$ ▯
```

Figure 3.D.6

When you select names for user-definable shell variables, be aware that the
shell recognizes seven special user-definable variables. These are listed and
explained below.

HOME   Typically your login directory. HOME's value is set when you login to the UNIX system. In addition, the change directory built-in command, cd, changes to the directory named by the HOME variable when invoked with no arguments. In other words:

    cd

is equivalent to:

    cd $HOME

PATH   The search path for commands. PATH names the directories to be used when the shell looks for program files referenced in commands. Directories are separated by colons.

CDPATH   The search path for the change directory built-in command. CDPATH names the directories to be used when looking for sub-directories referenced by the cd command. Directories are also separated by colons.

MAIL   The file name of your mail box. The shell checks the file named by the MAIL variable before displaying the prompt. If the file is non-zero in length and has been modified since the shell last looked at the file, the shell prints:

    you have mail

before printing the prompt. The MAIL variable reflects the file name that the **mail** program uses.

MAILCHECK   The MAILCHECK variable tells the shell how often in seconds it should look at the file named by the MAIL variable for new mail. The default is every 6 minutes, specified as 600 seconds, and an interval of 0 seconds causes the shell to look at the file named by MAIL before each prompt.

MAILPATH   The MAILPATH variable names the files to be checked for the receipt of mail. File names are separated by colons as in the PATH and CDPATH variables. To distinguish which file has received mail, the shell recognizes a % followed by text after the file name as a message to be printed when mail is received. For example,

```
$ MDIR = / usr / spool / mail
$ MAILPATH = "$MDIR / rogers%rogers-mail:$MDIR /
  writers:writers-mail"
$ MAILCHECK = 0
$ mail rogers
This is a test of mail
      .

rogers-mail
$ mail writers
How's the book coming?
      .

writers-mail
$ ▢
```

PS1   The primary prompt string. The PS1 variable defines the string used when the shell prompts for a command, and has a default value of $ followed by a single space.

PS2   The secondary prompt string. The PS2 variable defines the string used when the shell encounters a newline before the end of a command, and has a default value of > followed by a single space. For example, in:

```
$ echo "help
> me"
help
me
$ ▢
```

Figure 3.D.7

the shell displayed the secondary prompt because the command lacked the matching double quote when the newline at the end of help was entered.

IFS   Internal field separators. The IFS variable defines the set of characters that separate words and is used most often with the **read** built-in command explained in Chapter 8. IFS has a default value of space, tab, and newline.

D.2 Predefined Shell Variables

Predefined shell variables are variables that the shell sets for you in response to certain operations. Their values are substituted for references when their names are prefaced by $, just like user-definable shell variables. However, unlike user-definable shell variables, you cannot assign values to predefined shell variables.

The two predefined shell variables most commonly used with an interactive Bourne Shell are ? and !. The ? shell variable contains the decimal value returned by the last command run in the foreground. See Chapter 8, Section D, for a discussion of values returned by commands. For example, in:

```
$ grep root /etc/passwd
root:qWIFA9ZsYVcH.:0:1:0000-Admin(0000):/:
$ echo $?
0
$ grep Rogers /etc/passwd
$ echo $?
1
$ ▢
```

Figure 3.D.8

grep returns the value zero because the pattern specified, root, was found in the named file, */etc/passwd*. See Chapter 8 for the UNIX system conventions about return values.

The ! variable contains the process ID of the last program started in the background. Figure 3.D.9 shows an example.

```
$ cc test4.c &
602
$ ps -f
     UID   PID PPID  C   STIME TTY     TIME COMMAND
   rogers   65   1  0 17:16:22 tty12   0:06 -sh
   rogers  602  65  0 18:49:39 tty12   0:00 cc test4.c
   rogers  605  65  0 18:49:40 tty12   0:03 ps -f
$ echo $!
602
$ kill -9 $!
602 Killed
$ ▢
```

Figure 3.D.9

E. RE-DIRECTING INPUT AND OUTPUT

The UNIX system has many small, generic software tools. It seems reasonable to combine them to do some larger job. For example, you can connect the output of the **cat** program to the input of the **spell** program, and then send the list of misspelled words from the **spell** program to the line printer. The software tools approach to programming – where tools are combined to solve problems – is easy with the UNIX system because of input and output redirection.

It is easy in the UNIX system to *REDIRECT* a program's output to a file or another program instead of to the terminal screen. The shell contains special operators, called *REDIRECTION OPERATORS*, that are specified on the command line. Redirection eliminates the programming required to make individual programs flexible enough to send their output anywhere.

E.1 Redirection with Standard Files

When a program needs to interact with a file, the program must first open that file. The program supplies the file name to the UNIX kernel along with the operations, e.g. reading and writing, it wants to do on the file. If the operations are allowed, the kernel returns a *FILE DESCRIPTOR* and requires that all references to the opened file use this file descriptor. File descriptors, therefore, are the key to interacting with files in the UNIX system. Chapter 7 further explains file descriptors more fully.

When a program is started, the shell automatically opens three files for that program to use. These files are called *STANDARD INPUT*, *STANDARD OUTPUT*, and *STANDARD ERROR*; and their file descriptors are 0, 1, and 2 respectively. Recall from Chapter 1 that programs that use the the UNIX system software tool design philosophy read data from standard input, write data to standard output, and write diagnostics to standard error. Unless otherwise redirected as shown below, the shell connects these files to your terminal.

At times, you may want to change the source of input and the destination of output for a program. The Bourne Shell provides redirection operators that let you control the source and destination files from the command line. This means that programs don't have to be rewritten to interact with different files – only the command lines change.

The first redirection operator is > which causes the standard output of a command to be written to the file named as the next word in the command. Both the > operator and the following word are shell directives, and neither is passed to a program as an argument.

For example, in:

```
$ ls -l
total 0
-rw-r--r--   1 rogers   writers   0 Jun  1 12:28 programa.c
-rw-r--r--   1 rogers   writers   0 Jun  1 12:29 programd.c
-rw-r--r--   1 rogers   writers   0 Jun  1 12:29 programe.c
$ ls -l > /tmp/longlist
$ cat /tmp/longlist
total 0
-rw-r--r--   1 rogers   writers   0 Jun  1 12:28 programa.c
-rw-r--r--   1 rogers   writers   0 Jun  1 12:29 programd.c
-rw-r--r--   1 rogers   writers   0 Jun  1 12:29 programe.c
$ ☐
```

Figure 3.E.1

/tmp/longlist contains the standard output of the **ls** program as modified by the -l option.

If the file named by the > operator does not exist, the shell creates it; if it does exist, the shell deatroys the file's contents and replaces it with the command's standard output. If the shell cannot create a new or open the existing file, it prints a message and does not execute the command.

The second redirection operator is ≫ which is like the > operator except that the shell adds the standard output of the command onto the end of the named file rather than destroying and then replacing that file's contents. In the example below, the standard output of **echo** is added onto the end of the file named *message*.

```
$ echo This is a test. > message
$ cat message
This is a test.
$ echo Only a test. >> message
$ cat message
This is a test.
Only a test.
$ ☐
```

Figure 3.E.2

Again, if the file named by the ≫ operator does not exist, the shell creates it if possible.

44

Both the > and ≫ operators cause the shell to create the file referenced by the operator before the program named in the command is started. To see this, consider the following example:

```
$ ls
programa.c
programd.c
programe.c
$ ls > files
$ cat files
files
programa.c
programd.c
programe.c
$ □
```

Figure 3.E.3

files is created by the shell before the second **ls** command is started. **ls** finds *files* in the current directory and includes it in the list of files.

The standard error file can also be redirected just like the standard output file. Recall that file descriptor number 2 is associated with the standard error file. To redirect the standard error file from a program, preface the > or the ≫ redirection operator with a 2. There must be no white space between the 2 and the operator. The example below causes the standard output of the **grep** program to be saved in *found* and the standard error in *errors*. **grep** writes the lines that match the first argument on the standard output file and all error messages on the standard error file.

```
$ grep root /etc/passwd
root:qWIFA9ZsYVcH.:0:1:0000-Admin(0000):/:
$ grep root /etc/passwd > found 2> errors
$ cat found
root:qWIFA9ZsYVcH.:0:1:0000-Admin(0000):/:
$ cat errors
$ grep root /etc/passw > found 2> errors
$ cat found
$ cat errors
grep: can't open /etc/passw
$ □
```

Figure 3.E.4

Similarly, the standard input file can be redirected from a file with the <
redirection operator. Figure 3.E.5 shows an example.

```
$ cat message
The meeting today at 4 PM has been moved to tomorrow at 3PM.
Sorry for the inconvenience.
$ mail thomas rogers yates < message
$ □
```

Figure 3.E.5

The last type of redirection involves program-to-program communication.
Instead of creating temporary files to hold a program's output to be used
immediately by another program, the Bourne Shell lets you directly connect
commands together with *PIPELINES*. For example, instead of entering:

```
$ grep /bin/sh /etc/passwd > regshell
$ pr < regshell > print
$ lpr < print
$ rm regshell print
$ □
```

Figure 3.E.6

you can say:

46

```
$ grep /bin/sh /etc/passwd | pr | lpr
$ □
```

Figure 3.E.7

The pipeline symbol, |, forces the shell to connect the standard output of the command on the left of the pipeline symbol to the standard input of the command on the right of the pipeline symbol.

F. SHELL FUNCTIONS

The Bourne Shell in UNIX System V Release 2.0 provides a new feature called shell functions. A shell function is a collection of commands that is called by name and passed arguments from the command line. Shell functions are similar to shell procedures as described earlier in Section B, except that they are executed directly by the login shell. In contrast, shell procedures are executed by a new shell. Because of this, shell functions execute more quickly than shell procedures.

Shell functions are defined with either of the forms shown below.

---

function__name() *command*

function__name() {
command__list
}

DEFINITION 1. Bourne Shell Functions

---

where *function__name* is a name formed from alphabetic and numeric characters and the underscore character, and *command__list* is a list of commands to be executed. There is no white space between *function__name* and (). Figure 3.F.1 shows an example.

```
$ d() {
> date
> }
$ d
Mon Nov 19 15:18:40 EST 1984
$ ▢
```

Figure 3.F.1

With this shell function, the **d** command causes the **date** program to be executed. Notice that the shell continues to prompt for the contents of the *command_list* with the string defined by the PS2 shell variable.

The shell can also pass command line arguments to shell functions using positional parameter shell variables explained in Section C of Chapter 8. Briefly, the first nine arguments to a shell procedure and shell function are accessible as a positional parameter shell variable named according to the following scheme: $1 represents the value of the first argument, $2 represents the value of the second argument, etc, up to $9. Furthermore, all positional parameter shell variables can be referenced as $@, and the number of arguments passed to the shell function is represented by $#. Figure 3.F.2 shows another example.

```
$ lsl() {
> ls -l $@
> }
$ ls
programa.c
programd.c
programe.c
$ lsl
-rw-r--r--   1 rogers   writers   0 Jun  1 12:28 programa.c
-rw-r--r--   1 rogers   writers   0 Jun  1 12:29 programd.c
-rw-r--r--   1 rogers   writers   0 Jun  1 12:29 programe.c
$ ▢
```

Figure 3.F.2

Shell functions can reference other shell functions in *command_list*, but you must be careful of infinite recursion. For example:

```
$ x() {
echo testing
x
}
$ □
```

Figure 3.F.3

produces:

```
$ x
testing
testing
testing
testing
testing
testingDELETE
$ □
```

Figure 3.F.4

Finally, figure 3.F.5 shows another example where the **ls** shell function uses the **ls** program located in the */bin* directory to enable the C and F options while avoiding infinite recursion.

```
$ ls() {
> /bin/ls -CF $@
> }
$ /bin/ls
programa.c
programd.c
programe.c
$ ls
programa.c  programd.c  programe.c
$ □
```

Figure 3.F.5

A shell is the most visible program in the UNIX system because most commands are started by interacting directly with that shell. In particular, the Bourne Shell provides the capabilities necessary to control program execution and to specify the files used by these programs. Through variables and metacharacters, the Bourne Shell also provides an effective short-hand method that reduces the number of characters entered and therefore the number of errors made. While the Bourne Shell is not the only user-interface program available with the UNIX system, it is the most common. The Bourne Shell is an important part of the UNIX system, and understanding how to use it effectively cannot be overemphasized.

CHAPTER 4
BASIC C LANGUAGE
PROGRAM DEVELOPMENT TOOLS

A. INTRODUCTION

The **ex** and **vi** text editors, the C compiler system, library archives, and the **make** utility are among the most commonly used software development tools in the UNIX system. Combined, they provide a unified software development system highly regarded in the industry today.

In this chapter you will learn to use primarily the C compiler under the UNIX system while developing skills that apply to programming in general. For example, parts of the C compiler and all the library archive system also apply to FORTRAN-77, compiled Pascal, assembler, and other languages available under the UNIX system.

You should find the programming features provided by **ex** and **vi** - the screen editors we selected for software development - particularly helpful. Line numbering and automatic indenting are among several aids that **ex** and **vi** offer.

The C compiler system, the compiler most often used on the UNIX system, is also easy to use. Although it has a preprocessor pass, two compiler passes, an assembly pass, and a linking/loader pass, the C language system can be invoked with a single command. Of this set of passes, the only portion that is C language dependent is the first compiler pass. Other languages can work well in this system by substituting a different language processor for the C compiler. One such example is the FORTRAN-77 compiler.

The **ar** program combines object files into archives, also called libraries. Each archive is a single file that the linking/loader searches for needed subroutines. **ar** can be used to add, delete, move, update, and list files in libraries as necessary.

Also of interest is the **make** utility. To use this tool, you provide **make** with a simple description in **make**'s format that defines the way in which a software tool is made. The **make** utility is especially useful when you have several files that depend on other files, which in turn depend on still other files. In a large software product, it is difficult to remember how to create a specific piece of software. The **make** utility provides a convenient way to automate the entire creation process.

Throughout this chapter, two programming examples are used to show the features of the UNIX system's software development tools. These two examples are described in the sections that follow.

A.1 The copy Program

The first example program is a simple routine named **copy** that copies a stream of characters from a source file to a destination file. **copy** uses the **getchar**() subroutine to get a character from the standard input file and the **putchar**() subroutine to display the character on the standard output file. See Chapter 6 that describes the UNIX system subroutine library for a detailed explanation of these subroutines.

The **copy** program represents a class of programs known as filters as defined in Chapter 1. Recall that a filter takes its input from the standard input file and delivers its output to the standard output file. **copy** is shown in figure 4.A.1.

```
$ number copy.c
 1      / *
 2       * copy program
 3       *        copy standard input to standard output
 4       * /
 5
 6      #include                <stdio.h>
 7
 8      main()
 9      |
10              int c;
11
12              while ((c = getchar()) != EOF) |
13                      putchar(c);
14              |
15              exit(0);
16      |
$ □
```

Figure 4.A.1

A.2 The more Program

The second programming example, **more**, is an adaptation of **copy**. **more** passes one screenful of information from standard input to standard output and then prompts its user for instructions on how much more of the file to display. A space followed by a newline given in response to the prompt means that **more** should display the next screenful of the file, a newline means to display the next line, and any other response means to stop displaying immediately.

The **more** program is broken into three subroutines. One subroutine copies the standard input to the standard output. Another subroutine counts lines until a screenful has been displayed. The third subroutine displays a prompt, and accepts and interprets the response that defines the number of lines to be displayed next.

Figure 4.A.2 lists the file *main.c*, a variant of *copy.c* (see figure 4.A.1).

```
$ number main.c
1       / *
2        * more
3        *        main subroutine - copy input to output
4        * /
5
6       #include                <stdio.h>
7
8       main()
9       {
10              int c, colcnt, linecnt;
11
12              colcnt = 1;
13              linecnt = 0;
14              while ((c = getchar()) != EOF) {
15                      putchar(c);
16                      if (more(c, &colcnt, &linecnt) == 0) {
17                              break;
18                      }
19              }
20              exit(0);
21      }
$ ☐
```

Figure 4.A.2

In this variation of *copy.c*, *main.c* has been changed to include line and column variables used in other subroutines. These variables are passed to **more()** by address so that **more()** can change their values. In contrast, the character read is passed to **more()** by value, since its value in **main()** shouldn't be changed by **more()**.

The two remaining subroutines are shown in Figure 4.A.3 and Figure 4.A.4.

```
$ number more.c
1        /*
2         * more
3         *          more subroutine - controls command prompting
4         *          based on screen size
5         */
6
7        #include              "defs.h"
8
9        more(c, colcnt, linecnt)
10       int c, *colcnt, *linecnt;
11       {
12               int value;  /* returned by this function */
13
14               if (c == '\n' || *colcnt >= LINESIZE) {
15                       *colcnt = 1;
16                       (*linecnt)++;
17               } else {
18                       (*colcnt)++;
19               }
20               if (*linecnt == SCRNSIZE) {
21                       value = command(linecnt);
22               } else {
23                       value = 1;
24               }
25               return(value);
26       }
$
```

Figure 4.A.3

```
$ number command.c
1       /*
2        * more
3        *       command subroutine - prompts for command
4        */
5
6       #include                <stdio.h>
7       #include                "defs.h"
8
9       command(linecnt)
10      int *linecnt;
11      {
12              static FILE *fp = NULL;
13              int c, value;
14
15              if (fp == NULL) {
16                      fp = fopen("/dev/tty", "r");
17              }
18              printf("more?");
19              fflush(stdout);
20              if ((c = getc(fp)) == ONELINE) {
21                      *linecnt = SCRNSIZE - 1;
22                      value = 1;
23              } else if (c == ONESCREEN) {
24                      *linecnt = 0;
25                      value = 1;
26              } else {
27                      value = 0;
28              }
29              while (c != EOF && c != '\n') {
30                      c = getc(fp);
31              }
32              return(value);
33      }
$ ☐
```

Figure 4.A.4

The file *defs.h*, listed in Figure 4.A.5, contains definitions of MANIFEST CONSTANTS – that is, constants whose uses are obvious from their names.

```
$ number defs.h
1        / *
2        * more
3        *       definitions header file
4        * /
5
6        #define        SCRNSIZE         23
7        #define        LINESIZE         80
8        #define        ONELINE          '\n'
9        #define        ONESCREEN        ' '
$ ☐
```

Figure 4.A.5

In figure 4.A.6, these subroutines are compiled and then linked together. The executable version is stored in a file named *more*.

```
$ cc main.c more.c command.c -o more
main.c:
more.c:
command.c:
$ ☐
```

Figure 4.A.6

When **more** is executed, it accepts data from the standard input and sends it to the standard output. **main**() calls **more**() to calculate the column and line number after each character is output.

The **command**() subroutine, which is called from **more**(), interprets the response from the terminal after SCRNSIZE number of lines have been counted. Figure 4.A.7 shows an invocation of **more** using the on-line dictionary */usr/lib/w2006* as the input file.

```
$ more < /usr/lib/w2006
abilities
ability
able
about
above
absence
absent
absentee
absenteeism
absolute
absolutely
abstract
abstracts
academic
academically
academician
accept
acceptability
acceptable
acceptably
acceptance
acceptances
more?□
```

Figure 4.A.7

Notice that the cursor is poised after the more? prompt. If you type a space followed by a newline, another screenful is displayed. If you type a newline, one more line is displayed. To stop paging through the dictionary, type any other character followed by a newline.

Since **copy** and **more** will be used to show features of the UNIX system software development tools, you should understand how they work before reading the rest of this chapter.

B. EX AND VI FEATURES FOR EDITING PROGRAMS

You can use any of the UNIX system text editors for entering program text. However, the **ex** and **vi** text editors provide several options that make program entry easy. These options affect a program's format by encouraging you to enter source files organized with tabs and blank lines. This section

57

concentrates on the features of **ex** and **vi** that help you write programs using the UNIX system. For a complete description of **ex** and **vi**, see the *Ex Reference Manual* and *An Introduction to Display Editing with Vi*, both written by William N. Joy.

When the C compiler compiles a program, it is not concerned about the length and distribution of white space – that is blank lines, spaces, and tabs. The compiler treats any combination of consecutive blank lines, spaces, and tabs as a single delimiter that separates a symbol from the surrounding symbols.

The use of white space helps you to understand a program. Logically related expressions are physically grouped when surrounded by white space. White space is also used within expressions to improve readability. Indentation shows the relationship between sub-expressions.

This formatting style has a purpose: it improves readability which in turn helps to produce source files that have fewer bugs. For example, the C compiler does not give informative error diagnostics when braces ({}) are missing. If a pair of braces is missing, the entire sense of the program may be changed without the compiler even detecting an error. By using indentation, you can easily spot groups of statements that should be enclosed in braces.

The next six sections describe the **ex** and **vi** features that make entering and editing a program easier. These features are autoindent, line numbering, punctuation matching, cursor positioning, other useful features, and option enabling.

B.1 Autoindent

The autoindent option forces **ex** and **vi** to maintain the same level of indentation from one line to the next. At the beginning of each line, **ex** and **vi** add enough white space to align the new line with the previous line. When you enter more white space at the beginning of a line, the new indentation continues on the next line. White space is usually added one tab at a time, and tabs can be entered with the TAB key or the control-I (^I) key combination.

To decrease the level of indentation, use the end-of-file (EOF) character, usually entered by typing control-D (^D). Each time **ex** and **vi** receive an EOF character at the beginning of a line, they move the cursor back one tab stop meaning less indentation. This new level of indentation then continues on the next line.

Figure 4.B.1 illustrates the use of autoindent with the **ex** editor.

```
$ ex copy.c
"copy.c" [New file]
:set ai
:a
/*
 * copy program
 *          copy standard input to standard output
 */

#include        <stdio.h>

main()
{
^Iint c;

        while ((c = getchar()) != EOF) {
        ^Iputchar(c);
                ^D}
        exit(0);
        ^D}
.
:x
"copy.c" [New file] 16 lines, 167 characters
$ ▯
```

Figure 4.B.1

In this example, **ex** is used to create the *copy.c* file. The set ai command turns on the autoindent option, but initially **ex** assumes no level of indentation. Indentation begins with the body of the function **main**() in response to the ^I. **ex** then moves the cursor to the next tab stop and continues to indent one tab stop for each new line. Because the **putchar**() subroutine is part of the while loop, it should be indented one additional tab stop, so another ^I is typed.

The next line contains the closing brace (}) which is entered after first entering ^D. This command removes one tab and moves the cursor backward one tab stop, causing the brace to be vertically aligned with the while statement. Similarly, the closing brace of the program is placed at the left margin by prefacing it with another ^D.

Several **ex** and **vi** commands work with the autoindent facility. By entering zero control-D (0^D) at the beginning of a line, you can remove all indentation. **ex** and **vi** move the cursor to the left margin and forget the previous level of indentation for all new lines.

Using caret control-D (^^D) at the beginning of a line suspends indentation for the current line. **ex** and **vi** again move the cursor to the left margin, but they continue the previous indentation on the following lines.

Recall that you enter a tab character when you want to add white space for each indentation level. You can change the number of spaces that **ex** and **vi** display for a tab by changing the setting of tabstop (ts). By default, tabstop is set to 8. To change tabstop to 4, enter set ts=4, in command mode. This command reduces the amount of indentation **ex** and **vi** display for each tab to four spaces. This does not, however, affect the spacing of text outside the editor.

The shiftwidth is the complement of tabstop. Each time a ^D is entered, **ex** and **vi** reduce the indentation by the shiftwidth characters. Shiftwidth and tabstop are normally set to the same value.

For the next example, reinvoke **ex**, and give the command set sw=4 ts=4. This changes shiftwidth and tabstop to 4 spaces. As in figure 4.B.2, you will see that **ex** displays *copy.c* with tabs represented as 4 spaces instead of 8.

```
$ ex copy.c
"copy.c" 16 lines, 167 characters
:set ai
:set sw=4 ts=4
:%
/*
 * copy program
 *     copy standard input to standard output
 */

#include        <stdio.h>

main()
{
    int c;

    while ((c = getchar()) != EOF) {
       putchar(c);
    }
    exit(0);
}
:x
$ 
```

Figure 4.B.2

A shiftwidth of 4 is useful when entering programs that have many indentation levels. Most likely, all lines in a program will fit on the average terminal screen without wrapping around the screen.

Next are the ≪*n* and ≫*n* commands which work with both **ex** and **vi** to shift the *n* selected lines either left or right one shiftwidth, respectively. If *n* is

60

omitted, only the current line will be shifted. To use this feature with *copy.c*, first display the line main(). Next type one >> while in command mode and then display the contents of the edit buffer. Figure 4.B.3 shows this dialogue.

```
:/main()
main()
:>>
    main()
:%
/ *
 * copy program
 *      copy standard input to standard output
 */

#include                 <stdio.h>

    main()
}
    int c;

    while ((c = getchar()) != EOF) {
        putchar(c);
    }
    exit(0);
}
:□
```

Figure 4.B.3

The > command shifted the line main() one shiftwidth to the right.

If you use the **vi** editor, the $<x$ and $>x$ commands can be used to shift the display left or right one shiftwidth in terms of the objects x. Some objects useful when editing program source code include H, M, L, and nG. These shift all lines from the cursor to the top of the screen, the cursor to the middle of the screen, the cursor to the bottom of the screen, and the cursor to the nth line in the file. This feature is particularly useful when you add or delete a line that affects the indentation of other lines.

Figure 4.B.4 shows an example of the >L command. First, notice that the cursor is positioned over the i in int:

```
/*
 * copy program
 *     copy standard input to standard output
 */

#include      <stdio.h>

main()
{
        int c;

        while ((c = getchar()) != EOF)
                putchar(c);
        }
        exit(0);
}
~
~
~
~
~
~
~
"copy.c" 16 lines, 167 characters
```

Figure 4.B.4

While in the command mode, type >L to move every line between the cursor line and the end of the display one shiftwidth to the right:

```
/*
 * copy program
 *      copy standard input to standard output
 */

#include            <stdio.h>

main()
{
         int c;

         while ((c = getchar()) != EOF) {
                 putchar(c);
         }
         exit(0);
     }
~
~
~
~
~
~
~
7 lines >ed
```

Figure 4.B.5

The last line of the display – 7 lines >ed – tells you how many lines were changed by the >L command. By typing <L before you move the cursor, you can restore the screen to its original appearance.

B.2 Line Numbering

Another useful editing feature is line numbering. When you enable line numbering, a line number precedes each line of text that you enter. Line numbers are only printed on the terminal and are not part of the file. Line numbering is important because the C compiler reports errors by showing the line number in the file where the error occurred.

To enable line numbering, use the set nu command. This turns line numbering on for the duration of the editing session or until you enter the set nonu command.

Figure 4.B.6 shows what *copy.c* looks like when it is entered with automatic line numbering enabled.

```
$ ex copy.c
"copy.c" [New file]
:set nu
:a
    1  /*
    2   * copy program
    3   *     copy standard input to standard output
    4   */
    5
    6  #include                <stdio.h>
    7
    8  main()
    9  {
   10    int c;
   11
   12          while ((c = getchar()) != EOF) {
   13                  putchar(c);
   14          }
   15          exit(0);
   16  }
   17  .
:x
"copy.c" [New file] 16 lines, 167 characters
$ □
```

Figure 4.B.6

Both autoindent and line numbering may be set in the same command by entering set ai nu. To see which editing options have been changed from their default values, type set followed by a newline.

You can turn options off by using the set command and prefacing the option you want to disable with no. For example, you can turn off line numbering by entering set nonu. Figure 4.B.7 shows these **ex** and **vi** features.

```
:set ai nu
:set
autoindent number redraw term=c100
:set nonu
:set
autoindent term=c100
:□
```

Figure 4.B.7

64

The entry term=c100 displays the terminal name being used with the **ex** and **vi** editors.

To find the current value of a particular option, follow the option name, sw for example, with a question mark. To change the value of an option that accepts a value, use the command format set *option=value.* Do not use white space around the =. For example, type set sw=4 and set sw? while in command mode and observe the result that Figure 4.B.8 shows.

```
:set sw?
shiftwidth=8
:set sw=4
:set sw?
shiftwidth=4
:▢
```

Figure 4.B.8

The set *option*? command even works for options that do not have values. For example, set ai? shows if autoindent is currently enabled. That's why a ? is required with these so-called toggle options so that you can display their value without changing (by setting) it. You don't need the ? to display values for options that take a value. For instance, entering set sw displays the current value of shiftwidth without changing it.

You can list all options and their current values with set all. Figure 4.B.9 shows this.

:set all

noautoindent	open	tabstop=8
autoprint	nooptimize	taglength=0
noautowrite	paragraphs=IPLPPPQPP LIpplpipbp	tags=tags /usr/lib/tags
nobeautify	prompt	term=c100
directory=/tmp	noreadonly	noterse
noedcompatible	redraw	timeout
noerrorbells	remap	ttytype=c100
hardtabs=8	report=5	warn
noignorecase	scroll=4	window=8
nolisp	sections=NHSHH HUnhsh	wrapscan
nolist	shell=/bin/sh	wrapmargin=0
magic	shiftwidth=8	nowriteany
mesg	noshowmatch	
nonumber	noslowopen	

:□

Figure 4.B.9

For information on those options that are not discussed in this chapter, see the *Ex Reference Manual.*

B.3 Matching Parentheses, Braces, and Brackets with vi

A common mistake made in program entry is unbalanced parentheses, braces, and brackets. In a complicated expression, it is easy to lose track of the number of parentheses necessary to group a subexpression. Because the compiler finds symbols out of context, it often produces error messages that do not accurately pinpoint the missing parenthesis, brace, or bracket. For example, when the compiler reaches the end of a program that has one missing closing brace, it prints the misleading message *Unexpected end of file.*

You can use the **vi** command % to display the parenthesis, brace, or bracket that matches the one where the cursor is currently positioned. The editor moves the cursor to the matching punctuation character.

Intervening occurrences of the same symbol are counted by **vi** until the matching opposite symbol is found. Figures 4.B.10 and 4.B.11 show an example of this feature before and after the % key is entered.

```
/*
 * copy program
 *      copy standard input to standard output
 */

#include        <stdio.h>

main()
{
        int c;

        while ([](c = getchar()) != EOF) {
                putchar(c);
        }
        exit(0);
{
~
~
~
~
~
~
~
"copy.c" 16 lines, 167 characters
```

Figure 4.B.10

```
/*
 * copy program
 *      copy standard input to standard output
 */

#include              <stdio.h>

main()
{
        int c;

        while ((c = getchar()) != EOF[]) {
                putchar(c);
        }
        exit(0);
}
~
~
~
~
~
~
~
"copy.c" 16 lines, 167 characters
```

Figure 4.B.11

You can also force **vi** to point to the matching parenthesis, brace, or bracket automatically as you type the closing symbol. This option is called showmatch, and you turn it on by typing set sm while in the command mode. Each time a you enter), }, or], **vi** automatically positions the cursor over the matching (, {, or [for a short time. Unlike the % command, showmatch only works if the matching symbol is on the screen currently displayed. If the matching punctuation is not on the screen, the cursor will not move. In either case, **vi** rings the terminal bell if you enter a closing parenthesis, brace, or bracket when the matching open character cannot be found before it in the file.

B.4 Other Cursor Movement Commands

vi provides two more cursor positioning commands that let you move quickly through program files. These commands require that you place the first and last braces surrounding the body of a function on separate lines. These braces should be anchored to the beginning of those lines.

The commands [[and]], normally used for moving backwards and forwards to sections and paragraphs of text written using the -ms and -mm macro packages with **troff** and **nroff**, also recognize an open brace ({) in the first column as the beginning of a section of program text. When you enter]], the cursor moves forward to the next line that begins with a {. Similariy, when you enter [[, the cursor moves backward to the previous line beginning with {. To help you remember these commands, think of]] as a blunt, forward-pointing arrow and [[as a blunt, backward-pointing arrow.

B.5 Other Useful Editing Options

ex and **vi** provide several other options that are useful for programming. Some apply only to users with slow terminals – that is terminals operating at slow speeds. Others are generally helpful. These editor options are:

- beautify, bf – The beautify option forces the editor to refuse to accept nonprinting characters during inserts and appends, except for tabs, newlines, form feeds, and backspaces. This option is useful in noisy communication environments, for example when using higher speed modems.

- message, mesg – The message option prevents other users from writing on your screen using the **write** program.

- optimize, opt – The optimize option prevents the editor from doing an automatic carriage return after a linefeed when printing more than one line. For example, if the cursor is on column 20 and the next line begins in column 22, the editor can print a linefeed followed by a space to move to the next line instead of returning to the left margin and then advancing the cursor across 21 spaces.

- redraw – For terminals without cursor addressing, **vi** simulates an intelligent terminal using great amounts of output. This option is only useful at higher baud rates.

- scroll – **ex** and **vi** let you move rapidly through files without specifying line numbers or context patterns. When you enter a ^D as the first character on a line, **ex** and **vi** print the next scroll lines. scroll's value is settable.

- terse – The terse option forces the editors to print shorter error diagnostics.

- report – The report option specifies the threshold size before **ex** and **vi** report the number of lines effected by a command. The default value is 5, so that if a command changes more than 5 lines, a message appears stating the number of lines effected by that command.

- window – For terminals connected to machines at low baud rates, window should be set to a fraction of the screen's length. This reduces the time spent refreshing the screen. For example, setting window to 6 makes **vi** tolerable at 300 baud.

B.6 Installing Special Editing Options

You can enable autoindent, number, showmatch, and other special editing options by using the **set** command when in the editor command mode. These and any other editor options may also be installed automatically each time you start **ex** and **vi** by adding commands to your programming environment. There are different ways of doing this, and the method that you use depends on which shell you are using.

If you use the Bourne Shell, you should add two commands to the *.profile* file in your home directory. The *.profile* file is executed by the Bourne Shell each time you login to the UNIX system, but only if the Bourne Shell is to be used as your login shell. The commands you should add are:

EXINIT = 'set *options to be enabled and disabled*'
export EXINIT

Figure 4.B.12

If you use the Berkeley C Shell, you need to add only one command to the *.login* file, again found in your home directory. The *.login* file is the C Shell equivalent of the *.profile* file and its contents are executed each time you login to the UNIX system, but only if the C Shell is to be used as your login shell. The command to be added is:

---
setenv EXINIT "set *options to be enabled and disabled*"

Figure 4.B.13

No matter which shell you use, you won't be notified of an error in the option list you've defined until you start either **ex** or **vi**. Figure 4.B.14 shows what to expect if there is an error in the option list.

$ echo $EXINIT
set ai nu sm ax
$ ex copy.c
ax: No such option - 'set all' gives all option values
"copy.c" 16 lines, 167 characters
:☐

Figure 4.B.14

You can also place the desired commands to set, unset, and change editor option values in a file named *.exrc* located in your login directory. The **ex** and **vi** editors look for this file and execute the commands in it.

Once you've created a program file with **ex** or **vi**, you then need to compile it before you can run it. The next section discusses the C compiler and shows you how to compile a C language program source file.

C. The C Compiler System

COMPILERS are special programs used to translate programming language source files into working programs. If the programming language source files presented to the compiler follow the rules of the programming language, then the compiler produces an executable file that does what the programming language statements require. However, if the compiler finds statements in the file that do not adhere to the programming language rules, the compiler responds with error messages.

In addition to compilation and error detection, the compiler is also responsible for arranging the basic interfaces to the operating system by providing a suitable *RUNTIME ENVIRONMENT*. This environment includes file handling, basic I/O, and other connections with the operating system.

The **cc** program is the UNIX system compiler for the C language. The various tasks done by this compiler – macro expansion and file inclusion, compilation, optimization, assembling, and linking and loading – are divided among several UNIX system utilities. Figure 4.C.1 shows the flow of files through the utilities in the C compiler.

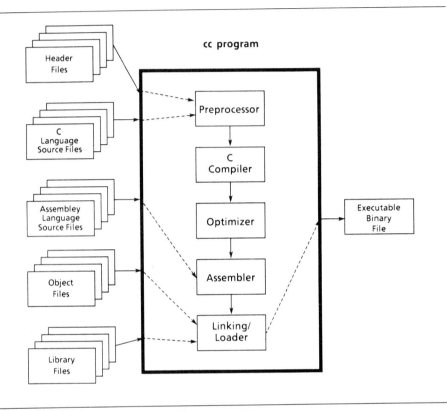

Figure 4.C.1

These utilities have been combined under the direction of a single program, named **cc**, that can be executed to compile a program. Figure 4.C.2 shows an example of the C compiler compiling *copy.c*.

Figure 4.C.2

The C compiler operates on the principle that "no news is good news." Since the compiler printed no messages, this means that *copy.c* was successfully compiled into a file named *a.out*, the default name of the binary executable file created by the loader, and that *a.out*'s permissions were changed to allow it to be executed.

To execute the **copy** program, type **a.out** as a command to the shell. To give **copy** some input, type a line of text followed by a newline. Finally, to send end-of-file to **copy**, type a ˆD on a separate line. **copy** ends and control returns to the shell. Figure 4.C.3 shows an example.

$ a.out
UNIX collects the line until a newline and copy echoes.
UNIX collects the line until a newline and copy echoes.
$ ☐

Figure 4.C.3

Note: The ˆD is not echoed by the UNIX system and will not be shown on any of the screens in this section.

The **cc** program controls a series of programs to produce an executable *a.out* file. Each program handles one stage in compiling a C language source program.

The programs **/lib/cpp**, **/lib/ccom** and **/lib/c2**, **as**, and **ld**, which represent the four primary stages in compiling a C language source file, can also be invoked separately. While this is often not practical, it is important to understand each stage of the compilation process. The four stages are:

- The preprocessor, **/lib/cpp**, is the first stage of compilation. It converts preprocessor directives, which begin with # in the first column of the source file, to a form suitable for the next stage of compilation. The preprocessor also optionally removes comments.

- The compiler, **/lib/ccom** and **/lib/c2**, next translates the preprocessor output to an assembly language source program.

- The assembler, **as**, reads an assembly language source program and creates an object file containing binary code and relocation information for the linking/loader.

- The linking/loader, **ld**, combines all relocatable object files given to the **cc** program with the standard libraries to produce an executable program file named *a.out*.

Options for the preprocessor, compiler, assembler, and linking/loader are given on the **cc** command line. This command line has the general form:

---

cc [-*option*...] *source_and_object_files* [-l*library*...]

DEFINITION 2. Suggested C Compiler Command Line

---

option are options for **cc**, **/lib/cpp**, **/lib/ccom**, **/lib/c2**, **as**, and **ld**. Options not recognized by **cc** are passed on to **/lib/cpp**, **/lib/ccom**, **/lib/c2**, **as**, and finally to **ld**. You can specify arguments for a specific part of the compilation process with the -W option to the **cc** program. This means that all utilities can be controlled by options on the original **cc** command line. The options that affect each stage of compilation are described during the discussion of each particular stage.

The **cc** program understands the options listed below that control the compilation process.

-c   Only compile the C language source program files, producing object files. Do not create an executable binary file by running the linking/loader.

-W*c,arg1[,arg2,...]*   Pass *arg1*, *arg2*, ... *argn* to pass *c* of the compilation process. Allowable values for *c* are: p02al, meaning the preprocessor, the compiler, the optimizer, the assembler, and the linking/loader.

The *source_and_object_files* are C language program source files, relocatable object files, and assembly language source files. They can be listed in any order on the command line. Last on the command line are any additional archive libraries selected by -l*library*.

C.1 The Preprocessor

The preprocessor is the first step in the compilation process. It interprets directives in the source code file, which always begin with a # in the first column, as commands that define how to change the source code. In particular, the preprocessor is capable of including named source files, macro substitution, and conditional compilation. The preprocessor produces a file that contains no directives.

C.1.a File inclusion The preprocessor creates a temporary file for the next stage in the compilation process by copying all files named in #include directives, see below, into the program code at the point where the directive occurs. These directives may be nested – that is, files that contain include directives may be named in other include directives. Nesting of include directives is not recommended because it is not clear to the program reader exactly which files are being included.

The syntax for an include directive is:

#include   *filename*

DEFINITION 3. Preprocessor include Statement

Include directives cause the preprocessors to look in a standard list of directories for the file to be included. If angle brackets (<>) surround the file name, the preprocessor uses */usr/include* as the standard directory. If double quotes ("") surround the file name, the preprocessor first uses the current directory as the standard directory, and then */usr/include*.

For example, most C programs use the Standard I/O library to do input and output. To use this library, the *stdio.h* header file, which is found in */usr/include*, must be included in the program source file. Figure 4.C.4 shows the correct include directive.

#include   <stdio.h>

Figure 4.C.4

Include directives belong at the beginning of a C program source file, following the initial comments section.

The preprocessor can be told to search other directories before the standard list by using the -I*dir* option. Include file names enclosed in quotes that do not begin with a slash (/) are first searched for in the current directory, then in the directory listed by the -I option, and finally in the standard directory. Each -I option names one search directory, and several -I options can be given on the command line.

For example, if you have a customized *stdio.h* in the *$HOME/Include* directory, you can cause the preprocessor to search this directory before it searches the standard directory by invoking **cc** as shown below:

$ **cc -I$HOME/Include copy.c**

Figure 4.C.5

If the preprocessor cannot find a file named in an include directive, the compilation stops. If the name *stdio.h* were changed to, say, *newio.h* in our file *copy.c*, the attempt to compile it would look like the figure below.

```
$ cc copy.c
copy.c: 7: Can't find include file newio.h
$ □
```

Figure 4.C.6

The line number reported by the command is the line number of the directive that failed.

C.1.b Macro substitution Macro definitions have the form:

#define *identifier token-string*

DEFINITION 4. Preprocessor define Statement

They direct the preprocessor to replace all occurrence of *identifier*, except those occurrences in a string or a character constant, by the string of tokens, *token-string*.

Macro substitution is most commonly used to define manifest constants. By convention, manifest constant names appear in upper case letters. In the **more** program example, four such constants – LINESIZE, SCRNSIZE, ONELINE, and ONESCREEN – use this convention, as can be seen by reviewing the include file *defs.h* found in Figure 4.A.5. These constants are used in *more.c*, figure 4.A.3, and in *command.c*, figure 4.A.4.

The preprocessor does a literal replacement of *identifier* with *token-string* without regard to the surrounding context. You must know how an identifier will be used in a program when you define its replacement token string.

For instance, a common programming mistake made with the #define directive is to add a trailing semicolon at the end of the *token-string*. If the EOF identifier was defined with:

```
#define EOF -1;
```

Figure 4.C.7

then its use in *copy.c* would cause a syntax error when compiled because the semicolon is in the wrong place. Since the preprocessor does not check the context of the substitutions it makes, poorly formed definitions may not be detected until the next stage of compilation.

76

So far, the macro definition examples shown directed the preprocessor only to replace an identifier with a string of tokens. The preprocessor can also do parameter substitutions during macro substitutions. For example, in the next figure, the directive defines the printd macro that expects a parameter.

```
#define printd(n) printf("%d\n", n)
```

Figure 4.C.8

When referenced as printd(36), the preprocessor substitutes all occurrences of the token n found in the token string with the parameter to the macro, here 36. The preprocessor then replaces printd(36) with printf("%d\n", 36).

When you define a macro that uses parameters, you must always specify the same number of parameters when you use the macro. The preprocessor complains if the counts disagree.

A long macro definition may be continued onto another line by prefacing the newline with a backslash (\). Figure 4.C.9 shows an example.

```
#define getc(p) (--(p)->__cnt>=0? \
        *(p)->__ptr++&037:__filbuf(p))
```

Figure 4.C.9

The #undef directive is the counterpart to the #define directive. Its syntax is:

#undef *identifier*

DEFINITION 5. Preprocessor undef Statement

---

and it causes the preprocessor to remove the definition of *identifier* from its internal tables. #undef should be used to remove a definition of an identifier before redefining that identifier.

C.1.c Conditional compilation The preprocessor allows conditional compilation with the #if, #ifdef, #ifndef, #else, and #endif directives. These are used to define source code that should be conditionally included or excluded from the compilation steps.

There are two types of conditional compilation directives. The first type has the form:

> #if *constant__expression*
>   *source__code__true*
> #else
>   *source__code__false*
> #endif
>
> **DEFINITION 6.** Preprocessor if Statement

---

where the #else *source__code__false* clause is optional. The preprocessor checks the value of *constant__expression*; and if the value is non-zero, *source__code__true* is passed on to the compiler and *source__code__false* is not. If the value of *constant-expression* is zero, *source__code__false* is passed to the compiler and *source__code__true* is not.

constant__expression can use any of the following binary C language operators: *, /, %, +, -, <<, >>, <, >, <=, >=, ==, !=, &, |, &&, ||, and expr?expr:expr. An expression can also use the -, !, and ~ operators. The preprocessor supports the **defined** operator which takes a single argument, and is true if the argument is defined, and false otherwise.

The second type has the form:

> #ifdef *identifier*
>   *source__code__true*
> #else
>   *source__code__false*
> #endif
>
> **DEFINITION 7.** Preprocessor ifdef Statement

---

and again the #else *source__code__false* clause is optional. The preprocessor checks whether *identifier* is currently defined; and if it is, *source__code__true* is passed to the compiler and *source__code__false* is not, and visa versa. The #ifndef directive may be used in place of #ifdef to check if the identifier is not defined.

Figure 4.C.10 shows an example of a debugging message conditionally added to the **copy** program.

```
$ number copy.c
   1       / *
   2        * copy program
   3        *     copy standard input to standard output
   4        * /
   5
   6       #include      <stdio.h>
   7       #define TEST 1
   8
   9       main()
  10       {
  11              int c;
  12
  13              while ((c = getchar()) != EOF) {
  14       #if TEST
  15                      printf("The octal value of c = %o\n", c);
  16       #endif
  17                      putchar(c);
  18              }
  19              exit(0);
  20       }
$ ☐
```

Figure 4.C.10

When recompiled, **copy** works as shown below.

```
$ cc copy.c
$ a.out
A
The octal value of c = 101
AThe octal value of c = 12


$ ☐
```

Figure 4.C.11

copy prints the line "The octal value of c = 12" because a newline was entered after the A.

Figure 4.C.12 shows *copy.c* changed to use an #ifdef instead of an #if.

79

```
$ number copy.c
 1       /*
 2        * copy program
 3        *    copy standard input to standard output
 4        */
 5
 6       #include     <stdio.h>
 7       #define TEST 0
 8
 9       main()
10       {
11               int c;
12
13               while ((c = getchar()) !=EOF) {
14       #ifdef TEST
15                       printf("The octal value of c = %o\n", c);
16       #endif
17                       putchar(c);
18               }
19           exit(0);
20       }
$ □
```

Figure 4.C.12

Irrespective of TEST's value, the debug print statement is passed on to the compilation step. The program created from this file operates identically to that created from the file shown in figure 4.C.10.

You can also control the compilation process by using the -D option to the **cc** program. For example, to define an identifier for *copy.c*, code:

$ **cc -D***identifier* **copy.c**

Figure 4.C.13

identifier is defined and has the value 1. The next figure shows a compilation of a version of *copy.c* that has no definition of TEST in the source code, but does have a definition of TEST on the command line.

```
$ cc -DTEST copy.c
$ a.out
A
The octal value of c = 101
AThe octal value of c = 12

$ ☐
```

Figure 4.C.14

An identifier can also be assigned a value from the command line by using the following:

cc -D*identifier=value source_file* ...

Figure 4.C.15

There must be no spaces in the command line definition – that is, between the -D and the identifier or around the =. However, *value* can contain spaces if they are forced with \ or if *value* is enclosed in either single quotes or double quotes. The next figure shows an example of an identifier defined to be a string containing spaces.

```
$ cc -DFATAL="Please call Lawrence R. Rogers for help" file.c
```

Figure 4.C.16

Recall that the #if, #ifdef, and #ifndef directives may be followed by any number of lines of source code file, ending with either an #else or an #endif directive. Furthermore, the #else directive may also be followed by any number of lines of source code, ending with an #endif directive. Figure 4.C.17 shows a slightly modified version of *copy.c* that uses an #else clause.

```
$ number copy.c
1        / *
2         * copy program
3         *    copy standard input to standard output
4         * /
5
6        #include       <stdio.h>
7
8        main()
9        {
10               int c;
11
12               while ((c = getchar()) !=EOF) {
13       #if TEST
14                       printf("The octal value of c = %o\n", c);
15       #else
16                       putchar(c);
17       #endif
18               }
19               exit(0);
20       }
$ []
```

Figure 4.C.17

The next two figures show how the **copy** program operates when TEST is
defined to be non-zero and zero respectively.

```
$ cc -DTEST=1 copy.c
$ a.out
A
The octal value of c = 101
The octal value of c = 12
$ []
```

Figure 4.C.18

```
$ cc -DTEST=0 copy.c
$ a.out
A
A
$ ▢
```

Figure 4.C.19

Like the include directives, the conditional compilation directives can also be nested. Figure 4.C.20 shows a change to the *defs.h* file that lets **more** use all the capabilities of a wide screen CRT.

```
$ number defs.h
 1       /*
 2        * more
 3        *    definitions header file
 4        */
 5
 6       #ifdef BIGSCRN
 7       #    ifndef LINESIZE
 8       #         define LINESIZE 132
 9       #    endif LINESIZE
10       #else
11       #    ifndef LINESIZE
12       #         define LINESIZE 80
13       #    endif LINESIZE
14       #endif BIGSCRN
15       #define SCRNSIZE       23
16       #define ONELINE             '\n'
17       #define ONESCREEN           ' '
$ ▢
```

Figure 4.C.20

If BIGSCRN is defined, LINESIZE is defined to be 132, if not otherwise defined. If BIGSCRN is not defined, LINESIZE is defined to be 80, if not otherwise defined. Notice the use of modifiers on the #endif directives. These help to document which directives the #endif directives belong to.

The preprocessor already has some symbols in its symbol table. These symbols define the name of the operating system, unix, and the type of CPU, for example vax or z8000. You should use these symbols to define those parts of your programs that are specific to the operating system and the CPU.

C.1.d Preprocessor options The preprocessor accepts several options from the **cc** command line. These are:

-P	Invoke the preprocessor only. This option causes the **cc** program to stop after preprocessing completes. Preprocessor output is stored in a file that has the same base name as the source file, but it ends with a *.i* instead of a *.c*.
-E	Invoke the preprocessor only. This option differs from -P in that the preprocessor output is directed to the standard output rather than to a file. This output is not suitable for further compilation. -E is useful when debugging preprocessor directives.
-D*identifier*[=*string*]	Define *identifier*. When *string* is not specified, *identifier* is defined to have the value 1. If *string* is specified, *identifier* is assigned the value of *string*. This option is similar to the #define *identifier token-string* directive usually found in a source file. The -D option takes precedence over any definitions in the source file. No spaces are allowed between -D and the identifier and around the =.
-U*identifier*	Undefine *identifier*. This option is similar to the #undef *identifier* directive usually found in a source file.
-I*directory*	Search *directory* for files named in #include directives. Only those file names enclosed in double quotes that do not begin with / are affected. This option forces the preprocessor to look in the specified directory for include files before searching the standard directory, */usr/include*.
-C	Preserve comments in the preprocessor's output file.

C.2 The Compiler

C.2.a The compiler processing stage The compiler next processes the code prepared by the preprocessor. The source code passes through two compiler passes. The first pass removes all white space and logically groups all remaining characters into tokens, a process called *TOKENIZING*. The second pass matches each logical grouping of tokens with one of several tables used to produce assembly language code. When the second pass fails to find a match in one of its tables, it prints an error message.

This description makes the compiler appear both simpler and more strict than it really is. The compiler was designed to produce efficient assembly language code. It must produce code from any combination of tokens allowed by the C language definition. This is the key to the power of C, but is also a source of trouble.

C.2.b Some examples of compiler errors The C compiler gives you much flexibility to produce code that works. However, even with this flexibility, you will make mistakes. For example, by adding a semicolon in the wrong place in the *copy.c* program file, the program changes from one that works to one that fails to compile. Figure 4.C.21 shows how the compiler reacts to this type of error.

```
$ number copy.c
 1      / *
 2       * copy program
 3       *      copy standard input to standard output
 4       * /
 5
 6      #include            <stdio.h>
 7
 8      main();
 9      ¦
10              int c;
11
12              while ((c = getchar()) != EOF) ¦
13                      putchar(c);
14              ¦
15              exit(0);
16      ¦
$ cc copy.c
"copy.c", line 9: syntax error
"copy.c", line 12: syntax error
"copy.c", line 12: syntax error
Fatal error in /lib/ccom
$ ▯
```

Figure 4.C.21

Adding a semicolon to the end of the **main**() statement changes the program and causes a compiler error. The compiler detects a syntax error when it finds the ¦ that begins the function body.

A missing semicolon is also likely to produce a compiler error message. If the semicolon after int c is removed, for example, the compilation produces the errors shown in Figure 4.C.22.

```
$ number copy.c
 1     / *
 2     * copy program
 3     *      copy standard input to standard output
 4     * /
 5
 6       #include              <stdio.h>
 7
 8       main()
 9       {
10             int c      / *semicolon missing here * /
11
12             while ((c = getchar()) != EOF) {
13                     putchar(c);
14             }
15             exit(0);
16       }
$ cc copy.c
"copy.c", line 12: syntax error
"copy.c", line 13: syntax error
"copy.c", line 15: syntax error
$ □
```

Figure 4.C.22

The missing semicolon produces three error messages, not one of which mentions the semicolon.

What has happened is this: the missing semicolon changed the way that the characters are logically grouped. The compiler interprets int c as either the beginning of a subroutine named **c**() that returns an int result, or the first variable declared in a list of declarations. The compiler reports no error for this line.

However, the compiler does expect that the next group of characters will begin with any of the following: a left parenthesis, a comma, a semicolon, a left bracket, an equals sign defining a function, another item in the list, the end of the declaration list, an array, or an assignment of a value respectively. Instead, the compiler finds the while keyword and reports this as an error. It is difficult what the compiler does next, except to say that it is no longer correctly synchronized with the meaning of some of the tokens in the rest of the file.

Unlike the example above, where one syntax error produced a cascade of errors, some errors do not have such long-reaching effects. For example, if a v was coded instead of a c in line 13 of the **copy** program, the compiler would produce the unambiguous message shown in figure 4.C.23.

```
$ cc copy.c
"copy.c", line 13: v undefined
$ □
```

Figure 4.C.23

C.2.c Compiler options The options that affect the compilation stage of **cc** are:

-g   The debug option. This option causes the compiler to include additional information about the variables and source code statements in the final executable object file. This information is necessary for the proper operation of the symbolic debugger **sdb**.

-p   The profile option. This option causes the compiler to add code to each subroutine to count the number of times it is called. These counts are written to a file named *mon.out*, to be processed by the **prof** program. **prof** produces a program profile that is used to decide which subroutines to improve.

-O   The optimization option. This option invokes the optimizer, an additional stage of the compiler used to produce more efficient code. The optimizer is a program that scans the assembly language program created by the compiler and replaces certain assembly language code sequences with more efficient code sequences. This usually has the effect of shortening the size of the object file and reducing execution time. For some programs, the optimizer has no effect. Figure 4.C.24 illustrates two compilations of example program *copy.c*.

```
$ cc copy.c
$ size a.out
2368 + 452 + 2232 = 5052
$ cc -O copy.c
$ size a.out
2356 + 452 + 2232 = 5040
$ □
```

Figure 4.C.24

The size of the optimized version of *copy.c* is smaller than the unoptimized version. This difference should be even more apparent for programs more complicated than *copy.c*.

-S   The assembler source option. This option preserves the assembly language temporary file created by the compiler. This file has the same base name as the source file, but it ends with a *.s* instead of a *.c*.

C.3 The Assembler

C.3.a The assembly stage The assembler's task is to produce an object module from the assembly language file created by the compiler step. This usually occurs uneventfully because the source file for the assembler is – theoretically – error free.

The object file created by the assembler has the same root name as the source file, but it ends with a *.o* instead of a *.s*. These object files remain after the compilation process only if the -c option is given to the **cc** command.

C.3.b The assembler option The **cc** command doesn't pass any options from the command line to the assembler, unless directed by a -Wa option to the **cc** command.

C.4 The Linking/Loader

The linking/loader, **ld**, is the last step in creating an executable program. This step usually involves combining object files and searching archive libraries to resolve undefined references.

C.4.a The link edit stage The linking/loader first scans its command line arguments for object files and archive files. When the linking/loader discovers an object file, it reads the file, relocates the program code, and adds this relocated code onto the end of the binary executable file. The linking/loader then merges the object file's symbol table with the binary executable file's symbol table.

When the linking/loader discovers an archive library, it searches the archive symbol table, looking for names that resolve any undefined names in the binary executable file's symbol table. The linking/loader searches the symbol table as many times as necessary to resolve all references, meaning that the order of object files in an archive is not important. Only the object modules that resolve undefined names in the symbol table are included in the binary executable file. The linking/loader reads each selected object file's code from the archive, relocates it, and adds this relocated code onto the end of the binary executable file. The symbol table from each included object file is merged with the binary executable file's symbol table.

Archive file names *must* appear after the object files that reference them on the **cc** command line. If an archive file appears on the command line before an object file that references a symbol in the archive, the linking/loader will be unable to resolve the reference. For example, the figure below shows what happens when the */lib/libc.a* archive file – the archive containing standard C subroutines – is given on the command line before the list of object files that reference subroutines in the archive.

$ ld /lib/crt0.o /lib/libc.a main.o more.o command.o
undefined   first referenced
 symbol   in file
____iob   main.o
____flsbuf   main.o
____filbuf   main.o
__fopen   command.o
__printf   command.o
ld fatal: Symbol referencing errors. No output written to a.out
$ ☐

Figure 4.C.25

When **ld** searched the archive, there were no undefined names in the symbol table. Undefined names only appeared in the symbol table after *main.o,* *more.o,* and *command.o* were processed. Since there were no more object files or archive libraries left to read when the linking/loader finished reading *command.o,* the names remained undefined. The linking/loader stopped creating the *a.out* binary executable file and displayed the names it could not resolve. Figure 4.C.26 illustrates a successful loading by listing the archive file last.

$ ld /lib/crt0.o main.o more.o command.o /lib/libc.a
$ ☐

Figure 4.C.26

/lib/crt0.o is added to the binary executable file first when **cc** invokes the linking/loader. This object file arranges for an orderly entrance into a C language program from the operating system. If **ld** is invoked explicitly, this object file *must* appear as the first file name in the list of file name arguments.

The **cc** command also adds the standard C library, */lib/libc.a,* to the list of archive files in the command line. The command in the figure above can be simplified by using **cc** instead of **ld**, as the figure below shows.

$ **cc main.o more.o command.o**

$ □

Figure 4.C.27

C.4.b The loading stage The loading stage starts when all object files and archive files listed on the command line have been read. The symbol table now contains all the identifier names from all object files that have been loaded. The linking/loader sorts this table, matches all undefined names with their definitions, and then resolves all references. Names that remain undefined after the matching process cause the linking/loader to quit without creating a binary executable file and to produce the error message **Undefined:**, followed by a list of all undefined identifiers.

C.4.c Archive libraries The archive program, **ar**, combines object files into a special format. This format is discussed in Section D of this chapter. Archives are used primarily as libraries that are searched by the linking/loader.

Some of the commonly used archive libraries include:

- *libc.a* – the standard C function library. This archive is automatically searched when **cc** is used to create binary executable files.

- *libm.a* – the special math functions library.

- *libl.a* – the library used with **lex**, the lexical analyzer generator.

- *liby.a* – the library used with **yacc**, the parser generator.

- *libcurses.a* and *libtermlib.a* – the libraries used to achieve terminal independence in programs.

- *libplot.a* – the plotting subroutine library. This library contains the plot subroutines described in Section 3 of the **UNIX System User's Manual System V**.

- *libF77.a* – the FORTRAN-77 library.

C.4.d Linking/loader options The linking/loader accepts several options from the **cc** command line. These options can appear in any order with the exception that all -l*x* options *must* appear after all object file arguments. Some of the available options are listed below.

-o *name*   This option causes the binary executable file to be named *name* instead of *a.out*.

-l*x*   This option is an abbreviation for the archive library named */lib/libx.a*. If that archive does not exist, **ld** then tries */usr/lib/libx.a*.

The order in which library names are given is significant because libraries are only searched at the point where they are specified on the command line. The *x* part of the option is a string, not necessarily a single character.

-s   This option causes the linking/loader to strip the symbol table from the binary executable file. While this causes the binary executable file to be shorter, it also removes the information needed by the **adb** and **sdb** debuggers.

-u *name*   Add the symbol *name* to the symbol table and mark it as undefined. This option is useful when building a binary executable file entirely from archive libraries. Recall that the linking/loader only includes an object file from an archive if an undefined symbol references a symbol in the symbol table of that object file.

-x   This option forces the linking/loader to exclude all non-global symbols from the symbol table of a binary executable file, thereby saving file space.

-L *dir*   Look in *dir* for archives given with -l before looking in */lib* and */usr/lib*.

The C compiler system lets you compile C language files and then combine them to create working programs that do a job. File inclusion, macro substitutions, and conditional compilation let you parameterize your programs so that you can easily customize them to any environment. Through archive libraries, you can eliminate much of the redundant programming often necessary to build a program for other systems. The next section first defines archive libraries and then explains how to use them.

D. ARCHIVES

An archive or library is a single file made from other files using the **ar** utility. Each file in an archive may be unrelated to other files in the archive. The UNIX system places no restrictions on the contents of files in an archive. By convention, archive file names begin with *lib* and end with *.a*.

Archives usually hold the object file versions of general purpose subroutines. These subroutines are explained in Chapters 7 of this guide and in Section 3 of the **UNIX System User's Manual System V**.

Archives are not only used for general purpose subroutines, but they can also be used to hold project-specific subroutines. To help you use archives, the next section describes how the linking/loader searches an archive for the subroutines it needs, and the following section explains how to maintain archives.

D.1 How the Linking/Loader Searches an Archive

When you compile a program, the linking/loader searches the C library archive and all other archives given on the command line to find the object files it needs to complete the *a.out* image. For example, if you use the **printf()** subroutine in a program, the object file built by the compiler contains a reference to **printf** as noted by a symbol table entry showing that the **printf** symbol is undefined.

The linking/loader tries to resolve the **printf** reference by searching these archives. When it searches the archive's symbol table and finds an object file that defines the **printf** symbol, the linking/loader extracts the file from the archive, relocates it, and adds this relocated code onto the end of the binary executable file. The linking/loader then merges the object file's symbol table with the binary executable file's symbol table, and continues looking through the archive symbol table to resolve other undefined symbols.

UNIX System V simplifies archive maintenance by embedding a table that relates external symbol definitions to the object files that define them in the archive. All operations on an archive that change the contents of that archive are automatically reflected in the symbol table.

D.2 Maintaining Archives

The **ar** utility is used to maintain archives. The next four sections describe how to create an archive, extract files from an archive, add to and replace files in an archive, and list the table of contents.

D.2.a Creating an archive To create an archive, use the command:

---

ar rv *archive_file object_files*

DEFINITION 8. Create Archive Command Line

---

ar automatically creates the symbol table relating external symbol names to object file names. The order of *object_files* is unimportant.

D.2.b Extracting files from an archive Files are extracted from an archive with the command:

---

ar xv *archive__file* [*object__file ...*]

DEFINITION 9. Extract From Archive Command Line

All files extracted are placed into the current directory. If no *object__files* are given, all files in the archive are extracted.

D.2.c Adding to and replacing files in an archive Files can be added and replaced in an archive with the command:

---

ar rv *archive__file object__files*

DEFINITION 10. Add To/Replace Archive Command

---

ar replaces those files already in the archive and adds those files not in the archive. The archive symbol table is automatically updated to reflect the change in the archive's contents.

D.2.d Listing the table of contents The command:

---

ar t *archive__file*

DEFINITION 11. Archive Table of Contents Command Line

---

causes **ar** to list the files in an archive. Figure 4.D.1 shows an example of part of the contents of the standard C library archive.

```
$ ar t /lib/libc.a
a64l.o
abs.o
acct.o
assert.o
abort.o
bsearch.o
bufctl.o
chdir.o
chmod.o
chown.o
chroot.o
clock.o
clrerr.o
crypt.o
ctermid.o
DELETE
$ ☐
```

Figure 4.D.1

To get more information from the archive, use the v option as shown in the next figure.

```
$ ar tv /lib/libc.a
rw-rw-r--    0/    3     366 Dec 19 23:36 1983 a64l.o
rw-rw-r--    0/    3     314 Dec 19 23:37 1983 abs.o
rw-rw-r--    0/    3     346 Dec 19 23:37 1983 acct.o
rw-rw-r--    0/    3     746 Dec 19 23:36 1983 assert.o
rw-rw-r--    0/    3     486 Dec 19 23:36 1983 abort.o
rw-rw-r--    0/    3     498 Dec 19 23:36 1983 atol.o
rw-rw-r--    0/    3     398 Dec 19 23:36 1983 bsearch.o
rw-rw-r--    0/    3     284 Dec 19 23:36 1983 bufctl.o
rw-rw-r--    0/    3     346 Dec 19 23:37 1983 chdir.o
rw-rw-r--    0/    3     346 Dec 19 23:37 1983 chmod.o
rw-rw-r--    0/    3     346 Dec 19 23:37 1983 chown.o
rw-rw-r--    0/    3     346 Dec 19 23:37 1983 chroot.o
rw-rw-r--    0/    3     458 Dec 19 23:36 1983 clock.o
rw-rw-r--    0/    3     328 Dec 19 23:36 1983 clrerr.o
rw-rw-r--    0/    3    4582 Dec 19 23:36 1983 crypt.o
rw-rw-r--    0/    3     432 Dec 19 23:36 1983 ctermid.o
rw-rw-r--    0/    3    2454 Dec 19 23:36 1983 ctime.o
rw-rw-r--    0/    3     596 Dec 19 23:36 1983 cuserid.o
DELETE
$ □
```

Figure 4.D.2

The tv option, in addition to being pleasantly mnemonic, lists the default permission masks, the user and group ID of the person who added the file to the archive, the size of the file in bytes, the date of the file's last change, and the file name.

Archives are the method used in the UNIX system to build libraries of subroutines for the linking/loader. Archives in UNIX System V are organized randomly, meaning that the ordering of files in the archive is not important. The **ar** utility builds a symbol table that relates symbol names to object files, and the linking/loader searches this table as many times as necessary to resolve all references.

The next section describes the **make** program that builds on the C compiler features shown in the last section and the archive features shown in this section. **make** further simplifies the programming job already made easier by the **ex** and **vi** text editors, the C compiler system, and library archives.

E. USING MAKE TO DEVELOP PROGRAMS

During program development, it is a good idea to divide a large programming project into subroutines with simple, well-defined interfaces. These subroutines can be written and tested independently and then combined to build a complete program. The program that results is much less sensitive to change because the changes are usually localized to individual subroutines. A subroutine can be completely overhauled without the other subroutines even knowing about the change as long as the well-defined interface remains unchanged.

While this "divide and conquer" technique reduces the time required to develop a large program, since subroutines can be developed by different programmers working in parallel, the program's administrative overhead increases. For example, if a change must be made to a constant defined in a header file and used in several subroutines, how do you decide which subroutines must be recompiled when the change is made?

One method is to use the **grep** utility to search through all source files for a certain string and then recompile only those files. This method certainly works, but it is cumbersome when the number of files is large and header files are shared by several programs whose source files are stored in several directories.

Another problem arises when a change is made to a file, but the file is not recompiled when the new version of the program is built. To decide which files to recompile, you must remember which files were changed. When several programmers work together on a project, you'd have to ask everyone working on the project which files they changed and make certain that the latest versions have been recompiled. This too is cumbersome in larger projects when several files are combined to build a program.

The **make** utility solves these and other program administration problems. For example, **make** can oversee the changes made to source files and insure that all object files have been recompiled since the last change. **make** can also recompile files that use other files that have changed. **make**'s ability to find the most recent modification date of source and object files and to understand which files use other files is the key to its operation.

E.1 What make Does

make is driven by an auxiliary file, also called a *MAKEFILE*, that defines which files make up a program. In addition, the makefile shows the relationship between files, also called the *DEPENDENCY*. **make** takes responsibility for recompiling any source file that has been changed since the last time it was compiled and also for recompiling any source file that depends on other source files that have changed. This means that you no longer have to remember which files have recently changed. You don't have to recompile everything in sight, just in case.

When compiling source files, **make** uses built-in rules to decide which language processor to use. For example, the *.c* suffix of a C language source file name tells **make** that the C compiler must be used to build a new version of the object file needed to build a new version of a program. Although this discussion focuses on the C language, **make** may be used with several other language processors.

make can also do other routine tasks often required in program administration. For example, **make** can be used to list and make backup copies of only those source files changed since their last printing and backup.

E.2 An Example Makefile

Figure 4.E.1 shows a simple makefile used to maintain the **more** program described earlier in this chapter. While the makefile does not use many of **make**'s intrinsic knowledge, it does show **make**'s basic functions.

```
$ number Makefile
1     ################################################
2     #       more
3     #              more program make file
4     #              version 1
5     ################################################
6
7     more:       main.o more.o command.o
8                 cc main.o more.o command.o -o more
9
10    main.o: main.c
11                cc -c main.c
12
13    more.o: defs.h more.c
14                cc -c more.c
15
16    command.o:  defs.h command.c
17                cc -c command.c
$ □
```

Figure 4.E.1

This simple makefile has two types of entries:

● *Dependency lines,* such as:

```
more:          main.o more.o command.o
main.o:        main.c
more.o:        defs.h more.c
command.o:     defs.h command.c
```

- *Command lines*, such as:

```
cc main.o more.o command.o -o more
cc -c main.c
cc -c more.c
cc -c command.c
```

A dependency line shows the relationship between a target file name, given to the left of the colon, and the files that the target depends on, given to the right of the colon. The command line(s), also called *RULES*, that follow a dependency line are assumed to transform the dependency files into the target file.

To invoke **make**, use the command:

$ **make** [*target__file...*]

Figure 4.E.2

In the example makefile, *target__file* can be any combination of more, main.o, more.o, and command.o. Since more is the first target file in the description file, **make** remakes the more target if no target is given on the command line.

make expects that the makefile is stored in a file named either *makefile* or *Makefile*. Of these two file names, *Makefile* is recommended because it stands out when a directory's contents are listed as shown below.

$ **ls**
Makefile
command.c
main.c
more.c
$ □

Figure 4.E.3

If you must use a different name for the makefile, for example when you have several such files in a single directory, use the command line form shown below.

> make -f *makefile* [*target__file*...]
>
> **DEFINITION 2.** make Command Line

Figure 4.E.4 shows an example of running **make** using this makefile.

$ **make**
```
        cc -c main.c
        cc -c more.c
        cc -c command.c
        cc main.o more.o command.o -o more
```
$ □

Figure 4.E.4

Since none of the object files needed to build **more** exist, **make** built them before building **more**.

E.3 Built-In Rules

In version 1 of the makefile example, all dependencies and rules have been stated explicitly. Most of this is unnecessary because **make** knows about the relationship between certain files. For example, if an object file is out of date, **make** searches the current directory for a source file with the same root name as the object file but with a different suffix. Some of the suffixes that **make** knows are *.c* for C language source files, *.l* for **lex** source files, *.y* for **yacc** source files, and *.s* for assembly language source files.

When **make** finds a file that ends with one of these suffixes, it uses the rule defined by **make** to transform that source file into an object file. The table below shows the rules built into **make** for the *.c*, *.l*, *.y*, and *.s* file name suffixes.

EXTENSION	LANGUAGE	RULE
.c	C	cc -c *source__file*.c
.l	Lex	lex *source__file*.l cc -c lex.yy.c rm lex.yy.c mv lex.yy.c *source__file*.o

99

EXTENSION	LANGUAGE	RULE
.y	Yacc	yacc *source__file*.y cc -c y.tab.c rm y.tab.c mv y.tab.o *source__file*.o
.s	Assembler	as -o *source__file*.o *source__file*.s

Figure 4.E.5 shows version 2 of the makefile rewritten to use these built-in rules.

```
$ number Makefile
1      ##################################################
2      #       more
3      #                   more program make file
4      #                   version 2
5      ##################################################
6
7      more:           main.o more.o command.o
8                      cc main.o more.o command.o -o more
9
10     more.o: defs.h
11
12     command.o:      defs.h
$ ☐
```

Figure 4.E.5

All dependency definitions and commands that relate source files to their object modules have been removed. The dependency lines relating *more.o* to *defs.h* and *command.o* to *defs.h* remain because their relationship needs to be stated explicitly.

E.4 Makefile Syntax

make is sensitive to the syntax of makefile, more so than the C compiler is to the syntax of a C language program. The next six sections describe the syntax of dependency lines, command lines, comments, macros, pre-defined macros, and built-in macros.

E.4.a Dependency lines Dependency lines are formed from a list of one or more target file names, separated by white space, followed by a colon. Each file name in the dependency list must be separated from other file names by white space. If a dependency line must extend to the next line, each line except the last line in the list must end with the backslash character.

100

make in UNIX System V has a notation for specifying archive member names as target names in a makefile. This notation is:

- *archive__name(file__name)*, referencing a specific file in an archive, and

- *archive__name((symbol__name))*, referencing the file in an archive that defines the symbol *symbol__name*.

The built-in rule that defines how to transform a C language source file into an archive member is:

```
cc -c source__file.c
ar rv archive__name source__file.o
rm -f source__file.o
```

The list of dependencies following a target may be null, allowing commands to be associated with a target that has no dependencies. When a target with a null dependency list is named on the **make** command line, the commands associated with the target are unconditionally executed. For example, figure 4.E.6 shows version 3 of the makefile. This version defines the print target that causes all source files to be printed.

```
$ number Makefile
1    # # # # # # # # # # # # # # # # # # # # # # # # # # # # # # # # # # # # # # # # # # # #
2    #       more
3    #               more program make file
4    #               version 3
5    # # # # # # # # # # # # # # # # # # # # # # # # # # # # # # # # # # # # # # # # # # # #
6
7    more:           main.o more.o command.o
8                    cc main.o more.o command.o -o more
9
10   more.o: defs.h
11
12   command.o:      defs.h
13               .
14   print:
15                   echo Printing all source files.
16                   for file in defs.h main.c more.c command.c; \
17                   do \
18                       pr -n $$file; \
19                   done
$ make print
        echo Printing all source files.
Printing all source files.
        for file in defs.h main.c more.c command.c; \
        do \
                pr -n $file; \
        done
[ Listings of defs.h, main.c, more.c, and command.c ]
$ □
```

Figure 4.E.6

When make print is entered, the commands that follow the print dependency line are unconditionally executed because print has a null dependency list.

E.4.b Commands The commands that follow a dependency line are executed when one or more of the target's dependents have been changed more recently than the target. **make** requires that each command line be indented at least one tab. If a command line does not begin with a tab, **make** displays the message:

Make: must be a separator on rules line n. Stop.

Figure 4.E.7

where n is the line number following the command line that did not begin with a tab character.

When command lines follow a dependency line, **make** abandons its use of built-in rules. **make** assumes that the command lines following a dependency line transform the dependents into the target.

A new shell is started to execute each command line. This means that those commands that affect the current shell process – for example, the **cd** (change directory) command – will not affect the commands given on other command lines. Figure 4.E.8 shows a simple makefile that illustrates this.

```
$ number Makefile
1       ###############################################
2       #       makefile showing how make
3       #       executes command lines
4       ###############################################
5
6       pathname:
7                       pwd; cd; pwd
8                       pwd
$ pwd
/usr/rogers/make.test
$ make
pwd; cd; pwd
/usr/rogers/make.test
/usr/rogers
pwd
/usr/rogers/make.test
$ ▯
```

Figure 4.E.8

The first **pwd** (print working directory) command displays the current directory. The **cd** command changes the current directory to the home directory, and the next **pwd** shows this change. Because these commands are on the same command line, they are executed by the same shell. When **pwd** is executed on the next command line, **make** starts a new shell to execute the command line; and the current working directory reverts to the directory where **make** was started.

make also recognizes that a backslash (\) at the end of a line means that the command is continued on the next line. All lines up to and including the line that does not end with a backslash are passed to the new shell started to execute the command line. The backslash character is only cosmetic because neither the backslash nor the following newline character are passed to the shell. This means that constructs such as the for loop in figure 4.E.6, must use the semicolon command separator character to end both the word list and the **pr** command. Chapter 8 describes where to place the semicolon in Bourne Shell structured constructs.

make normally displays each command that it executes. In the makefile example shown in figure 4.E.6, the display of the **echo** and the **cat** commands clog the source file listing. These displays can be eliminated three ways.

First, **make** does not display any command it executes that begins with the @ character. Figure 4.E.9 shows version 4 of the makefile that uses this feature.

```
$ number Makefile
1      #############################################
2      #       more
3      #                more program make file
4      #                version 4
5      #############################################
6
7      more:           main.o more.o command.o
8                      cc main.o more.o command.o -o more
9
10     more.o: defs.h
11
12     command.o:      defs.h
13
14     print:
15                     @echo Printing all source files.
16                     @for files in defs.h main.c more.c command.c; \
17                     do \
18                          pr -n $$file; \
19                     done
$ make print
Printing all source files.
[ Listings of defs.h, main.c, more.c, and command.c ]
$ ☐
```

Figure 4.E.9

Second, **make** recognizes the dummy dependency line .SILENT:. Because .SILENT: turns off the display of all commands executed by **make**, its position in the makefile does not matter. Furthermore, once command displays are turned off, they cannot be turned back on.

Third, **make** accepts the -s command line option, which is the same as the .SILENT: dummy dependency line in a makefile.

Every program run in the UNIX system returns a numeric value called the *RETURN CODE*. Chapter 8 describes the meaning of these numbers and how to set their values from a program and a shell procedure. To summarize the discussion from Chapter 8, a return code with the value zero means that the program completed its required job successfully. In contrast, a non-zero return code means that the program could not do what it was supposed to do, perhaps because the program was called incorrectly or because some needed files were missing.

make uses these program return codes to decide if it should continue executing the commands given in command lines and in built-in rules. If the command returns a non-zero return code, **make** stops processing the makefile and displays an error message.

Unfortunately, not all programs return values consistent with the jobs they do. Fortunately, **make** provides three ways that let you continue executing commands in the makefile even if some programs return non-zero values.

The first way is to add the dummy dependency line .IGNORE:. If this dependency line appears anywhere in a makefile, **make** ignores all program return codes.

The second way is to specify the -i command line option to **make**. This has the same effect as a .IGNORE: dummy dependency line.

The third way to ignore program return codes is to preface each command with a hyphen (-). The hyphen lets you selectively ignore program return codes.

Figure 4.E.10 shows version 5 of the makefile. This version uses the **test** built-in shell command to see if all source files are in the current directory. **test** is explained in Chapter 8. Briefly, **test** evaluates the expression given as its arguments. If the expression value is true, **test** returns zero; otherwise, **test** returns non-zero. In this version of the makefile, test -r *filename* returns zero if *filename* exists and is readable. Because **test** is built-in to the shell, it must appear as a command given to the shell's on standard input.

```
$ number Makefile
 1      ###############################################
 2      #       more
 3      #               more program make file
 4      #               version 5
 5      ###############################################
 6
 7      more:           main.o more.o command.o
 8                      cc main.o more.o command.o -o more
 9
10      more.o: defs.h
11
12      command.o:      defs.h
13
14      print:
15                      @echo Printing all source files.
16                      @for file in defs.h main.c more.c command.c; \
17                      do \
18                              pr -n $$file; \
19                      done
20
21      readable:
22                      -echo test -r defs.h | sh
24                      -echo test -r main.c | sh
25                      -echo test -r more.c | sh
26                      -echo test -r command.c | sh
$ []
```

Figure 4.E.10

If a source files is missing, **make** continues to test for the other files because **test**'s return codes are ignored. Figure 4.E.11 shows an example.

```
$ mv more.c MORE.c
$ make readable
        echo test -r defs.h | sh
        echo test -r main.c | sh
        echo test -r more.c | sh
*** Error code 1 (ignored)
        echo test -r command.c | sh
$ []
```

Figure 4.E.11

E.4.c Comments Comments in makefiles explain information in a makefile. Comments begin with a # and end with a newline character. Since **make** ignores everything between the # and the newline, you can (and should) use comments anywhere in a makefile.

E.4.d Macros Macros let you parameterize makefiles. Macros are commonly used to define lists of files, compiler options, libraries, and commands.

Macros are defined in a makefile with statements of the form:

```
STRING1 = string2
```

where the equal sign defines the entry as a macro definition. By convention, macro names are all upper case.

Macros should be defined at the beginning of the makefile, and they work like the user-definable shell variables explained in Chapter 3. Each macro reference begins with a $ followed by the macro name in parentheses. Parentheses are not required if the macro name is just a single character.

Figure 4.E.12 shows version 6 of the makefile that uses macros to define the names of the source, object, and header files in **more**.

```
$ number Makefile
 1     ###############################################
 2     #       more
 3     #               more program make file
 4     #               version 6
 5     ###############################################
 6
 7     OBJECTS     =       main.o more.o command.o
 8     SOURCES     =       main.c more.c command.c
 9     HEADERS     =       defs.h
10
11     more:       $(OBJECTS)
12                 cc $(OBJECTS) -o more
13
14     more.o: defs.h
15
16     command.o:  defs.h
17
18     print:
19                 @echo Printing all source files.
20                 @for file in $(HEADERS) $(SOURCES); \
21                 do \
22                     pr -n $$file; \
23                 done
24
25     readable:
26                 -echo test -r defs.h | sh
27                 -echo test -r main.c | sh
28                 -echo test -r more.c | sh
29                 -echo test -r command.c | sh
$ 
```

Figure 4.E.12

E.4.e Pre-defined macros The **make** program recognizes several pre-defined macros. Those of interest for C programming are listed below:

```
CC = cc          # The C compiler
AS = as          # The Assembler
CFLAGS =           # C compiler flags
LOADLIBES =          # Loader libraries
```

Figure 4.E.13

Figure 4.E.14 shows version 7 of the makefile that has been changed to use some of these pre-defined macros.

108

```
$ number Makefile
 1      ##################################################
 2      #       more
 3      #              more program make file
 4      #              version 7
 5      ##################################################
 6
 7      OBJECTS      =       main.o more.o command.o
 8      SOURCES      =       main.c more.c command.c
 9      HEADERS      =       defs.h
10      CFLAGS       =       -O -g
11
12      more:        $(OBJECTS)
13                   $(CC) $(OBJECTS) -o more
14
15      more.o: defs.h
16
17      command.o:   defs.h
18
19      print:
20                   @echo Printing all source files.
21                   @for file in $(HEADERS) $(SOURCES); \
22                   do \
23                        pr -n $$file; \
24                   done
25
26      readable:
27                   -echo test -r defs.h | sh
28                   -echo test -r main.c | sh
29                   -echo test -r more.c | sh
30                   -echo test -r command.c | sh
$ □
```

Figure 4.E.14

Macro definitions given on the command line supercede those in a makefile. Figure 4.E.15 shows an example. Recall that the -g option causes the C compiler to add the information required by the **sdb** symbolic debugger.

```
$ make "CFLAGS = -g"
        cc -g -c main.c
        cc -g -c more.c
        cc -g -c command.c
        cc main.o more.o command.o -o more
$ ▢
```

Figure 4.E.15

E.4.f Built-in macros **make** recognizes six special built-in macros. They are assigned values during dependency evaluation and are used in the related command lines. These macros are:

$*   the file name part of the current dependent with the suffix removed.

$@   the full target name. $@ is evaluated only for explicitly named dependencies.

$?   the full names – root and suffix – of the dependent files that are out of date with the target. $? is evaluated only when explicit rules are used.

$<   the full names of all dependent files, both out of date and up to date.

$$ the string $.

$%   when the target name is an archive of the form *lib(file.o)*, $@ evaluates to *lib* and $% evaluates to *file.o*.

Some of these built-in macros can be used to improve the makefile built so far. Figure 4.E.16 shows the next version.

```
$ number Makefile
  1     ###################################################
  2     #       more
  3     #               more program make file
  4     #               version 8
  5     ###################################################
  6
  7     OBJECTS    =       main.o more.o command.o
  8     SOURCES    =       main.c more.c command.c
  9     HEADERS    =       defs.h
 10     CFLAGS     =       -O
 11
 12     more:      $(OBJECTS)
 13                $(CC) $(OBJECTS) -o $@
 14
 15     more.o: defs.h
 16
 17     command.o:  defs.h
 18
 19     printall:
 20                @echo Printing all source files.
 21                @for file in $(HEADERS) $(SOURCES); \
 22                do \
 23                     pr -n $$file; \
 24                done
 25
 26     print:   $(HEADERS) $(SOURCES)
 27                @echo Printing modified source files.
 28                @for file in $?; \
 29                do \
 30                     pr -n $$file; \
 31                done
 32                @-touch $@
 33
 34     readable:
 35                -echo test -r defs.h | sh
 36                -echo test -r main.c | sh
 37                -echo test -r more.c | sh
 38                -echo test -r command.c | sh
$ ☐
```

Figure 4.E.16

In line 13, the $@ macro is used instead of the target name. If the **more** program must be renamed because of a conflict with another program named **more**, only the target name on line 12 needs to be changed to build and maintain the new program.

In line 19, the print target name has been renamed printall. **make** prints all source and header files in response to make printall.

111

Finally, the print target has been redefined to print only those source and header files that have changed since the last printing; print is now dependent on all source and header files, and the $? macro names the dependent files that are out of date with respect to the print target.

To make this work properly, **make** must remember when files were last printed. One way to remember this is to change an auxiliary file and then let **make** determine which source and header files are out of date with this time stamp file. The **touch** program is a utility designed to do this by changing a file's modification date without changing its contents. In the makefile, *print* is the target name used to decide which files are out of date and **touch** changes *print*'s modification date to remember when files were last printed.

Finally, the $< macro can be used to create new built-in rules and to override those already known to **make**. Figure 4.E.17 shows the default built-in rule used to transform a C language source file into an object file.

```
CC      =       cc
CFLAGS =
.c.o:
                $(CC) $(CFLAGS) -c $<
```

Figure 4.E.17

E.5 Make Options

Several options are available with **make**. These are:

-f *makefile* Defines the makefile file name. If not specified, **make** first looks for *makefile* and then for *Makefile*. If the -f option argument is a -, then the makefile is assumed to appear on the standard input. Furthermore, more than one -f *makefile* option is allowed.

-p **make** prints the complete set of macro definitions, built-in rules, and target descriptions.

-i Forces **make** to ignore non-zero return codes returned by commands. This option has the same effect as the the .IGNORE dummy dependency line.

-s Stops **make** from displaying commands before executing them. This option has the same effect as the .SILENT: dummy dependency line.

-r Forces **make** to ignore its built-in rules. This means that every target and the rules that create it must be described explicitly in the makefile, which has the effect of destroying much of **make**'s power. Since individual built-in rules may be redefined in a makefile, using the -r option is not recommended.

-n   **make** expands all shell metacharacters, makes all macro substitutions, and displays the commands it would execute, but it does not execute them. Even those commands preceded by the @ character are listed on standard output. Figure 4.E.18 shows an example using the makefile in figure 4.E.16.

```
$ touch defs.h
$ make -n print
        echo Print modified source files.
        for file in defs.h; \
        do \
                pr -n $file; \
        done
        touch print
$ ▢
```

Figure 4.E.18

-t   **make** touches all out-of-date target files instead of rebuilding them with the built-in rules and the commands given in command lines. This option forces all dependents to appear up to date without changing any file's contents. The -t option may be used in place of **touch**, but doing this subverts the intent of **make**, which is to change certain files by applying a well-defined set of rules. **touch** is the recommended program to use to make files appear up to date.

-q   **make** returns a zero return code if the named target files are up-to-date and non-zero otherwise. This option is intended for use in shell scripts.

The program development tools described in this chapter help you to build and to manage programs. The **ex** and **vi** text editors help you to enter and to edit program source files with commands that encourage you to format files in a readable fashion. The C compiler system lets you write programs that use other files that define constants and data structures and conditionally compile source files. Library archives provide a way to catalog general purpose and project-specific subroutines for users of your system. Finally, the **make** program helps tie together all files for a program into a manageable unit.

The next step in the process of developing software concentrates on how your programs interact with users. Chapter 5 defines seven guidelines for program development and then builds example programs using these guidelines. The tools explained in this chapter are used in Chapter 5 to edit and compile example programs.

CHAPTER 5

FORGING A SOFTWARE TOOL

A. INTRODUCTION

Now that you know how to edit program source files with **ex** and **vi**, how to compile programs with **cc**, and how to coordinate source files with **make**, it is time to focus on how to design a program, paying particular attention to how your programs interact with users. This chapter presents seven guidelines for writing software tools, and discusses the techniques used to build a generic type of tool called a filter. These guidelines will help you to build software tools using the UNIX system. They also show you how to combine subroutines with your software tool to make better programs while spending less time in front of the terminal.

The software tools you build should use the same conventions as the tools distributed with the UNIX system. When your programs adopt these conventions, they become as easy to use as the distributed tools, and other users of your system tend to use your software tools because of their similarities.

B. PROGRAMMING GUIDELINES

The seven guidelines, whose explanations follow, define the conventions for writing software tools with the UNIX system. These guidelines describe the Standard Command Format, metacharacters in command lines, standard files, program messages, input and output data formats, dot files and environment variables, and standard libraries.

B.1 Guideline 1 – Standard Command Format Equals Programming Efficiency and Power

When you build a new software tool, you should program that tool to understand arguments given to it in the Standard Command Format, described in detail in Section C. Those who use your tool won't have to learn a new command format when you use the format described below.

The Standard Command Format for invoking commands is:

   $ *program* [*option* ...] [*file* ...]

where *program* is the program to execute, *option* tells the command what to do and is optional, and *file* names the files for the program to use and is also optional.

Program options are always prefaced by a dash and can take the form:

-option(s)

or:

-option -option -option

An option may use an *option_argument* which is a number, a keyword, or a file name that further defines the action of the option. Options that do not require option arguments can be grouped together into a single program argument or specified as individual options, each prefaced with a dash. Option arguments are not optional and must be specified as individual arguments. The -- argument marks the end of the options and the - argument is considered a file name that names the standard input file.

Options and option arguments give more information to the program by specifying parameters for the actions of the program. For example, in the command line:

$ ls -l samplefile

Figure 5.B.1

ls is the name of the list files command to be invoked, -l is the option that tells **ls** to list in the long form, and *samplefile* is the name of the file to be listed.

Programs in the UNIX system typically operate without interactive prompting. They assume a set of default values that are usually appropriate for the job done by the program. You can change these default values with options.

Tools that do not interactively prompt for parameters when executed require foresight in coding, as reasonable default parameter values must be selected. As a recommendation, look at other software tools in the UNIX system to help you decide which default parameter values you should use. Also, select meaningful options and option arguments to help users learn how to use your tools.

The UNIX system programming philosophy assumes that you will use many programs – perhaps several hundred in a day. Frequently used program names are short and many options require only a single letter. Less frequently used program names are longer, but are still concise. Section C defines the standard command format and shows programming examples that use this format.

B.2 Guideline 2 – Metacharacters

Chapter 3 described how the shell expands words in commands that use metacharacters. For example, when you enter:

$ **rm a***

Figure 5.B.2

the shell expands the a* word into a sorted list of all the files whose names begin with *a*, and then passes the list to the **rm** program.

The tools you write should also be able to recognize several file arguments to encourage the use of metacharacters by those who use your software tools. Section D describes how to use the files given on the command line.

B.3 Guideline 3 – Standard I/O Equals Modularity and Flexibility

A program should take its input from the standard input, write its output to the standard output, and write error messages to the standard error output wherever possible. Programs that adopt this convention are called filters.

Error messages should not appear in the standard output file, but rather in the standard error file. If you send error messages on to the next program using pipelines as described in Chapter 3, they may be misinterpreted as data and cause unexpected and unwanted results.

B.4 Guideline 4 – Keep Messages and Prompts to a Minimum

To build software tools that operate similarly to the existing UNIX system tools, you should minimize prompts and on-screen descriptions. Your software tools shouldn't babble. By the third time you run a program, you shouldn't need reassurance about the program's ability to do its job. For example, the **diff** program doesn't print anything if the files it compares are identical. In contrast, the same command in DEC's VMS System prints a screenful of stars and a version number before printing the sentence:

    No differences were found.

At 300 baud this printing sequence takes a long time.

In general, a tool should do its work silently. A program's output should be informative without being verbose. However, you may want to provide a *verbose* option that gives information on every step. The letter v is recommended as the name of the verbose option.

Don't use identifying headers or titles for data printed by a program unless necessary. For example, the **who** program prints one line for each user logged onto the UNIX system. Because of this, the output of **who** can be piped directly into the **wc** program to count the number of users logged on. If **who** supplied a header such as:

WHO TERM LOGIN TIME

then you would have to subtract one from the count printed by **wc** to get the number of users logged on.

Error messages should be informative without being overly lengthy. They should instruct the user how to reenter the input to avoid repeating the error condition. A tool user shouldn't have to guess how a program should be used.

B.5 Guideline 5 – Input and Output Data Should be Text Wherever Possible

Wherever possible, input to and output from a tool should be text. Text is defined to be a string of ASCII characters, no longer than 255 characters, that ends with a newline character. Text should be formated so that all logical parts of a single record appear on the same line. A mailing list, for example, might be:

```
First:Last:Street:Town:State:Zip
Jack:Jones:123 Main Street:Smalltown:CA:90000
Linda:Lawrence:1 California St:San Francisco:CA:94115
Helen:Smith:4692 El Camino Real Suite 111:Los Altos:CA:94022
Jane:Brown: 8 Tenth Avenue:San Francisco:CA:94100
John:Doe:9 Anywhere Drive:Hicksville:NY:11801
Shelia:Webster:1 W. 72 St:New York:NY:10023
```

Colons delimit fields and fields can vary in length. Tab characters and commas can also be used as delimiters.

Many UNIX system utilities, such as **grep**, **awk**, and **sort**, use text as their input and output data format. You can build new and powerful software tools by combining these utilities with your own. It is easier to move data files containing only text from computer to computer, and this form is becoming a standard for file transfer.

B.6 Guideline 6 – Use Dot Files and Environment Variables for Often Needed Information

Your software tools should not prompt a user for information that is often the same. Instead, your tools should use dot files and environment variables to store the information for reuse.

Dot files usually reside in a user's home directory; and even though you don't see them when you use the **ls** program, they are there. Dot files contain commands that tell a program how it should run. Examples of commonly used dot files include *.login* (used by the Berkeley C Shell when you log in), *.profile* (used by Bourne Shell when you log in), and *.cshrc* (used by the Berkeley C Shell when invoked).

In contrast, environment variables usually contain information that many different programs can use. For example, the PATH environment variable described in Chapter 3 specifies the directory search path for use by all processes. Also, the name of your terminal is stored in the TERM environment variable. **vi** and other programs use this terminal name to identify the terminal's type and capabilities. Since a typical programming session has 20 to 30 editor invocations, it is inefficient to tell **vi** the terminal name each time you edit a file. Chapter 6 shows how to access environment variables from a program, and Chapters 8 and 9 show examples of shell procedures that use environment variables.

B.7 Guideline 7 – Use Standard Libraries and Tools to Save Coding Effort

The UNIX system comes complete with a standard I/O library, a math subroutine library, a set of terminal cursor manipulation routines, and many more useful subroutines. You can also create your own libraries using the **ar** program described in Chapter 4.

Programming is involved and time-consuming enough without reinventing the wheel each time you need it. Sorting an array of elements is, for example, a commonly needed – and therefore commonly programmed – subroutine. The UNIX system saves you the trouble of writing a sort subroutine by providing an efficient version of the quick-sort algorithm as a subroutine named **qsort**(). You may save a day or two of programming effort when you use **qsort**(). Furthermore, using subroutines lets you concentrate on solving the problem at hand. Chapter 6 gives more information on the standard subroutines available with the UNIX system and is a supplement to section 3 of the **UNIX System User's Manual System V**.

C. THE STANDARD COMMAND FORMAT

Inherent in the UNIX system is the notion of the command line as a basic, yet powerful, coding tool. Options, option arguments, and file names expand the power of the command line as they provide a means for changing both the way a command works and the files it uses.

Often, a program uses a default set of options when invoked. The **diff** program, for example, requires as arguments two file names which are then compared. Figure 5.C.1 shows a sample.

```
$ cat file1
this    is    a    test
only a test
$ cat file2
this is a test
$ diff file1 file2
1,2c1
< this    is    a    test
< only a test
---
> this is a test
$ ☐
```

Figure 5.C.1

diff lists the differences between the two files on the standard output file. **diff**'s default parameters cause the files to be compared literally, including spaces and tabs. Occasionally, however, you must compare two files that are identical, but have different indentation or use different tab stops. Ignoring spaces and tabs is important here.

Guideline 4 recommends that prompts be kept to a minimum. The **diff** user is likely to be annoyed if the program asks:

Would you like to ignore blanks? (yes or no)

every time it is used.

The software tools way to change how **diff** operates so that it ignores spaces is to provide the -b option on the command line. Figure 5.C.2 builds on the example shown in figure 5.C.1.

```
$ diff -b file1 file2
2d1
< only a test
$ ☐
```

Figure 5.C.2

diff's operation, like the operation of most other programs, may be further modified by using several other options.

The Standard Command Format described at the beginning of this chapter is the preferred way to specify options, option arguments, and file names for

120

program. The Standard Command Format, in detail, is:

SCF	→	program [options] [separator] [files]
program	→	*2-9 lower case letters and digits*
options	→	-option white_space options*
option	→	noarg_options* arg_option | noarg_options+
noarg_option	→	letter
arg_option	→	letter white_space string
string	→	character+
letter	→	*lower or upper case letter*
character	→	*ASCII character*
white_space	→	*blanks and tabs*
separator	→	--
files	→	file white_space files
file	→	- | name
name	→	*any valid UNIX file name*

DEFINITION 13. The Standard Command Format Grammar

where the symbol * means zero or more objects, + means one or more objects, [...] means optional, and | means or. The rest of this section concentrates on writing C language programs that recognize the Standard Command Format.

All C language programs begin execution at a subroutine named **main**(). The UNIX system makes all command line arguments available to a process by passing two parameters to **main**(). The first parameter, named argc by convention, is a count of the number of arguments passed to the process. The second parameter, named argv by convention, is a pointer to an array of pointers to strings. In the C language, this type of data structure is called a *STRING VECTOR*, and figure 5.C.3 shows a diagram of this structure.

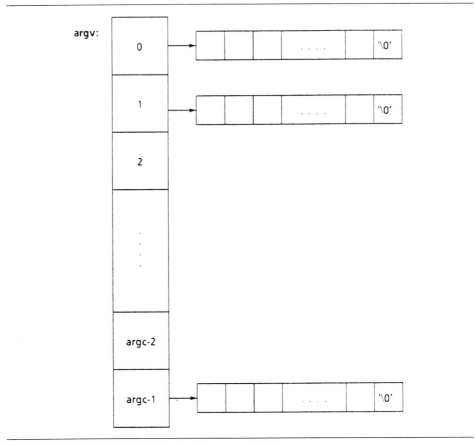

Figure 5.C.3

Figure 5.C.4 shows an example argv built by the UNIX system when executing the command ls −l filename.

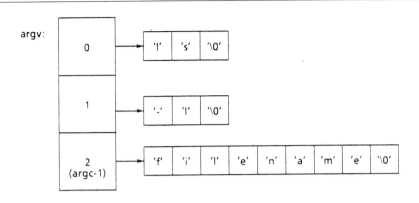

Figure 5.C.4

The program shown in figure 5.C.5 uses the information passed to it by the UNIX system to print the value of its arguments on the standard output file.

```
$ number printargs.c
 1   / *
 2    * printargs - print the command line arguments
 3    * /
 4
 5   #include    <stdio.h>
 6
 7   main(argc, argv)
 8   int argc;
 9   char *argv[];
10   {
11       int i;
12
13       for (i = 0; i < argc; i++) {
14           printf("Argument #%d is <%s>\n", i, argv[i]);
15       }
16       exit(0);
17   }
$ ☐
```

Figure 5.C.5

Figure 5.C.6 shows the compilation and examples with different command line arguments.

```
$ cc -o printargs printargs.c
$ printargs hello there
Argument #0 is <printargs>
Argument #1 is <hello>
Argument #2 is <there>
$ printargs -a -b -c -d
Argument #0 is <printargs>
Argument #1 is <-a>
Argument #2 is <-b>
Argument #3 is <-c>
Argument #4 is <-d>
$ ▢
```

Figure 5.C.6

You should use this example to clarify any questions about argument placement. Notice that the name of the program is argv[0].

Figure 5.C.7 shows the **printoptions** program that interprets the command line arguments passed to it by the UNIX system according to the Standard Command Format. **printoptions** recognizes the a, b, c, and d options and expects an option argument for the b option.

```
$ number printoptions1.c
 1   /*
 2    *    printoptions
 3    *         print option settings based on arguments
 4    *         version 1
 5    */
 6
 7   #include    <stdio.h>
 8
 9   main(argc, argv)
10   int argc;
11   char *argv[];
12   {
13       int ai, ci, errs = 0, rc = 0, aoption, boption, coption, doption;
14       char *bvalue;
15
16       aoption = boption = coption = doption = 0;
17       for (ai = 1; ai < argc && strcmp(argv[ai], "--"); ai++) {
18           if (argv[ai][0] == '-') {
19               for (ci = 1; ci < strlen(argv[ai]); ci++) {
20                   switch (argv[ai][ci]) {
21                   case 'a':
22                       aoption = 1;
23                       break;
24                   case 'b':
25                       boption = 1;
26                       if (argv[ai][ci + 1] != NULL) {
27                           fprintf(stderr, "%s: no white space before b option argument\n",
28                                   argv[0]);
29                           boption = 0;
30                       } else if (ai + 1 == argc) {
31                           fprintf(stderr, "%s: b option has no value\n", argv[0]);
32                           boption = 0;
33                       } else {
34                           bvalue = &(argv[ai + 1][0]);
35                           ai++;
36                           ci = strlen(argv[ai]);
37                       }
38                       if (boption == 0) {
39                           ci = strlen(argv[ai]);
40                           errs++;
41                       }
42                       break;
43                   case 'c':
44                       coption = 1;
45                       break;
46                   case 'd':
47                       doption = 1;
48                       break;
49                   default:
50                       errs++;
51                       break;
```

```
52                   |
53               |
54           |
55       |
56    if (errs) |
57        fprintf(stderr, "usage: %s [-a -c -d -b value] \n", argv[0]);
58        rc = 1;
59    | else |
60        printf("a option %d\n", aoption);
61        printf("b option %d\n", boption);
62        if (boption) |
63            printf("The value of b option is %s\n", bvalue);
64        |
65        printf("c option %d\n", coption);
66        printf("d option %d\n", doption);
67    |
68    exit(rc);
69 |
$ □
```

Figure 5.C.7

The program source file begins with comments that describe what the program is supposed to do. These commands are followed by all include directives, here including the standard input/output definitions.

printoptions recognizes four options, named a through d, and records the fact that it found an option in aoption through doption. Only the b option can have a value, and that value will be stored in bvalue. **printoptions** uses the ai variable to index through the argument string array and the ci variable to index through each character of an argument.

The argument processing code begins on line 19. Since argv[0] is always the program name, argument processing begins with argv[1].

The test in the for loop on line 19 verifies that ai has not exceeded the number of arguments (ai < argc) and that the argument is not the double dashes string that ends the option section, strcmp(argv[ai], "--"). If both conditions hold, line 20 tests whether the current argument is indeed an option.

On line 21, the program indexes through the argument string and analyzes options. Since argv[ai][0] is the dash that denotes an option, option analysis begins at argv[ai][1]. Each remaining character in the string is examined.

The switch statement dispatches to the appropriate action for each option. To add a new option to this program, add a variable that will show that the option has been recognized (e.g boption), a variable that contains the value of the option if the option uses an argument (e.g bvalue), and code a new case in the switch statement.

printoptions sets the appropriate option variable when it recognizes a legal option. The b option, however, has an option argument. The option argument must be in next argument string, if there is a next argument string. **printoptions** in line 26 verifies that the b option ends the argument and prints a diagnostic if it is not the end. Line 30 checks to see if the option argument value is in the next argument string. If this check also fails, **printoptions** in line 31 prints an error message on the standard error file. For the purposes of this example, **printoptions** displays the options and their values in lines 59 through 66.

Figure 5.C.8 shows some examples of execution.

```
$ printoptions -a -b buck -c -d
a option 1
b option 1
The value of b option is buck
c option 1
d option 1
$ printoptions -a -bbuck -c -d
printoptions: no white space before b option argument
usage: printoptions [-a -c -d -b value]
$ printoptions -a -b nobuk
a option 1
b option 1
The value of b option is nobuk
c option 0
d option 0
$ printoptions -a -b
printoptions: b option has no value
usage: printoptions [-a -c -d -b value]
$ printoptions -acdb buck
a option 1
b option 1
The value of b option is buck
c option 1
d option 1
$ printoptions -b buck -b newbuck
a option 0
b option 1
The value of b option is newbuck
c option 0
d option 0
$
$ □
```

Figure 5.C.8

Notice a side effect in the algorithm – multiple occurrences of the same option do not cause an error.

In the next example, the double dashes argument ends option processing, so **printoptions** treats both the -b argument and the newbuck option argument as file names instead of options.

```
$ printoptions -b buck -- -b newbuck
a option 0
b option 1
The value of boption is buck
c option 0
d option 0
$ ☐
```

Figure 5.C.9

printoptions shows how to process options, option arguments, and file names for a specific set of options and option arguments. Clearly, it would be appropriate to solve this argument processing problem in general.

UNIX System V provides the **getopt**() subroutine that helps parse command line arguments and supports a command line style that is common among the UNIX system utilities. The style is the command name, optionally followed by options which are optionally followed by list of files. Figure 5.C.10 shows **printoptions** rewritten to use **getopt**().

```
$ number printoptions2a.c
 1   /*
 2    *   printoptions
 3    *      print option settings based on arguments
 4    *      version 2a - uses getopt(1)
 5    */
 6
 7   #include   <stdio.h>
 8
 9   main(argc, argv)
10   int argc;
11   char *argv[];
12   {
13       int c, rc = 0, aoption, boption, coption, doption;
14       char *bvalue;
15       extern char *optarg;
16
17       aoption = boption = coption = doption = 0;
18       while ((c = getopt(argc, argv, "ab:cd")) != EOF) {
19           switch(c) {
20           case 'a':
21               aoption = 1;
22               break;
23           case 'b':
24               boption = 1;
25               bvalue = optarg;
26               break;
```

129

```
27          case 'c':
28              coption = 1;
29              break;
30          case 'd':
31              doption = 1;
32              break;
33          case '?':
34              rc = 1;
35              break;
36          }
37      }
38      if (rc == 1) {
39          fprintf(stderr, "usage: %s [-a -c -d -b value]\n", argv[0]);
40      } else {
41          printf("a option %d\n", aoption);
42          printf("b option %d\n", boption);
43          if (boption) {
44              printf("The value of b option is %s\n", bvalue);
45          }
46          printf("c option %d\n", coption);
47          printf("d option %d\n", doption);
48      }
49      exit(rc);
50  }
$
```

Figure 5.C.10

Each successive call to **getopt**() returns the next option letter taken from the argv string vector, or the special option ?, which means that **getopt**() found an option that was not in the list of allowable options given as the third argument to **getopt**(). When an option has an option argument, specified to **getopt**() as the option name followed by a colon (e.g. b:), **getopt**() sets the global variable optarg to point to the value of the option argument.

Unfortunately, not all versions of the UNIX system provide the **getopt**() subroutine. To help you write programs that recognize the Standard Command Format and are portable to many different versions of the UNIX system, the **scf**() subroutine was written. **scf**() translates program arguments given in the Standard Command Format into strings easily manipulated by C programs. The form into which **scf**() changes program arguments guarantees the following:

- All option and option arguments appear before any file names in the program arguments.

- The option and option argument program arguments are separated from the file name program arguments by the -- program argument.

- Each option program argument contains a single dash followed by the option.

- A single dash program argument is considered a file name and appears with any other file name program arguments.

Using the options and option arguments in **printoptions** as an example, the table below show examples of program arguments before and after processing by **scf**().

PROGRAM ARGUMENTS	TRANSLATED ARGUMENTS
-acd	-a -c -d --
-b value	-b value --
-acdb value	-a -c -d -b value --

Given how **scf**() changes program arguments, figure 5.C.11 shows a C program skeleton that process this new format.

```
$ number scfskel.c
 1   /*
 2    *   scfskel
 3    *       skeleton for scf subroutine
 4    */
 5
 6   main(argc, argv)
 7   int argc;
 8   char *argv[];
 9   {
10       int rc = 0, i;
11       char *options = "option__names";
12       char *optionargs = "option__arg__names";
13
14       if (scf(options, optionargs, &argc, &argv) == 0) {
15           fprintf(stderr, "usage: %s [%s] [files ...]\n", argv[0], options);
16           rc = 1;
17       } else {
18           for (i = 1; strcmp(argv[i], "--"); i++) {
19               switch(argv[i][1]) {
20               case 'option':   /* option without argument */
21                   option++;
22                   break;
...
35               case 'option':   /* option with argument */
36                   option++;
37                   option__value = argv[++i];
38                   break;
...
45               }
46           }
47           for (++i; i < argc; i++) {    /* process file names */
...
60           }
61       }
62   }
$
```

Figure 5.C.11

The options argument in line 14 defines the list of options that **scf**() searches for in the argv string vector and optionargs defines the subset of options that can accept option arguments. options and optionargs must be strings containing only letters, and all optionargs letters must appear in options. Both argv and argc are passed to **scf**() in line 14 as pointers because **scf**() creates a new set of arguments according to the Standard Command Format and may change the number of arguments to the program. Lines 18 through 46 process options, stopping when the -- program argument is found. Lines 20 through 22 process an option that has no option argument and lines 35 through 38 process

132

an option that has an option argument. Finally, lines 47 through 60 process all file names program arguments.

Figure 5.C.12 shows a revised version of **printoptions** rewritten to use the skeleton shown in figure 5.C.11.

```
$ number printoptions2b.c
 1   /*
 2    *    printoptions
 3    *         print option settings based on arguments
 4    *         version 2b - uses scf
 5    */
 6
 7   #include    <stdio.h>
 8
 9   main(argc, argv)
10   int argc;
11   char *argv[];
12
13       int i, rc = 0, aoption, boption, coption, doption;
14       char *bvalue;
15
16       aoption = boption = coption = doption = 0;
17       if (scf("abcd", "b", &argc, &argv) == 0) {
18           fprintf(stderr, "usage: %s [-a -c -d -b value]\n", argv[0]);
19           rc = 1;
20       } else {
21           for (i = 1; strcmp(argv[i], "--"); i++) {
22               switch(argv[i][1]) {
23               case 'a':
24                   aoption = 1;
25                   break;
26               case 'b':
27                   boption = 1;
28                   bvalue = argv[++i];
29                   break;
30               case 'c':
31                   coption = 1;
32                   break;
33               case 'd':
34                   doption = 1;
35                   break;
36               }
37           }
38           printf("a option %d\n", aoption);
39           printf("b option %d\n", boption);
40           if (boption) {
41               printf("The value of b option is %s\n", bvalue);
42           }
43           printf("c option %d\n", coption);
44           printf("d option %d\n", doption);
45       }
46       exit(rc);
47   }
$ ☐
```

Figure 5.C.12

134

Figure 5.C.13 shows this version of **printoptions**.

```
$ printoptions -a -b buck -c -d
a option 1
b option 1
The value of b option is buck
c option 1
d option 1
$ printoptions -a -b
printoptions: no option argument specified for b option
usage: printoptions [-a -c -d -b value]
$ printoptions -a -bbuck
printoptions: b option not followed by white space
usage: printoptions [-a -c -d -b value]
$ ▢
```

Figure 5.C.13

Finally, figure 5.C.14 shows **scf**() that uses several subroutines described in Chapter 6.

```
$ number scf.c
 1 /*
 2  *   scf
 3  *       translate arguments in the Standard Command Format
 4  *       into a form easily manipulated by C language programs
 5  */
 6
 7 #include    <stdio.h>
 8 #include    <ctype.h>
 9
10 #define     DASH        '-'
11 #define     OPTEND      "--"
12 #define     CNULL       (char **) NULL
13 #define     CSTAR       (char *)
14 #define     error(f, x)   rc = 0; fprintf(stderr, f, (*argv)[0], x)
15
16 static   char    **Nargv    = CNULL;
17
18 int
19 scf(options, optionargs, argc, argv)
20 char *options, *optionargs, **argv[];
21 int *argc;
22 {
23   int rc = 1, ai, ci, i;
24   unsigned na = 0, nf = 0;
25   char c, **nargv = CNULL, **files = CNULL;
```

135

```
26   extern char *strchr(), *malloc(), *realloc();
27
28   if ((nargv = (char **) malloc(sizeof CSTAR)) == CNULL) {
29     error("%s: memory allocation error in scf\n", "");
30   } else if (rc == goodargs(options, optionargs, (*argv)[0])) {
31     nargv[na++] = (*argv)[0];
32     for (ai = 1; rc == 1 && ai < *argc && strcmp((*argv)[ai], OPTEND); ai++) {
33       if ((*argv)[ai][0] == DASH && (*argv)[ai][1]) {
34         for (ci = 1; rc == 1 && ci < strlen((*argv)[ai]); ci++) {
35           c = (*argv)[ai][ci];
36           if (strchr(options, c) == CSTAR NULL) {
37             error("%s: illegal option %c\n", c);
38           } else if ((nargv = (char **) realloc(CSTAR nargv,
39                       (na + 1) * sizeof CSTAR)) == CNULL) {
40             error("%s: memory allocation error in scf\n", "");
41           } else if ((nargv[na] = malloc(3 * sizeof(char))) == CSTAR NULL) {
42             error("%s: memory allocation error in scf\n", "");
43           } else {
44             nargv[na][0] = DASH;
45             nargv[na][1] = c;
46             nargv[na++][2] = NULL;
47             if (strchr(optionargs, c) == CSTAR NULL) {
48               continue;
49             } else if ((nargv = (char **) realloc(CSTAR nargv,
50                         (na + 1) * sizeof CSTAR)) == CNULL) {
51               error("%s: memory allocation error in scf\n", "");
52             } else if ((*argv)[ai][ci+1] != NULL) {
53               error("%s: option %c not followed by white space\n", c);
54             } else if (ai + 1 < *argc) {
55               nargv[na++] = (*argv)[++ai];
56               ci = strlen((*argv)[ai]);
57             } else {
58               error("%s: no option argument specified for %c option\n", c);
59             }
60           }
61         }
62       } else if (nf == 0) {
63         if ((files = (char **) malloc(sizeof CSTAR)) == CNULL) {
64           error("%s: memory allocation error in scf\n", "");
65         } else {
66           files[nf++] = (*argv)[ai];
67         }
68       } else if ((files = (char **) realloc(CSTAR files,
69                   (nf + 1) * sizeof CSTAR)) == CNULL) {
70         error("%s: memory allocation error in scf\n", "");
71       } else {
72         files[nf++] = (*argv)[ai];
73       }
74     }
75     if (rc == 1) {
76       if (ai < *argc && !strcmp((*argv)[ai], OPTEND)) {
77         ai++;
78       }
```

```
79    if ((nargv = (char **) realloc(CSTAR nargv,
80                (na + nf + (*argc - ai) + 2) * sizeof CSTAR)) == CNULL) |
81      error("%s: memory allocation error in scf\n", "");
82    | else |
83      nargv[na++] = OPTEND;
84      for (i = 0; i < nf; i++) |
85        nargv[na++] = files[i];
86      |
87      for ( ; ai < *argc; ai++) |
88        nargv[na++] = (*argv)[ai];
89      |
90      nargv[na] = CSTAR NULL;
91    |
92    |
93    if (files) |
94      free(CSTAR files);
95    |
96  |
97  if (rc == 1) |
98    *argv = nargv;
99    Nargv = nargv;
100   *argc = na;
101 | else if (nargv != CNULL) |
102   free(CSTAR nargv);
103 |
104 return(rc);
105|
106
107 scfend()
108|
109
110   if (Nargv != CNULL) |
111     free(CSTAR Nargv);
112   |
113|
114
115 static int
116 goodargs(options, optionargs, name)
117 char *options, *optionargs, *name;
118|
119 register char *p;
120 register int rc = 1;
121
122 for (p = options; *p; p++) |
123   if (!isalpha(*p)) |
124     fprintf(stderr, "%s: option specifier %c is not a character\n", name, *p);
125     rc = 0;
126   |
127 |
128 for (p = optionargs; *p; p++) |
129   if (!strchr(options, *p)) |
130     fprintf(stderr, "%s: option argument specifier %c is not a legal option\n",
131       name, *p);
```

```
132     rc = 0;
133   }
134   }
135   return(rc);
136 }
$ ☐
```

Figure 5.C.14

---

scf() begins by validating the options and optionargs arguments with the **goodargs**() private subroutine. If valid, **scf**() then scans all option program arguments looking for valid options. Each option found is stored in a separate program argument in lines 44 through 46. If the option has an option argument, it too is stored in a separate program argument in line 55, after first verifying that the option is the last option in the program argument and that there is an option argument. **scf**() accumulates file names beginning in line 62 and because of the if in line 33, it treats a single dash as a file name. The double dash option/file name separator is added as a program argument in line 83 and the rearranged arguments are assigned to the argc and argv arguments in lines 98 through 100. **scf**() returns 1 if no errors were found and 0 otherwise. **scf**() also prints a message on the standard error output that explains the error it found. Because **scf**() allocates memory to hold the revised form of arguments and some program require this memory to do their jobs, **scfend**() should be called when argument processing completes to recover the memory allocated.

The **scf**() subroutine provides a way for programs to handle program arguments given in the Standard Command Format in a straightforward way. Its use is recommended in the software tools you build and is used in the programming examples shown in the rest of this book.

D. RECOGNIZING INPUT/OUTPUT FILES ON THE COMMAND LINE

The shell associates the standard input, the standard output, and the standard error files with each program. Unless you redirect the input or output on the command line, these files remain connected to your terminal. You can use redirection operators, also explained in Chapter 3, to feed a file to your program or to redirect your program's output to another file. Many programs also allow input and output file arguments. For example, the **sort** program has the following forms, all identical in operation:

```
$ sort file > newfile
$ sort < file > newfile
$ sort -o newfile file
$ sort -o newfile < file
```

Figure 5.D.1

When the redirection operators are used, the shell assumes the responsibility for program input and output. Otherwise, your program must open its own data files using the files named as arguments.

In the **sort** examples, the optional input file is the first argument after the options and option arguments. The output file is given as an option argument to the −o option. If no input file is specified, data is taken from the standard input file.

Chapter 3 discussed connecting the standard output file of one program to the standard input file of another with a technique called pipelines. For example, the following command line uses pipelines to produce a list of specific users on your system:

```
$ sort /etc/passwd | grep /bin/sh | pr -h "List of Users" | lpr
```

Figure 5.D.2

The **sort** program alphabetically sorts account name entries in the */etc/passwd* file. The **grep** program selects those sorted entries that contain the characters /bin/sh somewhere in the line, thus locating all accounts that use the Bourne Shell as their login shell. The **pr** program paginates its input and prints the title on each page of output. Finally, **lpr** causes the paginated file to be printed on the line printer.

The software tools you write should be designed to use the standard input, output, and error files where appropriate, but also be able to recognize file name arguments. For example, imagine that when files are sent between computers using a modem, spurious delete characters creep into the input stream. Your job is to write a software tool that copies its standard input to standard output and removes these delete characters.

The program shown below solves this problem by reading characters from the standard input, comparing each with the delete character, octal 177, and writing those characters that are not the delete character on the standard output file. Notice that this software tool only removes delete characters and

139

has no other function.

```
$ number clean1.c
 1   /*
 2    *    clean
 3    *        remove delete characters
 4    *        version 1
 5    */
 6
 7   #include    <stdio.h>
 8
 9   #define     DELETE     '\177'
10
11   main()
12   {
13       int c;
14
15       while ((c = getchar()) != EOF) {
16           if (c != DELETE) {
17               putchar(c);
18           }
19       }
20       exit(0);
21   }
$ cc -o clean clean1.c
$ □
```

Figure 5.D.3

Figure 5.D.4 shows a sample that uses redirection operators to name the input and output files.

```
$ clean < file > file.out
$ ls -l file file.out
total 2
-rw-r--r--   1 rogers   writers      44 Apr 21 12:23 file
-rw-r--r--   1 rogers   writers      40 Apr 21 12:24 file.out
$ □
```

Figure 5.D.4

As your software tool gains popularity, you may find that others on your system need to use **clean**. The first time they invoke **clean** with:

$ **clean file > file.out**

Figure 5.D.5

they will find that nothing happens because **clean** does not recognize the file argument. Instead, **clean** reads the standard input and waits until either a character is typed or the program is interrupted. **clean** must be extended to check for file arguments and to read those files instead of the standard input file. Figure 5.D.6 shows version 2 of **clean**, which uses **fopen**() to open the files given as arguments.

$ **number clean2.c**

```
 1   /*
 2    *    clean
 3    *          remove delete characters
 4    *          version 2
 5    */
 6
 7   #include    <stdio.h>
 8
 9   #define     DELETE     '\177'
10
11   main(argc, argv)
12   int argc;
13   char *argv[];
14   {
15       FILE *fp;
16       int i, rc = 0;
17
18       if (scf("", "", &argc, &argv) == 0) {
19           fprintf(stderr, "usage: %s [file ...]\n", argv[0]);
20           rc = 1;
21       } else if (argc == 1) {
22           clean(stdin);
23       } else {
24           for (i = 2; i < argc; i++) {
25               fp = strcmp(argv[i], "-") ? fopen(argv[i], "r") : stdin;
26               if (fp == NULL) {
27                   perror(argv[i]);
28                   rc = 1;
29                   break;
30               } else {
31                   clean(fp);
32                   if (!strcmp(argv[i], "-")) {
33                       fclose(fp);
34                   }
35               }
36           }
37       }
```

```
38        exit(rc);
39  }
40
41  clean(fp)
42  FILE *fp;
43  {
44        register int c;
45
46        while ((c = getc(fp)) != EOF) {
47              if (c != DELETE) {
48                    putchar(c);
49              }
50        }
51  }
$ cc -o clean clean2.c
$ clean file > file.out
$ ls -l file file.out
total 2
-rw-r--r--  1 rogers   writers     44 Apr 21 12:23 file
-rw-r--r--  1 rogers   writers     40 Apr 21 12:24 file.out
$ 
```

Figure 5.D.6

Recall from the definition of the Standard Command Format that the -
argument references the standard input file. If **fopen**() in line 25 cannot open
a file, it returns NULL. **perror**(), called in line 27 and described in Chapter 7,
prints an error message that explains why the file could not be opened. **clean**
returns a non-zero value with **exit**() to show that it could not do the job it was
designed to do.

```
$ clean nonexistentfile > file.out
nonexistentfile: No such file or directory
$ echo $?
1
$ 
```

Figure 5.D.7

clean is even more popular now. Stage 2 in the evolution of a software tool
begins: other users on your system use your **clean** program. The next step is
to make it more versatile.

For instance, **clean** could be revised to remove characters other than delete. It
should be modified so that it can accept an argument that defines the character
to be removed. Since **clean** tends to remove invisible control and delete

characters, the character to be deleted should be given to **clean** as a number. For example:

Representation	Definition
0177	Octal for the delete character (ASCII 127)
127	Decimal for the delete character (ASCII 127)
01	Octal for control-A (ASCII 1)
015	Octal representation for carriage return (ASCII 13)
0X0D	Hexadecimal representation for carriage return (ASCII 13)
13	Decimal representation for carriage return (ASCII 13)

In the example that follows, the decimal representation of ASCII is used.

Figure 5.D.8 shows version 3 of **clean** that uses the -c option to define the character to be deleted.

```
$ number clean3.c
 1  /*
 2   *   clean
 3   *        remove unwanted characters
 4   *        version 3
 5   */
 6
 7  #include    <stdio.h>
 8
 9  #define     DELETE    "127"
10  #define     NOTASCII  (-1)
11
12  main(argc, argv)
13  int argc;
14  char *argv[];
15  {
16      FILE *fp;
17      int i, rc = 0, delchar;
18      char *cvalue = DELETE;
19
20      if (scf("c", "c", &argc, &argv) == 0) {
21          fprintf(stderr, "usage: %s [-c value] [file ...]\n", argv[0]);
22          rc = 1;
23      } else {
24          for (i = 1; strcmp(argv[i], "--"); i++) {
25              switch(argv[i][1]) {
26              case 'c':
27                  cvalue = argv[++i];
28                  break;
29              }
30          }
31          if ((delchar = ckdec(cvalue)) == NOTASCII) {
```

143

```
32              fprintf(stderr, "%s: value to delete (%s) ", argv[0], cvalue);
33              fprintf(stderr, "not a legal decimal value for ASCII\n");
34              rc = 1;
35          } else if (++i == argc) {
36              clean(stdin, delchar);
37          } else {
38              for ( ; i < argc; i++) {
39                  fp = strcmp(argv[i], "-") ? fopen(argv[i], "r") : stdin;
40                  if (fp == NULL) {
41                      perror(argv[i]);
42                      rc = 1;
43                      break;
44                  } else {
45                      clean(fp, delchar);
46                      if (!strcmp(argv[i], "-")) {
47                          fclose(fp);
48                      }
49                  }
50              }
51          }
52      }
53      exit(rc);
54  }
55
56  clean(fp, delchar)
57  FILE *fp;
58  int delchar;
59  {
60      register int c;
61
62      while ((c = getc(fp)) != EOF) {
63          if (c != delchar) {
64              putchar(c);
65          }
66      }
67  }
68
69  int
70  ckdec(string)
71  char *string;
72  {
73      int value;
74
75      value = atoi(string);
76      if (value < 0 || value > 127) {
77          value = NOTASCII;
78      }
79      return(value);
80  }
$ cc -o clean clean3.c
$ echo abcdefghijklmnopqrstuvwxyz | clean -c 105
abcdefghjklmnopqrstuvwxyz
$ cat test
```

```
This is a test of clean
$ clean -c 105 test
Ths s a test of clean
$ □
```

Figure 5.D.8

This latest version of **clean** uses the **scf**() subroutine to decode the options. Lines 31 through 34 validate the option arguments, and lines 56 through 67 define the principal subroutine **clean**. The **ckdec**() subroutine, lines 69 through 80, converts its string argument to a decimal number and then checks to see if the number is a legal ASCII character. The execution example removes the letter i, decimal value 105, from the input stream.

This chapter discussed guidelines for building new software tools that use the same conventions as existing UNIX system software tools, and the guidelines used here are applied to the examples in the rest of this book to describe other aspects of the UNIX system. These guidelines address the standard command format, metacharacters in command lines, the standard input, output, and error files, error messages, input and output data formats, dot files and environment variables, and standard UNIX system libraries. Chapters 6 and 7 build on Guideline 7 by describing those subroutines and system calls available with the UNIX system and showing how to use them.

CHAPTER 6

THE STANDARD UNIX SUBROUTINE LIBRARY

A. INTRODUCTION

The UNIX system simplifies the job of building software tools not only because of the programming tools described in Chapter 4 but also because of the tool kit of subroutines described in this chapter. To use the subroutines provided with the UNIX system effectively, you must know what they can do. This chapter describes several of the more popular and useful subroutines, and section 3 of the **UNIX System User's Manual System V** describes all subroutine tools distributed with your system. You should also know how to add the tools you develop to your tool kit. Chapter 4 explains how to add subroutines to the standard libraries.

This chapter describes the subroutine level interface to the UNIX system made available to you through the archive libraries described in Chapter 4. The standard UNIX system library provides subroutines for doing buffered input and output, manipulating strings and memory, classifying and converting characters, manipulating time, allocating storage, and accessing variables in the environment. These software building blocks save you time when you program a problem solution. They also provide a portable, standard interface to the UNIX system and to other operating systems that support them. These subroutines are recommended in preference to the system calls defined and explained in Chapter 7.

The heart of the subroutine library is the Standard I/O library, referred to as *stdio*. The Standard I/O library is a large set of integrated I/O subroutines with a consistent interface and was designed to be called from C programs. Standard I/O also optimizes the size of data passed between such devices as disks, terminals, and programs. For example, Standard I/O knows that I/O operations involving disks are optimally handled in the logical block size of the disk, typically 1K byte blocks, and that output destined for a terminal is better handled in lines ending with a newline. The software tools you build should use the Standard I/O subroutines for all input and output.

To access the subroutines in the Standard I/O library, you must include the Standard I/O definition file in your program code, preferably at the beginning, directly after the comments section. The recommended way to include this file is with the directive shown below.

#include   <stdio.h>

Figure 6.A.1

Once you've included this file into your program code, you then have access to the macros, constants, and definitions you need to use the subroutines in the Standard I/O library.

Recall from Chapter 3 that the key to I/O at the system call level in the UNIX system is the file descriptor. A file descriptor is an index into an array of open files that the UNIX system kernel maintains for you.

In contrast, the key to I/O at the Standard I/O level is a structure that contains more information than just a file descriptor. This structure is of type FILE and is defined in the include file *stdio.h*.

The FILE type contains a file descriptor, the operations allowed on the file, and a pointer to the buffer that temporarily stores data. All accesses to a file using the Standard I/O subroutines uses a pointer to a FILE type. Figure 6.A.2 shows declarations of pointers using the FILE type.

FILE *filein, *fileout;
FILE *tempfile;

Figure 6.A.2

The *stdio.h* header file defines three files for you: the standard input, standard output, and standard error files. These files are represented by the constants stdin, stdout, and stderr, and are connected to file descriptors 0, 1, and 2 respectively. They form the high-level filter-oriented interface used by many software tools in the UNIX system.

The *stdio.h* header file also defines three important constants. They are EOF, meaning end-of-file and defined to be -1; NULL, a null pointer and defined to be 0; and BUFSIZ, the ideal input/output size for your system and defined to be the logical block size of the disk, typically 1K bytes.

The sections that follow explain the Standard I/O subroutines most often used for input and output, manipulating strings and memory, portable ASCII data conversions, manipulating time, allocating storage, and accessing variables in the environment. See Section 3 of the **UNIX System User's Manual System V** for a complete and concise explanation of the subroutines described here.

B. SUBROUTINES FOR INPUT AND OUTPUT

This section describes the subroutines available in the Standard I/O library to open and close files, do input and output at the line, character, and object levels, do formatted input and output,check the status of files, access files randomly, execute shell level commands from a process, and establish a pipe between two processes.

B.1 Opening and Closing a File

All files should be opened with either the **fopen**() or the **freopen**() subroutine, both of which require a file name and a mode that defines the operations you are going to do on the file. The **fopen**() and **freopen**() subroutines have the syntax:

FILE *
fopen(*file__name, option__string*)
char *file__name*;
char *option__string*;

FILE *
freopen(*file__name, option__string, stream*)
char *file__name*;
char *option__string*;
FILE *stream*;

DEFINITION 14. The fopen Subroutine

and the operations available are shown in the following table.

STRING	OPERATION
"r"	Open for reading from the beginning of the file.
"w"	Open for writing starting at the beginning of the file. If the file does not exist, it is created first. If the file does exist, its contents are discarded.
"a"	Open for writing at the end of the file, or create the file for writing.
"r+"	Open the file for reading and writing.
"w+"	Open for reading and writing. If the file does not exist, it is created first. If the file does exist, its contents are discarded.
"a+"	Open for reading and writing at the end of the file. If the file does not exist, a+ is the same as w+.

fopen() opens the file named by *file__name* according to *option__string* and returns a pointer to a FILE type. **freopen()** first closes the file identified by *stream* and then opens the file named by *file__name* according to *option__string*. **freopen()** is useful when you must redirect an already open stream file to another file. See **clean**, version 2 in Chapter 5 for an example.

If **fopen()** or **freopen()** cannot open a file, each returns a NULL file pointer, which should trigger some type of error recovery procedure in your program. You can use the C language skeleton shown in figure 6.B.1 as one way to react to **fopen()** returning an error.

```
if ((fp = fopen(filename, "a")) = = (FILE *) NULL) |
        perror (filename);
        rc = 1; / * save the error condition for the exit statement * /
| else |
              / * process this file * /

|
```

Figure 6.B.1

Figure 6.B.2 shows the **there** program which merely opens the files given as arguments. **there** can be used to show if a file is "there".

```
$ number there1.c
 1   /*
 2    *   there
 3    *       check if files are there
 4    *       version 1
 5    */
 6
 7   #include    <stdio.h>
 8
 9   main(argc, argv)
10   int argc;
11   char *argv[];
12   {
13       FILE *fp;
14       int rc = 0, i;
15
16       for (i = 1; i < argc; i++) {
17           if ((fp = fopen(argv[i], "r")) == (FILE *) NULL) {
18               perror(argv[i]);
19               rc = 1;
20           }
21       }
22       exit(rc);
23   }
$ cc -o there there1.c
$□
```

Figure 6.B.2

Line 7 includes the standard input and output library definitions, and line 13 declares fp to be a pointer to a FILE type. If a file named as an argument cannot be opened, the **fopen**() subroutine returns a null pointer. **there** displays the reason the file could not be opened with **perror**() and continues processing arguments.

Figure 6.B.3 shows the **there** program testing for the presence of files.

```
$ ls
prog
report
there1.c
there
$ there prog
$ there Prog
Prog: No such file or directory
$ □
```

Figure 6.B.3

ls first shows which files are in the current directory. **there** verifies that *prog* is there, but then shows that *Prog* is not.

The UNIX system kernel places a limit on the number of files that can be open at any instant, and although the limit – 20 – is generous, you can run into problems if files are not closed when they are no longer needed. To close a file and de-allocate the internal data structures built by **fopen**() and **freopen**(), use the **fclose**() subroutine whose syntax is shown below.

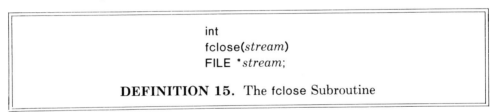

```
            int
            fclose(stream)
            FILE *stream;
```

DEFINITION 15. The fclose Subroutine

fclose() returns EOF if the close operation was unsuccessful.

Figure 6.B.4 shows version 2 of the **there** program that uses **fclose**().

```
$ number there2.c
 1  /*
 2   *   there
 3   *       check if files are there
 4   *       version 2
 5   */
 6
 7  #include    <stdio.h>
 8
 9  main(argc, argv)
10  int argc;
11  char *argv[];
12  {
13      FILE *fp;
14      int rc = 0, i;
15
16      for (i = 1; i < argc; i++) {
17          if ((fp = fopen(argv[i], "r")) == (FILE *) NULL) {
18              perror(argv[i]);
19              rc = 1;
20          } else if (fclose(fp) == EOF) {
21              perror(argv[i]);
22              rc = 1;
23          }
24      }
25      exit(rc);
26  }
$ □
```

Figure 6.B.4

If the file is opened for writing or appending, **fclose**() also flushes all data from the internal buffer to the related file. You can also explicitly flush the data with the **fflush**() subroutine. Its syntax is:

```
            int
            fflush(stream)
            FILE *stream;
```

DEFINITION 16. The fflush Subroutine

---

and it also returns EOF if the flush operation was unsuccessful.

B.2 Line Oriented I/O

Standard I/O provides two sets of line oriented I/O subroutines. One set, **gets**() and **puts**(), is used for the standard input and output files and the other set, **fgets**() and **fputs**(), is used for arbitrary files. The syntax for these subroutines is:

```
            char *
            gets(string);
            char *string;

            int
            puts(string);
            char *string;

            char *
            fgets(string, count, stream);
            char *string;
            int   count;
            FILE *stream;

            int
            fputs(string, stream);
            char *string;
            FILE *stream;
```

DEFINITION 17. Line Oriented I/O Subroutines

When **gets**() reads a line of characters and stores it in *string*, it replaces the line-ending newline character with a null character. The null character marks the end of the string pointed to by the *string* argument. Conversely, **puts**() adds a newline character onto the end of the *string* argument and then writes that string to the standard output. **gets**() returns its argument or NULL if it discovers end-of-file or an error. **puts**() returns EOF when it discovers an error.

The **fgets**() subroutine works like **gets**() except that it leaves the line-ending newline character intact and adds a null character directly after this newline in the buffer referenced by *string*. **fgets**() also reads no more than *count*-1 characters into *string*, stopping earlier if it finds a newline. **fputs**() complements **fgets**() because it does not add a newline character to the string that it writes to *stream*. Both **fgets**() and **fputs**() return the same values as **gets**() and **puts**().

Figure 6.B.5 shows another version of the **number** program that numbers the lines in its standard input file before copying them to the standard output file. **number** uses **fgets**() and **fputs**() to read and write information.

```
$ number number.c
 1   /*
 2    *   number
 3    *       preface lines with line numbers
 4    */
 5
 6   #include    <stdio.h>
 7
 8   main(argc, argv)
 9   int argc;
10   char *argv[];
11   {
12       char string[BUFSIZ], nums[BUFSIZ];
13       int number = 1, rc = 0;
14
15       while (fgets(string, sizeof(string), stdin) != (char *) NULL) {
16           itoa(number++, nums);
17           if (fputs(nums, stdout) == EOF || fputs("\t", stdout) == EOF ||
18               fputs(string, stdout) == EOF) {
19               perror("stdout");
20               rc = 1;
21               break;
22           }
23       }
24       exit(rc);
25   }
26
27   int
28   itoa(n, s)
29   int n;
30   char *s;
31   {
32       int c, i, j;
33       char *t = s;
34
35       do {
36           *s++ = n % 10 + '0';
```

```
37      | while ((n / = 10) > 0);
38      *s = NULL;
39      for (i = 0, j = s - t - 1; i < j; i++, j--) |
40          c = t[i];
41          t[i] = t[j];
42          t[j] = c;
43      |
44 |
$ cc -o number number.c
$ cat testfile
this is line 1
this is line 2
$ number < testfile
1    this is line 1
2    this is line 2
$ ☐
```

Figure 6.B.5

number reads and writes one line at a time. The **itoa**() subroutine converts its integer argument to an ASCII string. Since **fgets**() retains the newline character at the end of each input line in the variable string, **fputs**() should be called to write out the string. **fgets**() and **fputs**() are used in this example because they do not add a newline character at the end of the string they print. This means that the line number, a tab character, and the input line all appear on the same output line as directed by **fputs**() in lines 17 and 18.

B.3 Character I/O

Sometimes it is easier to handle characters individually instead of a line at a time. The **fgetc**() and **fputc**() subroutines and the **getchar**(), **getc**(), **putchar**(), and **putc**() macros let you read and write individual characters. Both **getc**() and **fgetc**() read a single character from an arbitrary file and **putc**() and **fputc**() write a single character to an arbitrary file. **getchar**() and **putchar**() work with standard input and output, respectively. The table below summarizes these Standard I/O subroutines.

FUNCTION	OPERATION	TYPE	FILE	SYNTAX
getchar	READ	Macro	Standard input	int c; c = getchar();
putchar	WRITE	Macro	Standard output	char c; int x; x = putchar(c);
getc	READ	Macro	Any	FILE *stream; int c; c = getc(stream);
putc	WRITE	Macro	Any	FILE *stream; char c; int x; x = putc(c, stream);
fgetc	READ	Function	Any	FILE *stream; int c; c = fgetc(stream);
fputc	WRITE	Function	Any	FILE *stream; char c; int x; x = fputc(c, stream);

DEFINITION 18. Character I/O Subroutines

putchar(), **putc**(), and **fputc**() all return their first argument or EOF on error.
The **repeatlines** program, figure 6.B.6, uses **getchar**() and **putchar**().

```
$ number repeatlines1.c
 1   /*
 2    *  repeatlines
 3    *      copy standard input to standard output
 4    *      version 1
 5    */
 6
 7   #include    <stdio.h>
 8
 9   main()
10   {
11       int c;
12
13       while ((c = getchar()) != EOF) {
14           putchar(c);
15       }
16       exit(0);
17   }
$ cc -o repeatlines repeatlines1.c
$ repeatlines
This program echoes characters.
This program echoes characters.
$ ▢
```

Figure 6.B.6

repeatlines copies characters from the standard input file to the standard output file until **getchar**() returns EOF. This happens when you enter the end-of-file code, a control-D, on a line by itself. Figure 6.B.7 shows the equivalent program built with **getc**() and **putc**().

```
$ number repeatlines2.c
 1   /*
 2    *   repeatlines
 3    *        copy standard input to standard output
 4    *        version 2
 5    */
 6
 7   #include    <stdio.h>
 8
 9   main()
10   {
11       int c;
12
13       while ((c = getc(stdin)) != EOF) {
14           putc(c, stdout);
15       }
16       exit(0);
17   }
$ cc -o repeatlines repeatlines2.c
$ repeatlines
This program also echoes characters.
This program also echoes characters.
$ □
```

Figure 6.B.7

B.4 Object Oriented I/O

The Standard I/O subroutines introduced so far are difficult to use when you must read and write files containing binary data and data stored as records. The best way to read and write this type of file is with the **fread**() and **fwrite**() subroutines.

These subroutines have the syntax:

```
        int
        fread((char *)ptr, sizeof(type), nitems, stream)
        type ptr;
        int nitems;
        FILE *stream;


        int
        fwrite((char *)ptr, sizeof(type), nitems, stream)
        type ptr;
        int nitems;
        FILE *stream;
```

DEFINITION 19. Object Oriented I/O Subroutines

where *nitems* defines the maximum number of items of type *type* to read from or write to *stream*. Both subroutines return the number of items read or written.

Figure 6.B.8 shows the C language structure that defines the format of records in the */etc/utmp* file. The UNIX system maintains this file to show who is logged into the system.

```
struct utmp {
      char      ut__user[8];
      char      ut__id[4];
      char      ut__line[12];
      short     ut__pid[2];
      struct exit__status {
          short  e__termination;
          short  e__exit;
      } ut__exit;
      time__t   ut__time;
};
```

Figure 6.B.8

When someone logs in, the UNIX system makes an entry in */etc/utmp* with the ut__type field set to USER__PROCESS, the user's name, the terminal name where the user logged in, and the time when the user logged in. When that user logs out, the UNIX system overwrites the user name entry with NULLs. The **Who** program, figure 6.B.9, reads */etc/utmp* with **fread**() and displays its contents.

```
$ number Who1.c
 1   /*
 2    *   Who
 3    *       who is currently logged in
 4    *       version 1
 5    */
 6
 7   #include    <stdio.h>
 8   #include    <sys/types.h>
 9   #include    <utmp.h>
10
11   #define     UTMPFILE  "/etc/utmp"
12
13   main(argc, argv)
14   int argc;
15   char *argv[];
16   {
17       FILE *fp;
18       struct utmp record;
19       int rc = 0;
20
21       if ((fp = fopen(UTMPFILE, "r")) == (FILE *) NULL) {
22           perror(UTMPFILE);
23           rc = 1;
24       } else {
25           while (fread((char *) &record, sizeof(record), 1, fp) == 1) {
26               if (record.ut_type == USER_PROCESS && record.ut_name[0] != NULL) {
27                   if (fputs(record.ut_name, stdout) == EOF ||
28                       fputs("\t", stdout) == EOF ||
29                       puts(record.ut_line) == EOF) {
30                           perror("stdout");
31                           rc = 1;
32                           break;
33                   }
34               }
35           }
36           if (fclose(fp) == EOF) {
37               perror(UTMPFILE);
38               rc = 1;
39           }
40       }
41       exit(rc);
42   }
$ cc -o Who Who1.c
$ Who
becca   ttya1
starr   ttya2
rogers  ttya3
ted     ttya4
$ ▯
```

Figure 6.B.9

161

The call to **fread**() on line 25 reads one record from the */etc/utmp* file, and if the record is of type USER__PROCESS and the record's name field is not null, the user and terminal names are displayed on the standard output file. The while loop ends when **fread**() finds end-of-file.

Notice especially the use of the sizeof operator provided by the C language. sizeof is an important C compiler directive that returns the size of a data structure. Its use helps to make your programs more portable by eliminating the need to code constants that reflect the specifics of a particular machine.

You can also use **fread**() and **fwrite**() to read an entire array of objects. The **fread**() call shown below reads an array of characters from a file.

```
FILE *fp;
char buffer[BUFSIZ];
int count;

count = fread(buffer, 1, sizeof(buffer), fp);
```

Figure 6.B.10

fread() returns the number of characters read.

B.5 Checking File Status

Standard I/O provides two subroutines that let you check the status of an open file. These subroutines are **feof**(), which returns the end-of-file status, and **ferror**(), which returns the error status. The syntax for **feof**() and **ferror**() is:

```
                            int
                            feof(stream)
                            FILE *stream;

                            int
                            ferror(stream)
                            FILE *stream;
```

DEFINITION 20. File Status Subroutines

The **feof**() subroutine can be used to control a loop. The program segment below shows an example.

```
$ number repeatlines3.c
 1   /*
 2    *    repeatlines
 3    *       copy standard input to standard output
 4    *    version 3
 5    */
 6
 7   #include   <stdio.h>
 8
 9   main()
10   {
11       int c;
12
13       c = getchar();
14       while (!feof(stdin)) {
15           putchar(c);
16           c = getchar();
17       }
18       exit(0);
19   }
$ □
```

Figure 6.B.11

Since the Standard I/O input subroutines return **EOF** when they reach end-of-file, you usually don't need to use **feof**(). Figure 6.B.6 shows the recommended version of **repeatlines**.

I/O errors resulting from hardware malfunctions are rare in the UNIX system, so the **ferror**() function is used infrequently. Any errors that do occur are likely to happen when the UNIX system cannot find a file or when a file is off-limits. Your programs should reflect these errors to the user with the **perror**() subroutine.

However, if you often use floppy disk media, you will probably encounter hardware errors. Your programs should expect these errors and handle them gracefully. Figure 6.B.12 shows the **floppy** program that was designed to do the more extensive error checking required when reading and writing floppy disks.

```
$ number floppy.c
 1   /*
 2    *   floppy
 3    *       copy standard input to standard output
 4    *       with error checking
 5    */
 6
 7   #include    <stdio.h>
 8
 9   main()
10   {
11       int c, rc = 0;
12
13       do {
14           if ((c = getchar()) == EOF) {
15               if (ferror(stdin)) {
16                   perror("stdin");
17                   rc = 1;
18               }
19           } else if (putchar(c) == EOF) {
20               perror("stdout");
21               rc = 1;
22           }
23       } while (c != EOF);
24       exit(rc);
25   }
$ ▢
```

Figure 6.B.12

B.6 Formatted I/O

In Chapter 5, Guideline 5 recommends that input and output data should be text wherever possible. The Standard I/O subroutines explained so far read and write information as text, but they do not convert that information to a form that lets your programs operate more efficiently. You need subroutines that do the conversions between the text form of information and a more efficient internal form.

This section describes the **printf**() and **scanf**() Standard I/O subroutine families. These subroutines convert information from an internal form to the text form and back again.

B.6.a Formatted output The **printf**() subroutine family is similar to a combination of the FORTRAN format and write statements and comes in the three related forms listed below.

printf()   Converts its arguments and writes the result on the standard output file.

164

fprintf()   Converts its arguments and writes the result on an arbitrary file or stream.

sprintf()   Converts its arguments and stores the result in a string.

The syntax for these forms is:

```
int
printf(format [ , arg ] ... );
char *format;


int
fprintf(stream, format [ , arg ] ... );
FILE *stream;
char *format;


int
sprintf(s, format [ , arg ] ... );
char *s, *format;
```

DEFINITION 21. The printf Subroutine Family

The *format* specification is a string that describes the internal form of the *arg* arguments and how they are to be converted to the text form. The string can contain literal characters that **printf**() displays without conversion and format specifiers, introduced with %, that tell **printf**() what type an argument is and how to convert it for printing. Integer, long, double, float, character, and string type variables can be converted with the **printf**() family of subroutines, and the format specifiers refer to the *arg* arguments following the *format* string argument. The table below shows the types of conversion available.

OUTPUT TYPE	C VARIABLE TYPE	FORMAT SPECIFICATION
String	pointer to char	%s
Character	int, char	%c
Exponent	float, double	%e, %E
Floating Point	float, double	%f
Integer as decimal	int unsigned int long long unsigned	%d %u %ld %lu

165

OUTPUT TYPE	C VARIABLE TYPE	FORMAT SPECIFICATION
Integer as octal	int	%o
	long	%lo
Integer as hex	int	%x, %X
	long	%lx

Figure 6.B.13 shows another version of the **Who** program that uses **printf**() to reformat the information in the */etc/utmp* file.

```
$ number Who2.c
 1   /*
 2    *   Who
 3    *       who is currently logged in
 4    *       version 2
 5    */
 6
 7   #include    <stdio.h>
 8   #include    <sys/types.h>
 9   #include    <utmp.h>
10
11   #define     UTMPFILE   "/etc/utmp"
12
13   main(argc, argv)
14   int argc;
15   char *argv[];
16   {
17       FILE *fp;
18       struct utmp record;
19       int rc = 0;
20
21       if ((fp = fopen(UTMPFILE, "r")) == (FILE *) NULL) {
22           perror(UTMPFILE);
23           rc = 1;
24       } else {
25           while (fread((char *) &record, sizeof(record), 1, fp) == 1) {
26               if (record.ut_type == USER_PROCESS && record.ut_name[0] != NULL) {
27                   printf("%s\t%s\n", record.ut_name, record.ut_line);
28               }
29           }
30           if (fclose(fp) == EOF) {
31               perror(UTMPFILE);
32               rc = 1;
33           }
34       }
35       exit(rc);
36   }
$ cc -o Who Who2.c
$ Who
becca   ttya1
starr   ttya2
rogers  ttya3
ted     ttya4
$ ▢
```

Figure 6.B.13

The format string specified in line 27 tells **printf**() that its arguments should be printed as follows:

%s   The first argument is a string; and all characters in the string, up to
       the string-ending null character, are to be printed without conversion.

%s   The second argument is also a string and should be printed like the
       first argument.

Figure 6.B.14 shows another example of the **printf**() subroutine.

```
$ number percent.c
 1   /*
 2    *   percent
 3    *      compute percents
 4    */
 5
 6   #include    <stdio.h>
 7
 8   main(argc, argv)
 9   int argc;
10   char *argv[];
11   {
12       int i;
13       double x, percent, atof();
14
15       for (i = 1; i + 1 < argc;) {
16           percent = atof(argv[i++]);
17           x = atof(argv[i++]);
18           printf("%f%% of %f is %f\n", percent, x, percent * x / 100.);
19       }
20       exit(0);
21   }
$ cc -o percent percent.c
$ percent 10 100 5 20 13.5 15000
10.000000% of 100.000000 is 10.000000
5.000000% of 20.000000 is 1.000000
13.500000% of 15000.000000 is 2025.000000
$ □
```

Figure 6.B.14

In this example, the format string in line 18 tells **printf**() to format its
arguments as listed below.

%f   Print the next (first) argument as a floating point number with 6 digits
       of precision, the default, since no precision specification was given.

%%   Print a single percent sign.

%f   Print the next (second) argument as a floating point number with 6
       digits of precision.

168

%f   Print the next (third) argument as a floating point number with 6 digits of precision.

printf() also lets you specify the adjustment, field width, precision, and data type for converted values. Figure 6.B.15 shows several examples where these format modifiers are used.

```
$ number pex.c
 1  /*
 2   *  pex
 3   *      printf examples
 4   */
 5
 6  #include    <stdio.h>
 7
 8  main(argc, argv)
 9  int argc;
10  char *argv[];
11  {
12      int i = 8916;
13      float f = 123.45;
14      double d = 6.023 * 100000000;
15      char *s = "Number of Atoms";
16
17      printf("%d, %f, %f, %s\n", i, f, d, s);
18      printf("%6d, %3.1f, %3.0f, %20s\n", i, f, d, s);
19      printf("%3d, %-6d, %06o\n",i, i, i);
20      printf("%5s\n", s);
21      exit(0);
22  }
$ cc -o pex pex.c
$ pex
8916, 123.449997, 602300000.000000, Number of Atoms
 8916, 123.4, 602300000,      Number of Atoms
8916, 8916  , 021324
Number of Atoms
$ ▯
```

Figure 6.B.15

The **printf**() in line 17 causes its arguments to be printed as a decimal number, a floating point number with 6 digits of precision, another floating point number, and a string. Each printed value takes as much space as it needs to hold the result.

Lines 18, 19, and 20 print the same arguments but they use the adjustment, field width, and precision capabilities of **printf**(). The form of these capabilities is defined and explained below.

> *%[flags][field__width][.precision][l]format__specifier*
>
> **DEFINITION 22.** Field Width and Precision

- The flags field can be any combination of the following:

  - The argument will be left adjusted in the field instead of right adjusted.

  + The formatted result will always have a sign, either + or -.

  space   If the first character of a signed conversion is not a sign, then the result will be prefaced by a space.

  #   For %o conversions, a zero will preface the result. For %x (%X) conversions, a 0x (OX) will preface the result. For %e, %E, %f, %g, and %G conversions, the result will always contain a decimal point. For %g and %G conversions, all trailing zeroes will remain.

- The *field__width* value defines the minimum width of the result. If the result has fewer than *field__width* characters, it is right or left adjusted in the field. **printf**() fills the remaining positions in the field with spaces or with zeroes if *field__width* begins with a 0.

- The *.precision* value defines the maximum number of digits to be printed after the decimal point with e and f format specifiers, or the maximum number of characters to be printed with the s format specifier.

- The l character modifies the d, o, u, X, and x format specifiers and tells **printf**() that the argument is a long integer.

Both the field width and the precision values may be given with an *. **printf**() uses the next argument in the *arg* list as the field width or precision value. Figure 6.B.16 shows an example.

```
$ number histo.c
 1  /*
 2   *  histo
 3   *      print a histogram of word lengths
 4   */
 5
 6  #include    <stdio.h>
 7
 8  #define     MAXSIZE     32
 9  #define     WIDTH       50
10
11  main(argc, argv)
12  int argc;
13  char *argv[];
14  {
15      int i, n, maxlen, maxcount, tick;
16      long lengths[MAXSIZE], total;
17      char buffer[BUFSIZ], *gets();
18
19      for (i = 0; i < MAXSIZE; i++) {
20          lengths[i] = 0;
21      }
22      maxlen = 0;
23      while (gets(buffer) != (char *) NULL) {
24          n = strlen(buffer);
25          if (n >= MAXSIZE) {
26              lengths[0]++;
27          } else {
28              lengths[n]++;
29              if (n > maxlen) {
30                  maxlen = n;
31              }
32          }
33      }
34      maxcount = 0;
35      for (i = 0; i <= maxlen; i++) {
36          if (lengths[i] > maxcount) {
37              maxcount = lengths[i];
38          }
39      }
40      printf("Length\t|");
41      for (i = 0; i <= WIDTH; i++) {
42          putchar('-');
43      }
44      printf("| Count\n");
45      tick = (maxcount + (WIDTH - 1)) / WIDTH;
46      total = 0;
47      if (lengths[0]) {
48          n = lengths[0] / tick;
49          printf("%5d+\t|%*s%*s%6d\n", i, n + 1, "*", (WIDTH - n + 1), "|", lengths[0]);
50          total += lengths[0];
51      }
```

171

```
52      for (i = maxlen; i > 0 ; i--) {
53          n = lengths[i] / tick;
54          printf("%5d\t|%*s%*s%6d\n", i, n + 1, "*", (WIDTH - n + 1), "|", lengths[i]);
55          total += lengths[i];
56      }
57      printf("TOTAL\t|");
58      for (i = 0; i <= WIDTH; i++) {
59          putchar('-');
60      }
61      printf("|%6d\n", total);
62      exit(0);
63  }
$ cc -o histo histo.c
$ □
```

Figure 6.B.16

When run with the on-line dictionary, */usr/lib/w2006*, **histo** displays the following:

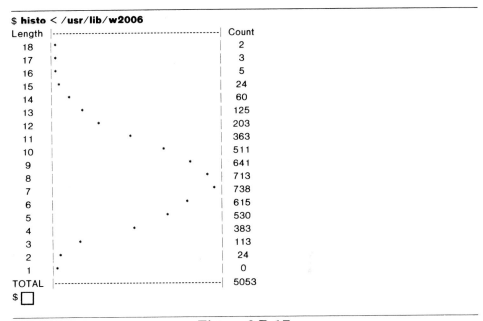

Figure 6.B.17

In the examples shown so far in this section, the **fprintf()** subroutine could be used in place of the **printf()** subroutine by replacing a call to **printf()** with a call to **fprintf()**, using stdout as the first argument.

172

Finally, the **sprintf**() subroutine provides the same type of functions available with **printf**() and **fprintf**() except that **sprintf**() leaves its result in a string pointed to by the first argument. Figure 6.B.18 shows an example where **sprintf**() is used to build the name of a temporary file. The **getpid**() system call, described in Chapter 7 and used in line 19, returns the process ID of the current process. A process ID is guaranteed to be unique among all processes in progress in the UNIX system and its use allows for unique file naming.

```
$ number renumber.c
 1   /*
 2    *   renumber
 3    *       add line numbers to a file
 4    */
 5
 6   #include    <stdio.h>
 7
 8   #define     TEMPDIR         "/tmp"
 9
10   main(argc, argv)
11   int argc;
12   char *argv[];
13   {
14       FILE *temp, *fp;
15       int i, number, rc = 0;
16       char filename[BUFSIZ], line[BUFSIZ];
17
18       if (argc > 1) {
19           sprintf(filename, "%s/%d", TEMPDIR, getpid());
20           for (i = 1; i < argc; i++) {
21               if ((temp = fopen(filename, "w")) == (FILE *) NULL) {
22                   perror(filename);
23                   rc = 1;
24                   break;
25               } else if ((fp = fopen(argv[i], "r")) == (FILE *) NULL) {
26                   perror(argv[i]);
27                   rc = 1;
28                   break;
29               }
30               while (fgets(line, sizeof(line), fp) != NULL) {
31                   fputs(line, temp);
32               }
33               fclose(fp);
34               fclose(temp);
35               if ((temp = fopen(filename, "r")) == (FILE *) NULL) {
36                   perror(filename);
37                   rc = 1;
38                   break;
39               } else if ((fp = fopen(argv[i], "w")) == (FILE *) NULL) {
40                   perror(argv[i]);
41                   rc = 1;
42                   break;
```

173

```
43              |
44              number = 1;
45              while (fgets(line, sizeof(line), temp) != NULL) |
46                      fprintf(fp, "%-4d\t%s", number++, line);
47              |
48              fclose(fp);
49              fclose(temp);
50          |
51      |
52      exit(rc);
53 |
$ []
```

Figure 6.B.18

```
$ cc -o renumber renumber.c
$ renumber nofile
nofile: No such file or directory
$ cat file
This is the first line.
This is the second line.
This is the third line.
$ renumber file
$ cat file
1       This is the first line.
2       This is the second line.
3       This is the third line.
$ []
```

Figure 6.B.19

B.6.b Formatted input The **scanf**() subroutine family is the Standard I/O counterpart to the **printf**() family. It too works with format specifiers and argument lists and also has three forms listed below.

scanf()   Converts input from the standard input and assigns the values to the variables given as arguments.

fscanf()   Converts input from an arbitrary file or stream and assigns the values to the variables given as arguments.

sscanf()   Converts input from a string and assigns the values to the variables given as arguments.

174

The syntax for the three forms is:

```
int
scanf(format [ , pointer ] ... );
char *format;

int
fscanf(stream, format [ , pointer ] ... )
FILE *stream;
char *format;

int
sscanf(s, format [ , pointer ] ... )
char *s, *format;
```

DEFINITION 23. The scanf Subroutine Family

These subroutines return EOF on end-of-file or the number of conversions made as directed by the *format* string.

Unlike **printf**(), **scanf**() requires the address of each variable in the argument list instead of the variable's value because it puts the data it reads into these variables. To do this in the C language, **scanf**() must be able to reference each variable by address.

The syntax of the *format* string in **scanf**() is similar to that of **printf**(), but different enough to cause problems. The table below lists the legal format specifiers for **scanf**().

INPUT TYPE	C VARIABLE TYPE	FORMAT SPECIFICATION
String	pointer to char	%s, %[]
Character	pointer to char	%c
Exponent	pointer to float	%e
	pointer to double	%le
Floating Point	pointer to float	%f
	pointer to double	%lf
Integer as decimal	pointer to short	%hd
	pointer to int	%d
	pointer to long	%ld

INPUT TYPE	C VARIABLE TYPE	FORMAT SPECIFICATION
Integer as octal	pointer to short pointer to int pointer to long	%ho %o %lo
Integer as hex	pointer to short pointer to int pointer to long	%hx %x %lx
Unsigned	pointer to short pointer to int pointer to long	%hu %u %lu

Though you can use the above formats in any combination, you should keep your statements as simple as possible. Figure 6.B.20 shows an example.

```
$ number scan1.c
 1  /*
 2   *   scan
 3   *       scanf example
 4   *       version 1
 5   */
 6
 7  #include    <stdio.h>
 8
 9  main(argc, argv)
10  int argc;
11  char *argv[];
12  {
13      int i, j, k, count;
14
15      i = j = k = 0;
16      if ((count = scanf("%d %d %d", &i, &j, &k)) != EOF) {
17          printf("Read %d items: i=%d, j=%d, k=%d\n", count, i, j, k);
18      }
19      exit(0);
20  }
$ cc -o scan scan1.c
$ scan
4 9898 9
Read 3 items: i=4, j=9898, k=9
$ scan
1 2 3
Read 3 items: i=1, j=2, k=3
$ □
```

Figure 6.B.20

scanf() reads three values and assigns the first to i, the second to j, and the third to k. **scanf**() returns 3 because it was able to make 3 assignments based on the format string.

If the input to **scan** was changed to the line

4, 9898, 9

only the 4 would be assigned to i because the next character in the format string is a space, matching any white space in the input stream, but the next character in the input stream is a comma. Because of this conflict, **scanf**() returns 1 meaning that only one value was assigned. To read this line with commas, commas must be included in the format statement. Figure 6.B.21 shows the revised version.

```
$ number scan2.c
 1  /*
 2   *    scan
 3   *        scanf example
 4   *        version 2
 5   */
 6
 7  #include    <stdio.h>
 8
 9  main(argc, argv)
10  int argc;
11  char *argv[];
12  {
13      int i, j, k, count;
14
15      i = j = k = 0;
16      if ((count = scanf("%d, %d, %d", &i, &j, &k)) != EOF) {
17          printf("Read %d items: i=%d, j=%d, k=%d\n", count, i, j, k);
18      }
19      exit(0);
20  }
$ cc -o scan scan2.c
$ scan
4, 9898, 9
Read 3 items: i=4, j=9898, k=9
$ scan
1 2 3
Read 1 items: i=1, j=0, k=0
$ □
```

Figure 6.B.21

Sometimes you may wish to ignore a specific value on an input line. You can do this by putting an asterisk after the percent sign in the format specifier that

177

corresponds to the ignored value, as figure 6.B.22 shows.

```
$ number scan3.c
 1   /*
 2    *   scan
 3    *        scanf example
 4    *        version 3
 5    */
 6
 7   #include    <stdio.h>
 8
 9   main(argc, argv)
10   int argc;
11   char *argv[];
12   {
13       int i, j, k, count;
14
15       i = j = k = 0;
16       if ((count = scanf("%d, %*d, %d", &i, &j, &k)) != EOF) {
17           printf("Read %d items: i=%d, j=%d, k=%d\n", count, i, j, k);
18       }
19       exit(0);
20   }
$ cc -o scan scan3.c
$ scan
4, 9898, 9
Read 2 items: i=4, j=9, k=0
$ scan
1, 2, 3
Read 2 items: i=1, j=3, k=0
$ □
```

Figure 6.B.22

When you read input to be assigned to strings, you can define which characters you want assigned by enclosing those characters in brackets. Furthermore, **scanf**() recognizes that when the first character in brackets is the caret (ˆ), all characters *except* those that follow the caret can be assigned if found in the input stream.

For example, a file of business accounts might consist of records separated by newlines and fields separated by colons. You can write a filter that prints a report of the accounts by using a combination of **printf**() and **scanf**(). The example below shows a program that reads and reformats a file in this format.

```
$ number labels.c
 1   /*
 2    *   labels
 3    *        print mailing labels
 4    */
 5
 6   #include <stdio.h>
 7
 8   main(argc, argv)
 9   int argc;
10   char *argv[];
11   {
12       FILE *fp;
13       int i, rc = 0;
14
15       if (scf("","", &argc, &argv) == 0) {
16           fprintf(stderr, "usage: %s [file ...]\n", argv[0]);
17           rc = 1;
18       } else if (argc == 2) {
19           format(stdin);
20       } else {
21           for (i = 2; i < argc; i++) {
22               fp = strcmp(argv[i], "-") ? fopen(argv[i], "r") : stdin;
23               if (fp == (FILE *) NULL) {
24                   perror(argv[i]);
25                   rc = 1;
26                   break;
27               } else {
28                   format(fp);
29                   if (fp != stdin) {
30                       fclose(fp);
31                   }
32               }
33           }
34       }
35       exit(rc);
36   }
37
38   format(fp)
39   FILE *fp;
40   {
41       struct {
42           char first[20];
43           char last[20];
44           char address[20];
45           char city[20];
46           char state[3];
47           char zip[20];
48       } c;
49
50       for (;;) {
51           fscanf(fp,"%[^:]%*c%[^:]%*c%[^:]%*c%[^:]%*c%[^:]%*c%s",
52               c.first, c.last, c.address, c.city, c.state, c.zip);
53           if (feof(fp)) {
54               break;
55           }
56           printf("%s %s\n%s\n%s %s %s\n\n",
57               c.first, c.last, c.address, c.city, c.state, c.zip);
```

179

```
58        ¦
59    ¦
$ cc -o labels labels.c
$ ☐
```

Figure 6.B.23

Line 45 uses the bracket notation to define the allowable strings. This statement reads and copies 6 colon-separated strings into a structure of type c. The first 5 strings require the format %[^:]%*c, where the %[^:] specifies a string that ends with a colon and the %*c specifies that a single character, here a colon, should be ignored. The last string ends with white space, so no explicit string-ending character set needs to be defined. Figure 6.B.24 shows a sample.

```
$ cat mailinglist
First:Last:Street:Town:St:Zip
Leon:Barr:123 Main Street:Santa Cruz:CA:90000
Ron:Silverstein:1 California St:San Francisco:CA:94115
Jean:Smith:4222 Sterling Rd:Los Sopranos:CA:94033
John:Doe:9 Anywhere Drive:Hicksville:NY:11801
Pete:Anonymous:1 W 72 St:New York:NY:10023
$ labels - mailinglist
Larry:Rogers:105 College Road:Princeton:NJ:08540
Larry Rogers
105 College Road
Princeton NJ 08540


ˆDFirst Last
Street
Town St Zip


Leon Barr
123 Main Street
Santa Cruz CA   90000


Ron Silverstein
1 California St
San Francisco CA   94115


Jean Smith
4222 Sterling Rd
Los Sopranos CA   94033


John Doe
9 Anywhere Drive
Hicksville NY   11801


Pete Anonymous
1 W 72 St
New York NY   10023


$ ▯
```

Figure 6.B.24

B.7 Random Access on Files

All Standard I/O subroutines explained so far use sequential access to read and write information. However, when you must manage large data files, sequential access is often inefficient. Random access, also available with Standard I/O, lets you quickly find and directly manipulate data anywhere in a file. Standard I/O provides random access capabilities with the **fseek()**, **ftell()**, and **rewind()** subroutines.

A file in the UNIX system resembles a (possibly large) array of characters, where each character in the file is directly addressable with the **fseek()** subroutine. One way to access information directly in the file is to compute where you want to be positioned, based on the size of objects in the file, and then use **fseek()** to move you there. Another way is to save your current location in a file, obtained with **ftell()**, and later reposition to that location with **fseek()**. To go to the beginning of a file, you can use the **rewind()** subroutine.

The syntax of **fseek()**, **ftell()**, and **rewind()** is as follows:

```
           int
           fseek(stream, offset, mode)
           FILE *stream;
           long offset;
           int mode;


           long
           ftell(stream)
           FILE *stream;


           void
           rewind(stream)
           FILE *stream;
```

DEFINITION 24. Direct Access Subroutines

The *mode* argument to **fseek()** can be any of the following:

0   Change the current position in the file to *offset*.

1   Change the current position in the file to *offset* plus the current position.

2   Change the current position in the file to *offset* plus the end-of-file position.

In the example that follows, **fseek()** is used to point to information in a database. The records are structured as figure 6.B.25 shows.

```
$ number cust.h
 1  /*
 2   *   cust
 3   *       format of balance due file
 4   */
 5
 6  #define    NAMESIZE  40
 7
 8  struct customer
 9  {
10      char    name[NAMESIZE];
11      float   due;
12  };
$ ☐
```

Figure 6.B.25

Records are organized sequentially by identification number and a customer's record is accessed by ID number. The next figure shows the **addcust** program, which adds records to the database, and the **prcust** program, which prints selected records in the database.

```
$ number addcust1.c
 1  /*
 2   *   addcust
 3   *       add a customer to the amount due database
 4   *       version 1
 5   */
 6
 7  #include <stdio.h>
 8  #include <ctype.h>
 9  #include "cust.h"
10
11  main(argc, argv)
12  int argc;
13  char *argv[];
14  {
15      int rc = 0;
16      FILE *fp;
17
18      if (scf("", "", &argc, &argv) == 0 || argc != 3) {
19          fprintf(stderr, "usage: %s database\n", argv[0]);
20          rc = 1;
21      } else if ((fp = fopen(argv[2], "r+")) == (FILE *) NULL &&
22              (fp = fopen(argv[2], "w+")) == (FILE *) NULL) {
23          perror(argv[2]);
24          rc = 1;
25      } else {
26          rc = add(argv[2], fp);
27          fclose(fp);
28      }
```

```
29         exit(rc);
30  }
31
32  int
33  add(filename, fp)
34  char *filename;
35  FILE *fp;
36  {
37         long id;
38         int rc = 0, n;
39         char buffer[BUFSIZ], *p;
40         struct customer newcust, oldcust;
41
42         while (1) {
43             printf("!D: ");
44             if ((n = scanf("%ld%*c", &id)) == EOF) {
45                 putchar('\n');
46                 break;
47             } else if (n != 1) {
48                 fprintf(stderr, "Invalid ID\n");
49                 while(getchar() != '\n');
50             } else if (fseek(fp, id * sizeof(newcust), 0)) {
51                 perror(filename);
52                 rc = 1;
53                 break;
54             } else {
55                 n = fread((char *) &oldcust, sizeof(oldcust), 1, fp);
56                 if (n == 1 && oldcust.name[0] != NULL) {
57                     fprintf(stderr, "Customer number %ld already added\n", id);
58                     continue;
59                 }
60                 while (1) {
61                     printf("Name: ");
62                     if (fgets(buffer, sizeof(buffer), stdin) == NULL) {
63                         fprintf(stderr, "\nCustomer must have a name\n");
64                     } else {
65                         for (p = buffer; !isalpha(*p); p++);
66                         for (n = 0; (n < NAMESIZE - 1) && *p != '\n'; n++) {
67                             newcust.name[n] = *p++;
68                         }
69                         newcust.name[n] = NULL;
70                         if (n == 0) {
71                             fprintf(stderr, "Invalid name\n");
72                         } else {
73                             break;
74                         }
75                     }
76                 }
77                 while (1) {
78                     printf("Amount due: ");
79                     if ((n = scanf("%f%*c", &newcust.due)) == EOF) {
80                         fprintf(stderr, "\nCustomer must have an amount due\n");
81                     } else if (n != 1) {
82                         fprintf(stderr, "Invalid amount\n");
83                         while(getchar() != '\n');
84                     } else {
85                         break;
86                     }
87                 }
```

184

```
88              if (fwrite((char *)&newcust, sizeof(newcust), 1, fp) != 1) {
89                  perror(filename);
90                  rc = 1;
91                  break;
92              }
93              if ((fflush(fp) == EOF || fseek(fp, 0L, 2)) {
94                  perror(filename);
95                  rc = 1;
96                  break;
97              }
98          }
99      }
100     return(rc);
101 }
```

$ **number prcust1.c**

```
1   /*
2    *  prcust
3    *       print selected customer records
4    *       version 1
5    */
6
7   #include <stdio.h>
8   #include "cust.h"
9
10  main(argc, argv)
11  int argc;
12  char *argv[];
13  {
14      int rc = 0;
15      FILE *rp;
16
17      if (scf("", "", &argc, &argv) == 0 || argc != 3) {
18          fprintf(stderr, "usage: %s database\n", argv[0]);
19          rc = 1;
20      } else if ((rp = fopen(argv[2], "r")) == (FILE *) NULL) {
21          perror(argv[21]);
22          rc = 1;
23      } else {
24          rc = pr(argv[2], rp);
25          fclose(rp);
26      }
27      exit(rc);
28  }
29
30  int
31  pr(filename, rp)
32  char *filename;
33  FILE *rp;
34  {
35      long id;
36      int rc = 0, n;
37      struct customer cust;
38
39      while (1) {
40          printf("ID: ");
41          if ((n = scanf("%ld%*c", &id)) == EOF) {
42              putchar('\n');
43              break;
44          } else if (n != 1) {
```

185

```
45              fprintf(stderr, "Invalid id\n");
46              while (getchar() != '\n');
47          } else if (fseek(rp, id * sizeof(cust), 0)) {
48              perror(filename);
49              rc = 1;
50              break;
51          } else if (fread((char *) &cust, sizeof(cust), 1, rp) != 1) {
52              fprintf(stderr, "No customer with id %ld\n", id);
53          } else if (cust.name[0] == NULL) {
54              fprintf(stderr, "No customer with id %ld\n", id);
55          } else {
56              printf("\tName:\t\t%s\n", cust.name);
57              printf("\tAmount due:\t$%5.2f\n", cust.due);
58          }
59      }
60      return(rc);
61  }
$ ▢
```

Figure 6.B.26

The **addcust** program adds customers to the database given as the first argument. If the database does not exist, **addcust** creates it with the **fopen()** subroutine. The **fflush()** and **fseek()** calls in line 93 of the **add()** subroutine are mandatory to make the information just written available to a future **fread()** call.

When adding a new customer to the database, the user can provide **addcust** with an identification number that causes **fseek()** to move beyond the current end-of-file, thereby extending the file. When the UNIX system extends a file in this way, the newly added part of the file is filled with null characters. For example, if a customer with identification number 10 was added to a new database, the UNIX system extends the file and sets the records for customers with identification numbers of 0 through 9 to nulls.

The **prcust** program formats the information in the database and uses the same algorithm for accessing customer records. It too relies on the UNIX system setting all unused customer records added to the database to nulls when the database is extended.

Figure 6.B.27 shows a sample.

```
$ cc -o addcust addcust1.c
$ cc -o prcust prcust1.c
$ addcust
usage: addcust database
$ addcust database
ID: 1
Name:^D
Customer must have a name
Name: Larry Rogers
Amount due: 125.53
ID: 1
Customer number 1 already added
ID: 273
Name: Jean Yates
Amount due: Fred Smith
Invalid amount
Amount due: 3250.28
ID: 1
Customer number 1 already added
ID: ^D
$ prcust database
ID: 1
      Name:        Larry Rogers
      Amount due:    $125.53
ID: 2
No customer with id 2
ID: 273
      Name:        Jean Yates
      Amount due:    $3250.28
ID: ^D
$ 
```

Figure 6.B.27

B.8 Invoking System Commands Within Programs

Standard I/O's **system**() subroutine lets your programs execute any command that you can execute from your terminal. The **system**() subroutine has the syntax:

187

```
                              int
                              system(command)
                              char *command;
```

DEFINITION 25. The system Subroutine

and the value returned by **system**() is the return code of the associated
command. **system**() passes the *command* string to a new copy of the shell.
Commands can therefore use all redirection and pipeline features described in
Chapter 3.

The example in figure 6.B.28 shows a data entry style program that uses the
system() subroutine to invoke the **ex** text editor when the user wishes to
correct an entry. When the user wants to call the text editor to edit the file, he
types the exclamation mark (!) in response to the Name: prompt. **dataentry**
then starts the **ex** text editor with the **system**() subroutine.

```
$ number dataentry1.c
 1  /*
 2   *   dataentry
 3   *       prompt for data entry
 4   *       version 1
 5   */
 6
 7  #include    <stdio.h>
 8
 9  #define     ESCAPE          '!'
10  #define     EDITOR      "ex"
11
12  main(argc, argv)
13  int argc;
14  char *argv[];
15  {
16      int rc = 0;
17      FILE *fp;
18      extern char *gets();
19
20      if (scf("", "", &argc, &argv) == 0 || argc != 3) {
21          fprintf(stderr, "usage: %s database\n", argv[0]);
22          rc = 1;
23      } else if ((fp = fopen(argv[2], "a")) == (FILE *) NULL) {
24          perror(argv[2]);
25          rc = 1;
26      } else {
27          rc = add(argv[2], fp);
28          if (fclose(fp) == EOF) {
29              perror(argv[1]);
```

188

```
30                  rc = 1;
31              }
32          }
33      exit(rc);
34 }
35
36 int
37 add(filename, fp)
38 char *filename;
39 FILE *fp;
40 {
41      char name[BUFSIZ], phone[BUFSIZ];
42      int done, rc = 0;
43
44      for (done = 0; done == 0;) {
45          while (!done) {
46              printf("Name: ");
47              if (fgets(name, BUFSIZ, stdin) == (char *) NULL) {
48                  putchar('\n');
49                  done++;
50              } else if (name[0] == ESCAPE) {
51                  fflush(fp);
52                  repair(filename);
53              } else {
54                  name[strlen(name) - 1] = NULL;
55                  break;
56              }
57          }
58          while (!done) {
59              printf("Phone Number: ");
60              if (fgets(phone, BUFSIZ, stdin) == (char *) NULL) {
61                  fprintf(stderr, "%s must have phone a number\n", name);
62              } else {
63                  phone[strlen(phone) - 1] = NULL;
64                  break;
65              }
66          }
67          if (!done) {
68              fprintf(fp, "%s:%s\n", name, phone);
69          }
70      }
71      return(rc);
72 }
73
74
75 repair(file)
76 char *file;
77 {
78      char command[BUFSIZ];
79
80      sprintf(command, "%s %s", EDITOR, file);
81      if (system(command)) {
82          perror(EDITOR);
```

189

```
83        ¦
84 ¦
$ cc -o dataentry dataentry1.c
$□
```

Figure 6.B.28

When **dataentry** recognizes the ! character in line 50, **add**() calls the **repair**() subroutine, lines 75 through 84, which in turn calls the editor and passes to it the name of the file to be edited. The **system**() subroutine takes as its only argument a pointer to a command string, and the **sprintf**() subroutine in line 80 builds this string.

Figure 6.B.29 shows an example of execution.

```
$ dataentry
usage: dataentry database
$ dataentry list
Name: Larry Rogers
Phone: 609-734-6559
Name: Jean yates
Phone: 415-424-8844
Name: !
"list" 2 lines, 50 characters
:.
Jean yates:415-424-8844
:s/y/Y
Jean Yates:415-424-8844
:w
"list" 2 lines, 50 characters
:q
Name: ^D
$ cat list
Larry Rogers:609-734-6559
Jean Yates:415-424-8844
$ □
```

Figure 6.B.29

B.9 Pipes to a Program

When you execute a command with the **system**() subroutine, you can capture that command's standard output by putting redirection operators in the string passed to **system**(). Your program can then read the file created by the command.

This mechanism is a bit clumsy because you must build a temporary file name and then remove that file when your program completes. A better way to use the output of a command in your program is with Standard I/O's **popen**() and **pclose**() subroutines. These subroutines let you easily manage and communicate with a command.

The syntax for **popen**() and **pclose**() is as follows:

```
FILE *
popen(command, operation);
char *command, *operation;


int
pclose(stream);
FILE *stream;
```

DEFINITION 26. The Pipe Subroutines

If *operation* is an r, then data is read from *command*. If the argument is a w, information is written to *command*. **popen**() returns NULL if *command* cannot be started and **pclose**() returns EOF if *stream* cannot be closed.

Figure 6.B.30 shows a diagram of the **grepex** program that uses the **grep** utility to find the line numbers of all lines that contain a string given as an option argument to the -e option. For each line, **grepex** starts the **ex** text editor with the cursor set to the line number returned by **grep**.

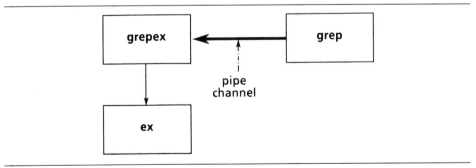

Figure 6.B.30

Figure 6.B.31 shows the **grepex** program.

```
$ number grepex1.c
  1   /*
  2    *    grepex
  3    *        edit files selected by grep
  4    *        version 1
  5    */
  6
  7   #include     <stdio.h>
  8
  9   #define      GREP    "grep -n"
 10   #define      EDITOR  "ex"
 11
 12   main(argc, argv)
 13   int argc;
 14   char *argv[];
 15   {
 16       char grepbuf[BUFSIZ], filename[BUFSIZ], line[BUFSIZ], *expr, *fixexpr();
 17       int rc = 0, c, i, eoption = 0, n, verbose = 0;
 18       FILE *pp, *popen();
 19
 20       if (scf("ev", "e", &argc, &argv) == 0) {
 21           rc = 1;
 22       } else {
 23           for (i = 1; strcmp(argv[i], "--"); i++) {
 24               switch (argv[i][1]) {
 25               case 'e':
 26                   eoption++;
 27                   expr = argv[++i];
 28                   break;
 29               case 'v':
 30                   verbose++;
 31                   break;
 32               }
 33           }
 34       }
 35       if (rc == 1 || eoption == 0 || ++i == argc) {
 36           fprintf(stderr, "usage: %s [-v] -e expression file [ ... ]\n", argv[0]);
 37       } else {
 38           expr = fixexpr(expr);
 39           sprintf(grepbuf, "%s \"%s\" /dev/null", GREP, expr);
 40           for ( ; i < argc; i++) {
 41               sprintf(grepbuf, "%s %s", grepbuf, argv[i]);
 42           }
 43           if (verbose) {
 44               printf("%s\n", grepbuf);
 45           }
 46           if ((pp = popen(grepbuf, "r")) == (FILE *) NULL) {
 47               perror(argv[0]);
 48               rc = 1;
 49           } else {
 50               while (fscanf(pp, "%[^:]%*c%d", filename, &n) != EOF) {
 51                   sprintf(line, "%s +%d %s", EDITOR, n, filename);
```

```
52              if (verbose) {
53                      printf("%s\n", line);
54              }
55              system(line);
56              while ((c = fgetc(pp)) != '\n');
57          }
58          pclose(pp);
59      }
60  }
61  exit(rc);
62  }
63
64  char *
65  fixexpr(e)
66  char *e;
67  {
68      char newe[BUFSIZ];
69      register char *ne;
70
71      for (ne = newe; *e; e++) {
72          switch (*e) {
73          case '\\':
74              *ne++ = *e++;
75              *ne++ = *e;
76              break;
77          case '"':
78              *ne++ = '\\';
79              *ne++ = *e;
80              break;
81          default:
82              *ne++ = *e;
83              break;
84          }
85      }
86      *ne = *e;
87      return(newe);
88  }
```

```
$ cc -o grepex grepex1.c
$ grepex -v -e include grepex1.c
grep -n "include" /dev/null grepex1.c
ex +7 grepex1.c
"grepex1.c" 88 lines, 1553 characters
:.
#include    <stdio.h>
:.=
7
:q
$
```

Figure 6.B.31

Lines 38 through 42 build the **grep** command line that was invoked with **popen**() in line 46. The file name */dev/null* is included in the command line because it forces **grep** to display matching lines in the form:

filename:line number:matching string

fscanf() in line 50 extracts the file name and the line number where the string was found. **grepex** then calls **ex**, passing to it the line number and the file name. When **ex** ends, **grepex** flushes the rest of the line from **grep**, and the process continues.

In conclusion, the Standard I/O library provides several different types of subroutines that simplify program input and output. The subroutines let you read and write characters, lines, and objects. Other subroutines let you convert information between a more efficient internal format and a more readable character format. The Standard I/O library also provides subroutines that let you start programs from within your program and let you set up a one-way communication channel with those programs. These subroutines are fundamentally important to the programs you write not only because they make your job easier but also because they improve the portability of your programs.

C. STRINGS AND MEMORY

A *STRING* in the C language is a set of characters that ends with a NULL character. Unfortunately, the C language does not provide a string data type nor any operators that let you work with strings. To work with strings, you must define a string with the following declaration:

---

char   *string*[*length*];

DEFINITION 27. C Language Character String

---

and you must use subroutines to operate on strings. The UNIX system does provide ten subroutines that let you operate on strings. These are listed in the following table.

SUBROUTINE	DESCRIPTION
char * strcpy(*string1, string2*) char *string1, *string2*;	Copies *string2*, including the NULL terminator, to the area in memory pointed to by *string1* and returns the value of *string1*.
int strcmp(*string1, string2*) char *string1, *string2*;	Compares *string1* and *string2* and returns less than zero, zero, or greater than zero if *string1* is lexicographically less than, equal to, or greater than *string2*.
char * strcat(*string1, string2*) char *string1, *string2*;	Adds a copy of *string2* onto the end of *string1* and returns the value of *string1*.
int strlen(*string*) char *string*;	Returns the length of *string* excluding the NULL terminator.
char * strchr(*string, character*) char *string, character*;	Returns a pointer to the first occurrence of *character* in *string*, or NULL if *character* does not appear in *string*.
char * strrchr(*string, character*) char *string, character*;	Returns a pointer to the last occurrence of *character* in *string*, or NULL if *character* does not appear in *string*.
char * strncpy(*string1, string2, n*) char *string1, *string2*; int *n*; strncmp(*string1, string2, n*) char *string1, *string2*; int *n*; char * strncat(*string1, string2, n*) char *string1, *string2*; int *n*;	These subroutines all use a third argument, *n*, that defines the size of the area in memory to be copied, compared, or added onto.
char * strpbrk(*string1 string2*) char *string1, *string2*;	Returns a pointer to the first occurrence of any character in *string2* in *string1*, or NULL if there are no characters from *string2* in *string1*.

DEFINITION 28. String Manipulation Subroutines

Figure 6.C.1 shows version 2 of the **grepex** program that uses string operations instead of **sprintf**() to build the **grep** command.

```
$ number grepex2.c
 1   /*
 2    *   grepex
 3    *        edit files selected by grep
 4    *        version 2
 5    */
 6
 7   #include    <stdio.h>
 8
 9   #define     GREP    "grep -n "
10   #define     EDITOR  "ex"
11
12   main(argc, argv)
13   int argc;
14   char *argv[];
15   {
16       char grepbuf[BUFSIZ], filename[BUFSIZ], line[BUFSIZ], *expr, *fixexpr();
17       int rc = 0, c, i, eoption = 0, n, verbose = 0;
18       FILE *pp, *popen();
19
20       if (scf("ev", "e", &argc, &argv) == 0) {
21           rc = 1;
22       } else {
23           for (i = 1; strcmp(argv[i], "--"); i++) {
24               switch (argv[i][1]) {
25               case 'e':
26                   eoption++;
27                   expr = argv[++i];
28                   break;
29               case 'v':
30                   verbose++;
31                   break;
32               }
33           }
34       }
35       if (rc == 1 || eoption == 0 || ++i == argc) {
36           fprintf(stderr, "usage: %s [-v] -e expression file [ ... ]\n", argv[0]);
37       } else {
38           strcpy(grepbuf, GREP);
39           strcat(grepbuf, "\"");
40           strcat(grepbuf, fixexpr(expr));
41           strcat(grepbuf, "\" /dev/null");
42           for ( ; i < argc; i++) {
43               strcat(grepbuf, " ");
44               strcat(grepbuf, argv[i]);
45           }
46           if (verbose) {
47               printf("%s\n", grepbuf);
48           }
```

196

```
49          if ((pp = popen(grepbuf, "r")) == (FILE *) NULL) {
50              perror(argv[0]);
51              rc = 1;
52          } else {
53              while (fscanf(pp, "%[^:]%*c%d", filename, &n) != EOF) {
54                  sprintf(line, "%s +%d %s", EDITOR, n, filename);
55                  if (verbose) {
56                      printf("%s\n", line);
57                  }
58                  system(line);
59                  while ((c = fgetc(pp)) != '\n');
60              }
61              pclose(pp);
62          }
63      }
64      exit(rc);
65 }
66
67 char *
68 fixexpr(e)
69 char *e;
70 {
71      char newe[BUFSIZ];
72      register char *ne;
73
74      for (ne = newe; *e; e++) {
75          switch (*e) {
76          case '\\':
77              *ne++ = *e++;
78              *ne++ = *e;
79              break;
80          case '"':
81              *ne++ = '\\';
82              *ne++ = *e;
83              break;
84          default:
85              *ne++ = *e;
86              break;
87          }
88      }
89      *ne = *e;
90      return(newe);
91 }
$ □
```

Figure 6.C.1

Sometimes, you need to work with arbitrarily sized sections of memory that do not conform to the definition of a string. Nonetheless, you still want to do the same operations that you can do with the string manipulation subroutines. The subroutines shown in the next table let you do string operations on memory areas.

SUBROUTINE	DESCRIPTION
char * memcpy(*mem1, mem2, n*) char *<i>mem1</i>, *<i>mem2</i>; int *n*;	Copies *n* characters from the area in memory pointed to by *mem2* to the area in memory pointed to by *mem1* and returns the value of *mem1*.
char * memccpy(*mem1, mem2, c, n*) char *<i>mem1</i>, *<i>mem2</i>; int *c, n*;	Copies characters from the area in memory pointed to by *mem2* to the area in memory pointed to by *mem1* and returns the value of *mem1*. The copy operation stops when either *n* characters have been copied or the *c* character has been copied.
int memcmp(*mem1, mem2, n*) char *<i>mem1</i>, *<i>mem2</i>; int *n*;	Compares the first *n* characters of *mem1* and *mem2* and returns less than zero, zero, or greater than zero if *mem1* is lexicographically less than, equal to, or greater than *mem2*.
char * memchr(*mem, character, n*) char *<i>mem</i>; int *character, n*;	Returns a pointer to the first occurrence of *character* in the first *n* characters of *mem*, or NULL if *character* does not appear in *mem*.
char * memset(*mem, c, n*) char *<i>mem</i>; int *c, n*;	Sets the first *n* characters in the area pointed to by *mem* to the character *c* and returns the value of *mem*.

DEFINITION 29. Memory Manipulation Subroutines

D. DATA CONVERSIONS

The UNIX system provides a library that contains macros you can use to classify and convert characters in a way that is independent of the CPU and the character encoding scheme. This library is not stored as an archive library as are the Standard I/O subroutines, but is stored instead as a header file named *ctype.h* in the */usr/include* directory. You must use the #include directive to gain access to these macros. The macros provided are listed below.

MACRO	OPERATION
isalnum(c)	returns true if c is an upper or lower case letter or a digit
isalpha(c)	returns true if c is an upper or lower case letter
isascii(c)	returns true if c is in the range from 0 to decimal 127 (octal 177)
iscntrl(c)	returns true if c is in the range from 0 to decimal 31 (octal 37) or is 127 (octal 177)
isdigit(c)	returns true if c is a digit
isxdigit(c)	returns true if c is a decimal digit or is a hexadecimal digit in the range from 0 through 9 and either A through F or a through f
islower(c)	returns true if c is a lower case letter
isupper(c)	returns true if c is an upper case letter
isprint(c)	returns true if c is an ASCII character but is not a control character
ispunct(c)	returns true if c is an ASCII character but is not a control character nor an alphanumeric character
isspace(c)	returns true if c is a horizontal or vertical tab, a linefeed, a formfeed, a carriage return, or a space
tolower(c)	returns the lower case equivalent of c, where c is an upper case letter
toupper(c)	returns the upper case equivalent of c, where c is a lower case letter

DEFINITION 30. Character Classification and Conversion Subroutines

You should design your software tools to accommodate all reasonable formats of input data. Software tools that accept only one precise format are not as generally useful as they could be. For example, there are many different ways to specify a telephone number. Some examples are:

```
(415) 424 8844
(415)4248844
4154248844
415-424-8844
415424 - 8844
4248844
```

The **trphone** program shown in figure 6.D.1 accepts these and any other format for the telephone numbers in the standard input file, translates them to only digits, and displays them on the standard output.

```
$ number trphone.c
 1  /*
 2   *   trphone
 3   *       strip telephone number of non-digits
 4   */
 5
 6  #include    <stdio.h>
 7  #include    <ctype.h>
 8
 9  main(argc, argv)
10  int argc;
11  char *argv[];
12  {
13      char line[BUFSIZ], *from, *to;
14      extern char *gets();
15
16      while (gets(line) != (char *) NULL) {
17          for (from = line, to = line; *from; from++) {
18              if (isdigit(*from)) {
19                  *to++ = *from;
20              }
21          }
22          *to = NULL;
23          switch (strlen(line)) {
24          case 7:
25          case 10:
26              puts(line);
27              break;
28          }
29      }
30      exit(0);
31  }
$ cc -o trphone trphone.c
$ trphone
(415) 424 8844
4154248844
(415)4248844
4154248844
4154248844
4154248844
415-424-8844
4154248844
415424 - 8844
4154248844
4248844
4248844
$ □
```

Figure 6.D.1

E. TIME SUBROUTINES

The UNIX system maintains the current time as the number of seconds since 00:00:00 GMT, January 1, 1970. You can sample the current time with the **time**() system call, and the Standard I/O library provides five subroutines that let you operate on the current time. These are listed below.

SUBROUTINE	DESCRIPTION
char * ctime(*time*) long *time*;	Converts its argument into a 26-character string, and returns a pointer to that string.
struct tm * localtime(*time*) long *time*;	Converts its argument to local time and then breaks that value into seconds, minutes, hours, day of the month, month of the year, day of the week, day of the year, and a logical value that shows if daylight savings time is in effect. These values are stored in a structure of type tm as defined in */usr/include/time.h*. **localtime**() returns a pointer to this structure.
struct tm * gmtime(*time*) long *time*;	Breaks its time argument, assumed to be in Greenwich Mean Time, into seconds, minutes, hours, day of the month, month of the year, day of the week, day of the year, and a logical value that shows if daylight savings time is in effect. These values are also stored in a structure of type tm and **gmtime**() returns a pointer to this structure.
char * asctime(*tm*) struct tm *tm*;	Converts its argument, assumed to be from either **localtime**() or **gmtime**(), into a 26-character string and returns a pointer to that string.
extern long timezone;	timezone contains the difference in seconds between Greenwich Mean Time and local time.
extern int daylight;	daylight contains non-zero if daylight savings time is in effect, according to the U.S.A. conventions.
extern char *tzname[2]; void tzset()	The environment variable TZ describes the time zone according to the format XXXYZZZ, where XXX is the standard local time zone abbreviation (e.g. EST), Y is the difference in hours from Greenwich Mean Time, and ZZZ is the dalight savings local time zone abbreviation (e.g. EDT). The **tzset**() subroutine extracts the value of TZ from the environment and sets tzname[0] to the local time zone abbreviation and tzname[1] to the daylight savings local time zone abbrevation.

DEFINITION 31. Time Subroutines

Figure 6.E.1 shows version 3 of the **Who** program that now also prints the time when each person logged in to the UNIX system.

```
$ number Who3.c
 1   /*
 2    *   Who
 3    *        who is currently logged in
 4    *        version 3
 5    */
 6
 7   #include    <stdio.h>
 8   #include    <sys/types.h>
 9   #include    <utmp.h>
10
11   #define     UTMPFILE  "/etc/utmp"
12
13   main(argc, argv)
14   int argc;
15   char *argv[];
16   {
17       FILE *fp;
18       struct utmp record;
19       int rc = 0;
20       extern char *ctime();
21
22       if ((fp = fopen(UTMPFILE, "r")) == (FILE *) NULL) {
23           perror(UTMPFILE);
24           rc = 1;
25       } else {
26           while (fread((char *) &record, sizeof(record), 1, fp) == 1) {
27               if (record.ut_type == USER_PROCESS && record.ut_name[0] != NULL) {
28                   printf("%s\t%s\t%s\n", record.ut_name, record.ut_line,
29                       ctime(&record.ut_time));
30               }
31           }
32           if (fclose(fp) == EOF) {
33               perror(UTMPFILE);
34               rc = 1;
35           }
36       }
37       exit(rc);
38   }
$ cc -o Who Who3.c
$ Who
becca  ttya1   Thu Mar 22 12:22:28 1984
starr  ttya2   Thu Mar 22 09:05:39 1984
rogers ttya2   Thu Mar 22 07:47:32 1984
ted    ttya4   Thu Mar 22 12:21:48 1984
$ ▢
```

Figure 6.E.1

Finally, figure 6.E.2 shows version 4 of the **Who** program that uses **localtime**() to compute the month, day, hour, and time from the information in the /etc/utmp file.

```
$ number Who4.c
 1  /*
 2   *  Who
 3   *      who is currently logged in
 4   *      version 4
 5   */
 6
 7  #include    <stdio.h>
 8  #include    <sys/types.h>
 9  #include    <utmp.h>
10  #include    <time.h>
11
12  #define     UTMPFILE  "/etc/utmp"
13
14  static  char *Months[] =
15  {
16      "Jan", "Feb", "Mar", "Apr", "May", "Jun",
17      "Jul", "Aug", "Sep", "Oct", "Nov", "Dec"
18  };
19
20  main(argc, argv)
21  int argc;
22  char *argv[];
23  {
24      FILE *fp;
25      struct utmp record;
26      struct tm *p;
27      int rc = 0;
28      extern char *ctime();
29      extern struct tm *localtime();
30
31      if ((fp = fopen(UTMPFILE, "r")) == (FILE *) NULL) {
32          perror(UTMPFILE);
33          rc = 1;
34      } else {
35          while (fread((char *) &record, sizeof(record), 1, fp) == 1) {
36              if (record.ut_type == USER_PROCESS && record.ut_name[0] != NULL) {
37                  p = localtime(&record.ut_time);
38                  printf("%s\t%s\t%s %2d %2d:%2d\n", record.ut_name, record.ut_line,
39                      Months[p->tm_mon], p->tm_mday, p->tm_hour, p->tm_min);
40              }
41          }
42          if (fclose(fp) == EOF) {
43              perror(UTMPFILE);
44              rc = 1;
45          }
46      }
47      exit(rc);
```

204

```
48 |
$ cc -o Who Who4.c
$ Who
becca   ttya1   Mar 22 12:22
starr   ttya2   Mar 22 09:05
rogers  ttya2   Mar 22 07:47
ted     ttya4   Mar 22 12:21
```

Figure 6.E.2

F. STORAGE MANAGEMENT

It's not always possible to know the storage requirements for data structures in your programs ahead of time. Furthermore, it is unreasonable to constrain tables, arrays, trees, and other data structures to some arbitrary maximum size. The UNIX system helps to solve this problem by providing four storage management subroutines that you can use to control dynamically the size of data structures used in a program. The syntax for each is shown next.

```
char *
malloc(area_size)
unsigned area_size;


char *
calloc(num_elements, element_size)
unsigned num_elements, element_size;


char *
realloc(area_pointer, new_size)
char *area_pointer;
unsigned new_size;


free(area_pointer)
char *area_pointer;
```

DEFINITION 32. Memory Management Subroutines

Notice that **malloc()**, **calloc()**, and **realloc()** all return pointers to a character string, which by definition can be any address in the address space. However, some machines require that certain data types be aligned on specific boundaries. On an IBM 370 machine, for example, all integers must be aligned on addresses that are integral multiples of four. To solve this alignment problem, all storage allocation subroutines always return a pointer to an area in

205

memory that satisfies the alignment requirements of all data types in the machine.

The simplest combination of these subroutines is **malloc()** and **free()**. You can use the **malloc()** subroutine to allocate an area of memory that is *area_size* bytes in length, and then use **free()** to return the allocated area to the storage management system. If the **malloc()**, subroutine is unable to allocate enough memory, it returns a NULL pointer. By convention, a NULL pointer means that the pointer is uninitialized. Hence, NULL can be used, for example, to signify the end of a linked list.

The **calloc()** subroutine is used most often to allocate space for an array of elements. **calloc()** guarantees that the space allocated is initialized to zeros. **free()** can also be used with **calloc()** to return the area previously allocated. **calloc()** also returns a NULL pointer when it cannot allocate enough memory.

Finally, the **realloc()** subroutine changes the size of the area previously allocated and may move the contents of the old area to the new area if necessary. Only the data in the old area, up to the smaller of the old and new sizes, remains in the new area. **realloc()** returns a NULL pointer when the request cannot be satisfied.

Figure 6.F.1 shows the **scf()** subroutine introduced in Chapter 5. Recall from Chapter 5 that **scf()** translates program arguments given in the Standard Command Format into a form easily manipulated by C language programs. **scf()** uses **malloc()**, **realloc()**, and **free()** to manage the new program arguments.

$ number scf.c

```
 1  /*
 2   *   scf
 3   *       translate arguments in the standard command format
 4   *       into a form easily manipulated by C language programs
 5   */
 6
 7  #include    <stdio.h>
 8  #include    <ctype.h>
 9
10  #define     DASH        '-'
11  #define     OPTEND      "--"
12  #define     CNULL       (char **) NULL
13  #define     CSTAR       (char *)
14  #define     error(f, x)   rc = 0; fprintf(stderr, f, (*argv)[0], x)
15
16  static   char    **Nargv    =   CNULL;
17
18  int
19  scf(options, optionargs, argc, argv)
20  char *options, *optionargs, **argv[];
21  int *argc;
22  {
23    int rc = 1, ai, ci, i;
24    unsigned na = 0, nf = 0;
25    char c, **nargv = CNULL, **files = CNULL;
26    extern char *index(), *malloc(), *realloc();
27
28    if ((nargv = (char **) malloc(sizeof CSTAR)) == CNULL) {
29      error("%s: memory allocation error in scf\n", "");
30    } else if (rc == goodargs(options, optionargs, (*argv)[0])) {
31      nargv[na++] = (*argv)[0];
32      for (ai = 1; rc == 1 && ai < *argc && strcmp((*argv)[ai], OPTEND); ai++) {
33        if ((*argv)[ai][0] == DASH && (*argv)[ai][1]) {
34          for (ci = 1; rc == 1 && ci < strlen((*argv)[ai]); ci++) {
35            c = (*argv)[ai][ci];
36            if (index(options, c) == CSTAR NULL) {
37              error("%s: illegal option %c\n", c);
38            } else if ((nargv = (char **) realloc(CSTAR nargv,
39                          (na + 1) * sizeof CSTAR)) == CNULL) {
40              error("%s: memory allocation error in scf\n", "");
41            } else if ((nargv[na] = malloc(3 * sizeof CSTAR)) == CSTAR NULL) {
42              error("%s: memory allocation error in scf\n", "");
43            } else {
44              nargv[na][0] = DASH;
45              nargv[na][1] = c;
46              nargv[na++][2] = NULL;
47              if (index(optionargs, c) == CSTAR NULL) {
48                continue;
49              } else if ((nargv = (char **) realloc(CSTAR nargv,
50                            (na + 1) * sizeof CSTAR)) == CNULL) {
51                error("%s: memory allocation error in scf\n", "");
```

207

```
52      } else if ((*argv)[ai][ci+1] != NULL) {
53          error("%s: option %c not followed by white space\n", c);
54      } else if (ai + 1 < *argc) {
55          nargv[na++] = (*argv)[++ai];
56          ci = strlen((*argv)[ai]);
57      } else {
58          error("%s: no option argument specified for %c option\n", c);
59      }
60          }
61      }
62      } else if (nf == 0) {
63      if ((files = (char **) malloc(sizeof CSTAR)) == CNULL) {
64      error("%s: memory allocation error in scf\n", "");
65      } else {
66      files[nf++] = (*argv)[ai];
67      }
68      } else if ((files = (char **) realloc(CSTAR files,
69                      (nf + 1) * sizeof CSTAR)) == CNULL) {
70      error("%s: memory allocation error in scf\n", "");
71      } else {
72      files[nf++] = (*argv)[ai];
73      }
74      }
75      if (rc == 1) {
76      if (ai < *argc && !strcmp((*argv)[ai], OPTEND)) {
77      ai++;
78      }
79      if ((nargv = (char **) realloc(CSTAR nargv,
80                      (na + nf + (*argc - ai) + 2) * sizeof CSTAR)) == CNULL) {
81      error("%s: memory allocation error in scf\n", "");
82      } else {
83      nargv[na++] = OPTEND;
84      for (i = 0; i < nf; i++) {
85      nargv[na++] = files[i];
86      }
87      for ( ; ai < *argc; ai++) {
88      nargv[na++] = (*argv)[ai];
89      }
90      nargv[na] = CSTAR NULL;
91      }
92      }
93      if (files) {
94      free(CSTAR files);
95      }
96      }
97      if (rc == 1) {
98      *argv = nargv;
99      Nargv = nargv;
100     *argc = na;
101     } else if (nargv != CNULL) {
102     free(CSTAR nargv);
103     }
104     return(rc);
```

```
105 |
106
107 scfend()
108 |
109
110   if (Nargv != CNULL) |
111     free(CSTAR Nargv);
112   |
113 |
114
115 static int
116 goodargs(options, optionargs, name)
117 char *options, *optionargs, *name;
118 |
119   register char *p;
120   register int rc = 1;
121
122   for (p = options; *p; p++) |
123     if (!isalpha(*p)) |
124       fprintf(stderr, "%s: option specifier %c is not a character\n", name, *p);
125       rc = 0;
126     |
127   |
128   for (p = optionargs; *p; p++) |
129     if (!index(options, *p)) |
130       fprintf(stderr, "%s: option argument specifier %c is not a legal option\n",
131         name, *p);
132       rc = 0;
133     |
134   |
135   return(rc);
136 |
$ □
```

Figure 6.F.1

scf() uses **malloc**() in line 28 to allocate space for a pointer to a character string used to hold the pointer to program's name, (*argv)[0]. This is the first step in building the new argv data structure named nargv. For each additional program argument, **scf**() uses **realloc**() in line 38 to extend the nargv array by one entry.

scf() uses **malloc**() again in line 41 to allocate memory for each option program argument and fills in this memory with the assignments in lines 44 through 46. If an option requires an option argument, **scf**() uses **realloc**() in line 49 to extend nargv by one entry. Once extended, **scf**() then copies the option argument pointer to this new array entry. Similarly, **scf**() uses **malloc**() in line 63 and **realloc**() in line 68 to create and extend the list of file name program arguments.

When **scf**() has processed all program arguments arguments or when it finds the double dash separator, **scf**() extends nargv with **realloc**() in line 79 to include all file name program arguments, the double dash separator, all arguments not yet processed, and one entry to be filled with NULL to mark the end of nargv. Lines 83 through 90 do the necessary assignments. **scf**() then uses **free**() in line 94 to return the memory used for the temporary copy of the pointers to the file name program arguments.

If **scf**() was unable to extend the nargv array at any time or if it discovered an error in the original program arguments, it frees the nargv array in line 102. **scf**() also uses **free**() in line 111 to free the new program argument array when directed by being called through **scfend**().

G. THE ENVIRONMENT

Each process in the UNIX system has available to it a array of strings called the *ENVIRONMENT*. Among the strings contained in the environment are the search path used to locate programs named in commands (PATH), the login directory (HOME), and the name of the terminal (TERM). The UNIX system passes a process' environment to the processes it starts as explained in section C of Chapter 7 that describes process creation and termination.

A process can sample these strings with the **getenv**() subroutine. Chapter 5 recommends using environment variables as one way to reduce the amount of information a software tools user must provide to run a tool. Also, Chapters 8 and 9 show how these variables can be placed in a process' environment with the **export** and **setenv** built-in shell commands. The subroutine **getenv**() has the syntax:

```
char *
getenv(name)
char *name;
```

DEFINITION 33. The getenv Subroutine

Recall that Bourne shell variables are defined or set with the shell assignment:

```
name=value
```

When a shell variable's name is supplied to **getenv**(), it returns a pointer to that variable's value if the variable is in the program's environment, or a NULL pointer if the variable is not in the environment.

The program below prompts for a variable's name and displays either the variable's value or the message:

name: not in environment

```
$ number envpr.c
 1   /*
 2    * envpr
 3    *  print selected environment variable values
 4    */
 5
 6   #include    <stdio.h>
 7   #include    <ctype.h>
 8
 9   main(argc, argv)
10   int argc;
11   char *argv[];
12   {
13       char name[BUFSIZ];
14       char *value, *p, *getenv(), *gets();
15
16       for (;;) {
17           printf("Name:  ");
18           if (gets(name) == (char *) NULL) {
19               break;
20           }
21           for (p = name; *p != NULL; p++) {
22               if (!isalpha(*p) && !isdigit(*p) && *p != '_') {
23                   fprintf(stderr, "Illegal character %c ", *p);
24                   fprintf(stderr, "in name %s\n", name);
25                   break;
26               }
27           }
28           if (*p == NULL) {
29               if((value = getenv(name)) == (char *) NULL) {
30                   printf("%s: not in environment\n", name);
31               } else {
32                   printf("%s=%s\n", name, value);
33               }
34           }
35       }
36       putchar('\n');
37       exit(0);
38   }
$ cc envpr.c -o envpr
$ echo $HOME $MAIL $LOGNAME $DATE
/usr/rogers /usr/spool/mail/rogers rogers
$ envpr
Name: *U*
Illegal character * in name *U*
Name: HOME
HOME=/usr/rogers
Name: MAIL
MAIL=/usr/spool/mail/rogers
Name: LOGNAME
```

```
LOGNAME = rogers
Name: DATE
DATE: not in environment
Name: ^D
$ □
```

Finally, figure 6.G.2 shows version 3 of the **grepex** program that uses the editor named in the EDITOR environment variable, or **ex** if EDITOR is not defined. If the editor selected by EDITOR is neither **ex** or **vi**, then the automatic positioning feature may not be available. **grepex** prints the line number where the match occurs, pauses to allow the user to read the message, and then starts the selected editor.

```
$ number grepex3.c
 1  /*
 2   *   grepex
 3   *       edit files selected by grep
 4   *       version 3
 5   */
 6
 7  #include    <stdio.h>
 8
 9  #define     GREP    "grep -n"
10  #define     EX "ex"
11  #define     VI  "vi"
12  #define     EDITOR  EX
13  #define     EDITORV "EDITOR"
14
15  main(argc, argv)
16  int argc;
17  char *argv[];
18  {
19      char grepbuf[BUFSIZ], filename[BUFSIZ], line[BUFSIZ], *expr,
20              *editor, *fixexpr();
21      int rc = 0, c, i, eoption = 0, n, verbose = 0;
22      FILE *pp, *popen();
23      extern char *getenv();
24
25      if (scf("ev", "e", &argc, &argv) == 0) {
26          rc = 1;
27      } else {
28          for (i = 1; strcmp(argv[i], "--"); i++) {
29              switch (argv[i][1]) {
30              case 'e':
31                  eoption++;
32                  expr = argv[++i];
33                  break;
```

```
34              case 'v':
35                  verbose++;
36                  break;
37              }
38          }
39      }
40      if (rc == 1 || eoption == 0 || ++i == argc) {
41          fprintf(stderr, "usage: %s [-v] -e expression file [ ... ]\n", argv[0]);
42      } else {
43          if ((editor = getenv(EDITORV)) == (char *) NULL) {
44              editor = EDITOR;
45          }
46          expr = fixexpr(expr);
47          sprintf(grepbuf, "%s \"%s\" /dev/null", GREP, expr);
48          for ( ; i < argc; i++) {
49              sprintf(grepbuf, "%s %s", grepbuf, argv[i]);
50          }
51          if (verbose) {
52              printf("%s\n", grepbuf);
53          }
54          if ((pp = popen(grepbuf, "r")) == (FILE *) NULL) {
55              perror(argv[0]);
56              rc = 1;
57          } else {
58              while (fscanf(pp, "%[^:]%*c%d", filename, &n) != EOF) {
59                  if (strcmp(editor, EX) && strcmp(editor, VI)) {
60                      printf("Match occurred on line %d\n", n);
61                      sleep(2);
62                      sprintf(line, "%s %s", editor, filename);
63                  } else {
64                      sprintf(line, "%s +%d %s", editor, n, filename);
65                  }
66                  if (verbose) {
67                      printf("%s\n", line);
68                  }
69                  system(line);
70                  while ((c = fgetc(pp)) != '\n');
71              }
72              pclose(pp);
73          }
74      }
75      exit(rc);
76 }
77
78 char *
79 fixexpr(e)
80 char *e;
81 {
82      char newe[BUFSIZ];
83      register char *ne;
84
85      for (ne = newe; *e; e++) {
86          switch (*e) {
```

213

```
87          case '\\':
88              *ne++ = *e++;
89              *ne++ = *e;
90              break;
91          case '"':
92              *ne++ = '\\';
93              *ne++ = *e;
94              break;
95          default:
96              *ne++ = *e;
97              break;
98          }
99      }
100     *ne = *e;
101     return(newe);
102 }
$ cc -o grepex grepex3.c
```

Figure 6.G.2

Figure 6.G.3 shows an example using the **vi** text editor. The boxed in area represents the screen after **grepex** starts **vi**.

```
$ EDITOR=vi
$ export EDITOR
$ grepex -e include grepex3.c
```

```
/*
 *  grepex
 *      edit files selected by grep
 *      version 3
 */

#include    <stdio.h>

#define    GREP    "grep -n"
#define    EX    "ex"
#define    VI    "vi"
#define    EDITOR  EX
#define    EDITORV "EDITOR"

main(argc, argv)
int argc;
char *argv[];
{
    char grepbuf[BUFSIZ], filename[BUFSIZ], line[BUFSIZ], *expr,
        *editor, *fixexpr();
    int rc = 0, c, i, eoption = 0, n, verbose = 0;
    FILE *pp, *popen();
    extern char *getenv();
"grepex3.c" 102 lines, 1907 characters
```

Figure 6.G.3

Figure 6.G.4 shows the same scenario but with the ed text editor.

```
$ EDITOR=ed
$ export EDITOR
$ grepex -e include grepex3.c
Match occurred on line 7
1907
7p
#include        <stdio.h>
q
$☐
```

Figure 6.G.4

In summary, the standard UNIX system subroutine library provides several valuable software building blocks that can save you time when you program a problem solution. Of prime importance are the subroutines in the Standard I/O library that simplify input and output operations. The subroutines provided by the UNIX system are recommended in preference to the system calls defined and explained in Chapter 7 because they provide a portable, standard interface to the UNIX system and to other operating systems that support them. However, sometimes you must write code using the low-level system call interface. Examples are when the subroutine library doesn't provide the necessary routine or when an existing library routine doesn't do the exact function you need. The system call interface gives you the control over the system you may need for added flexibility at the expense of addition coding overhead for buffering, error handling, etc.

CHAPTER 7

UNIX SYSTEM CALLS

A. INTRODUCTION

Chapter 6 described the higher level subroutine interface to the UNIX system. While this interface is recommended when you write your software tools, sometimes you need to use the elemental features of the UNIX system kernel available through the system call interface. This chapter describes this interface to the UNIX system kernel which is accessible from programs written in C and in assembly language.

Recall from Chapter 2 that the UNIX system kernel is a single large program that shares the CPU among competing processes and governs all access to disks, tapes, and terminals. In one way or another, all processes use the kernel through the UNIX system call interface to access files, to communicate with other processes, and to control processes.

Recall also from Chapter 2 that a *SYSTEM CALL* is a subroutine call that causes the kernel to do some operation for a process. A process makes a system call by using the system call interface described in Section 2 of the **UNIX System User's Manual System V**.

The UNIX system interface consists of about 80 system calls, and this guide describes 40 of the more important ones. As always, you should refer to Section 2 of the **UNIX System User's Manual System V** for a complete description of all system calls available with your version of the UNIX system.

IMPORTANT NOTE: The system call interface is that aspect of the UNIX system that has changed the most since the inception of the UNIX system. Therefore, when you write a software tool, you should protect that tool by putting system calls in other subroutines within your program and then calling only those subroutines. Should the next version of the UNIX system change the syntax and semantics of the system calls you've used, you need to change only your interface subroutines.

A.1 Classification of System Calls

UNIX system calls are used to manage the file system and to control processes. The following table shows the system calls described in this chapter.

GENERAL CLASS	SPECIFIC CLASS	SYSTEM CALL
File Structure Related Calls	Creating a Channel	creat() open() close()
	Input/Output	read() write()
	Random Access	lseek()
	Channel Duplication	dup()
	Aliasing and Removing Files	link() unlink()
	File Status	stat() fstat()
	Access Control	access() chmod() chown() umask()
	Device Control	ioctl()
Process Related Calls	Process Creation and Termination	exec() fork() wait() exit()
	Process Owner and Group	getuid() geteuid() getgid() getegid()
	Process Identity	getpid() getppid()
	Process Control	signal() kill() alarm()
	Change Working Directory	chdir()
Interprocess Communication	Pipelines	pipe()
	Messages	msgget() msgsnd() msgrcv() msgctl()
	Semaphores	semget() semop()
	Shared Memory	shmget() shmat() shmdt()

A.2 Error Handling

When a system call discovers an error, it returns -1 and stores the reason the call failed in an external variable named errno. The */usr/include/errno.h* file maps these error numbers to manifest constants, and it is these constants that you should use in your programs.

When a system call returns successfully, it returns something other than -1 but it does not clear errno. errno only has meaning directly after a system call that returns an error.

When you use system calls in your programs, you should check the value returned by those system calls. Furthermore, when a system call discovers an error, you should use the **perror**() subroutine to print a diagnostic message on the standard error file that describes why the system call failed. The syntax for **perror**() is:

```
                              void
                              perror(s)
                              char *s;
```

DEFINITION 34. The perror Subroutine

perror() displays the argument string, a colon, and then the error message, as directed by errno, followed by a newline. Typically, the argument given to **perror**() is the name of the program that incurred the error, argv[0]. However, when using subroutines and system calls on files, the related file name might be passed to **perror**().

Figure 7.A.1 shows the **errmesgs** program that uses **perror**() to display all possible error messages on the standard error file. The global variable sys__nerr is set to the maximum value that errno can assume.

```
$ number errmesgs.c
 1  /*
 2   *    errmesgs
 3   *        print all error messages from system calls
 4   */
 5
 6  #include    <stdio.h>
 7
 8  main(argc, argv)
 9  int argc;
10  char *argv[];
11  {
12      int i;
13      extern int errno, sys__nerr;
14
15      for (i = 0; i < sys__nerr; i++) {
16          fprintf(stderr, "%3d", i);
17          errno = i;
18          perror(" ");
19      }
20      exit(0);
21  }
$ cc -o errmesgs errmesgs.c
$ errmsgs
 0 : Error 0
 1 : Not owner
 2 : No such file or directory
 3 : No such process
 4 : Interrupted system call
 5 : I/O error
 6 : No such device or address
 7 : Arg list too long
 8 : Exec format error
 9 : Bad file number
10 : No child processes
11 : No more processes
12 : Not enough space
13 : Permission denied
14 : Bad address
15 : Block device required
16 : Device busy
17 : File exists
18 : Cross-device link
19 : No such device
20 : Not a directory
21 : Is a directory
22 : Invalid argument
23 : File table overflow
24 : Too many open files
25 : Not a typewriter
26 : Text file busy
27 : File too large
```

220

28 : No space left on device
29 : Illegal seek
30 : Read-only file system
31 : Too many links
32 : Broken pipe
33 : Argument out of domain
34 : Result too large
35 : No message of desired type
36 : Identifier removed
37 : Channel number out of range
38 : Level 2 not synchronized
39 : Level 3 halted
40 : Level 3 reset
41 : Link number out of range
42 : Protocol driver not attached
43 : No CSI structure available
44 : Level 2 halted
$ ☐

Figure 7.A.1

The rest of this chapter describes the system calls tabulated earlier.

B. FILE STRUCTURE RELATED SYSTEM CALLS

The file structure related system calls available in the UNIX system let you create, open, and close files, read and write files, randomly access files, alias and remove files, get information about files, check the accessibility of files, change the protections, owner, and group of files, and control devices. These operations use either a character string that defines the absolute or relative path name of a file, or a small integer called a file descriptor that identifies the I/O channel. A *CHANNEL* is a connection between a process and a file that appears to the process as an unformatted stream of bytes. The kernel presents and accepts data from the channel as a process reads and writes that channel. To a process then, all input and output operations are synchronous and unbuffered.

When doing I/O, a process specifies the file descriptor for an I/O channel, a buffer to be filled or emptied, and the maximum size of data to be transferred. An I/O channel may allow input, output, or both. Furthermore, each channel has a read/write pointer. Each I/O operation starts when the last operation finished and advances the pointer by the number of bytes transferred. A process can access a channel's data randomly by changing the read/write pointer.

The next eight sections describe those system calls used to manipulate files in the UNIX system. Even though the Standard I/O subroutines described in Chapter 6 are recommended in preference to these system calls, it is important to understand these system calls because Standard I/O uses them to do I/O.

B.1 Creating a Channel

All input and output operations start by opening a file using either the **creat**() or **open**() system calls. These calls return a file descriptor that identifies the I/O channel. A file descriptor is a small, non-negative integer that must be used in most other file structure related system calls. Recall that file descriptors 0, 1, and 2 refer to the standard input, standard output, and standard error files respectively, and that file descriptor 0 is a channel to your terminal's keyboard and file descriptors 1 and 2 are channels to your terminal's display screen.

The **creat**() system call creates and opens a file for writing. Its syntax is:

```
          int
          creat(file__name, mode)
          char *file__name;
          int mode;
```

DEFINITION 35. The creat System Call

where *file__name* is a pointer to the character string that names the file and *mode* defines the file's access permissions. If the file named by *file__name* does not exist, the UNIX system creates it with *mode* permissions. However if the file does exist, its contents are discarded and the *mode* value is ignored. The permissions of the existing file are retained. **creat**() fails if any of the following conditions holds:

- Part of the prefix of *file__name* is not a directory.

- Part of the prefix of *file__name* does not exist.

- A directory in *file__name* is not searchable.

- *file__name* is null.

- *file__name* cannot be created because the directory where the file is to be created is not writable.

- *file__name* resides or would reside on a read-only file system.

- *file__name* is a shared text file that is currently being executed.

- *file__name* exists and write permission is denied.

- *file__name* is a directory.

- There are already too many open files.

- *file__name* points to an invalid memory address.

Next is the **open**() system call. **open**() lets you open a file for reading, writing, or reading and writing. Its syntax is:

```
#include  <fcntl.h>

int
open(file__name, option__flags [ , mode ])
char *file__name;
int option__flags, mode;
```

DEFINITION 36. The open System Call

---

where *file__name* is a pointer to the character string that names the file, *option__flags* represents the type of channel, and *mode* defines the file's access permissions if the file is being created.

The allowable *option__flags* are:

O__RDONLY   *file__name* is opened for reading.

O__WRONLY   *file__name* is opened for writing.

O__APPEND   Each write to the file named by *file__name* will be at the end of the file.

O__CREAT   If *file__name* exists, O__CREAT is ignored. However, if *file__name* does not exist, it is created with mode *mode*.

O__TRUNC   If *file__name* exists, its contents will be discarded.

O__EXCL   If O__CREAT and O__EXCL are set, then **open**() fails if *file__name* exists.

open() returns a file descriptor that identifies the I/O channel. **open**() fails if any of the following conditions holds:

- Part of the prefix of *file__name* is not a directory.

- O__CREAT is cleared and *file__name* does not exist.

- A directory in *file__name* is not searchable.

- *option__flags* requests an access type that the permissions of *file__name* denies.

- There are already too many open files.

- *file__name* is a shared text file that is currently being executed.

223

- *file__name* points to an invalid memory address.

- O__CREAT and O__EXCL are set and *file__name* exists.

Because of the limit on the number of channels, currently 20, you should close a channel when you are finished. If you do not close an open channel, the UNIX will close it automatically when your program ends.

To close a channel, use the **close**() system call. Its syntax is:

```
int
close(file__descriptor)
int file__descriptor;
```

DEFINITION 37. The close System Call

where *file__descriptor* identifies a currently open channel. **close**() fails if *file__descriptor* does not identify a currently open channel.

B.2 Input/Output

The **read**() system call does all input and the **write**() system call does all output. When used together, they provide all the tools necessary to do input and output sequentially. When used with the **lseek**() system call, they provide all the tools necessary to do input and output randomly.

Both **read**() and **write**() take three arguments. Their syntax is:

```
int
read(file__descriptor, buffer__pointer, transfer__size)
int file__descriptor;
char *buffer__pointer;
unsigned transfer__size;

int
write(file__descriptor, buffer__pointer, transfer__size)
int file__descriptor;
char *buffer__pointer;
unsigned transfer__size;
```

DEFINITION 38. The read and write System Calls

where *file__descriptor* identifies the I/O channel, *buffer__pointer* points to the area in memory where the data is stored for a **read**() or where the data is taken for a **write**(), and *transfer__size* defines the maximum number of characters transferred between the file and the buffer. **read**() and **write**() return the number of bytes transferred, and they can fail if any of the following conditions holds:

- *file_descriptor* does not identify an open I/O channel.

- The I/O channel identified by *file_descriptor* does not allow reading or writing.

- The device accessed encountered some type of physical I/O error.

- The buffer as defined by *buffer_pointer* and *transfer_size* is not contained entirely within your process.

There is no limit on *transfer_size*, but you must make sure it's safe to copy *transfer_size* bytes to or from the memory pointed to by *buffer_pointer*. A *transfer_size* of 1 is used to transfer a byte at a time for so-called "unbuffered" input/output.

Your programs can gain some efficiency by buffering data to reduce the number of reads and writes. Efficiency is inversely proportional to the number of system calls and amount of data transferred. The most efficient value for *transfer_size* is the size of the largest physical record the I/O channel is likely to have to handle. Therefore, 1K bytes – the disk block size – is the most efficient general-purpose buffer size for a standard file. However, if you are writing to a terminal, the transfer is best handled in lines ending with a newline. The subroutines in the Standard I/O library transparently handle these two cases.

The example in figure 7.B.1 shows the **getchar**() and **putchar**() subroutines that use the **read**() and **write**() system calls to provide the same functions as their Standard I/O counterparts. Unlike those subroutines, these examples do not buffer the data. This figure also shows a standard error version of **putchar**().

```
$ number chario.c
 1   /*
 2    *   chario
 3    *       getchar, putchar, errchar subroutines
 4    *       build with system calls
 5    */
 6
 7   #include    <ctype.h>
 8
 9   #define     EOF     (-1)
10   #define     ERROR (-1)
11   #define     STDIN   0
12   #define     STDOUT    1
13   #define     STDERR    2
14
15   main(argc, argv)
16   int argc;
17   char *argv[];
18   {
19       int c, rc = 0;
20
21       while ((c = getchar()) != EOF) {
22           if (isupper(c)) {
23               if (errchar(c) == ERROR) {
24                   perror("stderr");
25                   rc = 1;
26                   break;
27               }
28           } else {
29               if (putchar(c) == ERROR) {
30                   perror("stdout");
31                   rc = 1;
32                   break;
33               }
34           }
35       }
36       exit(rc);
37   }
38
39   int
40   getchar()
41   {
42       char c;
43       int count;
44
45       if ((count = read(STDIN, &c, sizeof(c))) == 0) {
46           count = EOF;
47       } else {
48           count = (int) c;
49       }
50       return(count);
51   }
```

```
52
53  int
54  putchar(c)
55  char c;
56  {
57      int count;
58
59      if ((count = write(STDOUT, &c, sizeof(c))) != sizeof(c)) {
60          count = ERROR;
61      } else {
62          count = 0;
63      }
64      return(count);
65  }
66
67  int
68  errchar(c)
69  char c;
70  {
71      int count;
72
73      if ((count = write(STDERR, &c, sizeof(c))) != sizeof(c)) {
74          count = ERROR;
75      } else {
76          count = 0;
77      }
78      return(count);
79  }
```

$ cc -o chario chario.c
$ chario 2> UPPERCASE > LOWERCASE
This is a test of the CHARIO program that writes upper case
letters to STANDARD ERROR and all other characters to STANDARD OUTPUT.
$ cat LOWERCASE
his is a test of the program that writes upper case
letters to   and all other characters to .
$ cat UPPERCASE
TCHARIOSTANDARDERRORSTANDARDOUTPUT$ ▭

Figure 7.B.1

Note that the **getchar**() and **putchar**() subroutines in the Standard I/O library use macros and a special FILE data structure. See Chapter 6 on the Standard I/O library for further details.

Figure 7.B.2 shows another programming example that uses the **open**(), **close**(), **read**(), and **write**() system calls to copy the contents of the file named as the first argument to the file named as the second argument.

```
$ number copy.c
 1   /*
 2    *   copy
 3    *       copy one file to another
 4    */
 5
 6   #include    <stdio.h>
 7   #include    <fcntl.h>
 8
 9   #define     PMODE     0755
10   #define     STDIN     0
11   #define     ERROR     (-1)
12
13   main(argc, argv)
14   int argc;
15   char *argv[];
16   {
17       int infd, outfd, count, rc = 0;
18       char buf[BUFSIZ];
19
20       if (scf("", "", &argc, &argv) == 0 || argc != 4) {
21           fprintf(stderr, "usage: %s: file1 file2\n", argv[0]);
22           rc = 1;
23       } else if ((infd = (strcmp(argv[2], "-") ? open(argv[2], O_RDONLY) : STDIN)) == ERROR) {
24           perror(argv[2]);
25           rc = 1;
26       } else if ((outfd = creat(argv[3], PMODE)) == ERROR) {
27           perror(argv[3]);
28           if (close(infd) == ERROR) {
29               perror(argv[2]);
30           }
31           rc = 1;
32       } else {
33           do {
34               if ((count = read(infd, buf, sizeof(buf))) == ERROR) {
35                   perror(argv[2]);
36                   rc = 1;
37               } else if (count > 0 && write(outfd, buf, count) == ERROR) {
38                   perror(argv[3]);
39                   rc = 1;
40               }
41           } while (count > 0);
42           if (close(infd) == ERROR) {
43               perror(argv[2]);
44               rc = 1;
45           }
46           if (close(outfd) == ERROR) {
47               perror(argv[3]);
48               rc = 1;
49           }
50       }
51       exit(rc);
```

228

52 ¦
$ □

Figure 7.B.2

The file creation permission mode 755 gives read and execute access for all user categories as well as write permission for the file owner. All files are closed after the copy operation completes.

B.3 Random Access

The UNIX system file system treats an ordinary file as a sequence of bytes. No internal structure is imposed on a file by the operating system. Thus, a file of n bytes can be shown as:

| beginning of file | 1 | 2 | 3 | . . . . | n-2 | n-1 | n | end of file |

Figure 7.B.3

Generally, a file is read or written sequentially – that is, from the beginning to the end of the file. After a file is opened, characters are read one at a time starting at the beginning – shown at the left above – and proceeding to the end of the file to the right.

Sometimes sequential reading and writing is not appropriate. It may be inefficient, for instance, to read an entire file just to move to the end of the file to add characters. Fortunately, the UNIX system lets you read and write anywhere in the file. Known as *RANDOM ACCESS*, this capability is made possible with the **lseek**() system call.

During file I/O, the UNIX system uses a long integer, also called a *FILE POINTER*, to keep track of the next byte to read or write. This integer represents the number of bytes from the beginning of the file to that next character. Random access I/O is achieved by changing the value of this file pointer using the **lseek**() system call whose syntax is:

```
                    long
                    lseek(file__descriptor, offset, whence)
                    int file__descriptor;
                    long offset;
                    int whence;
```

DEFINITION 39. The lseek System Call

where *file__descriptor* identifies the I/O channel and *offset* and *whence* work together to describe how to change the file pointer according to the following table:

WHENCE	NEW POSITION
0	*offset* bytes into the file
1	current position in the file plus *offset*
2	current end-of-file position plus *offset*

If successful, **lseek**() returns a long integer that defines the new file pointer value measured in bytes from the beginning of the file. If unsuccessful, the file position does not change. **lseek**() fails if any of the following conditions holds:

- *file__descriptor* does not identify an open I/O channel.

- *file__descriptor* describes an I/O channel between two processes, namely a pipe.

- *whence* is none of 0, 1, and 2.

- The new file pointer value is negative.

Certain devices are incapable of seeking, namely terminals and the character interface to the tape drive. **lseek**() does not change the file pointer for these devices.

Figure 7.B.4 shows an example that uses the **lseek**() system call to position the file pointer to the end of the file named as an argument before adding the standard input file to that file.

```
$ number addto1.c
 1  /*
 2   *   addto
 3   *       add standard input to file argument
 4   *       version 1
 5   */
 6
 7  #include    <stdio.h>
 8  #include    <fcntl.h>
 9
10  #define     STDIN       0
11  #define     ERROR       (-1)
12  #define     PMODE       0644
13
14  main(argc, argv)
15  int argc;
16  char *argv[];
17  {
18      int fd, count, i, verbose = 0, rc = 0;
19      char buffer[BUFSIZ];
20      long posn, lseek();
21
22      if (scf("v", "", &argc, &argv) == 0) {
23          rc = 1;
24      } else {
25          for (i = 1; strcmp(argv[i], "--"); i++) {
26              switch (argv[i][1]) {
27              case 'v':
28                  verbose++;
29                  break;
30              }
31          }
32      }
33      if (rc == 1 || ++i != argc - 1) {
34          fprintf(stderr, "usage: %s [-v] file\n", argv[0]);
35          rc = 1;
36      } else if (!strcmp(argv[i], "-")) {
37          fprintf(stderr, "%s: file argument cannot be standard input\n", argv[0]);
38          fprintf(stderr, "usage: %s [-v] file\n", argv[0]);
39          rc = 1;
40      } else if ((fd = open(argv[i], O_WRONLY)) == ERROR &&
41              (fd = creat(argv[i], PMODE)) == ERROR) {
42          perror(argv[i]);
43          rc = 1;
44      } else if ((posn = lseek(fd, 0L, 2)) == ERROR) {
45          perror(argv[i]);
46          rc = 1;
47      } else {
48          if (verbose) {
49              printf("Old file size is %ld\n", posn);
50          }
51          do {
```

```
52              if ((count = read(STDIN, buffer, sizeof(buffer))) = = ERROR) {
53                  perror("stdin");
54                  rc = 1;
55              } else if (count > 0 && write(fd, buffer, count) = = ERROR) {
56                  perror(argv[i]);
57                  rc = 1;
58              }
59          } while (count > 0);
60          if (count != ERROR) {
61              if ((posn = lseek(fd, 0L, 2)) = = ERROR) {
62                  perror(argv[i]);
63                  rc = 1;
64              } else if (verbose) {
65                  printf("New file size is %ld\n", posn);
66              }
67          }
68          if (close(fd) = = ERROR) {
69              perror(argv[i]);
70              rc = 1;
71          }
72      }
73      exit(rc);
74  }
$ cc -o addto addto1.c
$ □
```

Figure 7.B.4

Figure 7.B.5 shows a sample of execution.

$ **ls -l testfile**
testfile not found
$ **addto**
usage: addto [-v] file
$ **addto testfile**
This is a test of the addto command.
$ **ls -l testfile**
-rw-rw-rw-   1 rogers   writers   37 Apr 2 11:55 testfile
$ **addto -v testfile**
Old file size is 37
This is another test of the addto command.
New file size is 80
$ **ls -l testfile**
-rw-rw-rw-   1 rogers   writers   80 Apr 2 11:56 testfile
$ **cat testfile**
This is a test of the addto command.
This is another test of the addto command.
$ ☐

Figure 7.B.5

B.4 Channel Duplication

The **dup**() system call duplicates an open file descriptor and returns the new file descriptor. This new file descriptor has the following properties in common with the original file descriptor:

- Refers to the same open file or pipe.

- Has the same file pointer – that is, both file descriptors share one file pointer.

- Has the same access mode, whether read, write, or read and write.

dup() has the syntax:

```
              int
              dup(file__descriptor)
              int file__descriptor;
```

DEFINITION 40. The dup System Call

where *file__descriptor* is the file descriptor describing the original I/O channel returned by the **creat**(), **open**(), **dup**(), or **pipe**() system calls. **dup**() is guaranteed to return a file descriptor with the lowest integer value available. **dup**() fails if any of the following conditions holds:

- *file__descriptor* does not identify an open I/O channel.

- There are already too many open files.

Figure 7.B.6 shows version 2 of the **addto** program that accepts the *-ifilename* argument as a redefinition of the input file. Recall that a file descriptor is a small non-negative integer that names the I/O channel, and that file descriptors 0, 1, and 2 name the I/O channels connected to your terminal's keyboard and its display. In the **open**(), **close**(), and **dup**() sequence beginning in line 52, the call to **dup**() is guaranteed to return file descriptor 0 if successful because file descriptor 0 was made available with the **close**() in line 55. This means that the standard input file, file descriptor 0, is redirected to the file given as the argument to the i option. The shell uses a similar sequence to redirect standard input when it finds the < redirection operator in a command.

$ **number addto2.c**

```
 1   /*
 2    *   addto
 3    *       add standard input to file argument
 4    *       version 2
 5    */
 6
 7   #include    <stdio.h>
 8   #include    <fcntl.h>
 9
10   #define     STDIN       0
11   #define     ERROR       (-1)
12   #define     PMODE       0644
13
14   main(argc, argv)
15   int argc;
16   char *argv[];
17   {
18       int fd, ifd, count, i, verbose = 0, rc = 0, ioption = 0;
19       char buffer[BUFSIZ], *file;
20       long posn, lseek();
21
22       if (scf("vi", "i", &argc, &argv) == 0) {
23           rc = 1;
24       } else {
25           for (i = 1; strcmp(argv[i], "--"); i++) {
26               switch (argv[i][1]) {
27               case 'v':
28                   verbose++;
29                   break;
30               case 'i':
31                   ioption++;
32                   file = argv[++i];
33                   break;
34               }
35           }
36       }
37       if (rc == 1 || ++i != argc - 1) {
38           fprintf(stderr, "usage: %s [-v] file\n", argv[0]);
39           rc = 1;
40       } else if (!strcmp(argv[i], "-")) {
41           fprintf(stderr, "%s: file argument cannot be standard input\n", argv[0]);
42           fprintf(stderr, "usage: %s [-v] file\n", argv[0]);
43           rc = 1;
44       } else if ((fd = open(argv[i], O_WRONLY)) == ERROR &&
45               (fd = creat(argv[i], PMODE)) == ERROR) {
46           perror(argv[i]);
47           rc = 1;
48       } else if ((posn = lseek(fd, 0L, 2)) == ERROR) {
49           perror(argv[i]);
50           rc = 1;
51       } else {
```

235

```
52          if (verbose) {
53              printf("Old file size is %ld\n", posn);
54          }
55          if (ioption) {
56              if ((ifd = open(file, O__RDONLY)) == ERROR) {
57                  perror(file);
58                  rc = 1;
59              } else if (close(STDIN) == ERROR) {
60                  perror("stdin");
61                  rc = 1;
62              } else if (dup(ifd) == ERROR) {
63                  perror(argv[0]);
64                  rc = 1;
65              } else if (close(ifd) == ERROR) {
66                  perror(file);
67                  rc = 1;
68              }
69          }
70          if (rc == 0) {
71              do {
72                  if ((count = read(STDIN, buffer, sizeof(buffer))) == ERROR) {
73                      perror("stdin");
74                      rc = 1;
75                  } else if (count > 0 && write(fd, buffer, count) == ERROR) {
76                      perror(argv[i]);
77                      rc = 1;
78                  }
79              } while (count > 0);
80              if (count != ERROR) {
81                  if ((posn = lseek(fd, 0L, 2)) == ERROR) {
82                      perror(argv[i]);
83                      rc = 1;
84                  } else if (verbose) {
85                      printf("New file size is %ld\n", posn);
86                  }
87              }
88              if (close(fd) == ERROR) {
89                  perror(argv[i]);
90                  rc = 1;
91              }
92          }
93      }
94      exit(rc);
95 }
$ cc -o addto addto2.c
```

Figure 7.B.6

Figure 7.B.7 shows another example.

```
$ addto -v x
Old file size is 0
This is a test of addto, version 2.
New file size is 36
$ addto -v y
Old file size is 0
This is another test of addto, version 2.
New file size is 42
$ addto -v -i y x
Old file size is 36
New file size is 78
$ cat x
This is a test of addto, version 2.
This is another test of addto, version 2.
$ ▢
```

Figure 7.B.7

The first invocation of **addto** creates x and stores 36 characters in it and the second invocation creates y with 42 characters in it. The last call adds the contents of y onto the end of x, and the **cat** command confirms the operation.

B.5 Aliasing and Removing Files

The UNIX system file structure allows more than one named reference to a given file, a feature called *ALIASING*. Making an alias to a file means that the file has more than one name, but all names of the file refer to the same data. Since all names refer to the same data, changing the contents of one file changes the contents of all aliases to that file.

Because of the way the UNIX system relates a file name to the file's contents, file aliasing is simple. To appreciate this simplicity, some terms must be defined. These are:

i-node An i-node is a data structure that defines all the specifics of a file except its name. The i-node contains a file's size, the number of links to the file, its permissions, owner, group, its last access, modification, and i-node change times, and pointers to the blocks in the file system that contain the data in the file. Within the UNIX system kernel, all access to a file is through its related i-node.

i-list All i-nodes are stored as an array in the file system named the i-list.

237

i-number   Access to a specific i-node in the i-list is by *I-NUMBER*. An i-number is a short integer field that starts at 1. Each file in a file system has an i-number.

link   Each i-number that names an i-node is called a *LINK* and the links field of the i-node tells how many i-numbers reference that i-node.

directory   A *DIRECTORY* is a specific file type in the UNIX system that relates a file name stored in ASCII to an i-number. Since the i-number 0 is not used, a directory entry with an i-number of 0 means that the entry is available.

Aliasing a file in the UNIX system amounts to the system creating a new directory entry that contains the alias file name and then copying the i-number of an existing file to the i-number position of this new directory entry. The diagram below shows two directory entries that reference the same file.

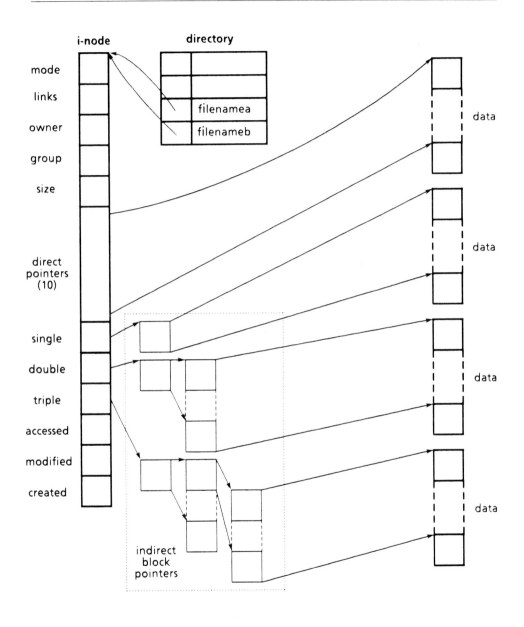

Figure 7.B.8

Notice especially that the only information retained by the alias file is the i-number of the original file. Since each file system has its own set of i-numbers that are unique only within a file system, files cannot be linked across file systems.

The **link**() system call links an existing file to a new file. Its syntax is:

```
int
link(original__name, alias__name)
char *original__name, *alias__name;
```

DEFINITION 41. The link System Call

where both *original__name* and *alias__name* are character strings that name the existing and the new files respectively. **link**() will fail and no link will be created if any of the following conditions holds:

- A path name component is not a directory.

- A path name component does not exist.

- A path name component is off-limits.

- *original__name* does not exist.

- *alias__name* does exist.

- *original__name* is a directory and you are not the superuser.

- A link is attempted across file systems.

- The destination directory for the file named by *alias__name* is not writable.

- The destination directory is contained in a file system mounted read-only.

- Either path argument points to an invalid memory address.

The opposite of the **link**() system call is the **unlink**() system call. **unlink**() removes a file by zeroing the i-number part of the file's directory entry, reducing the link count field in the file's i-node by 1, and releasing the data blocks and the i-node if the link count field becomes zero. **unlink**() is the only system call for removing a file in the UNIX system. The syntax for **unlink**() is:

```
                          int
                          unlink(file__name)
                          char *file__name;
```

DEFINITION 42. The unlink System Call

where *file__name* names the file to be unlinked. **unlink**() fails if any of the following conditions holds:

- A path name component is not a directory.

- A path name component does not exist.

- A path name component is off-limits.

- *file__name* does not exist.

- The directory for the file named by *file__name* is not writable.

- *file__name* is a directory and you are not the superuser.

- The directory is contained in a file system mounted read-only.

- *file__name* points to an invalid memory address.

It is important to understand that a file's contents and its i-node are not discarded until all processes close the unlinked file. This simplifies temporary file maintenance, as the skeleton in figure 7.B.9 shows.

```
$ number skeleton
1
2    #define    TMP      "/tmp"
3    #define    ERROR (-1)
4
5    char    filename[64];
6
...
30       /*
31        *  build temporary file name and unlink for later removal
32        */
33       sprintf(filename, "%s/%d", TMP, getpid());
34       if ((fd = open(filename, O__WRONLY)) == ERROR) {
35           perror(filename);
36           rc = 1;
37       } else if (unlink(filename) == ERROR) {
38           perror(filename);
39           rc = 1;
40       } else { /* use temporary file */
...
$ ☐
```

Figure 7.B.9

Since the file is unlinked just after it is created, the file name need not be saved for later use. When the process finishes using the temporary file, it need only close the file with **close**() and it will be discarded.

The example in figure 7.B.10 shows the **move** program that uses the **link**() and **unlink**() system calls to rename a file. **move** first creates a link between the original file and the new file and then unlinks the original file. Because **move** uses only **link**() and **unlink**() to rename a file, it can only move files from one place in a file system to another place in the same file system. Therefore, **move** is not as robust as the **mv** program distributed with the UNIX system. **mv** also uses **link**() and **unlink**() to rename a file in a file system, but it also copies the file from one place to another when linking is not possible.

```
$ number move.c
 1   /*
 2    *   move
 3    *      rename a file
 4    */
 5
 6   #include    <stdio.h>
 7
 8   #define     ERROR      (-1)
 9
10   main(argc, argv)
11   int argc;
12   char *argv[];
13   {
14       int rc = 0;
15
16       if (scf("", "", &argc, &argv) == 0 || argc != 4) {
17           fprintf(stderr, "usage: %s oldname newname\n", argv[0]);
18           rc = 1;
19       } else if (link(argv[2], argv[3]) == ERROR) {
20           perror(argv[0]);
21           rc = 1;
22       } else if (unlink(argv[2]) == ERROR) {
23           perror(argv[2]);
24           rc = 1;
25       }
26       exit(rc);
27   }
$ cc -o move move.c
$ □
```

Figure 7.B.10

Figure 7.B.11 shows a sample execution.

243

```
$ ls -l file
file not found
$ echo This is a test > file
$ ls -l file
-rw-rw-rw-   1 rogers   writers        15 Apr  2 117:23 file
$ move
usage: move oldname newname
$ move file newfile
$ ls -l file newfile
file not found
-rw-rw-rw-   1 rogers   writers        15 Apr  2 117:23 newfile
$ cat newfile
This is a test
$ □
```

Figure 7.B.11

B.6 File Status

The last section introduced the i-node as a data structure used by the file system to hold all information about a file except the file's name and its contents. Sometimes your programs need to use the information in the i-node structure to do some job. You can access this information with the **stat**() and **fstat**() system calls. **stat**() and **fstat**() return the information in the i-node for the file named by a string and by a file descriptor, respectively. The format for the i-node structure returned by these system calls is defined in */usr/include/sys/stat.h*. *stat.h* uses types built with the typedef C language construct and defined in the file */usr/include/sys/types.h*, so it too must be included and must be included before the inclusion of the *stat.h* file. **stat**() and **fstat**() have the following syntax:

```
#include        <sys/types.h>
#include        <sys/stat.h>

int
stat(file__name, stat__buf)
char *file__name;
struct stat *stat__buf;

int
fstat(file__descriptor, stat__buf)
int file__descriptor;
struct stat *stat__buf;
```

DEFINITION 43. The stat and fstat System Calls

where *file__name* names the file as an ASCII string and *file__descriptor* names the I/O channel and therefore the file. Both calls return the file's specifics in *stat__buf*. **stat**() and **fstat**() fail if any of the following conditions holds:

- A path name component is not a directory (**stat**() only).

- *file__name* does not exist (**stat**() only).

- A path name component is off-limits (**stat**() only).

- *file__descriptor* does not identify an open I/O channel (**fstat**() only).

- *stat__buf* points to an invalid address.

Figure 7.B.1 shows the **stat** program that gives information about the files named as arguments or the standard input file if no arguments are given.

```
$ number stat.c
1   /*
2   *   stat
3   *       display all stat information for a file
4   */
5
6   #include    <stdio.h>
7   #include    <sys/types.h>
8   #include    <sys/stat.h>
9
10  #define     STDIN    0
11  #define     ERROR    -1
12
13  main(argc, argv)
14  int argc;
15  char *argv[];
16  {
17      int rc = 0, i;
18      struct stat statb;
19
20      if (scf("", "", &argc, &argv) == 0) {
21              fprintf(stderr, "usage: %s [file ...]\n", argv[0]);
22              rc = 1;
23      } else if (argc == 2) {
24          if (fstat(STDIN, &statb) == ERROR) {
25              perror("stdin");
26              rc = 1;
27          } else {
28              display("stdin", &statb);
29          }
30      } else {
31          for (i = 2; i < argc; i++) {
32              if (!strcmp(argv[i], "-")) {
33                  if (fstat(STDIN, &statb) == ERROR) {
34                      perror("stdin");
35                      rc = 1;
36                  } else {
37                      display("stdin", &statb);
38                  }
39              } else if (stat(argv[i], &statb) == ERROR) {
40                      perror(argv[i]);
41                      rc = 1;
42              } else {
43                      display(argv[i], &statb);
44              }
45          }
46      }
47      exit(rc);
48  }
49
50  display(fname, sp)
51  char *fname;
```

```
52   struct stat *sp;
53   }
54       extern char *ctime();
55
56       printf("FILE: %s\n", fname);
57       printf("\tMajor device   = %d\n", major(sp->st_dev));
58       printf("\tMinor device   = %d\n", minor(sp->st_dev));
59       printf("\tI-node number  = %d\n", sp->st_ino);
60       printf("\tFile mode      = %o(8)\n", sp->st_mode);
61       printf("\tLinks          = %d\n", sp->st_nlink);
62       printf("\tOwner ID       = %d\n", sp->st_uid);
63       printf("\tGroup ID       = %d\n", sp->st_gid);
64       if (sp->st_mode & (S_IFCHR | S_IFBLK)) {
65           printf("\tMajor device   = %d\n", major(sp->st_rdev));
66           printf("\tMinor device   = %d\n", minor(sp->st_rdev));
67       }
68       printf("\tSize           = %ld\n", sp->st_size);
69       printf("\tLast access    = %s", ctime(&sp->st_atime));
70       printf("\tLast mod       = %s", ctime(&sp->st_mtime));
71       printf("\tLast change    = %s", ctime(&sp->st_ctime));
72   }
```

```
$ cc -o stat stat.c
$ stat
FILE: stdin
     Major device   = 0
     Minor device   = 0
     I-node number  = 188
     File mode      = 20622(8)
     Links          = 1
     Owner ID       = 541
     Group ID       = 2000
     Major device   = 1
     Minor device   = 11
     Size           = 0
     Last access    = Tue Dec 18 21:54:00 1984
     Last mod       = Tue Dec 18 21:54:00 1984
     Last change    = Tue Dec 18 21:54:00 1984
$ ls -l `tty`
crw--w--w-  1 rogers   writers   1, 11 Jun 21 19:42 /dev/tty11
$ stat /etc/passwd
FILE: /etc/passwd
     Major device   = 0
     Minor device   = 0
     I-node number  = 194
     File mode      = 100644(8)
     Links          = 1
     Owner ID       = 0
     Group ID       = 3
     Size           = 530
     Last access    = Tue Dec 18 21:56:01 1984
     Last mod       = Thu Nov 15 18:39:05 1984
     Last change    = Thu Nov 15 18:39:05 1984
$ ls -l /etc/passwd
```

```
-rw-r--r--  1 root    sys        530 Nov 15 18:39 /etc/passwd
$ stat < /etc/passwd
FILE: stdin
      Major device   = 0
      Minor device   = 0
      I-node number  = 194
      File mode      = 100644(8)
      Links       = 1
      Owner ID       = 0
      Group ID       = 3
      Size       = 530
      Last access    = Tue Dec 18 21:57:26 1984
      Last mod       = Thu Nov 15 18:39:05 1984
      Last change    = Thu Nov 15 18:39:05 1984
$ □
```

Figure 7.B.12

The first set of major and minor device descriptions for the *stdin* file names the device where the special file */dev/tty11* is stored. **stat**() and **fstat**() also return the major and minor device numbers for character and block special devices. **stat** prints these as the second set of major and minor devices in lines 57 and 58. Notice also that when the standard input file is redirected to another file, the information is the same as when that file is checked directly.

B.7 Access Control

Access to a file is determined by the file's permissions and the permissions of all directories searched to reach the file. The UNIX system provides four system calls that let you determine if you can access a file, let you change the protection modes, owner, and group of a file, and let you change the file creation permission mask.

Every file in the UNIX system has a mode field in the i-node that contains the file's permissions. This field is a short integer that is broken into the following sub-fields:

FIELD MASK	MEANING
0100000	Regular file
0040000	Directory file
0020000	Character special file
0060000	Block special file
0010000	Fifo file
0004000	Set user id
0002000	Set group id
0001000	Save text
0000400	Owner - read permission
0000200	Owner - write permission
0000100	Owner - execute/search permission
0000070	Group - read/write/execute/search permission
0000007	Other - read/write/execute/search permission

Of primary concern here are the permission fields that define who can do what to a file. There are three classes of protections in the UNIX system: those protections that apply to a file's owner, those that apply to the file's group, and those that apply to everyone else. Within each class, there are three things that a class can do: a class can read the file, a class can write to the file, and a class can execute the file if it is a regular file, or search the file if it is a directory file. Execution permission has no meaning for block and character special files.

Processes also have owner and group ID fields. The UNIX system uses these fields to determine if a process can access a file or search a directory.

As an example of a file's permissions and file and process IDs, consider what the UNIX system does when you say:

    cat /etc/passwd

and the **cat** program tries to open the *tetc/passwd* file. The steps the UNIX system goes through are listed below.

- File decoding starts at the root of the file system because the first character of the path name is /. / is a directory and to continue decoding the path name, you must be able to search it.

- Can you search /?

```
$ ls -ld /
drwxrwxr-x  14 bin     bin        288 Nov 15 19:21 /
$ □
```

Figure 7.B.13

Yes, / has search permission (x) for the owner class, the group class, and the other class.

● The next component of the path name is etc. It too is a directory – do you have permission to search it?

```
$ ls -ld /etc
drwxrwxr-x   3 root    sys       1328 Dec 18 19:17 /etc
$ □
```

Figure 7.B.14

Yes, it too has search permission enabled for the owner, the group, and the other classes.

● Finally, the file *passwd* in the */etc* directory is a regular file. Does it have *read* permission, since the **cat** command wants to read it and display its contents?

```
$ ls -l /etc/passwd
-rw-r--r--   1 root    sys        530 Nov 15 18:39 /etc/passwd
$ □
```

Figure 7.B.15

Yes, the *passwd* file in the */etc* directory has read permission for the owner, group, and other classes. Therefore the **cat** command will be able to display its contents.

Now, imagine that you said:

    rm /etc/passwd

instead of:

```
cat /etc/passwd
```

Would this command do the required job? Again, the steps are listed below.

- The / and /etc decoding steps are the same as with the **cat** command.

- Recall that the only way to remove a file in the UNIX system is with the **unlink**() system call. To remove a file, **unlink**() must be able to write into the directory where the file lives to write zeroes over its i-number entry. The question is: can you write into the /etc directory?

$ ls -ld /etc
drwxrwxr-x 3 root   sys   1328 Dec 18 19:17 /etc
$ ☐

Figure 7.B.16

The permissions only allow writing into the /etc directory for the file's owner, root, and the file's group, also root. If you are the root or superuser, then you can remove /etc/passwd; but if you are not the superuser, your **rm** program will not be successful and the /etc/passwd file will not be removed.

Your programs can check the accessibility of files and also change the owner and group of a file with the **access**(), **chmod**(), and **chown**() system calls. The first of these is **access**() and its syntax is:

```
           int
           access(file__name, access__mode)
           char *file__name;
           int access__mode;
```

DEFINITION 44. The access System Call

---

where *file__name* is the name of the file to which the access permissions given in *access__mode* are to be applied. The allowable modes are:

VALUE	MEANING
04	read
02	write
01	execute
00	existence

access() returns zero if you are allowed to access the file as specified by

251

access__mode and the standard -1 otherwise. **access**() fails if any of the following conditions holds:

- A path name component is not a directory.

- *file__name* does not exist.

- A path name component is off-limits.

- Write access is requested for a file on a file system mounted as read-only.

- Write access is requested for a shared text file that is being executed.

- The permission bits of the file mode do not permit the requested access.

- *file__name* points to an invalid memory address.

Figure 7.B.17 shows the **remove** program that uses the **access**() system call. **remove** removes files, after first checking that they exist, but does not remove a file that is not writable. **remove** recognizes the f option to mean that a non-writable file should be removed anyway.

```
$ number remove.c
 1  /*
 2   *  remove
 3   *      remove ordinary files
 4   */
 5
 6  #include   <stdio.h>
 7
 8  #define    EXIST  0
 9  #define    WRITE  2
10  #define    ERROR (-1)
11
12  main(argc, argv)
13  int argc;
14  char *argv[];
15  {
16      int foption = 0, rc = 0, i;
17
18      if (scf("f", "", &argc, &argv) == 0) {
19          rc = 1;
20      } else {
21          for (i = 1; strcmp(argv[i], "--"); i++) {
22              switch (argv[i][1]) {
23              case 'f':
24                  foption++;
25                  break;
26              }
27          }
28      }
29      if (rc == 1 | ++i == argc) {
30          fprintf(stderr, "usage: %s [-f] file ...\n", argv[0]);
```

```
31          rc = 1;
32      } else {
33          for ( ; i < argc; i++) {
34              if (!strcmp(argv[i], "-")) {
35                  fprintf(stderr, "%s: file argument cannot be standard input\n", argv[0]);
36                  rc = 1;
37              } else if (access(argv[i], EXIST) == ERROR) {
38                  perror(argv[i]);
39                  rc = 1;
40              } else if (access(argv[i], WRITE) == ERROR && !foption) {
41                  fprintf(stderr, "%s: %s write protected\n", argv[0], argv[i]);
42              } else if (unlink(argv[i])) {
43                  perror(argv[i]);
44                  rc = 1;
45              }
46          }
47      }
48      exit(rc);
49 }
$ cc -o remove remove.c
```

Figure 7.B.17

Figure 7.B.18 shows a sample.

```
$ echo testing > testfile
$ ls -l testfile
-rw-rw-rw-  1 rogers   writers        8 Apr  3 10:37 testfile
$ remove testfile
$ ls -l testfile
testfile not found
$ echo testing > testfile
$ chmod -w testfile
$ ls -l testfile
-r--r--r--  1 rogers   writers        8 Apr  3 10:37 testfile
$ remove testfile
remove: testfile write protected
$ remove -f testfile
$ ls -l testfile
testfile not found
$□
```

Figure 7.B.18

The example first creates a file that has write permission and then removes it with **remove**. The file is created again and write permission is removed with **chmod**. **remove** complains that the file is write-protected and does not remove it. The next invocation of **remove** specifies the f option that forces **remove** to remove the file even though it does not have write permission.

Next is the **chmod**() system call that lets you change a file's permissions. The syntax of **chmod**() is:

```
                          int
                          chmod(file__name, mode)
                          char *file__name;
                          int mode;
```

DEFINITION 45. The chmod System Call

where *file__name* names the file whose permissions are to be changed and *mode* defines the new permission modes as described at the beginning of this section. A file's mode can be changed only by the file owner or by the superuser. **chmod**() fails and the file mode remains unchanged if any of the following conditions hold:

- A path name component is not a directory.

- *file__name* does not exist.

- A path name component is off-limits.

- The process' owner ID does not match the owner of the file and the owner of the calling process is not the superuser.

- *file__name* resides on a file system mounted read-only.

- *file__name* points to an invalid memory address.

Figure 7.B.19 shows the **chmod** program that changes the modes of all files to the value given as the first argument.

```
$ number chmod.c
 1  /*
 2   *   chmod
 3   *      change the modes of files
 4   */
 5
 6  #include    <stdio.h>
 7
 8  #define     MODEMASK    0777
 9  #define     ERROR       (-1)
10
11  main(argc, argv)
12  int argc;
13  char *argv[];
14  {
15      int rc = 0, i, newmode;
16
17      if (scf("", "", &argc, &argv) == 0 | argc < 4) {
18          fprintf(stderr, "usage: %s mode file ...\n", argv[0]);
19          rc = 1;
20      } else {
21          if (sscanf(argv[2], "%o", &newmode) != 1) {
22              fprintf(stderr, "%s: mode argument (%s) not numeric\n", argv[0], argv[2]);
23              rc = 1;
24          } else {
25              for (i = 3; i < argc; i++) {
26                  if (!strcmp(argv[i], "-")) {
27                      fprintf(stderr, "%s: cannot change mode of standard input\n", argv[0]);
28                      rc = 1;
29                  } else if (chmod(argv[i], newmode) == ERROR) {
30                      perror(argv[i]);
31                      rc = 1;
32                  }
33              }
34          }
35      }
36      exit(rc);
37  }
$ cc -o chmod chmod.c
$ echo testing > y
$ ls -l y
-rw-rw-rw-  1 rogers   writers      8 Apr  3 10:57 y
$ chmod 0700 y
$ ls -l y
-rwx------  1 rogers   writers      8 Apr  3 10:57 y
$ chmod 0 y
$ ls -l y
----------  1 rogers   writers      8 Apr  3 10:57 y
$ ▢
```

Figure 7.B.19

The file *y* is created with a mode of 0666. The mode is changed to 0700 and the change is verified with **ls**. The mode is then changed and verified again.

The next system call is the **chown**() system call. **chown**() lets you change the owner and group of a file and its syntax is:

```
                   int
                   chown(file__name, owner, group)
                   char *file__name;
                   int owner, group;
```

DEFINITION 46. The chown System Call

where *file__name* names the file whose owner and group are to be changed and *owner* and *group* are the new owner and group ID for the file. **chown**() fails, leaving the owner and group fields of the file unchanged, if any of the following conditions holds:

- A path name component is not a directory.

- *file__name* does not exist.

- A path name component is off-limits.

- The process ID does not match the file's owner and the process' owner is not the superuser.

- *file__name* resides on a file system mounted read-only.

- *file__name* points to an invalid address.

Figure 7.B.20 shows the **chown** program that lets you change the owner and group IDs of the files given as arguments. If the new owner or group ID numbers are given as a plus sign, then the old owner or group is preserved, respectively. The **stat**() system call is used to find the current owner and group IDs for the file.

$ **number chown.c**

```
 1  /*
 2   *   chown
 3   *       change the owner and group of a file
 4   *       dash means do not change owner/group
 5   */
 6
 7  #include    <stdio.h>
 8  #include    <sys/types.h>
 9  #include    <sys/stat.h>
10
11  #define    OWNER      2
12  #define    GROUP      3
13  #define    FILENAME   4
14  #define    SAVE       '+'
15  #define    ERROR      -1
16
17  main(argc, argv)
18  int argc;
19  char *argv[];
20  {
21      int gid, uid, ngid, nuid, rc = 0, i;
22      char *fname;
23      struct stat statb;
24
25      if (scf("", "", &argc, &argv) == 0 | argc < 5) {
26          fprintf(stderr, "usage: %s owner group file ...\n", argv[0]);
27          rc = 1;
28      } else {
29          nuid = atoi(argv[OWNER]);
30          ngid = atoi(argv[GROUP]);
31          for (i = FILENAME; i < argc; i++) {
32              if (!strcmp(argv[i], "-")) {
33                  fprintf(stderr, "%s: file argument cannot be standard input\n", argv[0]);
34                  rc = 1;
35              } else if (stat(argv[i], &statb) == ERROR) {
36                  perror(argv[i]);
37                  rc = 1;
38              } else {
39                  uid = statb.st_uid;
40                  gid = statb.st_gid;
41                  if (argv[OWNER][0] != SAVE) {
42                      uid = nuid;
43                  }
44                  if (argv[GROUP][0] != SAVE) {
45                      gid = ngid;
46                  }
47                  if (chown(argv[i], uid, gid) == ERROR) {
48                      perror(argv[i]);
49                      rc = 1;
50                  }
51              }
```

```
52          |
53      |
54      exit(rc);
55  |
$ cc -o chown chown.c
$ ☐
```

Figure 7.B.20

```
$ echo testing > testfile
$ ls -l testfile
-rw-rw-rw-  1 rogers   writers     8 Apr  3 13:16 testfile
$ chown + + testfile
$ ls -l testfile
-rw-rw-rw-  1 rogers   writers     8 Apr  3 13:16 testfile
$ chown 1023 65 testfile
$ ls -l testfile
-rw-rw-rw-  1 1023     65          8 Apr  3 13:16 testfile
$ ☐
```

Figure 7.B.21

The **ls** program uses the **stat**() system call to find the owner and group IDs for a file. **ls** then looks for these IDs in the */etc/passwd* and */etc/group* files to print the owner and group for a file. If an ID cannot be found in */etc/passwd* or */etc/group*, **ls** prints the ID number, as is shown in figure 7.B.21.

Finally, the **umask**() system call lets you change the file creation mask. The value given to **umask**() defines the permissions that are *not* to be granted when a file is created. The UNIX system combines the *mode* value from the **creat**() system call with the value given to **umask**() according to the following formula:

file__permissions = mode & (!umask__value)

The syntax of the **umask**() system call is:

```
                        int
                        umask(cmask)
                        int cmask;
```

DEFINITION 47. The umask System Call

where *mask* defines the permissions to be denied when a file is created. **umask**() returns the old mask value and does not fail.

Figure 7.B.22 shows the **umask** program that shows how the **umask**() system call works. Relative path name addressing must be used to specify the **umask** command because the Bourne Shell has **umask** built-in.

```
$ number umask.c
 1  / *
 2   *   umask
 3   *       print the current umask value
 4   * /
 5
 6  #include    <stdio.h>
 7
 8  #define     TMP     "/tmp"
 9  #define     LS  "ls -l"
10  #define     ERROR -1
11  #define     PMODE 0666
12
13  main(argc, argv)
14  int argc;
15  char *argv[];
16  {
17      int rc = 0;
18      char filename[BUFSIZ], command[BUFSIZ];
19
20      if (scf("", "", &argc, &argv) = = 0 | argc != 2) {
21          fprintf(stderr, "usage: %s\n", argv[0]);
22          rc = 1;
23      } else {
24          sprintf(filename, "%s/%d", TMP, getpid());
25          sprintf(command, "%s %s", LS, filename);
26          umask(0);
27          if (creat(filename, PMODE) = = ERROR) {
28              perror(filename);
29              rc = 1;
30          } else {
31              system(command);
32              umask(022);
33              if (unlink(filename) = = ERROR) {
34                  perror(filename);
```

```
35              rc = 1;
36          | else if (creat(filename, PMODE) = = ERROR) |
37              perror(filename);
38              rc = 1;
39          | else |
40              system(command);
41              if (unlink(filename) = = ERROR) |
42                  perror(filename);
43                  rc = 1;
44              |
45          |
46      |
47  |
48  exit(rc);
49 |
$ cc -o umask umask.c
$ ./umask
-rw-rw-rw-  1 rogers  writers      0 Apr  3 13:45 /tmp/865
-rw-r--r--  1 rogers  writers      0 Apr  3 13:45 /tmp/865
$ □
```

Figure 7.B.22

The file creation mask is first set to 0 to preserve all bits in a **creat**() system call and then write permission for the group and other classes is removed. The **system**() subroutine explained in Chapter 6 lists the file's protection each time after the file is created.

B.8 Device Control

Certain devices in the UNIX system, namely terminals and other communication devices, provide a set of device-specific commands. These commands are executed by a part of the UNIX system kernel known as a *DEVICE DRIVER*. A device driver's mission in the UNIX system is to control a device and to do those jobs required by other parts of the kernel and by processes. For those devices that provide a set of device-specific commands, the **ioctl**() system call is the way that those commands are presented to the device driver and the way that the device driver returns information about the device.

Typically, **ioctl**() is used to determine and change the status of a terminal device. The terminal-specific commands are defined in the include file */usr/include/termio.h*, along with other useful manifest constants and data structures. The commands available should also be regarded as dependent on the UNIX system version.

The syntax for the **ioctl**() call is:

```
          #include       <termio.h>

          int
          ioctl(file__descriptor, request, arg__pointer)
          int file__descriptor;
          int request;
          struct termio *arg__pointer;
```

DEFINITION 48. The ioctl System Call

where *file__descriptor* identifies the I/O channel which must name a device that has some device-specific commands, *request* is the device-specific command, and *arg__pointer* defines a data structure used by the device driver when it executes *request*. When the device being controlled is a terminal, then *arg__pointer* must be a pointer to a structure named termio.

ioctl() fails if any of the following conditions holds:

- *file__descriptor* does not refer to an I/O channel connected to a character special device.

- Either the *request* or *arg__pointer* argument is invalid.

When you must program the terminal device with the **ioctl**() system call, refer to the **termio** manual page in Section 7 of the **UNIX System Administrator's Manual System V** for an explanation of the terminal-specific commands and the type of information expected in the *arg__pointer* structure.

C. PROCESS RELATED CALLS

The UNIX system provides several system calls to create and end programs, to send and receive software interrupts, to allocate memory, and to do other useful jobs from a process. This section describes these features of the UNIX system.

C.1 Process Creation and Termination

The UNIX system provides four systems calls for creating a process, ending a process, and waiting for a process to complete. These system calls are **fork**(), the **exec** family, **wait**(), and **exit**().

To understand how these system calls work, it is first necessary to understand the method the UNIX system uses to transform a program file built by the linking/loader **ld** into a process. Recall from Chapter 4 that the linking/loader is the last step in compiling a set of C language source files. The linking/loader

261

produces an executable binary file if the compilation is successful.

An executable binary file contains the following six sections:

HEADER
The header of an executable binary file defines the sizes of all other sections in the file and also identifies the entry point where execution is to begin when the program becomes a process. The header's format can be found in /usr/include/filehdr.h and /usr/include/a.out.h.

The header also contains a magic number that defines how the UNIX system is to transform the file into a process. Two of the more common magic numbers used in executable binary files are 0410, meaning that the program's instructions are to be made read-only when the program becomes a process, and 0407, meaning that the program's instructions are to be made readable and writable. If a process' instructions are read-only, then they cannot be changed as the process runs. Since they cannot be changed, the UNIX system allows them to be shared with any other process that is running the same executable binary file.

TEXT
The text part of a program is the instructions that the CPU will execute once the process created from the program runs.

DATA
The data part of a program consists of all initialized data items. An example from the C language is an explicitly initialized array defined outside a subroutine.

BSS
The bss part of a program consists of all uninitialized data items. When the program is transformed into a process, the UNIX system will set all variables in the bss part to zeroes. Because the bss part is zeroed, only the size of the bss area is kept in the binary executable file since its contents are known.

RELOCATION
The relocation part of a program defines how the linking/loader should change the program file when the file is linked with other program files. When the linking/loader successfully completes building an executable binary file, the relocation part of the program file is removed.

SYMBOL TABLE
The symbol table part of a program file relates symbols to locations in the process. This information is essential to debugging the program using **sdb** and **adb**. The symbol

table part of a program can be removed with the **strip** program or by specifying the s option to the linking/loader.

Similarly, a process is made of the four sections listed below.

TEXT

The text portion of a process is an image of the text portion of the program. In addition, the UNIX system uses the magic number in the header to set the hardware memory management protections. The text size of a process stays the same during the operation of the process.

DATA

The data portion of a process is made by zeroing and adding the bss part of the program file onto the end of the data part of the program file. The UNIX system always sets the hardware memory management protections to read and write for the data portion of a process. The data portion can grow and shrink as is necessary, and the **brk**() and **sbrk**() system calls control the size of the data portion of a process.

STACK

The stack portion of a process is something that the UNIX system creates when it builds the process. The stack is used to hold the following:

- All variables allocated when a subroutine begins and deleted when the same subroutine ends.

- The arguments to the program.

- The environment of the process, that is the set of name=value pairs made available to the process with the **export** and **setenv** built-in shell commands. See Chapters 8 and 9 for a complete discussion of **export** and **setenv**.

The UNIX system automatically makes the stack larger if necessary when you call subroutines and allocate variables in those subroutines.

USER BLOCK

The user block is a subset of the information the UNIX system maintains about the process. This information is resident in kernel address space and is not directly addressable by the process. The user block size stays the same during the operation of the process, and is swapped when the process is swapped.

Figure 7.C.1 shows how the parts of an executable binary file are transformed into a process.

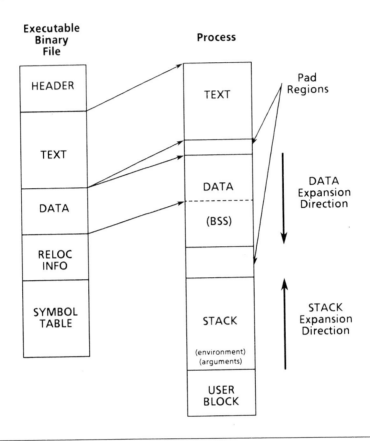

Figure 7.C.1

The pad region between the text and data portions of the process takes into account any rounding necessary to comply with hardware memory management restrictions. The pad region between the data and the stack portions of the process defines the free area used to expand both the data and the stack. The arrows to the right of these portions define the expansion direction of each portion.

The UNIX system calls that transform an executable binary file into a process are the **exec** family of system calls. The syntax for these calls is:

```
            int
            execl(file__name, arg0 [ , arg1, ..., argn ] , 0)
            char *file__name, *arg0, *arg1, ..., *argn;

            int
            execv(file__name, argv)
            char *file__name, *argv[];

            int
            execle(file__name, arg0 [ , arg1, ..., argn ] , 0, envp)
            char *file__name, *arg0, *arg1, ..., *argn, *envp[];

            int
            execve(file__name, argv, envp)
            char *file__name, *argv[], *envp[];

            int
            execlp(file__name, arg0 [ , arg1, ..., argn ] , 0)
            char *file__name, *arg0, *arg1, ..., *argn;

            int
            execvp(file__name, argv)
            char *file__name, *argv[];
```

DEFINITION 49. The exec Family System Calls

where *file__name* names the executable binary file to be transformed into a process, *arg0* through *argn* and *argv* define the arguments to be passed to the process, and *envp* defines the environment, also to be passed to the process. By convention, *arg0* and *argv[0]* name the last path name component of the executable binary file named by *file__name*. For **execl**(), **execv**(), **execle**(), and **execve**(), *file__name* must be the fully qualified path name of the executable binary file but for **execlp**() and **execvp**(), the PATH variable is used to find the executable binary file. When the environment is not explicitly given as an argument to an **exec** system call, the environment of the current process is used. Furthermore, the last array element in both *argv* and *envp* must be null to signify the end of the array.

Unlike the other system calls and subroutines, a successful **exec** system call does not return but instead gives control to the executable binary file named as the first argument. When that file is made into a process, that process replaces the process that executed the **exec** system call – the UNIX system does not create a new process. Figure 7.C.2 shows an example where **execl**() is used to

265

execute the **date** program. The **printf()** after **execl()** is never executed if **execl()** is successful because the **date** program overlays the **exec** process when **date** becomes a process.

```
$ number exec.c
 1  /*
 2   *  exec
 3   *        exec system call test
 4   */
 5
 6  #include    <stdio.h>
 7
 8  #define     DATEPATH "/bin/date"
 9  #define     DATE      "date"
10  #define     ERROR     (-1)
11
12  main(argc, argv)
13  int argc;
14  char *argv[];
15  {
16      int rc = 0;
17
18      if (execl(DATEPATH, DATE, 0) == ERROR) {
19          perror(DATEPATH);
20          rc = 1;
21      } else {
22          printf("This line is never printed\n");
23      }
24      exit(rc);
25  }
$ cc -o exec exec.c
$ ./exec
Wed Apr  4 09:50:41 EST 1984
$ □
```

Figure 7.C.2

An **exec** system call fails if any of the following conditions holds:

● A path name component of *file__name* is not a directory.

● *file__name* does not exist.

● A path name component is off-limits.

● *file__name* is a directory, a fifo file, a character special file, or a block special file.

● *file__name* does not have execute permissions.

- The header in *file__name* does not have a valid magic number.

- *file__name* is a shared text file which is open by another process for writing.

- The process created from *file__name* is bigger than the UNIX system allows.

- The arguments for the process created from *file__name* have too many characters.

- The header for *file__name* gives improper information about the file.

- Any of *file__name*, *arg0* through *argn*, *argv*, and *envp* points to an invalid address.

In the explanation of file permissions given in Section B that every process has an owner ID and a group ID that the UNIX system uses to determine if a process has the authority to access files. There are two sets of owner IDs and group IDs, called the *REAL IDs* and the *EFFECTIVE IDs*. The real ids define who you really are. Their values are taken from the owner ID and group ID fields of the */etc/passwd* file.

In contrast, the effective IDs define who you are for the duration of a process. Their values are taken from the owner and group IDs of the executable binary file you are executing, if that file's permissions say to do so. Recall from the explanation of file permissions that there are two bits in the permission field called the set user (owner) ID bit and the set group ID bit. If the set user or group ID bit is set, then the UNIX system sets the effective owner or group ID from the owner or group field of the executable binary file. If the set user or group ID bit is not set, then the UNIX system sets the effective owner or group ID to the real owner or group ID. The UNIX system uses the effective owner and group ID fields when checking to see if a process can access a file. Both the real IDs and the effective IDs are set when the executable binary file is transformed into a process.

You can obtain the real and effective IDs with the system calls shown below.

```
                              int
                              getuid()

                              int
                              geteuid()

                              int
                              getgid()

                              int
                              getegid()
```

DEFINITION 50. The getuid, geteuid, getgid, getegid System Calls

These system calls return the associated ID and none return errors.

When transforming an executable binary file into a process, the UNIX system preserves some characteristics of the replaced process. Among the items saved by the **exec** system call are:

- The nice value for scheduling.

- The process ID and the parent process ID.

- The time left until an alarm clock signal. See the section on signals.

- The current working directory and the root directory.

- The file creation mask as established with **umask**().

- All open files.

The last of these is the most interesting because the shell uses this feature to handle input/output redirection. The **redirect** program, figure 7.C.3, shows one way to mimic the shell's redirection technique. **redirect** expects that its first argument will be the new source of the standard input, its second argument will be the new source of the standard output, and its third argument will be the new source of the standard error output. **redirect** understands that a dash argument means that a file is not be reassigned.

```
$ number redirect.c
 1   /*
 2    *   redirect
 3    *       handle redirection in a non-standard way
 4    */
 5
 6   #include    <stdio.h>
 7   #include    <fcntl.h>
 8
 9   #define     ERROR      (-1)
10   #define     PROGRAM     5
11   #define     PRESERVE  "+"
12   #define     PMODE     0666
13
14   main(argc, argv)
15   int argc;
16   char *argv[];
17   {
18       int rc = 0, fd, i;
19
20       if (scf("", "", &argc, &argv) == 0 || argc < 6) {
21           fprintf(stderr, "usage: %s input output error arg ...\n", argv[0]);
22           rc = 1;
23       } else {
24           for (i = 0; i < 3; i++) {
25               if (!strcmp(argv[i+2], PRESERVE)) {
26                   continue;
27               } else if (i == 0 && (fd = open(argv[i+2], O_RDONLY)) == ERROR) {
28                   perror(argv[i+2]);
29                   rc = 1;
30                   break;
31               } else if (i != 0 && (fd = creat(argv[i+2], PMODE)) == ERROR) {
32                   perror(argv[i+2]);
33                   rc = 1;
34               } else if (close(i) == ERROR || dup(fd) == ERROR ||
35                   close(fd) == ERROR) {
36                   perror(argv[0]);
37                   rc = 1;
38                   break;
39               }
40           }
41           if (rc == 0) {
42               if (execvp(argv[PROGRAM], &argv[PROGRAM]) == ERROR) {
43                   perror(argv[PROGRAM]);
44                   rc = 1;
45               }
46           }
47       }
48       exit(rc);
49   }
$ cc -o redirect redirect.c
$ redirect + + + date
```

```
Wed Apr  4 09:50:41 EST 1984
$ redirect + x + date
$ cat x
Wed Apr  4 09:50:57 EST 1984
$ redirect x y + cat
$ cat y
Wed Apr  4 09:50:57 EST 1984
$ □
```

Figure 7.C.3

The first invocation of **redirect** does not change the standard input, output, and error files, so the **date** program writes its output on the terminal. The second invocation causes **date**'s output to be written to the file named x and the third invocation copies x to y.

The **exec** family of system calls transforms an executable binary file into a process that overlays the process that made the **exec** system call. The UNIX system does not create a new process in response to an **exec** system call. To create a new process, you must use the **fork**() system call whose syntax is:

---

int
fork()

DEFINITION 51. The fork System Call

---

fork() causes the UNIX system to create a new process, called the CHILD PROCESS, with a new process ID. The contents of the child process are identical to the contents of the parent process.

The new process inherits several of the characteristics of the old process. Among the characteristics inherited are:

● The environment.

● All signal settings. See the section on signals.

● The set user ID and set group ID status.

● The nice value.

● The time left until an alarm clock signal. See the section on signals.

● The current working directory and the root directory.

● The file creation mask as established with **umask**().

The child process begins executing and the parent process continues executing at the return from the **fork**() system call. This is difficult to understand at

270

first because you only call **fork**() once, yet it returns twice – once per process. To differentiate which process is which, **fork**() returns zero in the child process and non-zero (the child's process ID) in the parent process. The **fork** program in figure 7.C.4 shows a simple example that uses the **fork**() system call.

```
$ number fork1.c
 1   /*
 2    *   fork
 3    *       demonstrate the fork system call
 4    *       version 1
 5    */
 6
 7   #include    <stdio.h>
 8
 9   #define     ERROR      (-1)
10
11   main(argc, argv)
12   int argc;
13   char *argv[];
14   {
15       int rc = 0;
16
17       if (scf("", "", &argc, &argv) == 0 || argc != 2) {
18           fprintf(stderr, "usage: %s\n", argv[0]);
19           rc = 1;
20       } else if (fork()) {
21           sleep(1);
22           printf("I am the parent - pid = %d\n", getpid(), getppid());
23       } else {
24           printf("I am the child - pid = %d\n", getpid(), getppid());
25       }
26       exit(rc);
27   }
$ cc -o fork fork1.c
$ fork
I am the child - pid = 26772, ppid = 26771
I am the parent - pid = 26771, ppid = 9987
$ □
```

Figure 7.C.4

The **sleep**() subroutine in figure 7.C.4 causes the parent to sleep for at least 1 second before continuing. This should be enough time to let the child process print its message. Also, the **getpid**() and **getppid**() system calls, whose syntax are shown below, return a process' process ID and a process' parent process ID respectively.

```
                            int
                            getpid()

                            int
                            getppid()
```

DEFINITION 52. The getpid and getppid System Call

The **fork**() system call fails and does not create a new process if any of the following conditions holds:

- The limit on the number of processes in the system would be exceeded.

- The limit on the number of processes that can be under execution by a single user would be exceeded.

The **fork** program in figure 7.C.4 used the **sleep**() subroutine to wait long enough for the child process to finish before going on. To be certain that a child process has completed, use the **wait**() system call. Its syntax is:

```
                            int
                            wait(status)
                            int *status;
```

DEFINITION 53. The wait System Call

where *status* is a pointer to an integer where the UNIX system stores the value returned by the child process. **wait**() returns the process ID of the process that ended. **wait**() fails if any of the following conditions holds:

- The process has no children to wait for.

- *status* points to an invalid address.

Figure 7.C.5 shows an example that uses the **wait**() system call.

```
$ number fork2.c
 1   /*
 2    *   fork
 3    *        demonstrate the fork system call
 4    *        version 2
 5    */
 6
 7   #include    <stdio.h>
 8
 9   #define     ERROR      (-1)
10
11   main(argc, argv)
12   int argc;
13   char *argv[];
14   {
15       int status, rc = 0;
16
17       if (scf("", "", &argc, &argv) == 0 || argc != 2) {
18           fprintf(stderr, "usage: %s\n", argv[0]);
19           rc = 1;
20       } else if (fork()) {
21           wait(&status);
22           printf("I am the parent - pid = %d\n", getpid(), getppid());
23           printf("The child returned %d\n", status);
24       } else {
25           printf("I am the child - pid = %d\n", getpid(), getppid());
26       }
27       exit(rc);
28   }
$ cc -o fork fork2.c
$ fork
I am the child - pid = 290, ppid = 289
I am the parent - pid = 289, ppid = 89
The child returned 0
$ ▢
```

Figure 7.C.5

The parent process waits until the child finishes and then continues. The shell uses **wait**() for each command it executes that does not end with an &. The shell waits until the child finishes and then prompts you for another command.

The format of the information returned by **wait**() is as follows:

- If the process ended by calling the **exit**() system call, the second lowest byte of *status* is set to the argument given to **exit**() and the lowest byte of *status* is set to zeroes.

- If the process ended because of a signal, the second lowest byte of *status* is set to zeroes and the lowest byte of *status* contains the signal number that

273

ended the process. If the seventh bit of the lowest byte of *status* is set (i.e. status&0200==0200) then the UNIX system produced a core image of the process.

Finally, the **exit**() system call ends a process and returns a value to its parent. The syntax for **exit**() is:

```
                    void
                    exit(status);
                    int status;
```

DEFINITION 54. The exit System Call

where the lowest byte of *status* is made available to the parent process through the **wait**() system call. All C language program examples shown in this book use the **exit**() system call to return a value to the parent process. See Chapter 8 for the conventions on return values and why your programs should explicitly set a return value.

Figure 7.C.6 shows the **timer** program that computes the amount of wall clock time used by the command given as arguments. **timer** uses the **time**() system call in lines 23 and 32 to sample the current time before and after the specified command is executed.

```
$ number timer.c
 1  /*
 2   *    timer
 3   *        display the wall clock time for a the command
 4   *        given as arguments
 5   */
 6
 7  #include    <stdio.h>
 8
 9  #define     ERROR       (-1)
10  #define     NOEXEC       0177
11
12  main(argc, argv)
13  int argc;
14  char *argv[];
15  {
16      int rc = 0, pid, status;
17      long start, end;
18
19      if (scf("", "", &argc, &argv) == 0 || argc == 2) {
20          fprintf(stderr, "usage: %s command\n", argv[0]);
21          rc = 1;
22      } else {
23          time(&start);
24          if ((pid = fork()) == ERROR) {
25              perror(argv[0]);
26              rc = 1;
27          } else if (pid != 0) {
28              if (wait(&status) == ERROR) {
29                  perror(argv[0]);
30                  rc = 1;
31              } else if (((status >> 8) & 0377) != NOEXEC) {
32                  time(&end);
33                  end -= start;
34                  printf("Process took %02d:%02d:%02d\n",
35                      (end / 60 / 60) % 60, (end / 60) % 60, end % 60);
36              } else {
37                  rc = 1;
38              }
39          } else {
40              execvp(argv[2], &argv[2]);
41              perror(argv[2]);
42              rc = NOEXEC;
43          }
44      }
45      exit(rc);
46  }
$ cc -o timer timer.c
$ timer
usage: timer command
$ echo $?
1
```

```
$ timer sleep 2
Process took 00:00:02
$ timer speel 2
speel: No such file or directory
$ echo $?
1
$ ☐
```

Figure 7.C.6

If the child process cannot **execvp**() the program given as arguments, it returns NOEXEC as the value of the process. The parent, **timer**, reacts by not displaying the wall clock time taken by the child process. Coincidentally, the wall clock time taken by the **sleep** program corresponds to the time slept.

C.3 Software Interrupts

The UNIX system provides a facility for sending and receiving software interrupts, also called *SIGNALS*. Signals are sent to a process when a pre-defined condition happens. The table below shows nineteen signals along with a description that tells when the related signal happens. The signal name column shows the signal's name as defined in */usr/include/sys/signal.h*.

Your programs can respond to signals three different ways. These are:

1. You can ignore a signal. This means that your program will never be informed of the signal no matter how many times it occurs. The only exception to this is SIGKILL which can neither be ignored nor caught.

2. You can set a signal to its default state, which means that your process will be ended when it receives that signal. In addition, if your process receives any of SIGQUIT, SIGILL, SIGTRAP, SIGIOT, SIGEMT, SIGFPE, SIGBUS, SIGSEGV, or SIGSYS, the UNIX system will produce a core image, if possible, in the directory where the process was executing when it received the program-ending signal.

3. You can catch a signal. When the signal occurs, the UNIX system will transfer control to a previously defined subroutine where you can respond to the signal as is appropriate for your program.

You define how you want to respond to a signal with the **signal**() system call whose syntax is:

```
#include <sys/signal.h>

int (*
signal(signal__name, function))
int signal__name;
int (*function)();
```

DEFINITION 55. The signal System Call

where *signal__name* is the name of the signal from the table above and *function* is any of SIG__IGN, meaning that you wish to ignore the signal when it occurs; SIG__DFL, meaning that you wish the UNIX system to take the default action when your program receives the signal; or a pointer to a subroutine that returns an integer. This subroutine is given control when your program receives the signal, and the signal number is passed as an argument. **signal**() returns the previous value of *function*, and **signal**() fails if any of the following conditions holds:

- *signal__name* is an illegal signal name or SIGKILL.

- *function* points to an invalid memory address.

Figure 7.C.7 shows the **catcher** program that uses the **signal**() system call to stop printing the phrase:

No signal yet.

```
$ number catcher1.c
 1  /*
 2   *   catcher
 3   *       print a message until the SIGINT signal is caught.
 4   *       version 1
 5   */
 6
 7  #include    <stdio.h>
 8  #include    <sys/signal.h>
 9
10  #define     ERROR       (-1)
11
12  static  int  Caught = 0;
13
14  main(argc, argv)
15  int argc;
16  char *argv[];
17  {
18      int (*oldint)(), rc = 0, catcher();
19
20      if (scf("", "", &argc, &argv) == 0 || argc != 2) {
21          fprintf(stderr, "usage: %s\n", argv[0]);
22          rc = 1;
23      } else if ((oldint = signal(SIGINT, catcher)) == (int (*)()) ERROR) {
24          perror(argv[0]);
25          rc = 1;
26      } else {
27          for (Caught = 0; !Caught; ) {
28              printf("No signal yet\n");
29          }
30      }
31      exit(rc);
32  }
33
34  int
35  catcher(signo)
36  int signo;
37  {
38
39      Caught = 1;
40      printf("Caught signal number %d\n", signo);
41      fflush(stdout);
42  }
$ cc -o catcher catcher.c
$ catcher
No signal yet
No signal yet
No signal yet
No signal yet
No signal yet
No signal yet
No signal yet
```

278

```
No signal yet
DELETE
Caught signal number 2
$ ▢
```

Figure 7.C.7

The **signal**() system call in line 20 tells the UNIX system that when the SIGINT signal is received, control should be transferred to the **catcher**() subroutine. Notice the cast of the manifest constant ERROR to the correct type that **signal**() returns.

catcher() sets the global variable Caught to 1 when the SIGINT signal is received. **catcher**() then prints a message telling which signal it received, and returns. The UNIX system arranges for control to return to the location in the program where execution was interrupted when the signal handling subroutine finishes. Since **catcher**() changed the value of Caught, the for loop ends and **catcher** also ends.

When a caught signal has been received, it is reset to the default state. Figure 7.C.8 shows version 2 of **catcher** that shows this.

```
$ number catcher2.c
 1  /*
 2   *   catcher
 3   *       print a message until the SIGINT signal is caught.
 4   *       version 2
 5   */
 6
 7  #include    <stdio.h>
 8  #include    <sys/signal.h>
 9
10  #define     ERROR       (-1)
11
12  static  int  Caught = 0;
13
14  main(argc, argv)
15  int argc;
16  char *argv[];
17  {
18      int (*oldint)(), rc = 0, catcher();
19
20      if (scf("", "", &argc, &argv) == 0 || argc != 2) {
21          fprintf(stderr, "usage: %s\n", argv[0]);
22          rc = 1;
23      } else if ((oldint = signal(SIGINT, catcher)) == (int (*)()) ERROR) {
24          perror(argv[0]);
25          rc = 1;
26      } else {
27          for (Caught = 0; ; ) {
28              printf("No signal yet\n");
29          }
30      }
31      exit(rc);
32  }
33
34  int
35  catcher(signo)
36  int signo;
37  {
38
39      Caught = 1;
40      printf("Caught signal number %d\n", signo);
41      fflush(stdout);
42  }
$ cc -o catcher catcher.c
```

Figure 7.C.8

```
$ catcher
No signal yet
No signal yet
No signal yet
No signal yet
No signal yet
No signal yet
No signal yet
No signal yet
DELETE
Caught signal number 2
No signal yet
No signal yet
No signal yet
No signDELETE
$ ☐
```

Figure 7.C.9

The first instance of the SIGNIT signal causes **catcher**() to be called, but **catcher** continues printing its message. Since the signal was not redefined after being caught, the UNIX system resets it to its initial state. The next instance of SIGINT causes **catcher** to end.

In general, if you intend for your program to be able to catch a signal repeatedly, you need to re-arm the signal handling mechanism. You must do this as soon after receipt of the signal as possible, namely just after entering the signal handling routine.

You should use signals in your programs to isolate critical sections from interruption. For example, the subroutine in figure 7.C.10 defines a C language skeleton that insures that the data passed to the subroutine is written to the file.

```
$ number insure.c
 1   /*
 2    *   insure
 3    *        insure that the information passed as
 4    *        is written to the named file
 5    */
 6
 7   #include    <stdio.h>
 8   #include    <sys/signal.h>
 9   #include    "database.h"
10
11   #define     ERROR       (-1)
12
13   int
14   insure(dbrecord, file)
15   struct database *dbrecord;
16   FILE *file;
17   {
18       int (*oldint)(), (*oldquit)(), (*oldhup)(), (*oldterm)();
19       int rc = 0;
20
21       if ((oldint = signal(SIGINT, SIG__IGN)) == (int (*)()) ERROR ||
22          (oldquit = signal(SIGQUIT, SIG__IGN)) == (int (*)()) ERROR ||
23          (oldhup = signal(SIGHUP, SIG__IGN)) == (int (*)()) ERROR ||
24          (oldterm = signal(SIGTERM, SIG__IGN)) == (int (*)()) ERROR) {
25          rc = 1;
26       } else if (fwrite((char *) dbrecord, sizeof(struct database), 1, file) != 1) {
27          rc = 1;
28       } else if (fflush(file) == EOF) {
29          rc = 1;
30       } else {
31          signal(SIGINT, oldint);
32          signal(SIGQUIT, oldquit);
33          signal(SIGHUP, oldhup);
34          signal(SIGTERM, oldterm);
35       }
36       return(rc);
37   }
$ 
```

Figure 7.C.10

Finally, the state of all signals is preserved across a **fork**() system call, but all caught signals are set to SIG__DFL across an **exec** system call.

The UNIX system sends a signal to a process when something happens, such as typing the interrupt key on a terminal or attempting to execute an illegal instruction. Signals are also sent to a process with the **kill**() system call. Its syntax is:

```
int
kill(process__id, signal__name)
int process__id, signal__name;
```

DEFINITION 56. The kill System Call

---

where *process__id* is the ID of the process to be signaled and *signal__name* is
the signal to be sent to that process. If *process__id* has a positive value, that
value is assumed to be the process ID of the process to whom *signal__name*
signal is to be sent. If *process__id* has the value 0, then *signal__name* signal is
sent to all processes in the sending process' process group, that is all processes
that have been started from the same terminal. If *process__id* has the value -1
and the process executing the **kill**() system call is the superuser, then
signal__name signal is sent to all processes in the system except process 0, the
init process, and process 1, the kernel process. If *process__id* has the value -1
and the process executing the **kill**() system call is not the superuser, then
signal__name signal is sent to all processes excluding process 0 and process 1
that have the same user ID as the process executing the **kill**(). If *process__id*
is negative but not -1, the *signal__name* signal is set to all process whose
process group ID is equal to the absolute value of *process__id*. **kill**() fails if any
of the following conditions holds:

- *signal__name* signal is not a valid signal.

- There is no process in the system with process id *process__id*.

- Even though the process named by *process__id* is in the system, you cannot
  send it a signal because your effective user ID does not match either the
  real or effective user ID of *process__id*.

Figure 7.C.11 shows a condensed version of the **kill** program that uses the
kill() system call.

```
$ number kill.c
 1   /*
 2    *   kill
 3    *        mimic action of kill(1) command
 4    */
 5
 6   #include    <stdio.h>
 7   #include    <ctype.h>
 8   #include    <sys/signal.h>
 9
10   #define     ERROR       (-1)
11
12   static   char    *Names[] =
13   {
14       "",    "HUP", "INT", "QUIT","ILL", "TRAP","IOT", "EMT", "FPE",
15       "KILL","BUS", "SEGV","SYS", "PIPE","ALRM","TERM","USR1","USR2",
16       "CLD", "PWR", (char *) NULL
17   };
18
19   main(argc, argv)
20   int argc;
21   char *argv[];
22   {
23       int pid, signo, rc = 0, i, j;
24       char sig[BUFSIZ], *p, *t;
25
26       if (scf("s", "s", &argc, &argv) == 0 || argc < 3) {
27           fprintf(stderr, "usage: %s [-signo] pid ...\n", argv[0]);
28           rc = 1;
29       } else {
30           p = Names[SIGTERM];
31           for (i = 1; strcmp(argv[i], "--"); i++) {
32               switch (argv[i][1]) {
33               case 's':
34                   p = argv[++i];
35                   break;
36               }
37           }
38           if (isdigit(*p)) {
39               signo = atoi(p);
40               if (signo < 1 || signo > NSIG) {
41                   fprintf(stderr, "%s: invalid signal number %d\n", argv[0], p);
42                   rc = 1;
43               }
44           } else {
45               for (t = sig; *p; p++, t++) {
46                   *t = islower(*p) ? toupper(*p) : *p;
47               }
48               for (j = 1; Names[j]; j++) {
49                   if (!strcmp(Names[j], sig)) {
50                       break;
51                   }
```

```
52                 }
53                 if (Names[j] == (char *) NULL) {
54                     fprintf(stderr, "%s: invalid signal name %s\n", argv[0], sig);
55                     rc = 1;
56                 } else {
57                     signo = j;
58                 }
59             }
60         if (rc == 0) {
61             for (++i; i < argc; i++) {
62                 for (j = 0; argv[i][j]; j++) {
63                     if (!isdigit(argv[i][j])) {
64                         fprintf(stderr, "%s: invalid process ", argv[0]);
65                         fprintf(stderr, "id %s\n", argv[i]);
66                         break;
67                     }
68                 }
69                 if (argv[i][j]) {
70                     continue;
71                 }
72                 pid = atoi(argv[i]);
73                 if (kill(pid, signo) == ERROR) {
74                     perror(argv[0]);
75                     rc = 1;
76                 }
77             }
78         }
79     }
80     exit(rc);
81 }
$ cc -o kill kill.c
$ sleep 10 &
1325
$ kill -s 1 1325
1325 Hangup
$ sleep 10 &
1333
$ kill -s HUP 1333
1333 Hangup
$ ☐
```

Figure 7.C.11

The **sleep** process sleeps for 10 seconds, but is killed first with **kill**. The shell receives notification of **sleep** ending and prints the reason it ended on the terminal.

The programs shown in this book that read the standard input assume that the user will eventually enter some data that will allow the program to continue. When you are sharing a critical resource such as a database among several users, this approach can cause problems. For example, if a user locks a database through a program and is then called away from the terminal without first unlocking that database, all other users of that database cannot continue until the database is unlocked.

The recommended way to solve this type of problem is to use the **alarm**() system call to arrange for the program to be signaled some time in the future. The syntax of **signal**() is:

```
                        unsigned
                        alarm(seconds)
                        unsigned seconds;
```

DEFINITION 57. The alarm System Call

where *seconds* defines the time after which the UNIX system sends the SIGALRM signal to the calling process. Each successive call to **alarm**() nullifies the previous call, and **alarm**() returns the number of seconds until that alarm would have gone off. If *seconds* has the value 0, the alarm is canceled. **alarm**() has no error conditions.

Figure 7.C.12 shows version 2 of the **prcust** program as an example of the **alarm**() system call. **prcust** gracefully ends if the user does not enter an ID after the 5 tries.

$ number prcust2.c

```
 1  /*
 2   *    prcust
 3   *        print selected customer records
 4   *        version 2
 5   */
 6
 7  #include    <stdio.h>
 8  #include    <setjmp.h>
 9  #include    <sys / signal.h>
10  #include    "cust.h"
11
12  #define     MAXTRIES  5
13  #define     TIMEOUT         10
14  #define     FROMTIMEOUT 1
15
16  main(argc, argv)
17  int argc;
18  char *argv[];
19  {
20      int rc = 0;
21      FILE *rp;
22
23      if (scf("", "", &argc, &argv) = = 0 || argc != 3) {
24          fprintf(stderr, "usage: %s database\n", argv[0]);
25          rc = 1;
26      } else if ((rp = fopen(argv[2], "r")) = = (FILE *) NULL) {
27          perror(argv[2]);
28          rc = 1;
29      } else {
30          rc = pr(argv[0], argv[2], rp);
31          fclose(rp);
32      }
33      exit(rc);
34  }
35
36  static   jmp__buf        Jmp;
37
38  int
39  pr(progname, filename, rp)
40  char *progname, *filename;
41  FILE *rp;
42  {
43      long id;
44      int rc = 0, n, tries, timeout();
45      struct customer cust;
46
47      while (1) {
48          tries = MAXTRIES;
49          if (setjmp(Jmp) = = FROMTIMEOUT && --tries = = 0) {
50              printf("No response - %s ends\n", progname);
51              break;
```

287

```
52            }
53            signal(SIGALRM, timeout);
54            alarm(TIMEOUT);
55            printf("ID: ");
56            if (scanf("%ld%*c", &id) == EOF) {
57                 putchar('\n');
58                 break;
59            } else {
60                 alarm(0);
61                 if (fseek(rp, id * sizeof(cust), 0) == -1) {
62                      perror(filename);
63                      rc = 1;
64                      break;
65                 } else if (fread((char *) &cust, sizeof(cust), 1, rp) != 1) {
66                      fprintf(stderr, "No customer for id %ld\n", id);
67                 } else if (cust.name[0] == NULL) {
68                      fprintf(stderr, "No customer for id %ld\n", id);
69                 } else {
70                      printf("\tName:\t\t%s\n", cust.name);
71                      printf("\tAmount due:\t$%5.2f\n", cust.due);
72                 }
73            }
74       }
75       return(rc);
76  }
77
78  int
79  timeout()
80  {
81
82       putchar('\n');
83       longjmp(Jmp, FROMTIMEOUT);
84  }
$ cc -o prcust prcust2.c
$ ▢
```

Figure 7.C.12

The program also uses the **setjmp**() and **longjmp**() subroutines. Their syntax
is:

```
                    #include  <setjmp.h>

                    int
                    setjmp(state)
                    jmp__buf state;

                    void
                    longjmp(state, value)
                    jmp__buf state;
                    int    value;
```

DEFINITION 58. The setjmp and longjmp Subroutines

where *state* is a data structure defined in */usr/include/setjmp.h* where **setjmp()** stores the current state of the process (i.e., the machine registers, the stack pointer, and the program counter) and *value* defines the value returned by **setjmp()** when **longjmp()** is called.

setjmp() and **longjmp()** are difficult to understand at first because they act differently from other subroutines. When you call **setjmp()**, it saves the current state of the process in *state* and then returns 0. However when you call **longjmp()**, it never returns but instead passes control to the return address stored in *state* by **setjmp()**. **setjmp()** then returns *value* which **longjmp()** guarantees to be non-zero. Together, **setjmp()** and **longjmp()** form an intersubroutine goto statement.

In figure 7.C.12, **setjmp()** in line 49 saves the state of the process in Jmp and returns 0. Since **setjmp()** is called directly, the rest of the if statement on lines 49 through 52 are not executed now. **signal()** in line 53 then arms the signal handling mechanism to expect the SIGALRM signal and **alarm()** in line 54 schedules the signal to be sent in TIMEOUT seconds. **scanf()** in line 56 waits for input from the standard input file.

If the user does not respond in TIMEOUT seconds, the alarm goes off and the UNIX system transfers control to **timeout()** in line 79. **timeout()** prints a newline and then calls **longjmp()** to transfer control to the location stored in Jmp and to make **setjmp()** return FROMTIMEOUT.

When control transfers to the return from **setjmp()** in line 49, the first part of the condition is true so the --tries == 0 part is evaluated. If this part is also true, **pr()** prints a message and returns to **main()**. Otherwise, the signal is re-armed, a new time-out is scheduled and the user is again asked for an ID.

Should the user provide some input before the alarm goes off, it is necessary to cancel the pending alarm. The **alarm()** call in line 60 does this. Figure 7.C.13

289

shows an example.

$ **prcust database**
ID: **1**
         Name: Larry Rogers
         Amount due: $125.53
ID: **273**
         Name: Jean Yates
         Amount due: $3250.28
ID:
ID:
ID:
ID:
ID:
No response - prcust ends
$ ☐

Figure 7.C.13

Signals in the UNIX system allow a program to respond to external events, such as a program user hitting the DELETE key, and unusual conditions, such as attempting to execute an illegal instruction. Wherever possible, your programs should explicitly handle all signals gracefully by printing a message that tells the user who to call and what to do next.

C.4 Change Working Directory

The **chdir**() system call changes the current working directory. Recall that Chapter 2 defines the current working directory to be the starting point for all relative path names.

The syntax for **chdir**() is:

```
            int
            chdir(directory__name)
            char *directory__name;
```

DEFINITION 59. The chdir System Call

---

where *directory__name* points to the path name of the desired directory.
chdir() fails and the current directory remains unchanged if any of the
following conditions holds:

- A path name component is not a directory.

- A path name component does not exist.

- A path name component is off-limits.

- *directory__name* does not exist.

- *directory__name* points to an invalid memory address.

The program in figure 7.C.14 uses the **chdir**() system call to walk down the file
system listing the files found at each level.

```
$ number walk.c
 1   /*
 2    *   walk
 3    *        walk a directory hierarchy
 4    */
 5
 6   #include    <stdio.h>
 7   #include    <sys/types.h>
 8   #include    <sys/stat.h>
 9   #include    <sys/dir.h>
10
11
12   #define    CURRENT      "."
13   #define    PARENT       ".."
14   #define    MAXLEVELS  15
15   #define    ERROR        (-1)
16
17   main(argc, argv)
18   int argc;
19   char *argv[];
20   {
21       int rc = 0;
22       char *d = CURRENT;
23
24       if (scf("", "", &argc, &argv) == 0 || argc > 3) {
25           fprintf(stderr, "usage: %s [directory]\n", argv[0]);
```

```
26          rc = 1;
27      } else {
28          if (argc == 3) {
29              d = argv[2];
30          }
31          printf("%s\n", d);
32          rc = print(d);
33      }
34      exit(rc);
35  }
36
37  int
38  print(d)
39  char *d;
40  {
41      static int level = 0;
42      int i, rc = 0;
43      char *entry[DIRSIZ+1];
44      struct direct dir;
45      struct stat st;
46      FILE *fp;
47
48      if (++level <= MAXLEVELS) {
49          if (stat(d, &st) == ERROR || chdir(d) == ERROR) {
50              perror(d);
51              rc = 1;
52          } else if ((fp = fopen(CURRENT, "r")) == (FILE *) NULL) {
53              perror(d);
54              rc = 1;
55          } else {
56              fread((char *) &dir, sizeof(dir), 1, fp);
57              fread((char *) &dir, sizeof(dir), 1, fp);
58              while (fread((char *) &dir, sizeof(dir), 1, fp) == 1) {
59                  sprintf(entry, "%.*s", DIRSIZ, dir.d_name);
60                  if (dir.d_ino == 0) {
61                      continue;
62                  }
63                  if (stat(entry, &st) == ERROR) {
64                      perror(entry);
65                  } else {
66                      for (i = 0; i < level; i++) {
67                          putchar('\t');
68                      }
69                      printf("%s\n", entry);
70                      if ((st.st_mode & S_IFMT) & S_IFDIR) {
71                          if (rc = print(entry)) {
72                              break;
73                          }
74                      }
75                  }
76              }
77              fclose(fp);
78              if (chdir(PARENT) == ERROR) {
```

292

```
79              perror(PARENT);
80              rc = 1;
81          }
82        }
83      }
84    level--;
85    return(rc);
86  }
$ cc -o walk walk.c
$ ▢
```

Figure 7.C.14

Figure 7.C.15 shows an example of execution.

```
$ mkdir A
$ cd A
$ mkdir B
$ cd B
$ mkdir C
$ cd C
$ mkdir D
$ cd D
$ cp /dev/null E
$ cd ..
$ mkdir F
$ cd ..
$ mkdir G
$ cd ..
$ mkdir H
$ cd ..
$ walk A
A
        B
            C
                D
                    E
                F
            G
        H
$ ☐
```

Figure 7.C.15

walk recursively descends the directory structure from the current directory or the directory given as the first and only argument.

D. INTERPROCESS COMMUNICATION

UNIX System V allows processes to communicate with one another using pipes, messages, semaphores, and shared memory. This section describes how to use these features of UNIX System V.

D.1 Pipes

The first way to establish a communications channel between two processes is to create a pipeline with the **pipe()** system call. **pipe()** builds the channel, but it is up to you to connect the standard input of one process to the standard output of the other process. The syntax of **pipe**() is:

---

int
pipe(*file__descriptors*)
int *file__descriptors*[2];

DEFINITION 60. The pipe System Call

---

where *file__descriptors*[2] is an array that **pipe**() fills with a file descriptor opened for reading, *file__descriptor*[0], and a file descriptor opened for writing, *file__descriptor*[1]. **pipe**() fails if the following condition holds:

● There are too many open I/O channels.

Figure 7.D.1 shows version 4 of the **grepex** program where the channel to the **grep** program is built by the **piperead**() subroutine instead of the **popen**() subroutine as in version 3. The **fdopen**() subroutine in line 83 returns a pointer to a FILE type given a file descriptor and the type of operations allowed (i.e. reading or writing).

$ **number grepex4.c**

```
 1  /*
 2   *   grepex
 3   *       edit files selected by grep
 4   *       version 4
 5   */
 6
 7  #include    <stdio.h>
 8
 9  #define     GREP    "grep -n"
10  #define     VI  "vi"
11  #define     EX  "ex"
12  #define     EDITOR  EX
13  #define     EDITORV "EDITOR"
14
15  main(argc, argv)
16  int argc;
17  char *argv[];
18  {
19      char grepbuf[BUFSIZ], filename[BUFSIZ], line[BUFSIZ], *expr,
20          *editor, *fixexpr();
21      int rc = 0, c, i, eoption = 0, n, verbose = 0;
22      FILE *pp, *piperead();
23      extern char *getenv();
24
25      if (scf("ev", "e", &argc, &argv) == 0) {
26          rc = 1;
```

```
27        } else }
28            for (i = 1; strcmp(argv[i], "--"); i++) }
29                switch (argv[i][1]) }
30                case 'e':
31                    eoption++;
32                    expr = argv[++i];
33                    break;
34                case 'v':
35                    verbose++;
36                    break;
37                }
38            }
39        }
40        if (rc == 1 || eoption == 0 || ++i == argc) }
41            fprintf(stderr, "usage: %s  [-v] -e expression file [ ... ]\n", argv[0]);
42        } else }
43            if ((editor = getenv(EDITORV)) == (char *) NULL) }
44                editor = EDITOR;
45            }
46            sprintf(grepbuf, "%s \"%s\" /dev/null", GREP, fixexpr(expr));
47            for ( ; i < argc; i++) }
48                sprintf(grepbuf, "%s %s", grepbuf, argv[i]);
49            }
50            if (verbose) }
51                printf("%s\n", grepbuf);
52            }
53            if ((pp = piperead(grepbuf, "r")) == (FILE *) NULL) }
54                perror(argv[0]);
55                rc = 1;
56            } else }
57                while (fscanf(pp, "%[^:]%*c%d", filename, &n) != EOF) }
58                    if (strcmp(editor, EX) && strcmp(editor, VI)) }
59                        printf("Match occurred on line %d\n", n);
60                        sleep(2);
61                        sprintf(line, "%s %s", editor, filename);
62                    } else }
63                        sprintf(line, "%s +%d %s", editor, n, filename);
64                    }
65                    if (verbose) }
66                        printf("%s\n", line);
67                    }
68                    system(line);
69                    while ((c = fgetc(pp)) != '\n');
70                }
71                pipeclose(pp);
72            }
73        }
74        exit(rc);
75 }
76
77 char *
78 fixexpr(e)
79 char *e;
```

```
 80 |
 81     char newe[BUFSIZ];
 82     register char *ne;
 83
 84     for (ne = newe; *e; e++) |
 85        switch(*e) |
 86        case '\\':
 87            *ne++ = *e++;
 88            *ne++ = *e;
 89            break;
 90        case '"':
 91            *ne++ = '\\';
 92            *ne++ = *e;
 93            break;
 94        default:
 95            *ne++ = *e;
 96            break;
 97        |
 98     |
 99     *ne = *e;
100     return(newe);
101|
102
103 #define    ERROR       (-1)
104 #define    STDOUT      1
105 #define    READ        0
106 #define    WRITE       1
107
108 FILE *
109 piperead(command)
110 char *command;
111|
112     int pfd[2], pid;
113     FILE *fp = (FILE *) NULL;
114
115     if (pipe(pfd) == ERROR) |
116        perror("");
117     | else if ((fp = fdopen(pfd[READ], "r")) != (FILE *) NULL) |
118        if ((pid = fork()) == ERROR) |
119            perror("");
120            if (fclose(fp) == EOF || close(pfd[WRITE]) == ERROR) |
121                perror("");
122            |
123            fp = (FILE *) NULL;
124        | else if (pid == 0) |
125            if (close(STDOUT) == ERROR || dup(pfd[WRITE]) == ERROR ||
126                close(pfd[WRITE]) == ERROR || close(pfd[READ]) == ERROR ||
127                execl("/bin/sh", "sh", "-c", command, 0) == ERROR) |
128                perror("");
129                exit(1);
130            |
131        | else if (close(pfd[WRITE]) == ERROR) |
132                perror("");
```

```
133        }
134     }
135     return(fp);
136 }
137
138 pipeclose(fp)
139 FILE *fp;
140 {
141
142     fclose(fp);
143 }
$ cc -o grepex grepex4.c
$ EDITOR=ex
$ export EDITOR
$ grepex -v -e include grepex4.c
grep -n "include" /dev/null grepex4.c
ex +7 grepex4.c
"grepex4.c" 143 lines, 2688 characters
:.
#include      <stdio.h>
:.=
7
:q
$ □
```

Figure 7.D.1

Version 4 of **grepex** is for illustrative purposes only. Version 3 shown at the end of Chapter 6 is recommended because it does not rely on system calls but instead uses subroutines.

The **sortwho** program shown in figure 7.D.3 is another program that shows a pipeline created between two processed to execute the who | sort command. Figure 7.D.2 shows a diagram of the processes created by **sortwho**.

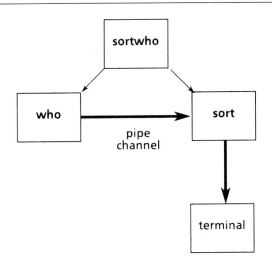

Figure 7.D.2

```
$ number sortwho.c
 1   /*
 2    *   sortwho
 3    *        set up communication between two children
 4    */
 5
 6   #include    <stdio.h>
 7
 8   #define     ERROR      (-1)
 9   #define     READ       0
10   #define     WRITE      1
11   #define     STDIN      0
12   #define     STDOUT        1
13
14   main(argc, argv)
15   int argc;
16   char *argv[];
17   {
18       int pidA, pidB, rc = 0;
19       int fd[2];
20
21       if (scf("", "", &argc, &argv) == 0 || argc != 2) {
22           fprintf(stderr, "usage: %s\n", argv[0]);
23           rc = 1;
24       } else if (pipe(fd) == ERROR) {
25           perror(argv[0]);
```

```
26        rc = 1;
27    } else if ((pidA = fork()) == ERROR) {
28        perror(argv[0]);
29        rc = 1;
30    } else if (pidA != 0) {
31        if ((pidB = fork()) == ERROR) {
32            perror(argv[0]);
33            rc = 1;
34        } else if (pidB != 0) {
35            if (close(fd[READ]) == ERROR || close(fd[WRITE]) == ERROR ||
36                wait((int *) 0) == ERROR || wait((int *) 0) == ERROR) {
37                perror(argv[0]);
38                rc = 1;
39            }
40        } else {
41            if (close(STDIN) == ERROR || dup(fd[READ]) == ERROR ||
42                close(fd[READ]) == ERROR || close(fd[WRITE]) == ERROR ||
43                execl("/bin/sort", "sort", 0) == ERROR) {
44                perror(argv[0]);
45                rc = 1;
46            }
47        }
48    } else {
49        if (close(STDOUT) == ERROR || dup(fd[WRITE]) == ERROR ||
50            close(fd[READ]) == ERROR || close(fd[WRITE]) == ERROR ||
51            execl("/bin/who", "who", 0) == ERROR) {
52            perror(argv[0]);
53            rc = 1;
54        }
55    }
56    exit(rc);
57 }
$ cc -o sortwho sortwho.c
$ sortwho
becca   ttya1   Thu 22 12:22
rogers  ttya2   Thu 22 07:47
starr   ttya3   Thu 22 09:05
ted     ttya4   Thu 22 12:21
$ ▯
```

Figure 7.D.3

sortwho first creates a new process identified by pidA. This process will become the **who** program, and lines 49 and 50 connect the standard output of **who** to the writing end of the pipeline. The process created by **sortwho** and identified by pidB then becomes the **sort** process, and it is connected to the reading end of the pipeline in lines 41 and 42. **sortwho** then closes the unneeded I/O channel in line 35 and waits for both child processes to end in line 36.

300

D.3 Messages

UNIX System V provides improved interprocess communication features that allow processes to more easily communicate with one another. Unlike pipelines that require a parent-child relationship for establishing a communication path, the System V interprocess communication features do not require that communicating processes be related. This section describes the message interprocess communication feature of UNIX System V.

A *MESSAGE* is a variable sized unit of information with no predefined format. Messages are stored on queues, and message queues have names, called *KEYS*, that processes use to gain access to a queue. Each message queue has an owner, a group, and a set of permissions that define whether the owner, group, and all others can read and write messages on a queue.

All message queue operations use a message queue identifier that is conceptually similar to a file descriptor. A message queue identifier is created with the **msgget**() system call whose syntax is:

```
#include    <sys/types.h>
#include    <sys/ipc.h>
#include    <sys/msg.h>

int
msgget(key, flag)
key_t key;
int   flag;
```

DEFINITION 61. The msgget System Call

where *key* is the name of the message queue, and *flag* is a combination of the following:

IPC_CREAT   The message queue named *key* is to be created if it does not already exist. If the queue does not exist, then the mode field, defined below, becomes the access mode of the message queue. If the queue does exist, IPC_CREAT is ignored, except as noted next.

IPC_EXCL   When combined with IPC_CREAT, IPC_EXCL forces **msgget**() to return an error when the message queue already exists.

mode   The low order 9 bits of *flag* define the access mode of the message queue when created with **msgget**(). The grouping of bits in mode is identical to the grouping of bits in the *mode* argument to the **creat**() system call, but only the read and write permission bits have meaning. If the message queue exists, then mode must be a subset of the access mode of the message queue.

msgget() fails if any of the following conditions holds:

- The message queue named by *key* does not exist and IPC__CREAT was not specified.

- The message queue named by *key* does exist, but IPC__CREAT and IPC__EXCL were specified.

- The message queue named by *key* does exist, but mode is not a subset of the access mode of that message queue.

- A new message queue is to be created, but the system wide limit on the number of message queues would be exceeded.

Figure 7.D.4 shows the **makeq** program that uses the **msgget**() system call to make message queues.

```
$ number makeq.c
 1  /*
 2   *   makeq
 3   *       make message queues with keys given as arguments
 4   */
 5
 6  #include    <stdio.h>
 7  #include    <sys/types.h>
 8  #include    <sys/ipc.h>
 9  #include    <sys/msg.h>
10  #include    <sys/errno.h>
11
12  #define     ERROR    (-1)
13  #define     DEFMODE  0666
14
15  main(argc, argv)
16  int argc;
17  char *argv[];
18  {
19      key_t key;
20      int i, rc = 0;
21      extern int errno;
22      extern key_t getkey();
23
24      if (scf("", "", &argc, &argv) == 0 || argc < 3) {
25          fprintf(stderr, "usage: %s key [key ...]\n", argv[0]);
26          rc = 1;
27      } else {
28          for (i = 2; i < argc; i++) {
29              key = getkey(argv[i]);
30              if ((msgget(key, 0) == ERROR && errno == ENOENT) &&
31                  msgget(key, IPC_CREAT | (DEFMODE & ~umask(0))) == ERROR) {
32                  perror(argv[0]);
33                  rc = 1;
34              }
35          }
36      }
37      exit(rc);
38  }
$ ▢
```

Figure 7.D.4

In line 30, **makeq** first checks to see if the message queue exists. If the queue does not exist, that is **msgget**() returned -1 and sets errno to ENOENT meaning that there is no message queue with name key, the message queue is created in line 31 with an access mode derived from the **umask**() value.

makeq makes the message queues using the keys given as arguments. **makeq** uses **getkey**(), shown in figure 7.D.5, to construct the key.

303

```
$ number getkey.c
 1   /*
 2    *   getkey
 3    *       make a key from the argument
 4    */
 5
 6   #include    <sys/types.h>
 7
 8   key_t
 9   getkey(p)
10   register char *p;
11   {
12       key_t key;
13       register int i;
14
15       if (isnumber(p)) {
16           key = (key_t) atol(p);
17       } else {
18           key = (key_t) 0;
19           for (i = 0; i < sizeof(key_t) && p[i]; i++) {
20               key = (key << 8) | p[i];
21           }
22       }
23       return(key);
24   }
$ □
```

Figure 7.D.5

getkey() converts either a numeric argument to a key using the **atol**() subroutine or an alphanumeric argument to a key using the ASCII value of each character in the argument. This scheme allows mnemonic keys.

getkey() uses the **isnumber**() subroutine shown in figure 7.D.6.

```
$ number isnumber.c
 1
 2  /*
 3   *   isnumber
 4   *       test string for all numbers
 5   */
 6
 7  #include    <ctype.h>
 8
 9  int
10  isnumber(p)
11  register char *p;
12  {
13
14      for ( ; *p && isdigit(*p); p++) ;
15      return(*p ? 0 : 1);
16  }
$ ▯
```

Figure 7.D.6

Figure 7.D.7 shows an example of making a message queue with **makeq**. The **ipcs** program, provided with UNIX System V, lets you examine the status of an interprocess communication facility. The -q option tells **ipcs** to report the status of all message queues.

```
$ makeq 1 fred
$ ipcs -q
IPC status from /dev/kmem as of Tue Dec 18 22:18:16 1984
T   ID   KEY        MODE        OWNER   GROUP
Message Queues:
q    0 0x00000001 --rw-rw-rw-  rogers  writers
q    1 0x66726564 --rw-rw-rw-  rogers  writers
$ ▯
```

Figure 7.D.7

getkey() translates 1 to 1 and fred to 66726564, which is the concatenation of the hexidecimal values of the ASCII characters f (66), r (72), e (65), and d (64). **makeq** uses these keys to make two message queues, and **ipcs** shows that they have been created.

UNIX System V lets you remove a message queue with the **ipcrm**, but unfortunately **ipcrm** only accepts a numeric argument. **getkey** shown in figure 7.D.8 transforms its arguments into numeric keys so that you can use

305

mnemonic keys to name message queues.

```
$ number getkey.c
 1  /*
 2   *   getkey
 3   *        transform arguments into keys
 4   */
 5
 6  #include    <stdio.h>
 7  #include    <sys/types.h>
 8
 9  main(argc, argv)
10  int argc;
11  char *argv[];
12  {
13      key__t key;
14      register int i;
15      extern key__t getkey();
16
17      for (i = 1; i < argc; i++) {
18          printf("%ld%c", getkey(argv[i]), i + 1 == argc ? '\n' : ' ');
19      }
20      exit(0);
21  }
$ □
```

Figure 7.D.8

Finally, figure 7.D.9 removes the message queues created in figure 7.D.7.

```
$ ipcs -q
IPC status from /dev/kmem as of Tue Dec 18 22:18:16 1984
T   ID  KEY         MODE         OWNER   GROUP
Message Queues:
q    0 0x00000001 --rw-rw-rw-   rogers  writers
q    1 0x66726564 --rw-rw-rw-   rogers  writers
$ ipcrm -Q 1
$ ipcs -q
IPC status from /dev/kmem as of Tue Dec 18 22:19:49 1984
T   ID  KEY         MODE         OWNER   GROUP
Message Queues:
q    1 0x66726564 --rw-rw-rw-   rogers  writers
$ ipcrm -Q 'getkey fred'
$ ipcs -q
IPC status from /dev/kmem as of Tue Dec 18 22:21:22 1984
T   ID  KEY         MODE         OWNER   GROUP
Message Queues:
$ ☐
```

Figure 7.D.9

Once a message queue has been created, you can send and receive messages
with the **msgsnd**() and **msgrcv**() system calls whose syntax is:

```
                #include   <sys/types.h>
                #include   <sys/ipc.h>
                #include   <sys/msg.h>


                int
                msgsnd(id, message, size, flag)
                int id, size, flag;
                struct msgbuf *message;


                int
                msgrcv(id, message, size, type, flag)
                int id, size, flag;
                long type;
                struct msgbuf *message;
```

DEFINITION 62. The msgsnd and msgrcv System Calls

307

where *id* is the message queue identifier returned by **msgget**(), *message* is the message sent and is assumed to be of the form:

```
struct msgbuf
{
    long    mtype;
    char    mtext[];
};
```

and *size* is the size of mtext in bytes. *flag* can assume a combination of the following:

IPC_NOWAIT   For **msgsnd**(), IPC_NOWAIT means that if there is no room in the kernel to store the message, return immediately with the value -1. Processes normally wait until there is room for a message to be stored. For **msgrcv**(), IPC_NOWAIT means that if there are no messages to read, return immediately with the value -1. Processes normally wait until there are messages to read.

MSG_NOERROR   For **msgrcv**(), MSG_NOERROR means that any messages bigger than *size* bytes will be silently shortened to *size* bytes and no error will be returned. Normally, a message bigger than *size* is not received but an error is returned by **msgrcv**(). MSG_NOERROR is ignored by **msgsnd**().

Finally, *type* defines which messages are to be received according to the following table.

VALUE	DESCRIPTION
0	Return the first message on the queue, irrespective of its type.
>0	Return the first message on the queue of type *type*.
<0	Return the first message on the queue that has the lowest value less than or equal to the absolute value of *type*. This means that messages of type 0 are returned first.

msgrcv() returns the number of bytes received and **msgsnd**() returns zero. Both **msgsnd**() and **msgrcv**() fail and return -1 if any of the following conditions holds:

• *id* is not a valid message queue identifier.

• The operation (sending or receiving) is not allowed according to the access modes of the message queue.

- *size* is less than zero (for **msgsnd**() and **msgrcv**()) or greater than a system imposed limit (for **msgsnd**()).

- *message* points to an invalid memory address.

- *type* is less than 1 (for **msgsnd**()).

- The message cannot be sent and IPC_NOWAIT is specified in *flag* (for **msgsnd**()).

- There are no messages of the specified type and IPC_NOWAIT is specified in *flag* (for **msgrcv**()).

- The next message to be received is bigger than *size*, but MSG_NOERROR is not specified in *flag* (for **msgrcv**()).

Figures 7.D.10 and 7.D.11 show the **writeq** and **readq** programs that use **msgsnd**() and **msgrcv**() to send and receive messages on message queues.

```
$ number writeq.c
1    /*
2     *   writeq
3     *       write to a message queue
4     */
5
6    #include    <stdio.h>
7    #include    <sys/types.h>
8    #include    <sys/ipc.h>
9    #include    <sys/msg.h>
10
11   #define     ERROR      (-1)
12   #define     DEFTYPE    1
13
14   main(argc, argv)
15   int argc;
16   char *argv[];
17   {
18       key_t key;
19       int type, rc = 0;
20       extern key_t getkey();
21
22       if (scf("", "", &argc, &argv) == 0 || (argc != 3 && argc != 4)) {
23           fprintf(stderr, "usage: %s key [type]\n", argv[0]);
24           rc = 1;
25       } else {
26           key = getkey(argv[2]);
27           if (argc == 4) {
28               if (sscanf(argv[3], "%d", &type) != 1) {
29                   fprintf(stderr, "%s: invalid key (%s)\n", argv[0], argv[2]);
30                   rc = 1;
31               }
32           } else {
```

```
33                  type = DEFTYPE;
34              |
35          if (rc == 0) |
36              rc = send(argv[0], key, type);
37          |
38      |
39      exit(rc);
40 |
41
42 static int
43 send(progname, key, type, verbose)
44 char *progname;
45 key__t key;
46 int type;
47 |
48      int msgqid, length, rc = 0;
49      struct message |
50          long type;
51          char text[BUFSIZ];
52      | msg;
53
54      if ((msgqid = msgget(key, 0)) == ERROR) |
55          perror(progname);
56          rc = 1;
57      | else |
58          msg.type = type;
59          while (fgets(msg.text, sizeof(msg.text), stdin) != (char *) NULL) |
60              if ((length = strlen(msg.text)) == 0) |
61                  length = 1;
62              |
63              if (msgsnd(msgqid, &msg, length, 0) == ERROR) |
64                  perror(progname);
65                  rc = 1;
66                  break;
67              |
68          |
69      |
70      return(rc);
71 |
$ □
```

Figure 7.D.10

$ number readq.c

```
 1  /*
 2   *   readq
 3   *       read from a message queue
 4   */
 5
 6  #include    <stdio.h>
 7  #include    <sys/types.h>
 8  #include    <sys/ipc.h>
 9  #include    <sys/msg.h>
10
11  #define     ERROR       (-1)
12  #define     DEFTYPE     1
13
14  main(argc, argv)
15  int argc;
16  char *argv[];
17  {
18      key_t key;
19      int type, rc = 0;
20      extern key_t getkey();
21
22      if (scf("", "", &argc, &argv) == 0 || (argc != 3 && argc != 4)) {
23          fprintf(stderr, "usage: %s key [type]", argv[0]);
24          rc = 1;
25      } else {
26          key = getkey(argv[2]);
27          if (argc == 4) {
28              if (sscanf(argv[3], "%d", &type) != 1) {
29                  fprintf(stderr, "%s: invalid key (%s)\n", argv[0], argv[2]);
30                  rc = 1;
31              }
32          } else {
33              type = DEFTYPE;
34          }
35          if (rc == 0) {
36              rc = receive(argv[0], key, type);
37          }
38      }
39      exit(rc);
40  }
41
42  static int
43  receive(progname, key, type)
44  char *progname;
45  key_t key;
46  int type;
47  {
48      int msgqid, count, c, rc = 0;
49      struct message {
50          long type;
51          char text[BUFSIZ];
```

```
52        | msg;
53
54        if ((msgqid = msgget(key, 0)) == ERROR) |
55            perror(progname);
56            rc = 1;
57        | else |
58            do |
59                if ((count = msgrcv(msgqid, &msg, sizeof(msg.text),
60                            type, MSG__NOERROR)) > 0) |
61                    printf("(%d)\t", msg.type);
62                    fputs(msg.text, stdout);
63                |
64                if (isatty(fileno(stdin))) |
65                    printf("More? ");
66                    if ((c = getchar()) != '\n') |
67                        if (c == EOF) |
68                            putchar('\n');
69                        |
70                        break;
71                    |
72                |
73            | while (1);
74        |
75        return(rc);
76  |
$☐
```

Figure 7.D.11

writeq first gets the message queue identifier for the message queue named by the first argument and then prompts for lines from the standard input. Each line is put on the message queue as an individual message, using the type given as the optional second argument.

readq also begins by getting the message queue identifier. **readq** prints a message, prefacing the text of the message by the message type. **readq** then asks if more messages should be printed, and prints more in response to a newline. **readq** only prompts if the standard input file (stdio) is connected to a terminal.

Figure 7.D.12 shows an example of **writeq** and **readq**.

```
$ makeq test
$ writeq test 10
This is a message of type 10.
^D
$ writeq test
This is a message of type 1.
This is another message of type 1.
^D
$ writeq test 2
This is a message of type 2.
^D
$ ipcs -qo
IPC status from /dev/kmem as of Tue Dec 18 22:23:02 1984
T    ID   KEY        MODE      OWNER   GROUP CBYTES  QNUM
Message Queues:
q    50 0x74657374 --rw-rw-rw-  rogers  writers    123     4
$ readq test 2
(2)    This is a message of type 2.
More?^D
$ ipcs -qo
IPC status from /dev/kmem as of Tue Dec 18 22:23:40 1984
T    ID   KEY        MODE      OWNER   GROUP CBYTES  QNUM
Message Queues:
q    50 0x74657374 --rw-rw-rw-  rogers  writers     94     3
$ readq test -10
(1)    This is a message of type 1.
More?
(1)    This is another message of type 1.
More?
(10)   This is a message of type 10.
More?^D
$ □
```

Figure 7.D.12

Finally, the **msgctl**() system call lets you change the owner, group, and permissions of a message queue, and lets you remove a message queue. The syntax of **msgctl**() is:

```
                    #include   <sys/types.h>
                    #include   <sys/ipc.h>
                    #include   <sys/msg.h>

                    int
                    msgctl(id, command, buffer)
                    int id, command;
                    struct msqid_ds *buffer;
```

DEFINITION 63. The msgctl System Call

where *id* is the message queue identifier returned by **msgget**() and *command* is one of the following:

IPC_STAT Store the information shown below in a structured pointed to by *buffer* and defined as the following:

```
struct  msqid_ds
{
    struct  Ipc_perm
    {
        ushort  cuid;         /* creator user id         */
        ushort  cgid;         /* creator group id        */
        ushort  uid;          /* user id            */
        ushort  gid;          /* group id           */
    } msg_perm;
    ushort  msg_qnum;            /* number of messages on queue */
    ushort  msg_qbytes;          /* max number of bytes on queue */
    ushort  msg_lspid;         /* process id of last msgsnd   */
    ushort  msg_lrpid;         /* process id if last msgrcv   */
    ushort  msg_stime;         /* last msgsnd time       */
    ushort  msg_rtime;         /* last msgrcv time      */
    ushort  msg_ctime;         /* last change time      */
};
```

IPC_SET Change only the msg_perm.uid, msg_perm.gid, msg_perm.mode, and msg_qbytes fields of the structure pointed to by *buffer*.

IPC_RMID Remove the message queue identifier named by *id*.

msgctl() fails if any of the following conditions holds:

● *id* is not a valid message queue identifier.

● *command* is not a valid command.

● *command* is IPC_STAT, but read permission is denied.

314

- *command* is either IPC__SET or IPC__RMID, but the effective user ID is not the superuser or msg__perm.uid.

- *command* is IPC__SET and msg__qbytes is to be increased, but the effective user ID is not the superuser.

- *buffer* points to an invalid memory address.

Figure 7.D.13 shows the **chownq** utility that changes the owner of the message queue named by the second through the last arguments to the owner named as the first argument.

```
$ number chownq.c
 1  /*
 2   *   chownq
 3   *        change the owner of a message queue
 4   */
 5
 6  #include    <stdio.h>
 7  #include    <sys/types.h>
 8  #include    <sys/ipc.h>
 9  #include    <sys/msg.h>
10  #include    <sys/errno.h>
11  #include    <pwd.h>
12
13  #define    ERROR       (-1)
14
15  main(argc, argv)
16  int argc;
17  char *argv[];
18  {
19      key__t key;
20      int owner, msgqid, i, rc = 0;
21      char *op;
22      struct passwd *pwd, *getpwuid(), *getpwnam();
23      struct msqid__ds buf;
24      extern int errno;
25      extern key__t getkey();
26
27      if (scf("", "", &argc, &argv) == 0 || argc < 4) {
28          fprintf(stderr, "usage: %s owner key [key ...]\n", argv[0]);
29          rc = 1;
30      } else {
31          if (isnumber(op = argv[2])) {
32              owner = atoi(op);
33              if ((pwd = getpwuid(owner)) == (struct passwd *) NULL) {
34                  fprintf(stderr, "%s: owner (%s) not in password file\n", argv[0], op);
35                  rc = 1;
36              }
37          } else if ((pwd = getpwnam(op)) == (struct passwd *) NULL) {
38              fprintf(stderr, "%s: owner (%s) not in password file\n", argv[0], op);
39              rc = 1;
```

```
40          | else |
41              owner = pwd->pw__uid;
42          |
43          for (i = 3; i < argc; i++) |
44              key = getkey(argv[i]);
45              if ((msgqid = msgget(key, 0)) == ERROR ||
46                  msgctl(msgqid, IPC__STAT, &buf) == ERROR) |
47                  perror(argv[i]);
48                  rc = 1;
49              | else |
50                  buf.msg__perm.uid = owner;
51                  if (msgctl(msgqid, IPC__SET, &buf) == ERROR) |
52                      perror(argv[i]);
53                      rc = 1;
54                  |
55              |
56          |
57      |
58      exit(rc);
59 |
$ □
```

Figure 7.D.13

chownq accepts either a numeric or an alphanumeric owner whose existence is validated with **getpwuid**() or **getpwnam**(). The owner field of all message queues named as arguments are changed to the owner named as the first argument. Figure 7.D.14 shows an example.

```
$ makeq 1
$ ipcs -q
IPC status from /dev/kmem as of Tue Dec 18 22:25:46 1984
T   ID  KEY      MODE       OWNER    GROUP
Message Queues:
q   51 0x00000001 --rw-rw-rw-   rogers   writers
$ chownq root 1
$ ipcs -q
IPC status from /dev/kmem as of Tue Dec 18 22:26:21 1984
T   ID  KEY      MODE       OWNER    GROUP
Message Queues:
q   51 0x00000001 --rw-rw-rw-   root   writers
$ □
```

Figure 7.D.14

316

D.4 Semaphores

Semaphores are another type of interprocess communication available in UNIX System V. A *SEMAPHORE* is a data structure shared by several processes. It is used by those processes to synchronize their operations on a resource so that those operations do not interfere with each other.

For example, imagine that a file must be shared among several processes. Each process accessing the file must synchronize with all other processes accessing the file so that the read and write operations of one process do not interfere with the read and write operations of any other process.

One way for a process to synchronize with all other processes competing for access to the file is to first gain exclusive access to that file. Once a process has exclusive access, it can operate on the file. The prototype shown below defines the steps that each process must go through to gain exclusive access to the file.

```
while (not done)
        get exclusive access to the file
        use the file
        release exclusive access to the file
end
```

As processes execute and attempt to gain exclusive access to the file, only one process is granted the right to continue. All other processes are suspended waiting for that process to finish. The process that has been granted the right to continue then uses the file. A part of a process that uses the file is called a *CRITICAL REGION*.

When finished, the process releases its right to the file. Exclusive access is then granted to a suspended process.

In UNIX System V, the semaphore family of system calls provides the operations required to grant a single process the right to continue while suspending all other processes requesting the same right. All access to semaphores begins by allocating a semaphore identifier with the **semget**() system call whose syntax is:

```
#include  <sys/types.h>
#include  <sys/ipc.h>
#include  <sys/sem.h>

int
semget(key, number, flag)
key_t key;
int number, flag;
```

DEFINITION 64. The semget System Call

where *key* is the name of the semaphore set, *number* defines the number of semaphores in the set, and *flag* is a combination of the following:

IPC_CREAT   The semaphore set named *key* is to be created if it does not already exist. If the set does not exist, then the mode field, defined below, becomes the access mode of the semaphore set. If the set does exist, IPC_CREAT is ignored, except as noted next.

IPC_EXCL   When combined with IPC_CREAT, IPC_EXCL forces **semget()** to return an error when the semaphore set already exists.

mode   The low order 9 bits of *flag* define the access mode of the semaphore set when created with **semget()**. The grouping of bits in mode is identical to the grouping of bits in the *mode* argument in the **creat()** system call, but only the read and write permission bits have meaning. If the semaphore set exists, then mode must be a subset of the access mode of the semaphore set.

semget() fails if any of the following conditions holds:

- *number* is less than or equal to zero, or greater than a system imposed limit.

- The semaphore set named by *key* does not exist and IPC_CREAT was not specified.

- The semaphore set named by *key* does exist, but IPC_CREAT and IPC_EXCL were specified.

- The semaphore set named by *key* does exist, but mode is not a subset of the access mode of that semaphore set.

- The semaphore set named by *key* does exist, but the number of semaphores in the set is less than *number*.

- A new semaphore set is to be created, but the system wide limit on the number of semaphore sets would be exceeded.

- A new semaphore set is to be created, but the system wide limit on the number of semaphores would be exceeded.

semget() returns a semaphore identifier to be used in the **semop**() and **semctl**() system calls.

Once a set of semaphores is created, the **semop**() system call is used to operate on the set. Its syntax is:

```
#include   <sys / types.h>
#include   <sys / ipc.h>
#include   <sys / sem.h>


int
semop(id, operations, number)
int id;
struct sembuf (*operations)[];
int number;
```

DEFINITION 65. The semop System Call

where *id* is the semaphore identifier returned by **semget**(), *operations* is the array of semaphore operation structures, and *number* defines the number of entries in *operations*. The C language structure sembuf has the following format:

```
struct  sembuf {
      ushort  sem__num;
      short   sem__op;
      short   sem__flg;
};
```

The operation defined by sem__op[i], as modified by sem__flg[i], is done to the semaphore numbered sem__num[i] in the semaphore set named by *id*. The operations allowed depend on the value of sem__op[i], and can be any of the following:

>0   The value of sem__op[i] is added to the semaphore named by sem__num[i] in the semaphore set. If SEM__UNDO is set in sem__flg[i], then sem__op[i] is subtracted from the process's semaphore adjustment value for that semaphore. When the process ends, the semaphore adjustment value for a semaphore is added to that semaphore. This mechanism provides the means to

319

reverse a semaphore operation so that all processes that have been
suspended waiting for the semaphore's value to change will not be
suspended "forever."

0

— If sem__num[i] semaphore is zero, **semop()** returns immediately.

— If sem__num[i] semaphore is not zero and IPC__NOWAIT is set
in sem__flg[i], **semop()** returns immediately.

— If sem__num[i] semaphore is not zero and IPC__NOWAIT is not
set in sem__flg[i], then the process that made the **semop()**
system call is suspended until that semaphore becomes zero.

<0

— If sem__num[i] semaphore is greater than or equal to the
absolute value of sem__op[i], the absolute value of sem__op[i] is
subtracted from that semaphore. If SEM__UNDO is set in
sem__flg[i], then the absolute value of sem__op[i] is added to
the semaphore adjustment value for that semaphore.

— If sem__num[i] semaphore is less than the absolute value of
sem__op[i] and IPC__NOWAIT is set in sem__flg[i], **semop()**
returns immediately.

— If sem__num[i] in the semaphore set is less than the absolute
value of sem__op[i] and IPC__NOWAIT is not set in sem__flg[i],
then the process that made the **semop()** system call is
suspended until that semaphore becomes greater than or equal
to the absolute value of sem__op[i]. When this happens, the
absolute value of sem__op[i] is added to the semaphore
adjustment value for that semaphore if SEM__UNDO is set in
sem__flg[i].

semop() fails if any of the following conditions holds:

● *id* is not a valid semaphore identifier.

● *operations*.sem__num[i] is less than zero or greater than or equal to the
number of semaphores in the semaphore set named by *id*.

● *number* is greater than the system imposed maximum.

● The operation is not allowed according to the access modes of the
semaphore set.

● The semaphore operation would cause the process to suspend, but
IPC__NOWAIT is set in *operations*.sem__flg[i].

- A system wide limit on the number of processes requesting undo operations would be exceeded.

- A system wide limit on the number of undo operations per process would be exceeded.

- A semaphore value would be exceeded.

- A semaphore adjustment value would be exceeded.

- *operations* points to an invalid memory address.

The prototype that defined the steps a process must go through to gain exclusive access to the file can be revised by adding the **semop**() and **semget**() references as the prototype below shows. Assume that the semaphore set has been created with a single semaphore, and the semaphore has been set to 1.

```
semget(semaphore set with one semaphore)
while (not done)
      semop(-1)   / * lock the file   * /
      use the file
      semop(1)    / * unlock the file * /
end
```

The first process that executes semop(-1) continues because the semaphore value (1) is equal to the absolute value of the operation value (-1). The absolute value of the operation value (-1) is subtracted from the semaphore value resulting in a semaphore value of 0. All other processes are suspended because the semaphore value (0) is less than the absolute value of the operation value (-1).

When the process that continued finishes, it executes semop(1), causing one of the suspended processes continue. That process immediately subtracts the absolute value of the operation value (-1) from the semaphore value (1), again resulting in a semaphore value of 0. All other suspended processes remain suspended until the continued process executes semop(1).

This prototype is used in the system shown in figure 7.D.15. The figure shows a diagram of a database-oriented system derived from the **addcust** and **prcust** programs first shown in Chapter 6.

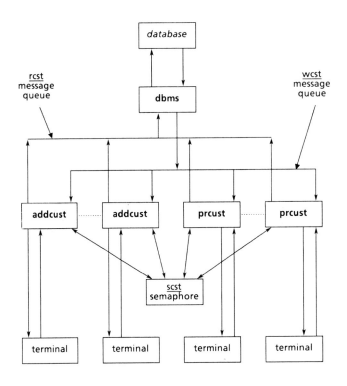

Figure 7.D.15

All access to the database is through messages sent between the database manager, **dbms**, and applications programs, **addcust** and **prcust**. Each application requires exclusive control of the message queues to send requests to and receive information from the database manager. The message queues, named rcst and wcst, are the resource to be shared among several processes. The semaphore set, named scst, is the data structure used to arbitrate the allocation of the message queues to a single process.

Figure 7.D.16 shows the file that defines the database format, the message format, and manifest constants used by **dbms**, **addcust**, and **prcust.**

```
$ number dbms1.h
 1  /*
 2   *      dbms
 3   *              constants for distributed dbms
 4   *              version 1
 5   */
 6
 7  #define    ERROR       (-1)
 8  #define    READQ       "rcst"
 9  #define    WRITEQ      "wcst"
10  #define    SEMAPHORE   "scst"
11  #define    SEMCOUNT    1
12  #define    RMODE       0644
13  #define    WMODE       0666
14  #define    DEFTYPE     1
15  #define    UNLOCK      0,1,SEM__UNDO
16  #define    LOCK        0,-1,SEM__UNDO
17
18  #define    NAMESIZE    40
19  #define    READCUST    1
20  #define    WRITECUST   2
21  #define    DBMSERR     3
22  #define    ALREADY     4
23  #define    NOCUSTOMER  5
24  #define    OK          ALREADY
25  #define    SIGNAL      0100
26
27  struct cust
28  {
29      char    name[NAMESIZE];
30      float   due;
31  };
32
33  struct message
34  {
35      long    request;
36      long    id;
37      long    status;
38      struct cust cust;
39  };
40
41  struct ms
42  {
43      long    type;
44      struct message m;
45  };
$ □
```

Figure 7.D.16

Figure 7.D.17 shows the **dbms** program that runs as a daemon process, servicing application program requests.

```
$ number dbms1.c
  1 /*
  2  *   dbms
  3  *       data base manager for amount due database
  4  *       version 1
  5  */
  6
  7 #include    <stdio.h>
  8 #include    <sys/types.h>
  9 #include    <sys/ipc.h>
 10 #include    <sys/msg.h>
 11 #include    <sys/sem.h>
 12 #include    <sys/signal.h>
 13 #include    <setjmp.h>
 14 #include    "dbms1.h"
 15
 16 main(argc, argv)
 17 int argc;
 18 char *argv[];
 19 {
 20     int rc = 1, rqid, wqid, sid;
 21     FILE *fp;
 22
 23     if (scf("", "", &argc, &argv) == 0 || argc != 3) {
 24         fprintf(stderr, "usage: %s database\n", argv[0]);
 25     } else if ((fp = fopen(argv[2], "r+")) == (FILE *) NULL &&
 26             (fp = fopen(argv[2], "w+")) == (FILE *) NULL) {
 27         perror(argv[1]);
 28     } else if ((rqid = msgget(getkey(READQ), IPC_CREAT|IPC_EXCL|RMODE)) == ERROR) {
 29         fprintf(stderr, "%s cannot create \"%s\" message queue\n", argv[0], READQ);
 30         perror(READQ);
 31     } else if ((wqid = msgget(getkey(WRITEQ), IPC_CREAT|IPC_EXCL|WMODE)) == ERROR) {
 32         fprintf(stderr, "%s cannot create \"%s\" message queue\n", argv[0], WRITEQ);
 33         perror(WRITEQ);
 34     } else if ((sid = semget(getkey(SEMAPHORE), 1, IPC_CREAT|IPC_EXCL|WMODE)) == ERROR) {
 35         fprintf(stderr, "%s cannot create \"%s\" semaphore\n", argv[0], SEMAPHORE);
 36         perror(SEMAPHORE);
 37     } else {
 38         rc = update(argv[2], fp, rqid, wqid, sid);
 39     }
 40     (void) fclose(fp);
 41     (void) msgctl(rqid, IPC_RMID);
 42     (void) msgctl(wqid, IPC_RMID);
 43     (void) semctl(sid, 0, IPC_RMID);
 44     exit(rc);
 45 }
 46
 47 static jmp_buf Jmp;
 48 struct sembuf Qunlock = {UNLOCK};
```

```
49
50 static int
51 update(filename, fp, rqid, wqid, sid)
52 char *filename;
53 FILE *fp;
54 int rqid, wqid, sid;
55 {
56      int rc = 0, n, catch();
57      struct ms msg;
58
59      (void) signal(SIGHUP,  SIG__IGN);
60      (void) signal(SIGINT,  SIG__IGN);
61      (void) signal(SIGQUIT, catch);
62      (void) signal(SIGILL,  catch);
63      (void) signal(SIGTRAP, catch);
64      (void) signal(SIGIOT,  catch);
65      (void) signal(SIGEMT,  catch);
66      (void) signal(SIGFPE,  catch);
67      (void) signal(SIGBUS,  catch);
68      (void) signal(SIGSEGV, catch);
69      (void) signal(SIGSYS,  catch);
70      (void) signal(SIGPIPE, catch);
71      (void) signal(SIGALRM, catch);
72      (void) signal(SIGTERM, catch);
73      (void) signal(SIGUSR1, catch);
74      (void) signal(SIGUSR2, catch);
75      if ((rc = setjmp(Jmp)) == 0) {
76          if (semop(sid, &Qunlock, 1) == ERROR) {
77              perror(SEMAPHORE);
78              rc = 1;
79          } else {
80              while (rc == 0) {
81                  if (receive(READQ, rqid, &msg) <- 0) {
82                      rc = 1;
83                  } else {
84                      switch (msg.m.request) {
85                      case READCUST:
86                          msg.m.status = rcust(filename, fp, &msg.m);
87                          break;
88                      case WRITECUST:
89                          msg.m.status = wcust(filename, fp, &msg.m);
90                          break;
91                      }
92                      rc = send(WRITEQ, wqid, &msg);
93                      if (msg.m.status == DBMSERR) {
94                          rc = 1;
95                      }
96                  }
97              }
98          }
99      } else {
100         rc |= SIGNAL;
101     }
```

```
102     return(rc);
103 }
104
105 static int
106 rcust(filename, fp, p)
107 char *filename;
108 FILE *fp;
109 struct message *p;
110 {
111     int rc;
112
113     if (fseek(fp, p->id * sizeof(struct cust), 0)) {
114         perror(filename);
115         rc = DBMSERR;
116     } else if (fread((char *) &p->cust, sizeof(struct cust), 1, fp) == 1 &&
117             p->cust.name[0] != NULL) {
118         rc = ALREADY;
119     } else {
120         rc = NOCUSTOMER;
121     }
122     return(rc);
123 }
124
125 static int
126 wcust(filename, fp, p)
127 char *filename;
128 FILE *fp;
129 struct message *p;
130 {
131     int rc = OK;
132
133     if (fseek(fp, p->id * sizeof(struct cust), 0) ||
134         fwrite((char *) &p->cust, sizeof(struct cust), 1, fp) != 1 ||
135         fflush(fp) == EOF || fseek(fp, 0L, 2)) {
136         perror(filename);
137         rc = DBMSERR;
138     }
139     return(rc);
140 }
141
142 static int
143 catch(signo)
144 int signo;
145 {
146
147     longjmp(Jmp, signo);
148 }
$ ▢
```

Figure 7.D.17

dbms is explained below.

326

25-37	Allocate the message queues and the semaphore set. The message queues and the semaphore set cannot exist when **dbms** starts.
38	Update the database in response to application program requests.
40-43	Close the database and remove the message queues and the semaphore set.
59-74	Handle all signals so that **dbms** never ends without first removing the message queues and the semaphore set.
75	Arrange for control to be transferred here after a signal has been caught.
76-79	Unlock the semaphore used for arbitrating access to the message queues.
80-99	Process application program requests, sending an acknowledgement for each request. Stop if there is a message error or a database error.
100-101	If a signal prematurely ends **dbms**, return the signal number caught.
105-123	Read a record from the database and return the status of the operation.
125-140	Write a record to the database and return the status of the operation. Force the record to be written to the database from the in-process buffer.
142-148	Transfer control on all caught signals to the location stored in Jmp and return the number of the caught signal.

dbms, **addcust**, and **prcust** use the **receive**() and **send**() subroutines, figure 7.D.18, to receive and send message on the message queues.

```
$ number rdwr.c
 1  /*
 2   *   rdwr
 3   *       read and write messages from the amount due database
 4   *       message queue
 5   */
 6
 7  #include    <stdio.h>
 8  #include    "dbms1.h"
 9
10  int
11  receive(name, id, p)
12  char *name;
13  int id;
14  struct ms *p;
15  {
16      register int rc;
17
18      if ((rc = msgrcv(id, p, sizeof(p->m), DEFTYPE, 0)) == ERROR) {
19          perror(name);
20          rc = 0;
21      } else if (rc != sizeof(p->m)) {
22          fprintf(stderr, "short record received");
23          fprintf(stderr, "size = %d, type = %ld\n", rc, p->type);
24          rc = 0;
25      }
26      return(rc);
27  }
28
29  int
30  send(name, id, p)
31  char *name;
32  int id;
33  struct ms *p;
34  {
35      register int rc = 0;
36
37      p->type = DEFTYPE;
38      if (msgsnd(id, p, sizeof(p->m), 0) == ERROR) {
39          perror(name);
40          rc = 1;
41      }
42  }
$ ▢
```

Figure 7.D.18

Figure 7.D.19 shows the **addcust** program that adds customers to the database.

328

$ **number addcust3.c**

```
 1  /*
 2   *    addcust
 3   *        add a customer to the amount due database
 4   *        version 3
 5   */
 6
 7  #include    <stdio.h>
 8  #include    <sys/types.h>
 9  #include    <sys/ipc.h>
10  #include    <sys/msg.h>
11  #include    <sys/sem.h>
12  #include    <ctype.h>
13  #include    "dbms.1h"
14
15  main(argc, argv)
16  int argc;
17  char *argv[];
18  {
19      int rc = 1, rqid, wqid, sid;
20      FILE *fp;
21
22      if (scf("", "", &argc, &argv) == 0 || argc > 2) {
23          fprintf(stderr, "usage: %s\n", argv[0]);
24      } else if ((wqid = msgget(getkey(READQ), 0)) == ERROR ||
25              (rqid = msgget(getkey(WRITEQ), 0)) == ERROR ||
26              (sid = semget(getkey(SEMAPHORE), 1, 0)) == ERROR) {
27          fprintf(stderr, "%s: start-up error - ", argv[0]);
28          fprintf(stderr, "database manager appears inactive\n");
29      } else {
30          rc = add(rqid, wqid, sid);
31      }
32      exit(rc);
33  }
34
35  struct sembuf Qunlock = {UNLOCK};
36  struct sembuf Qlock   = {LOCK};
37
38  static int
39  add(rqid, wqid, sid)
40  int rqid, wqid, sid;
41  {
42      int n, rc = 0;
43      char buffer[BUFSIZ], *p;
44      struct ms msg;
45
46      while (rc == 0) {
47          printf("ID: ");
48          if ((n = scanf("%ld%*c", &msg.m.id)) == EOF) {
49              putchar('\n');
50              break;
51          } else if (n != 1) {
```

329

```
52              fprintf(stderr, "Invalid ID\n");
53              while(getchar() != '\n');
54          } else if (semop(sid, &Qlock, 1) == ERROR) {
55              perror(SEMAPHORE);
56              rc = 1;
57          } else {
58              msg.m.request = READCUST;
59              if (send(WRITEQ, wqid, &msg) || receive(READQ, rqid, &msg) == 0) {
60                  rc = 1;
61              } else if (msg.m.status == ALREADY) {
62                  fprintf(stderr, "%ld: customer already added\n", msg.m.id);
63              } else if (msg.m.status == DBMSERR) {
64                  fprintf(stderr, "Database error trying to read id %ld\n", msg.m.id);
65                  rc = 1;
66              } else {
67                  while (1) {
68                      printf("Name: ");
69                      if (fgets(buffer, sizeof(buffer), stdin) == NULL) {
70                          fprintf(stderr, "\nCustomer must have a name\n");
71                      } else {
72                          for (p = buffer; !isalpha(*p); p++);
73                          for (n = 0; (n < NAMESIZE - 1) && *p != '\n'; n++) {
74                              msg.m.cust.name[n] = *p++;
75                          }
76                          msg.m.cust.name[n] = NULL;
77                          if (n == 0) {
78                              fprintf(stderr, "Invalid name\n");
79                          } else {
80                              break;
81                          }
82                      }
83                  }
84                  while (1) {
85                      printf("Amount due: ");
86                      if ((n = scanf("%f%*c", &msg.m.cust.due)) == EOF) {
87                          fprintf(stderr, "\nCustomer must have an amount due\n");
88                      } else if (n != 1) {
89                          fprintf(stderr, "Invalid amount\n");
90                          while (getchar() != '\n');
91                      } else {
92                          break;
93                      }
94                  }
95                  msg.m.request = WRITECUST;
96                  if (send(WRITEQ, wqid, &msg) || receive(READQ, rqid, &msg) <= 0) {
97                      rc = 1;
98                  } else if (msg.m.status == DBMSERR) {
99                      fprintf(stderr, "Database error trying to write id %ld\n", msg.m.id);
100                     rc = 1;
101                 }
102             }
103             if (semop(sid, &Qunlock, 1) == ERROR) {
104                 perror(SEMAPHORE);
```

```
105                rc = 1;
106            }
107         }
108      }
109   return(rc);
110 }
$ □
```

Figure 7.D.19

addcust is explained below.

24-29	The message queue IDs and semaphore ID are allocated. If they cannot be allocated, **addcust** assumes that the database manager is inactive and exits.
30	New customers are added to the database.
46-53	A customer ID can be provided by the user before exclusive control of the message queues is required. This reduces the size of the critical region to only that part of the **add**() subroutine that uses the database manager.
54-57	Request exclusive access to the message queues with the **semop**() system call. SEM__UNDO is specified in the flags field of the Qlock semaphore operation so that if **addcust** prematurely ends, the lock semaphore operation is undone. Recall that the **semop**() system call causes the absolute value of the semaphore value (1) to be added to the semaphore adjustment value. When **addcust** ends, the semaphore adjustment value is added to the semaphore. This means that the semaphore has the value of 1 if **addcust** ends before doing an unlock operation.
58-66	The beginning of the critical region. The customer record for the specified ID is read from the database.
67-94	If the customer to be added is not in the database, the user is prompted for the customer's name and the amount due.
95-102	The new customer record is sent to the database manager to be written to the database.
103-106	The end of the critical region. The message queues are no longer needed. They are released for use by other application programs. SEM__UNDO is again specified in the flags field of the Qunlock semaphore operation. This causes the semaphore value (1) to be subtracted from the semaphore adjustment value (also 1 because of the lock operation in line 55), yielding

331

> the value 0. When **addcust** ends, the semaphore adjustment value (0) is added to the semaphore value. Since this does not change the semaphore value, nothing happens.

Finally, figure 7.D.20 shows the **prcust** program that prints information in the database.

```
$ number prcust3.c
 1   /*
 2    *    prcust
 3    *        print selected customer records
 4    *        version 3
 5    */
 6
 7   #include    <stdio.h>
 8   #include    <sys/types.h>
 9   #include    <sys/ipc.h>
10   #include    <sys/msg.h>
11   #include    <sys/sem.h>
12   #include    "dbms1.h"
13
14   main(argc, argv)
15   int argc;
16   char *argv[];
17   {
18       int rc = 1, rqid, wqid, sid;
19       FILE *fp;
20
21       if (argc > 1) {
22           fprintf(stderr, "usage: %s\n", argv[0]);
23       } else if ((wqid = msgget(getkey(READQ), 0)) == ERROR ||
24           (rqid = msgget(getkey(WRITEQ), 0)) == ERROR ||
25           (sid = semget(getkey(SEMAPHORE), SEMCOUNT, 0)) == ERROR) {
26           fprintf(stderr, "%s: start-up error - ", argv[0]);
27           fprintf(stderr, "database manager appears inactive\n");
28       } else {
29           rc = pr(rqid, wqid, sid);
30       }
31       exit(rc);
32   }
33
34   struct sembuf  Qunlock = {UNLOCK};
35   struct sembuf  Qlock   = {LOCK};
36
37   static int
38   pr(rqid, wqid, sid)
39   int rqid, wqid, sid;
40   {
41       int rc = 0, n;
42       struct ms msg;
43
44       while (rc == 0) {
```

332

```
45         printf("ID: ");
46         if ((n = scanf("%ld%*c", &msg.m.id)) == EOF) {
47             putchar('\n');
48             break;
49         } else if (n != 1) {
50             fprintf(stderr, "Invalid ID\n");
51             while(getchar() != '\n');
52         } else if (semop(sid, &Qlock, 1) == ERROR) {
53             perror(SEMAPHORE);
54             rc = 1;
55         } else {
56             msg.m.request = READCUST;
57             if (send(WRITEQ, wqid, &msg) || receive(READQ, rqid, &msg) == 0) {
58                 rc = 1;
59             } else if (msg.m.status == NOCUSTOMER) {
60                 fprintf(stderr, "No customer for id %ld\n", msg.m.id);
61             } else if (msg.m.status == DBMSERR) {
62                 fprintf(stderr, "Database error trying to read id %ld\n", msg.m.id);
63                 rc = 1;
64             } else {
65                 printf("\tName:\t\t%s\n", msg.m.cust.name);
66                 printf("\tAmount due:\t$%5.2f\n", msg.m.cust.due);
67             }
68             if (semop(sid, &Qunlock, 1) == ERROR) {
69                 perror(SEMAPHORE);
70                 rc = 1;
71             }
72         }
73     }
74     return(rc);
75 }
$
```

Figure 7.D.20

prcust's explanation follows.

23-28   The message queue IDs and semaphore ID are allocated. If they cannot be allocated, **prcust** assumes that the database manager is inactive and exits.

29   Customer information in the database is printed.

45-51   A customer ID can be provided by the user before exclusive control of the message queues is required. This reduces the size of the critical region to only that part of the **pr**() subroutine that uses the database manager.

52-55   Request exclusive access to the message queues with the **semop**() system call. Again, SEM_UNDO is specified in the flags field of the Qlock semaphore operation so that if **prcust**

	prematurely ends, the lock semaphore operation is undone.
56-67	The beginning of the critical region. The customer record for the specified ID is read from the database. If the record is in the database, it is printed.
68-71	The end of the critical region. The message queues are no longer needed. They are released for use by other application programs. Again, SEM__UNDO is again specified in the flags field of the Qunlock semaphore operation.

Figure 7.D.21 shows the dialogue between the **dbms** program and two application programs running at two different terminals. The information shown for each terminal is in sequence. Blank entries show delays that result when requesting exclusive control of the message queues.

LINE	TERMINAL A	TERMINAL B
1	$ **dbms accrcvdb &**	
2	4768	
3	$ **addcust**	$ **prcust**
4	ID: **1**	ID: **1**
5		No customer for id 1
6	Name: **Larry Rogers**	ID: **1**
7	Amount Due: **125.53**	
8	ID: **1**	Name: Larry Rogers
9		Amount Due: $125.53
10	1: customer already added	ID: **273**
11	ID: **273**	No customer for id 273
12	Name: **Jean Yates**	ID: **273**
13	Amount Due: **3250.28**	
14	ID: **^D**	Name: Jean Yates
15	$ ☐	Amount Due: $3250.28
16		ID: **^D**
17		$ ☐

Figure 7.D.21

1. The **dbms** program is started as a background process to service requests made by application programs.

2. The shell responds with the process ID of **dbms**.

3. **addcust** and **prcust** are started.

4. **addcust** and **prcust** request a customer ID.

5. **prcust** is given exclusive control of the message queues and exchanges messages with **dbms**. **prcust** discovers that there is no database record for customer number 1. Because **prcust** has exclusive control of the message queues, **addcust** is suspended.

6. When **prcust** finishes using the message queues, it frees them which causes **addcust** to continue. **addcust** gains exclusive control and prompts for the customer's name. **prcust** prompts for another customer ID.

7. **addcust** next prompts for the amount due. Because **addcust** has control of the message queues, **prcust** is suspended.

8. **addcust** causes **dbms** to add the new customer record to the database, gives up the message queues, and prompts for another ID. **prcust** is given control of the queues and displays the information for customer 1.

9. **prcust** continues displaying information. **addcust** is suspended.

10. **prcust** gives up the message queues, and **addcust** is restarted and prints a diagnostic message. **prcust** asks for another ID.

11. **prcust** gets control of the message queues and reports that there is no customer record numbered 273. **addcust** asks for an ID.

12. **addcust** gets control of the message queues and asks for a customer name. **prcust** prompts for a customer ID.

13. **addcust** prompts for the amount due. **prcust** is suspended waiting for the message queues.

14. **addcust** gives up the message queues and ends. **prcust** displays the customer's name for record number 273.

15. **prcust** displays the amount due for record number 273.

16. **prcust** gives up the message queues and ends.

Semaphores in UNIX System V provide a means for sharing resources among competing processes. The kernel is responsible for suspending and restarting processes, and for undoing semaphore operations when processes end abnormally. Processes need only agree to use semaphores to guard a resource and on semaphore values.

D.5 Shared Memory

The last new interprocess communication facility available in UNIX System V is shared memory. *SHARED MEMORY* is main computer memory shared by one

335

or more processes. That is, the same physical portion of main memory appears in the address space of one or more processes. Figure 7.D.22 shows two processes sharing the same section of main computer memory.

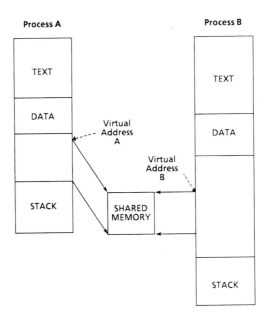

Figure 7.D.22

Notice especially that while process A and process B use the same piece of shared memory, that memory appears at a different address in each process.

Access to shared memory begins with the **shmget**() system call whose syntax is:

```
#include   <sys/types.h>
#include   <sys/ipc.h>
#include   <sys/shm.h>

int
shmget(key, size, flag)
key_t key;
int size, flag;
```

DEFINITION 66. The shmget System Call

where *key* is the name of the shared memory, *size* is the size of the shared memory segment in bytes, and *flag* is a combination of the following:

IPC_CREAT   The shared memory segment named *key* is to be created if it does not already exist. If the segment does not exist, then the mode field, defined below, becomes the access mode of the segment. If the segment does exist, IPC_CREAT is ignored, except as noted next.

IPC_EXCL   When combined with IPC_CREAT, IPC_EXCL forces **shmget**() to return an error when the shared memory segment already exists.

mode   The low order 9 bits of *flag* define the access mode of the shared memory segment when created with **shmget**(). The grouping of bits in mode is identical to the grouping of bits in the *mode* argument in the **creat**() system call, but only the read and write permission bits have meaning. If the shared memory segment exists, then mode must be a subset of the access mode of the segment.

shmget() fails if any of the following conditions holds:

- *size* is less than the system imposed minimum, or greater than a system imposed maximum.

- The shared memory segment named by *key* does not exist and IPC_CREAT was not specified.

- The shared memory segment named by *key* does exist, but IPC_CREAT and IPC_EXCL were specified.

- The shared memory segment named by *key* does exist, but mode is not a subset of the access mode of that shared memory segment.

337

- The shared memory segment named by *key* does exist, but the segment is less than *size* and *size* is not zero.

- A new shared memory segment is to be created, but the system wide limit on the number of shared memory segments would be exceeded.

- A new shared memory segment is to be created, but the amount of physical memory required is not available.

Once a shared memory segment is created, the **shmat**() and **shmdt**() system calls are used to insert it into and remove it from a process' address space. Their syntax is:

```
#include   <sys/types.h>
#include   <sys/ipc.h>
#include   <sys/shm.h>


char *
shmat(id, at__address, flag)
int id;
char *at__address;
int flag;


int
shmdt(dt__address)
char *dt__address;
```

DEFINITION 67. The shmat and shmdt System Calls

where *id* is the shared memory segment identifier returned by **shmget**(). *at__address* is the address in process address space where the shared memory segment is to be attached and can be zero if the UNIX system is to decide where to attach the segment. *dt__address* is the address in process address space of a shared memory segment to be detached and is the value returned by a successful **shmat**() system call. *flag* can be SHM__RDONLY, meaning that the shared memory segment named by *id* is read-only, or zero, meaning that the shared memory segment named by *id* is readable and writable. A shared memory segment is zeroed the first time a process attaches it. **shmat**() returns the address in the process' address space where the shared memory segment was attached, and **shmat**() returns zero.

shmat() and **shmdt**() fail if any of the following conditions holds:

- *id* is not a valid shared memory identifier.

- The operation is not allowed according to the access modes of the shared memory segment.

- The process' address space is not large enough to hold the shared memory segment.

- *at_address* or *dt_address* are illegal.

- The system imposed limit on the number of shared memory segments would be exceeded.

Figure 7.D.23 shows an update diagram of the database system described in the last section. The new version uses shared memory for exchanging information between **dbms** and applications, a semaphore for allocating the shared memory to applications, and another semaphore for arbitrating access to the shared memory between **dbms** and an application.

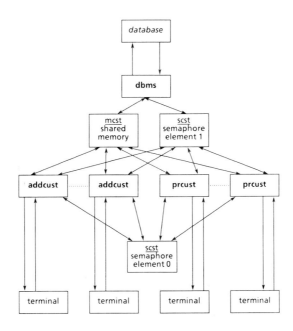

Figure 7.D.23

The technique for allocating a resource among competing processes was described in the last section. The same technique is used here to allocate the shared memory segment among the application processes. However, this version of the database system also needs a method for arbitrating access to the shared memory once an application has gained exclusive control of the shared memory. The next prototypes show the steps each process must go through to access the shared memory segment in an orderly fashion.

```
/ * this is the dbms program * /
semget(one semaphore)
semop(1)            / * unlock shared memory * /
while (not done)
     semop(-2)      / * lock shared memory   * /
     use shared memory
     semop(1)       / * unlock shared memory * /
end

/ * this is an application program * /
semget(one semaphore)
while (not done)
     semop(-1)      / * lock shared memory   * /
     use shared memory
     semop(2)       / * unlock shared memory * /
end
```

dbms creates the semaphore, initializes it to 1, and begins processing application program requests. Because all requests are started by an application, **dbms** must suspend until a request is made. A semaphore operation value of -2 suspends **dbms** until the semaphore value is 2 or greater.

When an application does a semaphore operation with the value -1, it continues because the semaphore has the value 1. The absolute value of -1 (1) is subtracted from 1 yielding 0. The semaphore value remains at 0 and **dbms** remains suspended until the application sets the semaphore to 2.

When the application finishes building a request, it sets the semaphore to 2. This starts **dbms**, where the absolute value of -2 (2) is subtracted from 2 yielding 0, and continues the application. The application suspends when it does the semaphore operation with the value -1.

Similarly, when **dbms** finishes processing a request, it sets the semaphore to 1. This starts the application and **dbms** continues. **dbms** suspends when it does the semaphore operation with the value -2.

These prototypes are used by **dbms, addcust**, and **prcust** to exchange information in the same way that messages were used in the last version. The programs for this version begin with the constants and data structures shown in figure 7.D.24.

340

```
$ number dbms2.h
 1  /*
 2   *      dbms
 3   *              constants for distributed dbms
 4   *              version 2
 5   */
 6
 7  #define     ERROR           (-1)
 8  #define     SEMAPHORE       "scst"
 9  #define     SEMCOUNT        2
10  #define     MEMORY          "mcst"
11  #define     WMODE           0666
12  #define     UNLOCK          0,1,SEM__UNDO
13  #define     LOCK            0,-1,SEM__UNDO
14  #define     DBMSUNLOCK      1,1,SEM__UNDO
15  #define     DBMSLOCK        1,-2,SEM__UNDO
16  #define     APPLUNLOCK      1,2,0
17  #define     UAPPLLOCK       1,-1,SEM__UNDO
18  #define     APPLLOCK        1,-1,0
19
20  #define     NAMESIZE        40
21  #define     READCUST        1
22  #define     WRITECUST       2
23  #define     DBMSERR         3
24  #define     ALREADY         4
25  #define     NOCUSTOMER      5
26  #define     OK              ALREADY
27  #define     SIGNAL          0100
28
29  struct  cust
30  {
31      char    name[NAMESIZE];
32      float   due;
33  };
34
35  struct  message
36  {
37      long    request;
38      long    id;
39      long    status;
40      struct  cust cust;
41  };
$ ▢
```

Figure 7.D.24

Figure 7.D.25 shows the **dbms** program, followed by highlights of the changes made in this version.

$ number dbms2.c

```
 1  /*
 2   *   dbms
 3   *        data base manager for amount due database
 4   *        version 2
 5   */
 6
 7  #include   <stdio.h>
 8  #include   <sys/types.h>
 9  #include   <sys/ipc.h>
10  #include   <sys/shm.h>
11  #include   <sys/sem.h>
12  #include   <sys/signal.h>
13  #include   <setjmp.h>
14  #include   "dbms2.h"
15
16  main(argc, argv)
17  int argc;
18  char *argv[];
19  {
20      int rc = 1, mid, sid;
21      struct message *p;
22      FILE *fp;
23
24      if (scf("", "", &argc, &argv) == 0 || argc != 3) {
25          fprintf(stderr, "usage: %s database\n", argv[0]);
26      } else if ((fp = fopen(argv[2], "r+")) == (FILE *) NULL &&
27              (fp = fopen(argv[2], "w+")) == (FILE *) NULL) {
28          perror(argv[2]);
29      } else if ((mid = shmget(getkey(MEMORY), sizeof(struct message),
30          IPC_CREAT|IPC_EXCL|WMODE)) == ERROR) {
31          fprintf(stderr, "%s: cannot create \"%s\" shared memory\n", argv[0], MEMORY);
32          perror(MEMORY);
33      } else if ((p = (struct message *) shmat(mid, (char *) 0, 0)) == (struct message *) ERROR) {
34          fprintf(stderr, "%s: cannot attach shared memory\n", argv[0]);
35      } else if ((sid = semget(getkey(SEMAPHORE), SEMCOUNT, IPC_CREAT|IPC_EXCL|WMODE)) == ERROR
36          fprintf(stderr, "%s: cannot create \"%s\" semaphore\n", argv[0], SEMAPHORE);
37          perror(SEMAPHORE);
38      } else {
39          rc = update(argv[2], fp, mid, p, sid);
40          (void) fclose(fp);
41          if (shmctl(mid, IPC_RMID) == ERROR) {
42              fprintf(stderr, "%s: cannot remove \"%s\" shared memory\n", argv[0], MEMORY);
43              perror(MEMORY);
44          }
45          if (semctl(sid, 0, IPC_RMID) == ERROR) {
46              fprintf(stderr, "%s: cannot remove \"%s\" semaphore\n", argv[0], SEMAPHORE);
47              perror(SEMAPHORE);
48          }
49      }
50      exit(rc);
51  }
```

342

```
52
53 static jmp__buf Jmp;
54 struct sembuf Unlock[2] =      |UNLOCK, DBMSUNLOCK|;
55 struct sembuf Sunlock =        |DBMSUNLOCK|;
56 struct sembuf Slock   =        |DBMSLOCK|;
57
58 #define SERROR  perror(SEMAPHORE); rc = 1
59
60
61 static int
62 update(filename, fp, mid, p, sid)
63 char *filename;
64 FILE *fp;
65 int mid, sid;
66 struct message *p;
67 |
68     int rc = 0, n, catch();
69
70     (void) signal(SIGINT, SIG__IGN);
71     (void) signal(SIGHUP, catch);
72     (void) signal(SIGQUIT, catch);
73     (void) signal(SIGILL, catch);
74     (void) signal(SIGTRAP, catch);
75     (void) signal(SIGIOT, catch);
76     (void) signal(SIGEMT, catch);
77     (void) signal(SIGFPE, catch);
78     (void) signal(SIGBUS, catch);
79     (void) signal(SIGSEGV, catch);
80     (void) signal(SIGSYS, catch);
81     (void) signal(SIGPIPE, catch);
82     (void) signal(SIGALRM, catch);
83     (void) signal(SIGTERM, catch);
84     (void) signal(SIGUSR1, catch);
85     (void) signal(SIGUSR2, catch);
86     if (setjmp(Jmp) == 0) |
87         if (semop(sid, Unlock, 2) == ERROR) |
88             SERROR;
89         | else |
90             while (rc == 0) |
91                 if (semop(sid, &Slock, 1) == ERROR) |
92                     SERROR;
93                 | else |
94                     switch (p->request) |
95                     case READCUST:
96                         p->status = rcust(filename, fp, p);
97                         break;
98                     case WRITECUST:
99                         p->status = wcust(filename, fp, p);
100                        break;
101                    |
102                    if (semop(sid, &Sunlock, 1) == ERROR) |
103                        SERROR;
104                    | else if (p->status == DBMSERR) |
```

```
105                      rc = 1;
106                  }
107               }
108            }
109         }
110      }
111      return(rc);
112 }
113
114 static int
115 rcust(filename, fp, p)
116 char *filename;
117 FILE *fp;
118 struct message *p;
119 {
120      int rc;
121
122      if (fseek(fp, p->id * sizeof(struct cust), 0)) {
123          perror(filename);
124          rc = DBMSERR;
125      } else if (fread((char *) &p->cust, sizeof(struct cust), 1, fp) == 1 &&
126              p->cust.name[0] != NULL) {
127          rc = ALREADY;
128      } else {
129          rc = NOCUSTOMER;
130      }
131      return(rc);
132 }
133
134 static int
135 wcust(filename, fp, p)
136 char *filename;
137 FILE *fp;
138 struct message *p;
139 {
140      int rc = OK;
141
142      if (fseek(fp, p->id * sizeof(struct cust), 0) ||
143          fwrite((char *) &p->cust, sizeof(struct cust), 1, fp) != 1 ||
144          fflush(fp) == EOF || fseek(fp, 0L, 2)) {
145          perror(filename);
146          rc = DBMSERR;
147      }
148      return(rc);
149 }
150
151 static int
152 catch(signo)
153 int signo;
154 {
155
156      longjmp(Jmp, signo);
157 }
```

$□

Figure 7.D.25

87   Unlock the shared memory for allocation to an application and for an application making a request. These two semaphore operations are combined in a single call to **semop**().

91   Wait for an application's request.

102   When the request has been processed, start the application by unlocking the shared memory.

Figure 7.D.26 shows the **addcust** program.

```
$ number addcust4.c
 1  /*
 2   *  addcust
 3   *      add a customer to the amount due database
 4   *      version 4
 5   */
 6
 7  #include    <stdio.h>
 8  #include    <sys/types.h>
 9  #include    <sys/ipc.h>
10  #include    <sys/shm.h>
11  #include    <sys/sem.h>
12  #include    <ctype.h>
13  #include    "dbms2.h"
14
15  main(argc, argv)
16  int argc;
17  char *argv[];
18  {
19      int rc = 1, mid, sid;
20      FILE *fp;
21      struct message *p;
22      extern char *shmat();
23
24      if (scf("", "", &argc, &argv) == 0 || argc > 2) {
25          fprintf(stderr, "usage: %s\n", argv[0]);
26      } else if ((mid = shmget(getkey(MEMORY), sizeof(struct message), 0)) == ERROR ||
27          (p = (struct message *) shmat(mid, (char *) 0, 0)) == (struct message *) ERROR ||
28          (sid = semget(getkey(SEMAPHORE), SEMCOUNT, 0)) == ERROR) {
29          fprintf(stderr, "%s: start-up error - ", argv[0]);
30          fprintf(stderr, "database manager appears inactive\n");
31      } else {
32          rc = add(mid, p, sid);
33          (void) shmdt(p);
34      }
```

```
35      exit(rc);
36 }
37
38 struct  sembuf  Unlock[2]     =       {DBMSUNLOCK, UNLOCK};
39 struct  sembuf  Lock[2]       =       {LOCK, APPLLOCK};
40 struct  sembuf  Sunlock       =       {APPLUNLOCK};
41 struct  sembuf  Slock         =       {APPLLOCK};
42
43 #define SERROR    perror(SEMAPHORE); rc = 1
44
45 static int
46 add(mid, p, sid)
47 int mid, sid;
48 struct message *p;
49 {
50      int n, rc = 0;
51      long tid;
52      char buffer[BUFSIZ], *t;
53
54      while (rc == 0) {
55          printf("ID: ");
56          if ((n = scanf("%ld%*c", &tid)) == EOF) {
57              putchar('\n');
58              break;
59          } else if (n != 1) {
60              fprintf(stderr, "Invalid ID\n");
61              while(getchar() != '\n');
62          } else if (semop(sid, Lock, 2) == ERROR) {
63              SERROR;
64          } else {
65              p->request = READCUST;
66              p->id = tid;
67              if (semop(sid, &Sunlock, 1) == ERROR || semop(sid, &Slock, 1) == ERROR) {
68                  SERROR;
69              } else if (p->status == ALREADY) {
70                  fprintf(stderr, "%ld: customer already added\n", tid);
71              } else if (p->status == DBMSERR) {
72                  fprintf(stderr, "Database error trying to read id %ld\n", tid);
73                  rc = 1;
74              } else {
75                  while (1) {
76                      printf("Name: ");
77                      if (fgets(buffer, sizeof(buffer), stdin) == NULL) {
78                          fprintf(stderr, "\nCustomer must have a name\n");
79                      } else {
80                          for (t = buffer; !isalpha(*t); t++);
81                          for (n = 0; (n < NAMESIZE - 1) && *t != '\n'; n++) {
82                              p->cust.name[n] = *t++;
83                          }
84                          p->cust.name[n] = NULL;
85                          if (n == 0) {
86                              fprintf(stderr, "Invalid name\n");
87                          } else {
```

346

```
88                              break;
89                          }
90                      }
91                  }
92              while (1) {
93                  printf("Amount due: ");
94                  if ((n = scanf("%f%*c", &p->cust.due)) == EOF) {
95                      fprintf(stderr, "\nCustomer must have an amount due\n");
96                  } else if (n != 1) {
97                      fprintf(stderr, "Invalid amount\n");
98                      while (getchar() != '\n');
99                  } else {
100                     break;
101                 }
102             }
103             p->request = WRITECUST;
104             if (semop(sid, &Sunlock, 1) == ERROR || semop(sid, &Slock, 1) == ERROR) {
105                 SERROR;
106             } else if (p->status == DBMSERR) {
107                 fprintf(stderr, "Database error trying to write id %ld\n", tid);
108                 rc = 1;
109             }
110         }
111     if (semop (sid, Unlock, 2) == ERROR) {
112         SERROR;
113     }
114     }
115 }
116 return(rc);
117 }
$ □
```

Figure 7.D.26

62   The Lock semaphore operation first allocates the shared memory to the process (LOCK) and then it arbitrates access to the application (UAPPLLOCK). Both of these semaphore operations are undone if **addcust** ends prematurely.

67   Unlocking sends the request and relocking waits until the request has been completed. Neither of these semaphore operations are undone because the undo operations in line 62 correctly reset the semaphore if **addcust** ends prematurely.

104   Again, unlocking sends the request and relocking waits until the request has been completed. These semaphore operations are also not undone.

111   The Unlock semaphore operation first arbitrates access to neither the application or the **dbms** (DBMSUNLOCK) and then

it unlocks the shared memory so that it can be allocated to another process (UNLOCK). These semaphore operations are undone, in effect negating the undone operations in line 62.

Finally, figure 7.D.27 shows the **prcust** program.

```
$ number prcust4.c
 1  /*
 2   *  prcust
 3   *      print selected customer records
 4   *      version 4
 5   */
 6
 7  #include    <stdio.h>
 8  #include    <sys/types.h>
 9  #include    <sys/ipc.h>
10  #include    <sys/shm.h>
11  #include    <sys/sem.h>
12  #include    "dbms2.h"
13
14  main(argc, argv)
15  int argc;
16  char *argv[];
17  {
18      int rc = 1, mid, sid;
19      FILE *fp;
20      struct message *p;
21      extern char *shmat();
22
23      if (scf("", "", &argc, &argv) == 0 || argc > 2) {
24          fprintf(stderr, "usage: %s\n", argv[0]);
25      } else if ((mid = shmget(getkey(MEMORY), sizeof(struct message), 0)) == ERROR ||
26          (p = (struct message *) shmat(mid, (char *) 0, 0)) == (struct message *) ERROR ||
27          (sid = semget(getkey(SEMAPHORE), SEMCOUNT, 0)) == ERROR) {
28          fprintf(stderr, "%s: start-up error - ", argv[0]);
29          fprintf(stderr, "database manager appears inactive\n");
30      } else {
31          rc = pr(mid, p, sid);
32          (void) shmdt(p);
33      }
34      exit(rc);
35  }
36
37  struct sembuf Unlock[2]=    {DBMSUNLOCK, UNLOCK};
38  struct sembuf Lock[2] =     {LOCK, APPLLOCK};
39  struct sembuf Sunlock =     {APPLUNLOCK};
40  struct sembuf Slock   =     {APPLLOCK};
41
42  #define SERROR  perror(SEMAPHORE); rc = 1
43
44  static int
45  pr(mid, p, sid)
```

```
46  int mid, sid;
47  struct message *p;
48  {
49      int rc = 0, n;
50      long tid;
51
52      while (rc == 0) {
53          printf("ID: ");
54          if ((n = scanf("%ld%*c", &tid)) == EOF) {
55              putchar('\n');
56              break;
57          } else if (n != 1) {
58              fprintf(stderr, "Invalid ID\n");
59              while(getchar() != '\n');
60          } else if (semop(sid, Lock, 2) == ERROR) {
61              SERROR;
62          } else {
63              p->request = READCUST;
64              p->id = tid;
65              if (semop(sid, &Sunlock, 1) == ERROR || semop(sid, &Slock, 1) == ERROR) {
66                  SERROR;
67              } else if (p->status == NOCUSTOMER) {
68                  fprintf(stderr, "No customer for id %ld\n", tid);
69              } else if (p->status == DBMSERR) {
70                  fprintf(stderr, "Database error trying to read id %ld\n", tid);
71              } else {
72                  printf("\tName:\t\t%s\n", p->cust.name);
73                  printf("\tAmount due:\t$%5.2f\n", p->cust.due);
74              }
75          }
76          if (semop(sid, Unlock, 2) == ERROR) {
77              SERROR;
78          }
79      }
80      return(rc);
81  }
$ □
```

Figure 7.D.27

60   The Lock semaphore operation first allocates the shared memory to the process (LOCK) and then it arbitrates access to the application (UAPPLLOCK). Both of these semaphore operations are undone if **prcust** ends prematurely.

65   Unlocking sends the request and relocking waits until the request has been completed. Neither of these semaphore operations are undone because the undo operations in line 62 correctly reset the semaphore if **addcust** ends prematurely.

76   The Unlock semaphore operation first arbitrates access to neither the application or the **dbms** (DBMSUNLOCK) and then it unlocks the shared memory so that it can be allocated to another process (UNLOCK). These semaphore operations are undone, in effect negating the undone operations in line 60.

This version of the database system operates identically to the version that uses semaphores and message queues. However, it operates more quickly because no data is copied between an application and the kernel, and between the kernel and **dbms.**

By sharing physical memory, processes can communicate with one another by reading and writing that memory. Sharing memory is not enough, however, as a protocol that defines who has access to memory at any point must be used. The examples shown in this section again used semaphores to arbitrate access to a resource.

In summary, system calls form the lower level interface to the UNIX system, but they are both a blessing and a curse. For some programs, system calls are a blessing because they provide the control necessary to do some operations either not available in the Standard I/O library or available but not efficient enough to meet the program's needs. System calls are also a curse for these programs because system calls are known to be one of the more volatile aspects of the UNIX system and therefore subject to change as the UNIX system matures. Without question, system calls should be used only when no other programming option is available and then only by insulating the system call with a subroutine that has well defined inputs and outputs and a well defined function.

CHAPTER 8

PROGRAMMING THE BOURNE SHELL

A. INTRODUCTION

The software tools built so far have used subroutines and system calls to operate on data structures. These components have been "glued" together with the C language. You can also build software tools by gluing together system commands with the Bourne Shell programming language.

You might ask, "When should I use a command language to program a problem solution, and when should I use a conventional language?" There are no hard and fast rules for selecting one language over another, but the questions below can help you decide which approach is appropriate when developing a problem solution.

QUESTION 1: Does a tool or a combination of tools already exist that solves my problem? If one does, use it instead of writing your own. You should keep track of the tools in your tool kit, be they programs or subroutines.

QUESTION 2: Can some parts of my problem be solved with existing tools? If partial solutions do exist, use those tools, forge the ones you don't have with a programming language, and connect them together with a command language.

When you must forge a new tool, make sure you understand the problem you're trying to solve. A well-written program – one that adheres to the rules of structured programming and uses data structures in an efficient and elegant way – is of little use to anyone if it doesn't solve the defined problem.

Some command languages are good for building prototype versions of problem solutions. The prototype can be shown to those defining the problem as a way of achieving better understanding of the problem. Because command languages are usually interpreted rather than compiled by a command language processor, many different solutions can be built quickly. This is important when you are trying to understand a problem needing a computerized solution.

This chapter shows how to forge new tools using the Bourne Shell programming language. It complements the chapter on using the Bourne Shell interactively. Many of the techniques shown here also apply when you use the shell interactively.

A.1 Command Languages

Command languages provide a means for controlling the execution of programs by a computer. Some command languages offer few functions, for example, argument passing. Other languages offer several, such as file creation, conditional and iterative program execution, and operations on variables. Typically, programs written with command languages have limited portability and are usually customized to a specific computer environment.

One example of a command language is IBM's Job Control Language, also called JCL. Figure 8.A.1 shows the JCL procedure used to assemble, link-edit, and execute a program written in IBM's Basic Assembly Language.

```
 1  //ASM EXEC    PGM=IEUASM,PARM=LOAD
 2  //SYSLIB  DD DSNAME=SYS1.MACLIB,DISP=OLD
 3  //SYSUT1 DD UNIT=SYSSQ,SPACE=(1700,(400,50))
 4  //SYSUT2 DD UNIT=SYSSQ,SPACE=(1700,(400,50))
 5  //SYSUT3 DD UNIT=(SYSSQ,SEP=(SYSUT2,SYSUT1,SYSLIB)),
 6  //       SPACE=(1700,(400,50))
 7  //SYSPRINT    DD SYSOUT=A
 8  //SYSPUNCH DD SYSOUT=B
 9  //SYSGO  DD DSNAME=&LOADSET,UNIT=SYSSQ,SPACE=(80,(100,50)),
10  //       DSP=(MOD,PASS)
11  //LKEDEXEC    PGM=IEWL,PARM='XREF,LET,LIST,NCAL',
12  //       COND=(8,LT,ASM)
13  //SYSLIN  DD DSNAME=&LOADSET,DISP=(OLD,DELETE)
14  //       DD DDNAME=SYSIN
15  //SYSLMOD    DD DSNAME=&GOSET(GO),UNIT=SYSDA,
16  //       SPACE=(1024,(50,20,1)),DISP=(MOD,PASS)
17  //SYSUT1 DD UNIT=(SYSDA,SEP=(SYSLIN,SYSLMOD)),
18  //       SPACE=(1024,(50,20))
19  //SYSPRINT    DD SYSOUT=A,DCB=(BLKSIZE=121)
20  //GO       EXEC   PGM=*.LKED.SYSLMOD,COND=((8,LT,ASM),(4,LT,LKED))
```

Figure 8.A.1

This procedure contains three steps, named ASM, LKED, and GO. The first step executes the assembler, IEUASM, with the LOAD option enabled. The DD statements in this step define files needed by the assembler. The assembler's output is written to the file identified on the SYSGO DD statement.

Step 2, LKED, executes the linkage editor, IEWL, but only if the condition code returned by the ASM step is less than 8. The parameters XREF, LET, LIST, and NCAL are passed to IEQL via the PARM parameter. The assembler's output becomes input to the linkage editor as defined by the SYSLIN DD statement. When the linkage editor step ends, the assembler's output file is deleted as the DISP parameter shows.

The last step executes the load module created by the linkage editor, but only if the assembly step returned a condition code less than 8 and the linkage editor returned a condition code less than 4. The EXEC statement uses a backward reference to define the program to be executed.

JCL allows parameter passing, conditional execution, parameter substitution, and file creation and deletion. These features are common in command languages and provide the user enough flexibility to control program execution.

A.2 The Bourne Shell Command Language

The Bourne Shell language is a command language because it has features common to many command languages. These features let you control program execution. The Bourne Shell language is also a programming language because it has features common to many programming languages. These features let you write programs in a straightforward and structured way. Because of this union of features, the Bourne Shell is well-suited to writing structured programs that control program execution.

The command language features of the Bourne Shell are briefly explained below.

- PROGRAM EXECUTION - The Bourne Shell lets you execute programs sequentially and in parallel.

- FILE CREATION - The Bourne Shell can create new files and add to existing files.

- ARGUMENT PASSING - The Bourne Shell lets you pass arguments to the programs it invokes via the command line and the environment.

- CONDITIONAL PROGRAM EXECUTION - The Bourne Shell lets you execute programs based on the success or lack of success of other programs.

- PREDEFINED PROCEDURES - The Bourne Shell lets you build scripts that define a sequence of programs to be executed.

- PARAMETERIZATION - The Bourne Shell lets you write scripts using shell variables so that your scripts are more general.

Similarly, the Bourne Shell programming language features are listed and explained below.

- VARIABLES - The Bourne Shell lets you define variables and do operations on them.

- STRUCTURED LANGUAGE CONSTRUCTS - The Bourne Shell provides sequence, selection, and iteration language constructs.

- SCOPE - The Bourne Shell lets you restrict the places where variables and programs are known.

- MACRO SUBSTITUTION - The Bourne Shell provides a macro expansion and file include facility.

- SUBROUTINES - The Bourne Shell lets you write and call subroutines and it allows recursion.

This chapter concentrates on the programming language features of the Bourne Shell and builds on the command language features described in Chapter 3.

You can build command files that control program execution. These files are called shell procedures, shell scripts, or simply scripts. We refer to a special class of shell procedures to as simple shell procedures because they use only the command language features of the Bourne Shell. Figure 8.A.2 shows a simple shell procedure, named **numon**, that prints the number of people currently logged in to the UNIX system. **numon** uses **who** to report on who is logged into the system and wc to count the lines in the report. The result is the number of people currently logged in.

```
$ number numon
1    ###############################
2    #    numon
3    #    print number of people
4    #    currently logged in
5    ###############################
6    who | wc -l
7    exit 0
$ ▯
```

Figure 8.A.2

B. SIMPLE SHELL PROCEDURES

A shell procedure is a file that contains commands for the shell to execute. We define a simple shell procedure as a shell procedure that uses only the command language features of the Bourne Shell.

Shell procedures are called by many names such as shell programs, shell scripts, shell command files, shell files, and shells. All are synonymous with the name shell procedure as defined above.

B.1 Command Files

Figure 8.B.1 shows a simple shell procedure that prints information useful at login time.

```
$ number loginfo1
1   ###############################
2   #   loginfo
3   #   print information useful
4   #   at login time - version 1
5   ###############################
6   echo "The current date and time: \c"
7   date
8   echo "The number of users: \c"
9   who | wc -l
10  echo "Personal stat: \c"
11  who am I
12  exit 0
$ ▢
```

Figure 8.B.1

loginfo1 reformats the date and time, the number of people currently logged in, and a brief description of who you are into a more readable form. This file is nothing more than a list of commands that could be individually entered each time you login to the UNIX system. For convenience, they have been collected into a file named **loginfo1** and can be executed by typing **loginfo1** in response to the shell's prompt.

Similarly, **fcount**, shown below, prints the number of files in the current directory.

```
$ number fcount1
1   ###############################
2   #   fcount
3   #   count files in current
4   #   directory - version 1
5   ###############################
6   ls -l | sed 1d | wc -l
7   exit 0
$ ▢
```

Figure 8.B.2

fcount1 uses ls to list all files in the current directory, **sed** to remove the total line printed by **ls**, and **wc** to count the remaining lines. **fcount1** is a file that contains a list of commands that can be collectively referred to by a single name.

B.2 Executing Shell Files

There are two ways to execute shell files. Both are important to understand because the steps you explicitly follow in the first method are identical to the steps implicitly taken by the shell in the second method.

B.2.a Invoking with sh You can cause the shell to execute a shell file by giving the shell file name as an argument to another instance of the shell. This new shell reads the file, executes the commands listed, and ends when all commands have been executed. Figure 8.B.3 shows how **fcount** can be executed using this method.

```
$ sh fcount
14
$ □
```

Figure 8.B.3

This method has advantages and disadvantages. The advantages are that various debugging and tracing options can be selected without changing the commands listed in the shell file. At times this is important, especially if you don't have permission to edit the shell file to add the debugging commands you need.

There are two disadvantages, however. The first is that you must remember that you are trying to execute a shell file instead of a binary file. You must remember to start a new shell and give it the name of the file you want to execute.

The second disadvantage is that the new shell expects a full path name as the name of the file to execute. You must also remember where the shell file is stored in the file system.

Because of these disadvantages, the method described next is common and recommended. However, explicitly invoking the shell to execute a shell file does have its place when debugging that file.

B.2.b Using chmod to make a file executable A shell procedure file can be made executable by adding execute and read permissions to that file. Figure 8.B.4 shows how to make the **fcount** shell file executable using the **chmod** program.

```
$ chmod u=rwx,go=rx fcount
$ ls -l fcount
total 1
-rwxr-xr-x   1 rogers   writers      37 May  5 13:55 fcount
$ □
```

Figure 8.B.4

Notice that write permission is given only to the owner of the shell procedure file. On your system, you may want to allow others to change the commands listed in the file, so add write permission as appropriate.

When a shell file is made executable with **chmod**, you can invoke it as though it were an executable binary file, as shown below.

```
$ fcount
14
$ □
```

Figure 8.B.5

The login shell searches all directories listed in the PATH variable, just as it does when you invoke an executable binary file. The only difference between the modes of an executable shell file and the modes of an executable binary file is the requirement for read permission.

To understand why read permission is important, recall from the last section that a new instance of the shell must be started to read the file to execute commands. When you invoke a command, the login shell first assumes that the command is stored as a binary file. The login shell tells the operating system to execute it. If the operating system can't execute the file, the login shell then assumes the command is a shell file. It starts a new instance of the shell and gives the command's file name to that shell. This new shell must be able to read the file to execute the commands listed in the file. If the new shell can't read the file, it ends without executing anything, even though the file was marked executable. Therefore, to let someone execute a software tool you have forged using the shell, add read and execute permissions to the shell procedure file.

B.3 Some Simple Shell Procedures

Two more examples of simple shell procedures are shown below. The first, **mkjob**, is a simple shell procedure that remakes an executable binary file named *job*. This type of simple shell procedure is useful in maintaining other commands.

```
$ number mkjob
 1  ##############################
 2  #    mkjob
 3  #    build system
 4  ##############################
 5  cd
 6  cd compile/p1
 7  cc -c *.c
 8  cd ../p2
 9  cc -c *.c
10  cd ..
11  cc p1/*.o p2/*.o
12  cp a.out job
13  strip job
14  chmod 755 job
15  echo Job remake complete
16  exit 0
$ ▢
```

Figure 8.B.6

The second, **lsl**, is a simple shell procedure that merely enables the l option for the **ls** command. This type of shell procedure reduces the number of characters you need to enter at the keyboard and is useful when certain combinations of programs and options are often required.

```
$ number lsl
 1  ##############################
 2  #    lsl
 3  #    ls command with long
 4  #    listing enabled
 5  ##############################
 6  ls -l
 7  exit 0
$ ▢
```

Figure 8.B.7

C. SHELL VARIABLES REVISITED

To this point, all shell procedures shown as examples are simple shell procedures and each does only a single function. As a way of review and as a way to make these shell procedures more versatile, some will be revised to use shell variables as introduced in Chapter 3.

There are five basic types of shell variables. They are listed below, along with a short definition.

1. USER-DEFINABLE - These are variables defined as needed by the syntax name=value.

2. POSITIONAL PARAMETER - These are variables given as arguments to a shell procedure.

3. PREDEFINED - These are variables defined by the shell. Examples are the number of arguments passed to a shell procedure and the current process identification number.

4. COMMAND SUBSTITUTION - These are variables made from commands surrounded by grave accents. A variable's value is the standard output of the enclosed command.

5. PARAMETER SUBSTITUTION - These are variables whose values are dependent on other variables.

C.1 User-Definable

Figure 8.C.1 below shows version 2 of the **loginfo** command from section B.

```
$ number loginfo2
 1  ##############################
 2  #   loginfo
 3  #   print information useful
 4  #   at login time - version 2
 5  ##############################
 6  TIME="The current date and time: \c"
 7  USERS="The number of users: \c"
 8  ME="Personal stat: \c"
 9  echo "$TIME"
10  date
11  echo "$USERS"
12  who | wc -l
13  echo "$ME"
14  who am I
15  exit 0
$ loginfo2
The current date and time: Thu Jun 21 18:55:36 EDT 1984
The number of users: 1
Personal stat: rogers     tty11      Jun 21 18:18
$ □
```

Figure 8.C.1

In this version, all strings are first defined as variables on lines 6, 7, and 8, and then used in lines 9, 11, and 13. Because each string contains blanks, each definition value is enclosed in double quotes. Each string reference is also enclosed in double quotes. This forces the shell to pass the \c substring to the **echo** command without first removing the \.

C.2 Positional Parameters

Figure 8.C.2 shows version 2 of the **fcount** shell procedure.

```
$ number fcount2
 1  ##############################
 2  #   fcount
 3  #   count files in current
 4  #   directory - version 2
 5  ##############################
 6  ls -l $1 | sed 1d | wc -l
 7  exit 0
$ ls
csubs
fcount
loginfo
psubs
svtest
$ fcount2
5
$ ☐
```

Figure 8.C.2

This version uses the first positional parameter, named $1 and assumed to be a directory file name, as an argument to the **ls** command. Notice that if no arguments are given to **fcount**, the command assumes a reasonable default, the current directory.

Chapter 5 recommends that you select reasonable default values. Don't assume that the user of your software tools will always supply all the information you need. **fcount** benefits from this programming philosophy by letting **ls** use its built-in default values if no arguments are given.

C.3 Predefined

svtest, figure 8.C.3, is a new example that uses the predefined shell variables.

```
$ number svtest
 1  ###############################
 2  #    svtest
 3  #    predefined shell
 4  #    variables test
 5  ###############################
 6  echo The number of arguments is $#.
 7  date&
 8  echo The process id of the date command was $!.
 9  wait
10  echo The process id of this shell is $$.
11  grep root /etc/passwd
12  echo The return code from grep was $?.
13  echo The current set of options is $-.
$ ▯
```

Figure 8.C.3

Running **svtest** produces the following:

```
$ chmod u=rwx,go=rx svtest
$ ls -l svtest
total 1
-rwxr-xr-x   1 rogers  writers      374 May  9 12:09 svtest
$ svtest a b c
The number of arguments is 3.
Thu Jun 21 18:57:54 EDT 1984
The process id of the date command was 413.
The process id of this shell is 411.
root::0:1:0000-Admin(0000):/:
The return code from grep was 0.
The current set of flags is .
$ sh -ek svtest
The number of arguments is 0.
Thu Jun 21 18:58:12 EDT 1984
The process id of the date command was 421.
The process id of this shell is 419.
root::0:1:0000-Admin(0000):/:
The return code from grep was 0.
The current set of flags is ek.
$ ▯
```

Figure 8.C.4

The first invocation passes 3 arguments to **svtest** and the second enables the e and k options before executing **svtest**.

C.4 Command Substitution

csubs, figure 8.C.5, uses command substitution to add information to the **echo** commands in lines 5 and 7.

```
$ number csubs
1    ###############################
2    #   csubs
3    #   Command substitution
4    ###############################
5    echo The number of people currently logged in is 'who | wc -l'.
6    VT100='cat /etc/ttytype | grep vt100 | sed "s/vt100 //"'
7    echo VT100 terminals are: $VT100
8    exit 0
$ □
```

Figure 8.C.5

In line 5, the: **who I wc -l** command is executed first and its standard output replaces the string:

    `who | wc -l`

The **echo** command is then invoked as:

    echo The number of people currently logged in is 1.

and prints:

    The number of people currently logged in is 1.

In line 6, the *letc/ttytype* file is assumed to contain lines with two elements per line. Each line relates a terminal name (e.g., tty00, tty7), to a terminal type (e.g., vt100 for a Digital Equipment Corporation VT-100 crt). Elements are separated by a single space character.

When line 6 is executed, **grep** first selects from its standard input all lines containing the string vt100. **grep** passes the selections on to the stream editor **sed**. **sed** then removes the string vt100 and the space character. This produces a list of terminal names separated by newline characters. The shell replaces newlines by spaces when it assigns the resulting string to VT100. When executed, **csubs** prints:

$ **csubs**
The number of people currently logged in is 1.
VT100 terminals are: tty11
$ ☐

Figure 8.C.6

C.5 Parameter Substitution

The Bourne Shell provides a parameter substitution facility that lets you conditionally test the value of parameters and shell variables. The substitutions allowed are:

SYNTAX	DESCRIPTION
${*parameter-word*}	If *parameter* is set, then substitute its value; otherwise substitute *word*.
${*parameter=word*}	If *parameter* is not set, then set it to *word*; the value of the parameter is then substituted. Positional parameters ($1, $2, etc.) may not be assigned to in this way.
${*parameter?word*}	If *parameter* is set, then substitute its value; otherwise, print *word* and exit from the shell. If *word* is omitted, then a standard message is printed.
${*parameter+word*}	If *parameter* is set, then substitute *word*; otherwise substitute nothing.

Figure 8.C.7 shows the **psubs** shell procedure that uses parameter substitution variables.

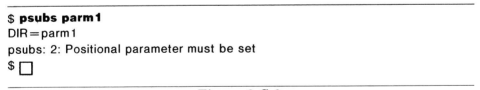

```
$ number psubs
 1  ##############################
 2  #   psubs
 3  #   parameter substitution
 4  ##############################
 5  DIR=${1-$HOME}
 6  echo DIR=$DIR
 7  echo 2=${2?"Positional parameter must be set"}
 8  TMP=/tmp/$$
 9  T=${TMP+"a legal value"}
10  echo TMP=$T
11  T=${FRED+nothing}
12  echo FRED=$FRED
13  exit 0
$ □
```

Figure 8.C.7

In line 5, DIR is assigned the value of HOME variable or the value of the first positional parameter, depending on whether the first positional parameter is set to any value, including the null string. DIR is printed in line 6.

Line 7 shows how you can use parameter substitution to display an error message. If the second positional parameter is not set, the phrase:

  Positional parameter must be set

is printed as shown below.

```
$ psubs parm1
DIR=parm1
psubs: 2: Positional parameter must be set
$ □
```

Figure 8.C.8

Notice that the shell procedure exits immediately after printing the message. This is useful when a shell procedure requires a variable to be set before going on.

Finally, lines 8 through 12 use another type of parameter substitution. The shell tests if the parameters TMP and FRED are set and if so, substitutes the word after the plus operator. Figure 8.C.9 shows an example of execution.

```
$ psubs parm1 parm2
DIR=parm1
2=parm2
TMP=/tmp/1375
FRED=
$ ▢
```

Figure 8.C.9

Shell variables should be used when writing shell procedures because they help to make your programs easier to read and understand. You should follow the programming guidelines for naming shell variables – use lower case letters only – and defining manifest constants – use upper case letters only – when you forge a software tool with the shell.

D. CONDITIONAL TESTS

You can specify that certain commands will be executed depending on the results of other commands. Often, you need this kind of control when you are writing a shell procedure. For example, you may want to print an error message when commands can't do a required job. Conditional tests are one way in the shell to execute commands based on the results of other commands.

Every command executed in the UNIX system returns a number that the shell's conditional tests can use to control the execution of other commands. The number zero, also called true, means that the command executed successfully. All other numbers, collectively called false, mean that the command was unsuccessful. Unfortunately, this assignment of zero for true and non-zero for false is opposite from the conventions used when evaluating C language expressions, where zero means false and non-zero means true. This chapter uses the terms true and false rather than specific numbers in its explanations of conditional tests and structured looping.

A program written using the C language and a program written using the shell both return true and false with the **exit** statement. Figure 8.D.1 shows two C language programs that return true and false respectively, and figure 8.D.2 shows the equivalent programs written with the shell.

```
$ number true.c
 1  /*
 2   *   C language version of the command true
 3   */
 4
 5  #define     TRUE        0
 6
 7  main()
 8  {
 9      exit(TRUE);
10  }
$ number false.c
 1  /*
 2   *   C language version of the command false
 3   */
 4
 5  #define     FALSE       1
 6
 7  main()
 8  {
 9      exit(FALSE);
10  }
$ ▯
```

Figure 8.D.1

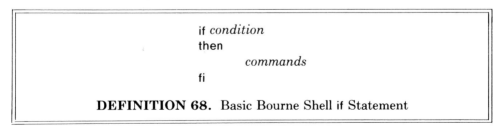

```
$ number true
1   ###############################
2   #   true
3   #   Shell version of the
4   #   true command - always
5   #   returns true
6   ###############################
7   TRUE=0
8   exit $TRUE
$ number false
1   ###############################
2   #   false
3   #   Shell version of the
4   #   false command - always
5   #   returns false
6   ###############################
7   FALSE=1
8   exit $FALSE
$ ☐
```

Figure 8.D.2

Every software tool you forge should clearly define true and false. Each tool should use **exit** statements to return the appropriate value. Unfortunately, not all commands in the UNIX system return true and false consistent with the job they do. Those commands that treat true and false inconsistently cannot be used in conditional tests and structured loops in shell scripts.

D.1 Simple Conditional - if

The first shell programming statement that uses true and false is the if statement. Its basic syntax is:

---

if *condition*
then
      commands
fi

DEFINITION 68. Basic Bourne Shell if Statement

If the command *condition* returns true, *commands* are executed. Notice especially the coding style that places the then and if keywords on separate lines and indents all commands in *commands*.

Figure 8.D.3 shows the **inpass1** shell procedure as an example of the if statement.

```
$ number inpass1
1    ################################
2    #   inpass
3    #   check password file for
4    #   login - version 1
5    ##############################
6    NAME=${1-root}
7    BB=/dev/null
8    if grep $NAME /etc/passwd > $BB 2> $BB
9    then
10       echo $NAME is in password file
11   fi
12   exit 0
$ □
```

Figure 8.D.3

inpass1 determines if the login name specified by the NAME variable is in the */etc/passwd* file and prints a message if it is. NAME defaults to root if no argument is given. **inpass1** uses the **grep** command, which returns true if the pattern given as the first argument occurs anywhere in the file given as the second argument, and false otherwise. Both the standard output and standard error files from **grep** are redirected to the "bit bucket" so that **inpass1** prints only a specific message or no message at all. **inpass1** always returns true.

inpass1 prints a message only if the login name occurs in */etc/passwd*, i.e. when **grep** returns true. Printing a message when **grep** returns false may be equally important. The shell also provides the ability to execute commands when a *condition* command returns false by specifying an else clause to the if statement. A more complete syntactic specification of the if statement is:

---

if *condition*
then
        true__commands
else
        false__commands
fi

DEFINITION 69. Advanced Bourne Shell if Statement

If the *condition* command returns true, the *true__commands* are executed; but if the *condition* returns false, the *false__commands,* which are optional, are executed. Again, notice the recommended coding style that places the else keyword on a separate line and indents *false__commands.*

Figure 8.D.4 shows version 2 of **inpass**.

```
$ number inpass2
 1  ###############################
 2  #   inpass
 3  #   check password file for
 4  #   login - version 2
 5  ###############################
 6  NAME=${1-root}
 7  BB=/dev/null
 8  if grep $NAME /etc/passwd > $BB 2> $BB
 9  then
10      echo $NAME is in password file
11  else
12      echo $NAME is not in password file
13  fi
14  exit 0
$ ☐
```

Figure 8.D.4

In version 2, a message is also printed if the login name cannot be found in */etc/passwd*.

Imagine that **inpass2** must be extended to check the group file, */etc/group*, for the login name, but only if the name cannot be found in the password file. Because the shell allows nesting of if statements, **inpass2** can be revised, as figure 8.D.5 shows, to do this job.

```
$ number inpass3
 1  ###############################
 2  #   inpass
 3  #   checks password file
 4  #   for login, and failing
 5  #   that, checks group file
 6  #   version 3
 7  ###############################
 8  NAME=${1-root}
 9  BB=/dev/null
10  if grep $NAME /etc/passwd > $BB 2> $BB
11  then
12      echo $NAME is in password file
13  else
14      if grep $NAME /etc/group > $BB 2> $BB
15      then
16          echo $NAME is in group file
17      else
18          echo $NAME is not in either
19          echo password or group file
20      fi
21  fi
22  exit 0
$ □
```

Figure 8.D.5

The shell provides an alternative way to code version 3 of **inpass** by using the keyword elif. elif is a "contraction" of else and if that does not introduce a new if statement. The complete syntax of the if statement is as follows.

```
             if condition__1
             then
                      commands__1
             elif condition2
             then
                      commands__2
             elif condition__3
             then
                      commands__3

                  .

                  .

                  .

             else
                      commands__n
             fi
```

DEFINITION 70. Complete Bourne Shell if Statement

All

```
    elif condition__i
    then
             commands__i
```

clauses are optional as is the

```
    else
             commands__n
```

clause. There is no limit to the number of elif clauses attached to an if statement.

inpass4 is shown below and its operation is identical to that of version 3.

```
$ number inpass4
 1   ################################
 2   #   inpass
 3   #   checks password file
 4   #   for login, and failing
 5   #   that, checks group file
 6   #   version 4
 7   ################################
 8   NAME=${1-root}
 9   BB=/dev/null
10   if grep $NAME /etc/passwd > $BB 2> $BB
11   then
12       echo $NAME is in password file
13   elif grep $NAME /etc/group > $BB 2> $BB
14   then
15       echo $NAME is in group file
16   else
17       echo $NAME is not in either
18       echo password or group file
19   fi
20   exit 0
$ ☐
```

Figure 8.D.6

Finally, certain programs in the UNIX system – most notably the **make** program – allow shell procedures but restrict them to only a single line. The syntax below shows how to "punctuate" a single-line if statement.

> if *condition*; then *command__a; command__b; ...;* fi
>
> **DEFINITION 71.** Single Line Bourne Shell if Statement

While single-line if statements are not recommended, sometimes there is no choice, so you should be familiar with the correct syntax.

D.2 Conditional Control - test

The last section described the shell's if statement and used the notation *condition* to reference any command that returns true and false. One program that is especially useful as a *condition* in an if statement is the **test** program. **test** is a program that evaluates the expression given as arguments to **test** and returns true if the expression is true and false otherwise. Expressions can be simple, such as testing two numbers for equality, or complex, such as testing several sub-conditions and relating them with logic operators. The **test** program is particularly useful when writing shell procedures.

Simply stated, the **test** program tests things. Among the things that can be tested are:

- Command Execution
- Numeric Values
- String Values
- Files

These types are explained in the next four sections.

D.2.a Command execution **inpass** can be further revised to use the **test** program as figure 8.D.7 shows.

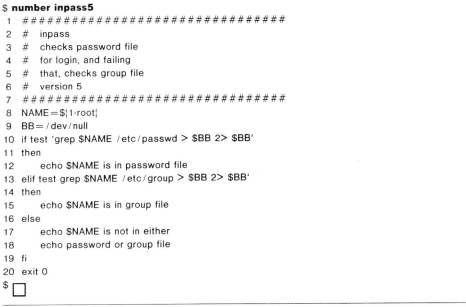

```
$ number inpass5
 1  ###############################
 2  #   inpass
 3  #   checks password file
 4  #   for login, and failing
 5  #   that, checks group file
 6  #   version 5
 7  ###############################
 8  NAME=${1-root}
 9  BB=/dev/null
10  if test 'grep $NAME /etc/passwd > $BB 2> $BB'
11  then
12      echo $NAME is in password file
13  elif test grep $NAME /etc/group > $BB 2> $BB'
14  then
15      echo $NAME is in group file
16  else
17      echo $NAME is not in either
18      echo password or group file
19  fi
20  exit 0
$ ☐
```

Figure 8.D.7

In this example, **test** returns true if **grep** returns true, or false if **grep** returns false. Using **test** and command substitution is unnecessary, as **grep** returns true or false as appropriate.

D.2.b Numeric values You can compare two numbers algebraically with the **test** program. Six operators are available and they are:

-eq   Equal
-ne   Not equal
-gt   Greater than

-ge   Greater than or equal to
-lt   Less than
-le   Less than or equal to

You can combine expressions comparing numbers with the logic operators and (-a), or (-o), and not (!). Figure 8.D.8 shows the shell procedure **postage** that computes the postage for a third class letter weighing less than 16 ounces. It uses the numeric value comparison operators and logic operators.

```
$ number postage
1  ##############################
2  #   postage
3  #   compute third class postage rate
4  ##############################
5  if test $# -ne 1 -o "$1" -lt 1 -o "$1" -gt 16
6  then
7       echo usage: $0 weight
8       RC=1
9  else
10      if test $1 -le 1
11      then
12          cost=.20
13      elif test $1 -gt 1 -a $1 -le 2
14      then
15          cost=.37
16      elif test $1 -gt 2 -a $1 -le 3
17      then
18          cost=.54
19      elif test $1 -gt 3 -a $1 -le 4
20      then
21          cost=.71
22      elif test $1 -gt 4 -a $1 -le 6
23      then
24          cost=.85
25      elif test $1 -gt 6 -a $1 -le 8
26      then
27          cost=.95
28      elif test $1 -gt 8 -a $1 -le 10
29      then
30          cost=1.05
31      elif test $1 -gt 10 -a $1 -le 12
32      then
33          cost=1.15
34      elif test $1 -gt 12 -a $1 -le 14
35      then
36          cost=1.25
37      elif test $1 -gt 14 -a $1 -le 16
38      then
39          cost=1.35
40      fi
41      echo The cost of a $1 ounce, third class item is \$cost.
42      RC=0
43  fi
44  exit $RC
$ □
```

Figure 8.D.8

Quotes surround the positional parameter in line 5 so that the arguments passed to **test** can be correctly checked. See the next section for a complete explanation. Figure 8.D.9 shows an example.

```
$ postage
usage: postage weight
$ echo $?
1
$ postage 5
The cost of a 5 ounce, third class item is $.85.
$ echo $?
0
$ postage 9
The cost of a 9 ounce, third class item is $1.05.
$ ☐
```

Figure 8.D.9

Notice that **postage** returns false when you invoke it improperly and true when called correctly.

D.2.c String values You can also compare strings with the **test** command, but only for equality, inequality, zero, and non-zero length. To distinguish between numeric comparisons and string comparisons, **test** provides a different set of operators. They are:

=	Equality
!=	Inequality
-z string	Zero length
-n string	Non-zero length

As a word of caution, always enclose string variables used in comparisons in quotes. If the string variable STRING is of zero length, coding

```
test -z $STRING
```

will produce the diagnostic

```
test: argument expected
```

because the shell substitutes the null string for $STRING. The proper way to code the expression is:

```
test -z "$STRING"
```

Enclosing a string variable in quotes insures a proper test, even if the variable contains spaces or tabs.

376

Figure 8.D.10 shows a shell procedure that uses string comparisons.

```
$ number namer
1   ##############################
2   #   namer
3   #   makes comments on the first
4   #   argument, assumed to be
5   #   a name
6   ##############################
7   if test $# -ne 1 -o -z "$1"
8   then
9       echo usage: $0 non__zero__string
10      RC = 1
11  else
12      echo "The name you have selected is\c"
13      if test "$1" = bob -o "$1" = Bob
14      then
15          echo " $1."
16      elif test "$1" != tom -a "$1" != Tom
17      then
18          echo "n't tom or Tom, it's $1."
19      else
20          echo " $1."
21      fi
22      RC = 0
23  fi
24  exit $RC
$ □
```

Figure 8.D.10

Figure 8.D.11 shows **namer**.

```
$ namer
usage: namer non__zero__string
$ echo $?
1
$ namer tom
The name you have selected is tom.
$ echo $?
0
$ namer Tom
The name you have selected is Tom.
$ namer fred
The name you have selected isn't tom or Tom, it's fred.
$ ☐
```

Figure 8.D.11

Again, notice that **namer** returns true if invoked properly, and false otherwise. Also notice that more than one string is recognized for tom and bob. Where possible, accept variations on a correct answer, especially when both upper and lower case mean the same thing to your tool. It's only a small amount of extra work for you to add alternatives, but the users of your tool will appreciate your efforts.

D.2.d Files **test** can also test file characteristics, such as file type, file size, and protections. The table below shows the attributes that can be checked.

ATTRIBUTE	MEANING
-r *file*	*file* exists and is readable
-w *file*	*file* exists and is writable
-f *file*	*file* exists and is not a directory
-d *file*	*file* exists and is a directory
-s *file*	*file* exists and has a size greater than zero
-c *file*	*file* exists and is a character special file
-b *file*	*file* exists and is a block special file
-p *file*	*file* exists and is a fifo file
-u *file*	*file* exists and has the set-user-ID bit set
-g *file*	*file* exists and has the set-group-ID bit set
-k *file*	*file* exists and has the sticky bit set

Checking a file before accessing it in a shell procedure is recommended. If a file cannot be accessed, you can print a message so that the user can fix the problem before re-running your tool. Chapter 5 recommends that you always tell a user how to fix an error. This self-teaching nature of a tool is important because the user doesn't have to refer to an auxiliary document to find what he or she did wrong. Your tool has told what's wrong and how to fix it.

Figure 8.D.12 shows the shell procedure **filet** that makes comments on the file given as the first argument.

```
$ number filet
 1  ##############################
 2  #   filet
 3  #   comment on a file
 4  ##############################
 5  if test $# != 1 -o -z "$1"
 6  then
 7      FILE=.
 8  else
 9      FILE="$1"
10  fi
11  echo $FILE is:
12  if test -r "$FILE"
13  then
14      echo " readable, "
15  fi
16  if test -w "$FILE"
17  then
18      echo " writable, "
19  fi
20  if test -f "$FILE"
21  then
22      echo " a regular file, "
23  fi
24  if test -d "$FILE"
25  then
26      echo " a directory, "
27  fi
28  if test -s "$FILE"
29  then
30      echo " and has more than zero bytes."
31  else
32      echo " and is zero bytes long."
33  fi
34  exit 0
$ ☐
```

Figure 8.D.12

Running **filet** produces:

$ **filet**
. is:
 readable,
 writable,
 a directory,
 and has more than zero bytes.
$ **filet /bin/ls**
/bin/ls is:
 readable,
 a regular file,
 and has more than zero bytes.
$ ☐

Figure 8.D.13

Finally, **test** also has an alias that you may see in shell procedures. Instead of coding:

    if test $# -ne 1 -o "$1" -lt 1 -o "$1" -gt 10

you can say

    if [$# -ne 1 -o "$1" -lt 1 -o "$1" -gt 10]

It must be surrounded by spaces just like **test** or any other command name. The right bracket (]) serves as a delimiter. It is required and must be preceded by a space, but can be followed by a space, tab, or newline.

E. STRUCTURED LOOPING

The examples shown in the last section used one kind of conditional control statement available in the Bourne Shell. Unfortunately, those examples allowed commands to be executed only once. This section describes the three iteration control statements in the Bourne Shell, namely while, until, and for. These statements allow commands to be executed as long as the specified condition holds.

E.1 The while Loop

The first looping control statement we discuss is the while statement. Its operation is identical to that of the while construct in the C language, and its syntax is shown below.

> while *condition*
> do
>   *commands*
> done
>
> **DEFINITION 72.** The Bourne Shell while Statement

The *commands* inside the while loop are repeatedly executed as long as the *condition* command returns true. *commands* should effect the *condition* command in some way so that *condition* eventually returns false, otherwise an infinite loop will result.

Notice the coding style. Both the do and done keywords are on separate lines and *commands* are indented.

Figure 8.E.1 shows another variation of the **inpass** shell procedure.

```
$ number inpass6
1   ################################
2   #   inpass
3   #   check password file for
4   #   login - version 6
5   ################################
6   BB = /dev/null
7   echo "Name: \c"
8   while read NAME
9   do
10      if grep "$NAME" /etc/passwd > $BB 2> $BB
11      then
12          echo "$NAME" is in password file
13      else
14          echo "$NAME" is not in password file
15      fi
16      echo "Name: \c"
17  done
18  echo
19  exit 0
$ ▯
```

Figure 8.E.1

This version uses the **read** command that is built into the shell. **read** is explained in section H of this chapter. For now, assume that **read** reads a line from standard input and assigns that line to the shell variable named as the argument. **read** returns false when end-of-file (^D) is read from standard input, and true otherwise.

inpass6 is executed below.

```
$ inpass6
Name: bin
bin is in password file
Name: root
root is in password file
Name: fred
fred is not in password file
Name: ^D
$ ☐
```

Figure 8.E.2

The until loop has no corresponding construct in the C language, but is similar to the shell's while loop. Its syntax is:

---

until *condition*
do
         commands
done

DEFINITION 73. The Bourne Shell until Statement

The until loop causes the enclosed commands to be executed until *condition* is true. Expressed as a while loop, the until control statement is identical to the following:

while [*!condition*]
do
         commands
done

Recall that [] is an alias for the **test** program and that ! is the negation logical operator. This loop continues to execute while the negated value of *condition* is true, i.e. until *condition* returns true.

parg is an example of a shell procedure using the until loop. It uses a new program, **expr**, and another built-in command, **shift**.

```
$ number parg
 1  ##############################
 2  #   parg
 3  #   print arguments to a
 4  #   shell file
 5  ##############################
 6  NUMBER=0
 7  until [ $# = 0 ]
 8  do
 9      NUMBER='expr $NUMBER + 1'
10      echo Argument $NUMBER is $1
11      shift
12  done
13  exit 0
$ ▢
```

Figure 8.E.3

expr is a program whose arguments are taken as an expression and after evaluation, it writes the result on the standard output. In **parg**, **expr** is used to increment the shell variable NUMBER. **expr** also allows subtraction, division, and multiplication of its arguments.

shift is a built-in command that renames all positional parameters variables as follows: $2 becomes $1, $3 becomes $2, etc. Further, the count of arguments to a shell procedure, $#, is decreased by one each time **shift** is executed, until it becomes zero.

In **parg**, the until loop continues until no arguments remain. An example of execution is shown below.

```
$ parg arg1 arg2 arg3
Argument 1 is arg1
Argument 2 is arg2
Argument 3 is arg3
$ parg
$ ▢
```

Figure 8.E.4

The while and until loops can also be coded on a single line when required. The correct syntax is:

384

while *condition*; do *command_1; command_2; ...;* done

DEFINITION 74. Single Line Bourne Shell while Statement

E.2 The for Loop

The last iterative loop is the for loop. It is different from the for loop in the C language, where you provide an initialization, a condition, and a modification. With the Bourne Shell's for loop, you must provide a list of values that the loop variable will assume. The for loop will be executed once for each value in the list.

The syntax of the for loop is:

for *name* [in *word* ...]
do
        commands
done

DEFINITION 75. The Bourne Shell for Statement

The shell variable *name* assumes the value of each *word* in the list, and *commands* are executed once per *word*. Notice especially the coding style that places the do and done keywords on separate lines and indents commands.

A for loop that prints all integers between 1 and 10 inclusive is shown below.

```
1    for integer in 1 2 3 4 5 6 7 8 9 10
2    do
3            echo $integer
4    done
```

Figure 8.E.5

Another version of **inpass** that uses a for loop is shown in figure 8.E.6.

```
$ number inpass7
 1  ###############################
 2  #   inpass
 3  #   check password file for
 4  #   login - version 7
 5  ###############################
 6  BB = / dev / null
 7  for NAME in $@
 8  do
 9      if grep "$NAME" /etc/passwd > $BB 2> $BB
10      then
11          echo "$NAME" is in password file
12      else
13          echo "$NAME" is not in password file
14      fi
15  done
16  exit 0
$ inpass7 bin root fred
bin is in password file
root is in password file
fred is not in password file
$ □
```

Figure 8.E.6

This version checks to see if each login name argument is in the password file. The predefined variable $@ is short-hand for "$1" "$2" ..., and is used in for loops to specify a *word* list.

The for loop can also be expressed as a single line as shown below.

for *name* [in *word* ...]; do *command; command; ...;* done

DEFINITION 76. Single Line Bourne Shell for Statement

A final example of the for loop is shown in figure 8.E.7.

```
$ number OD1
 1   ###############################
 2   #   OD
 3   #   general interface to
 4   #   the od command
 5   #   version 1
 6   ###############################
 7   BB = / dev / null
 8   for arg
 9   do
10       if expr "$arg" : "^-.*" > $BB 2> $BB
11       then
12           OPTIONS = "$OPTIONS'echo $arg | sed s/.//'"
13           PREFIX = -
14       else
15           NAMES = "$NAMES$arg "
16       fi
17   done
18   if [ -z "$NAMES" ]
19   then
20       od $PREFIX$OPTIONS
21   else
22       for file in $NAMES
23       do
24           echo " = = = = =$file"
25           od $PREFIX$OPTIONS $file
26       done
27   fi
28   exit 0
$ □
```

Figure 8.E.7

This shell procedure was written because the octal dump program, **od**, does not understand command lines given according to the Standard Command Format defined in Chapter 5. **OD1** translates this standard format into a format that **od** understands.

OD1 highlights several new ideas, the first of which is an alternate form of the for loop. The for loop that begins on line 8 does not use the in keyword or the *word* list. Instead, the shell successively assigns each argument given to **OD1** to the shell variable arg, one per iteration through the *commands* contained in the for loop. This form is especially useful in handling shell procedure arguments individually.

OD1 also uses a different form of the **expr** program. **expr** is used in line 10 to compare two strings, where one string is defined by a regular expression. Regular expressions are used frequently by UNIX system commands, so you should become familiar with them. Examples of commands that use regular expressions are the text editors **ex** and **vi** and the selector program **grep**. Their manual pages explain the syntax and meaning of regular expressions.

The regular expression shown in this example matches all strings, here shell procedure arguments, that begin with a dash (-). Recall from Chapter 5 that an option begins with a dash. **expr** returns true if the current shell procedure argument, $arg, is an option, and false otherwise. The if statement on line 10 then selects all options given to **OD1**.

Lines 12 and 15 use what is called a string accumulator. A string accumulator builds a new string by adding a new element onto the end of the old string. Line 12 accumulates all options given to **OD1**, after first removing the leading dash, in the variable OPTIONS. Line 15 accumulates all file name arguments in the variable NAMES. Notice that individual elements in NAMES are separated by a single space, but options saved in OPTIONS are not.

When the for loop completes, OPTIONS contains all options and NAMES contains all file names. The variable PREFIX shows that there are options stored in OPTIONS and is used in lines 20 and 25. PREFIX must be dependent on the presence of options stored in OPTIONS because **od** does not understand a single dash as an option selecting no options.

Line 18 tests for file names. If no file names were given, **od** is invoked with only the options accumulated in OPTIONS. **od** then dumps standard input according to these options.

If file names were given, the for loop in line 22 is executed. The variable file assumes each file name stored in the NAMES word list. Remember that all file names were separated by spaces when accumulated in NAMES. The for loop is necessary because **od** can dump only one file per invocation. **echo** is used to display the file name passed to each invocation of **od**. Figure 8.E.8 shows a sample execution.

```
$ echo this is a test > testfile
$ OD1 -c -b testfile
= = = = =testfile
0000000   t   h   i   s       i   s       a       t   e   s   t  \n  \0
        164 150 151 163 040 151 163 040 141 040 164 145 163 164 012 000
0000017
$ □
```

Figure 8.E.8

E.3 Loop Control

The Bourne Shell also provides the break and continue loop control statements analogous to those found in the C language. break exits the enclosing while, until, or for loop and continue resumes the next iteration for such a loop. break and continue apply to only while, until, and for loops. The shell ignores break and continue in all other contexts.

Figure 8.E.9 shows the **getnum** shell procedure as an example of a procedure that uses break.

```
$ number getnum
 1  ###############################
 2  #   getnum
 3  #   prompts, reads, and
 4  #   validates a number from
 5  #   standard input
 6  ###############################
 7  BB = /dev/null
 8  TTY = /dev/tty
 9  while true
10  do
11      echo "Enter a number: \c" > $TTY
12      read NUMBER
13      if [ $? = 1 ]
14      then
15          NUMBER=$1
16      fi
17      if expr "$NUMBER" : "^[0-9][0-9]*\$" > $BB 2> $BB
18      then
19          break
20      else
21          echo "Number ($NUMBER) not all digits" > $TTY
22      fi
23  done
24  echo $NUMBER
25  exit 0
$ 
```

Figure 8.E.9

getnum prompts for a string containing characters drawn only from the digits 0 through 9 inclusive. If no string is given, then the first argument is used. **expr** on line 17 insures that the string entered is a legal number, that is a non-null string that has at least one digit drawn from the characters 0 through 9 inclusive. Illegal numbers produce a message as line 21 shows.

getnum prints the number entered on standard output, so **getnum** can be used as a command substitution variable. For example, in

389

NUM='getnum 15'

NUM contains either the number entered through the keyboard or the value of the argument, here 15, if end-of-file is entered.

Notice that lines 11 and 21 connect all standard output references to the terminal where **getnum** is running. This lets **getnum** display messages no matter where **getnum**'s standard output file has been redirected. The special file /dev/tty always refers to the terminal where a process is running, and it cannot be redirected.

E.4 Unstructured Looping

The Bourne Shell does not provide a goto statement or a label definition statement. Sometimes, even well-structured shell procedures need some form of a goto to end a loop or a procedure. For example, a goto would be helpful when an error condition occurs and the appropriate action is to clean up and end the script.

As one solution to this problem, the Bourne Shell does provide variations on the break and continue statements. These variations use break and continue as defined in the last section, but add to them a numeric argument. The argument tells how many levels of enclosing while, until, and for loops are to be exited if the statement is a break, or where to resume the next iteration of a loop if the statement is a continue.

A second solution to this problem is to use **exit** statements throughout a shell procedure. Every shell procedure shown in this chapter uses only one **exit** statement, and it is always at the end of the procedure. Each could use **exit** statements when it was impossible to continue in the procedure. Instead, conditional statements were used to deal with error conditions. A shell variable RC was used to contain the value to be returned by the procedure. While the latter method is recommended, sometimes an **exit** statement is appropriate and does not sacrifice the shell procedure's readability.

E.5 Multi-Way Branching - The case Statement

The Bourne Shell also provides a case statement which selectively executes a set of commands from a list of commands. The syntax of the case statement is:

```
                    case word  in
                    pattern__1 )
                              commands__1
                              ;;
                    pattern__2 )
                              commands__2
                              ;;
                      .
                      .
                      .
                    esac
```

DEFINITION 77. The Bourne Shell case Statement

pattern__i is a regular expression that uses the special characters defined for file name generation in Chapter 3, namely *, ?, and []. Further, *pattern__i* can be made from several regular expressions, each separated by a vertical bar, |. The shell interprets the vertical bar as a logical OR operator, and *word* is said to match *pattern__i* if it matches any regular expression in *pattern__i*. The pattern * matches every *word* and can be thought of as the way to specify the default case.

When the shell executes a case statement, it compares *word* with each successive pattern until either *word* matches *pattern__i* or the shell finds the keyword esac. The shell then executes the commands associated with the matching pattern and transfers control to the first command after esac, if no other transfer statements (i.e., break, continue, or **exit**) are executed.

The shell's case statement differs from the switch statement in the C language in the following ways:

1. A case in the shell cannot fall through to another case as it can in the C language.

2. The default case should be last in the shell. In the C language, the default case can be anywhere within a switch statement.

3. Multiple patterns are given with | in the shell. The C language also allows multiple case entrance expressions, but the syntax is different.

4. The break statement does not effect the shell's case statement directly, but it may end a case if the case statement resides in a structured loop. In the C language, break causes an immediate exit from a switch statement irrespective of its context.

Figure 8.E.10 shows version 2 of the **OD** command developed previously.

```
$ number OD2
 1   ###############################
 2   #   OD
 3   #   general interface to
 4   #   the od command
 5   #   version 2
 6   ###############################
 7   for arg
 8   do
 9       case $arg in
10       -*)
11           OPTIONS="$OPTIONS'echo $arg | sed s/.//'"
12           PREFIX=-
13           ;;
14       *)
15           NAMES="$NAMES$arg "
16           ;;
17       esac
18   done
19   if [ -z "$NAMES" ]
20   then
21       od $PREFIX$OPTIONS
22   else
23       for file in $NAMES
24       do
25           echo "=====$file"
26           od $PREFIX$OPTIONS $file
27       done
28   fi
29   exit 0
$ □
```

Figure 8.E.10

This version uses the case statement instead of an if statement and **expr** to match a string with a pattern. Version 2 is faster than version 1 because the case statement, and therefore all pattern matching, is executed entirely in the shell. Version 1 had to execute the **expr** command to determine if an argument begins with a dash.

Since shell procedures can be invoked just like executable binary files, shell procedures should also recognize arguments given in the Standard Command Format as defined in Chapter 5. Unfortunately, even with the if, while, until, for, and case statements and shell variables, it is difficult to write a shell procedure that recognizes this format.

The **scf** program, shown in figure 8.E.11, is a useful program that translates arguments given in the Standard Command Format to a form easily managed by shell procedures. This form is identical to the form produced by the **scf**() subroutine.

```
$ number scf.c
 1   /*
 2    *   scf
 3    *       translate arguments into the standard command
 4    *       format and print on standard output
 5    */
 6
 7   #include    <stdio.h>
 8
 9   #define    USAGE       "option__names option__arg__names arguments"
10
11   main(argc, argv)
12   int argc;
13   char *argv[];
14   {
15       int rc = 0, i;
16       char *t, **nargv;
17
18       if (argc < 4) {
19           fprintf(stderr, "usage: %s %s\n", argv[0], USAGE);
20           rc = 1;
21       } else {
22           t = argv[0];
23           argv[0] = argv[2];
24           argv[2] = t;
25           nargv = argv;
26           nargv += 2;
27           argc -= 2;
28           if (scf(argv[1], argv[0], &argc, &nargv)) {
29               for (i = 1; i < argc; i++) {
30                   fputs(nargv[i], stdout);
31                   fputc((i + 1 != argc ? ' ' : '\n'), stdout);
32               }
33               scfend();
34           } else {
35               rc = 1;
36           }
37       }
38       exit(rc);
39   }
$ □
```

Figure 8.E.11

Figure 8.E.12 shows version 3 of **OD** that uses the **scf** program.

```
$ number OD3
 1  ###############################
 2  #   OD
 3  #   general interface to
 4  #   the od command
 5  #   version 3, using scf
 6  ###############################
 7  set -- 'scf bcdox "" $*'
 8  if [ $? -ne 0 ]
 9  then
10      echo "usage: $0 -bcdox [file]"
11      RC=1
12  else
13      RC=0
14      for arg in $*
15      do
16          case $arg in
17          --)
18              shift
19              break
20              ;;
21          -[bcdox])
22              OPTIONS="$OPTIONS'echo $arg | sed s/.//'"
23              PREFIX=-
24              shift
25              ;;
26          esac
27      done
28      if [ $# -eq 0 ]
29      then
30          od $PREFIX$OPTIONS
31      else
32          for file in $*
33          do
34              echo "=====$file"
35              od $PREFIX$OPTIONS $file
36          done
37      fi
38  fi
39  exit $RC
$ □
```

Figure 8.E.12

In line 7, **scf** is invoked to reformat the arguments according to the option string, bcdox, and the option argument string, "". The option string lists all valid options, and the option argument string names all options that take an option argument. All other arguments are assumed to be file names, and options and file names are separated by double dashes in the reformatted version.

The **set** built-in function used in line 7 redefines the positional parameters to the string returned by **scf**. The first argument – -- – forces **set** to treat the rest of the line as arguments and not options for **set**. For example, if:

```
$1 = -a
$2 = -bvalue
$3 = file
```

then **set** and **scf**, called as:

```
set -- 'scf ab b $*'
```

redefines the positional parameters as:

```
$1 = -a
$2 = -b
$3 = value
$4 = --
$5 = file
```

These arguments can be easily handled with a for loop and a case statement.

The for loop in line 14 scans the new list of arguments as established in line 7. The case statement beginning in line 16 looks at each argument individually. Two argument types are expected: options and the double dash separator.

The for loop beginning in line 15 defines the word list to be the arguments as reformatted by **scf** in line 7. The **shift** commands in lines 18 and 24 do not affect the argument list that defines the word list in line 15 but they do affect the argument list that defines the word list in line 32 and the number of file names as defined by $# in line 28.

When the options and the separator are recognized by the for loop and case statement, all that remains are the names of the files to be dumped by **od**. If no file names are given, i.e. when $# equals 0, **od** dumps the standard input file, as line 30 shows. If there are file names, the for loop on line 32 assigns each file name to the file variable, and the commands in the loop display the file name and cause **od** to dump the file's contents according to the specified options.

F. DEBUGGING SHELL PROCEDURES

Debugging shell procedures uses two basic techniques: enabling the **x** option and adding **echo** statements to the shell procedure. The **x** option, enabled as:

```
sh -x shell_procedure options option_arguments file_names
```

causes the shell to show the commands as executed, but does not show flow-control statements. Adding **echo** statements to display information is analogous to adding **printf**() calls to programs written in C. Each basic technique is applied to the example shown in figure 8.F.1.

```
$ number OD4a
 1   ###############################
 2   #   OD
 3   #   general interface to
 4   #   the od command
 5   #   version 4a
 6   ###############################
 7   RC=0
 8   for arg
 9   do
10       case $arg in
11       --)
12           shift
13           break
14           ;;
15       -*)
16           shift
17           echo $arg is not a legal option
18           RC=1
19           ;;
20       -[bcdox])
21           shift
22           OPTIONS="$OPTIONS'echo $arg | sed s/.//'"
23           PREFIX=-
24           ;;
25       *)
26           break
27           ;;
28       esac
29   done
30   if [ $RC -eq 1 ]
31   then
32       echo "usage: $0 [-bcdox] [file ...]"
33   elif [ $# = 0 ]
34   then
35       od $PREFIX$OPTIONS
36   else
37       for file
38       do
39           echo "=====$file"
40           od $PREFIX$OPTIONS $file
41       done
42   fi
43   exit $RC
$ ☐
```

Figure 8.F.1

This example is another version of **OD**. It does not use **set** and **scf** to reformat arguments, but chooses instead to handle arguments directly.

A sample execution is shown below.

$ **echo testing** | **OD4a -c -b**
-c is not a legal option
-b is not a legal option
usage: OD4a [-bcdox] [file ...]
$ ☐

Figure 8.F.2

Whoops! **OD4a** says that c and b are not legal options, but then shows it to be legal in the usage error message. There must be a bug in **OD4a**.

As a first way to isolate the problem, explicitly invoke the shell to execute **OD** and turn on the x option. This is shown below.

$ **echo testing** | **sh -x OD4a -c -b**
RC=0
+ shift
+ echo -c is not a legal option
-c is not a legal option
RC=1
+ shift
+ echo -b is not a legal option
-b is not a legal option
RC=1
+ [1 -eq 1]
+ echo usage: OD4a [-bcdox] [file ...]
usage: OD4a [-bcdox] [file ...]
+ exit 1
$ ☐

Figure 8.F.3

All lines beginning with plus signs (+) represent commands as they are executed by the shell.

When the case statement on line 10 is executed, both the -c and -b arguments match the -* pattern, so the associated commands on lines 16 through 18 are executed. Why are these commands executed instead of those on lines 21 through 23? More specifically, why do -c and -b match -* and not -[bcdox]?

The problem is that some of the patterns and commands in the case statement are in the wrong order. Recall that the shell finds -* first, and since

398

-c and -b match it, the associated commands are executed. Patterns should progress from most restrictive to least restrictive, and -[bcdox] is more restrictive than -*.

Another way to enable the x option is with the **set** statement. The command:

    set -*options*

enables options and the command:

    set +*options*

disables them.

In long shell procedures, you can be swamped by unnecessary debugging information produced by the shell when the x option is enabled for the entire procedure. You can reduce debugging output by bracketing the section of code in question with set −x / set +x. This technique lets you concentrate your efforts where you suspect the problem is in a shell procedure.

The second technique for debugging shell procedures is to add **echo** statements to display additional information and to show the flow of control through a procedure. **OD4b**, modified by **echo** statements, is shown below.

```
$ number OD4b
 1  ###############################
 2  #  OD
 3  #  general interface to
 4  #  the od command
 5  #  version 4
 6  ###############################
 7  RC=0
 8  for arg
 9  do
10      case $arg in
11      --)
12          echo "= = = = =$arg matches --"
13          shift
14          break
15          ;;
16      -*)
17          echo "= = = = =$arg matches -*"
18          shift
19          echo $arg is not a legal option
20          RC=1
21          ;;
22      -[bcdox])
23          echo "= = = = =$arg matches -[bcdox]"
24          shift
25          OPTIONS="$OPTIONS'echo $arg | sed s/.//'"
26          PREFIX=-
27          ;;
28      *)
29          echo "= = = = =$arg matches *"
30          break
31          ;;
32      esac
33  done
34  if [ $RC -eq 1 ]
35  then
36      echo "usage: $0 [-bcdox] [file ...]"
37  elif [ $# = 0 ]
38  then
39      od $PREFIX$OPTIONS
40  else
41      for file
42      do
43          echo "= = = = =$file"
44          od $PREFIX$OPTIONS $file
45      done
46  fi
47  exit $RC
$ □
```

Figure 8.F.4

When executed, **OD4b** displays:

```
$ echo testing | OD4b -c -b
=====-c matches -*
-c is not a legal option
=====-b matches -*
-b is not a legal option
usage: OD4b [-bcdox] [file ...]
$ ▢
```

Figure 8.F.5

From this, we see that -c and -b match a different pattern than intended, and conclude that cases are in the wrong order.

The debugged version is shown below.

```
$ number OD4
1  ##################################
2  #   OD
3  #   general interface to
4  #   the od command
5  #   version 4
6  ##################################
7  RC=0
8  for arg
9  do
10    case $arg in
11    --)
12        shift
13        break
14        ;;
15    -[bcdox])
16        shift
17        OPTIONS="$OPTIONS'echo $arg | sed s/.//'"
18        PREFIX=-
19        ;;
20    -*)
21        shift
22        echo $arg is not a legal option
23        RC=1
24        ;;
25    *)
26        break
27        ;;
28    esac
29  done
30  if [ $RC -eq 1 ]
31  then
32      echo "usage: $0 [-bcdox] [file ...]"
33  elif [ $# = 0 ]
34  then
35      od $PREFIX$OPTIONS
36  else
37      for file
38      do
39          echo "=====$file"
40          od $PREFIX$OPTIONS $file
41      done
42  fi
43  exit $RC
$ □
```

Figure 8.F.6

When executed, **OD4** produces:

```
$ echo testing | OD4 -c -b
0000000  t   e   s   t   i   n   g  \n
        164 145 163 164 151 156 147 012
0000010
```

$ ☐

Figure 8.F.7

which is as expected.

G. TRAP HANDLING

A *TRAP* is a mechanism used to catch something, be it a trap used to catch an animal or a trap used to catch a UNIX system signal. In both examples, *springing* the trap causes something to happen.

Traps in the Bourne Shell are conceptually identical to the **signal**() system call interface used in C language programs. The only difference is in the things that can happen when a trap or signal is sprung.

In the system call interface, reception of a signal causes control to be transferred to a previously identified subroutine. That subroutine then *handles* the signal and can cause control to be returned to where it came from. The interrupted code segment need not be aware of the signal.

In the Bourne Shell, reception of a signal causes control to be transferred to a previously identified set of commands. These commands can also handle the signal, as can the subroutine in C, but the commands cannot cause control to be returned to where it came from. The interrupted command must be restarted, if possible, to recover from the signal.

G.1 Review of Signals

The UNIX system defines nineteen signals. These are listed in Section C of Chapter 7.

Restarting an interrupted command in a shell procedure is difficult. Because of this, traps are typically used to disable signal reception in critical sections of a shell procedure and to remove temporary files built by shell procedures. The signals commonly used to stop shell procedures are hangup, interrupt, and software termination.

G.2 Syntax of the trap Command

The syntax of the **trap** command is:

---

trap *commands signals*

DEFINITION 78. The Bourne Shell trap Command

---

commands is a list of commands to be executed when *signals* are received by a shell procedure. *signals* is a list of signal numbers separated by spaces. When a signal in the *signals* list is received, *commands* are executed.

Neither the segmentation violation signal (11) nor the kill signal (9) are allowed in *signals*. Further, a special signal, numbered 0, is triggered when a shell procedure exits.

A signal can be handled in three different ways. A signal can be ignored, caught, or reset to its original value. The **trap** command allows for each, as the following shell procedure segment shows:

```
$ number traptest
 1     ###############################
 2     #       Ignore interrupt and
 3     #       software termination
 4     ###############################
 5     trap "" 2 15
 6     ###############################
 7     #       Reset hangup to its
 8     #       default value
 9     ###############################
10     trap 1
11     ###############################
12     #       Catch zero to remove
13     #       a temporary file
14     ###############################
15     trap "rm /tmp/$$; exit 0" 0
...
$ 
```

Figure 8.G.1

G.4 Special Considerations

Not all signals have meaning when caught with the **trap** command. For example, if a command executed by a shell procedure raises a floating point exception, the shell procedure is not informed of the condition via the trap mechanism. Instead, the shell procedure must examine the command's return code. Unfortunately, the command may have been designed so that the return code does not reflect the floating point exception if it was caught by the command with the **signal**() system call. The key point is that signals received by a shell procedure are sent from outside the procedure rather than from within. Those signals that are usually sent from outside a procedure are hangup, interrupt, quit, and software termination.

trap is especially useful when temporary files must be removed before a shell procedure exits. The shell procedure segment below shows a recommended way of naming temporary files and setting traps to insure their removal when signals are received.

```
1       TMP = /tmp/$$
2       trap "rm -f $TMP; trap 0; exit 1" 1 2 3 15
3       trap "rm -f $TMP; exit 0" 0
4       cat /dev/null > $TMP
...
```

Figure 8.G.2

Temporary files should be placed in the */tmp* directory and file names should use the process number of the creating process, available as the $$ predefined shell variable, to insure a unique file name, as line 1 shows. Traps should be set to remove temporary files when hangup, interrupt, quit, and software termination signals are received, and on procedure exit.

Line 2 defines that when any of the hangup, interrupt, quit, or the software termination signals are received, the temporary file is removed with **rm**, the special trap is canceled, and the shell procedure exits with false. Line 3 defines that when the shell procedure ends and raises signal 0, the temporary file is removed and the command returns true. If the special trap had not been canceled in line 2, the **exit** statement in line 2 would raise signal 0. This would cause the trap set in line 3 to be sprung, resulting in the removal of the temporary file and the value true to be returned as the value of the shell procedure.

Line 4 shows a command that uses the temporary file defined in line 1. Shell procedures should not use temporary files before executing **trap** statements to remove them. If the example above were coded as below, the temporary file could be created before the **trap** statements in lines 3 and 4 were executed.

```
1    TMP = /tmp/$$
2    cat /dev/null > $TMP
3    trap "rm -f $TMP; trap 0; exit 1" 1 2 3 15
4    trap "rm -f $TMP; exit 0" 0
```

Figure 8.G.3

If a hangup, interrupt, or software termination signal were received before the **trap** commands were executed, the temporary file would remain after the shell procedure exited. This practice is not recommended, so follow the example shown in figure 8.G.2 when using temporary files.

H. BUILT-IN SHELL COMMANDS

The Bourne Shell contains several built-in commands. Those discussed in the following sections are **eval**, **exec**, **shift**, **read**, **readonly**, **export**, **trap**, **wait**, and dot (.).

H.1 eval

When the shell executes the **eval** statement, **eval**'s arguments are read by the shell and the commands specified are executed. Under certain conditions, **eval** is the only way to execute certain types of command strings. For example, consider the shell procedure segment in the figure below.

```
1    PRINT = "| lpr"
2    pr /etc/passwd $PRINT
```

Figure 8.H.1

The shell passes both the pipe symbol, |, and the string lpr as arguments to the **pr** program. To force the shell to interpret the information in PRINT as a command, use **eval** as shown below.

```
1    PRINT = "| lpr"
2    eval pr /etc/passwd $PRINT
```

Figure 8.H.2

eval's arguments are read and interpreted by the shell. All commands found are then executed.

406

H.2 exec

When the shell encounters the **exec** statement, it executes the commands given as arguments by starting those commands in place of the shell. For example, in the following shell procedure:

```
$ number mydate
1   ##############################
2   #   mydate
3   #   execute the date command
4   #   indirectly
5   ##############################
6   exec date
7   echo "This command is never executed."
$ mydate
Mon May  7 08:29:28 EDT 1984
$
```

Figure 8.H.3

the **date** program replaces the shell which was started to read and execute the commands listed in the **mydate** shell procedure. When **date** completes, the process created to execute the shell procedure – originally the shell – also completes. When a new command is started in place of the shell, the rest of the shell procedure is discarded. Therefore, the **echo** statement in line 7 is never executed.

H.3 shift

shift causes the positional parameters $2, $3, ..., to be renamed $1, $2, ... Further, the number of shell parameters, $#, is reduced by one. See figure for an example of a shell procedure that uses the **shift** command.

H.4 read

The **read** command causes one line to be read from the standard input and divided into words. The first word is assigned to the first argument to **read**, the second word to the second argument, and so on. All remaining words are assigned to the last argument. **read** returns true unless end-of-file is read.

Figure 8.H.4 shows how the IFS variable can be redefined to control how an input line is divided into words.

```
$ number pwfmt
 1   ##############################
 2   #   pwfmt
 3   #   reformat the password
 4   #   file
 5   ##############################
 6   IFS=":"
 7   sed "s/$IFS$IFS/$IFS $IFS/g" < /etc/passwd | \
 8   while read LOGIN PASSWORD UID GID GCOS DIR SHELL
 9   do
10       if [ -z "$SHELL" ]
11       then
12           SHELL=/bin/sh
13       fi
14       echo "Name: $LOGIN"
15       echo "User ID: $UID"
16       echo "Group ID: $GID"
17       echo "GCOS Field: $GCOS"
18       echo "Directory: $DIR"
19       echo "Shell: $SHELL"
20   done
21   exit 0
$ ex /etc/passwd
"/etc/passwd" 11 lines, 317 characters
:1p
root::0:0::/:
:q
$ pwfmt
Name: root
User ID: 0
Group ID: 0
GCOS Field:
Directory: /
Shell: /bin/shell
DELETE
$□
```

Figure 8.H.4

IFS is defined to be only colon, the character that separates fields in
/etc/passwd. Because the shell treats consecutive field separators as a single
separator, the stream editor **sed** must precondition the password file by adding
a non-separator – space – between consecutive separators. Line 7 shows this.
Notice also that the standard input of the while loop that begins in line 8 is
changed to the output of the **sed** command using a pipe line.

read in line 8 then reads lines from the output of **sed**. Each line is broken
into words and assigned to the parameters given to **read**. The if statement in
line 10 assigns the string /bin/sh to SHELL, the default command to be

408

executed if the shell field is left blank in *etc/passwd*. The **echo** statements in lines 14 through 19 print the reformatted version of the password file.

H.5 readonly

The **readonly** built-in shell command lets you mark user-defined shell variables as unchangeable. The value of the variables named as arguments to **readonly** are fixed at the time **readonly** is executed. If an assignment statement attempts to change a **readonly** shell variable, the shell prints

> *name*: is read only

and does not do the assignment. **readonly** with no arguments lists all read-only shell variables. There is no way to "un-readonly" a shell variable.

H.6 export

Each process in the UNIX system has an environment. An environment is a list of name/value pairs that are passed to each child process from its parent process. User-defined shell variables are placed into the environment of a process by naming them as arguments to the **export** built-in command in the parent process.

For example, figure 8.H.5 shows the **childproc** shell procedure that prints the value of the EDITOR variable from the environment.

```
$ number childproc
1   ################################
2   #   childproc
3   #      display editor selected
4   ################################
5   echo The editor you have selected is $EDITOR.
6   exit
$ export
export HOME PATH MAIL
$ childproc
The editor you have selected is .
$ EDITOR=vi
$ export EDITOR
$ export
export HOME PATH MAIL EDITOR
$ childproc
The editor you have selected is vi.
$ □
```

Figure 8.H.5

The first time **childproc** is invoked, EDITOR is not in the environment because it is not in the list of variables named when **export** is invoked with no arguments. **childproc** prints an incomplete message. The second time it is invoked, EDITOR is in the environment, so **childproc** prints its value.

Recall that Chapter 5 emphasizes that a software tool user may not always provide all information needed by a program. Reasonable default values should be defined. The **echo** statement in line 5 should be coded as shown below to use this concept.

```
echo The editor you have selected is ${EDITOR-vi}.
```

The parameter substitution variable ${EDITOR-vi} has the value $EDITOR, if defined, or **vi**, if $EDITOR is undefined. In either case, **echo** prints a complete message.

If a child process changes the value of an exported variable, the new value is passed to its child processes only by re-executing the **export** command. Variables placed in the environment by a child process are NOT inherited by the parent process.

H.7 trap

The **trap** built-in command has been explained in section G. Section J shows an extended example of shell procedures that use the **trap** command.

H.8 wait

The **wait** built-in command causes the shell to wait for completion of all child processes started with &. **wait** always returns true. Figure 8.H.6 below shows a shell procedure that starts the **date** command with & and prints a message before **date** completes. The shell procedure then waits for **date** to finish before going on.

```
$ number nowait
1  ###############################
2  #   nowait
3  #   start command without
4  #   waiting for last to finish
5  ###############################
6  (sleep 5; date)&
7  echo This is a test of the wait command
8  wait
9  echo Date is now finished
10 exit 0
$ nowait
This is a test of the wait command
Mon May  7 08:31:11 EDT 1984
Date is now finished
$ □
```

Figure 8.H.6

H.9 . (dot)

The dot built-in command causes the shell to read and execute the commands listed in the file named as the argument. This file is assumed to be a shell procedure. The shell looks in the directories listed in the PATH variable for the file named as the argument.

The file is executed as though the commands listed in the file were entered in place of the dot command. For example, if *filea* contains:

```
$ number filea1
1   # # # # # # # # # # # # # # # # # # # # # # # # # # # # # #
2   #   filea
3   #   print a short message
4   #   version 1
4   # # # # # # # # # # # # # # # # # # # # # # # # # # # # # #
5   . fileb
6   echo $A $B $C
$
```

Figure 8.H.7

and *fileb* contains:

```
$ number fileb
1   # # # # # # # # # # # # # # # # # # # # # # # # # # # # # #
2   #   fileb
3   #   set shell variables
4   # # # # # # # # # # # # # # # # # # # # # # # # # # # # # #
5   A = This
6   B = "is an"
7   C = example
$
```

Figure 8.H.8

then executing *filea* is the same as executing the following:

411

```
$ number filec
1    ###############################
2    #    filec
3    #    a merge of filea and fileb
4    ###############################
5    A = This
6    B = "is an"
7    C = example
8    echo $A $B $C
$ □
```

Figure 8.H.9

When *filea1* is executed it produces:

```
$ filea1
This is an example
$ □
```

Figure 8.H.10

If *filea2* invoked *fileb* normally, as shown below:

```
$ number filea2
1    ###############################
2    #    filea
3    #    print a short message
4    #    version 2
4    ###############################
5    fileb
6    echo $A $B $C
$ □
```

Figure 8.H.11

the user-defined shell variables A, B, and C would be set in *fileb*, but would not affect the A, B, and C variables in *filea2*. The **echo** statement in *filea2* wouldn't print anything, as the variables would have no values in that shell procedure.

The shell procedure shown in figure 8.J.2 uses the dot command as a way to define variables needed other places in that procedure and in other procedures. Dot resembles a subroutine call in a conventional programming language and is especially useful when many shell procedures must share a common set of variables. A single file that defines the value of the variables can be created. Dot commands can then be used in each shell procedure to execute the variable-defining file. When a variable's value must be changed, the change is localized to one file. All shell procedures that use the file need not be altered.

I. ERROR HANDLING

The Bourne Shell can detect several different types of errors that shell procedures must be prepared to handle. Among these errors are:

- Non-existent or unexecutable commands.

- Failed redirection.

- Commands ending abnormally.

- Commands returning false values.

For the first three error types, the shell displays a message on the standard error file of the shell procedure, and the shell procedure continues. To force a shell procedure to end when any of these types of errors occur, enable the e option with the **set** command. A message will still be printed, but the shell will stop executing commands from the shell procedure immediately.

The last type of error occurs when a command returns false. Treatment of these errors depends on the command used and its context. With some commands, false means that the command could not do the job requested. For example, if the **grep** command cannot find any lines in its input stream containing a specific pattern, it returns false. In the **inpass** shell procedures shown earlier in this chapter, false causes a message to be displayed or some other action to be taken. False in this context means something to the shell procedure and is not an "error."

When false does imply some type of error, a shell procedure may display a message explaining the problem and proposing a solution. These messages are error messages and should appear in the standard error file. Commands that normally write to standard output can be redirected to standard error with the 1>&2 redirection operator. Figure 8.I.1 shows another version of the **OD** command where all error messages are written on standard error.

```
$ number OD3
 1  ################################
 2  #   OD
 3  #   general interface to
 4  #   the od command
 5  #   version 3, using scf
 6  ################################
 7  set -- `scf bcdox "" $*`
 8  if [ $? -ne 0 ]
 9  then
10      echo "usage: $0 -bcdox [file]" 1>&2
11      RC=1
12  else
13      RC=0
14      for arg in $*
15      do
16          case $arg in
17          --)
18              break
19              shift
20              ;;
21          -[bcdox])
22              OPTIONS="$OPTIONS`echo $arg | sed \"s/.//\"`"
23              PREFIX=-
24              shift
25              ;;
26          esac
27      done
28      if [ $# -eq 0 ]
29      then
30          od $PREFIX$OPTIONS
31      else
32          for file in $*
33          do
34              echo "=====$file"
35              od $PREFIX$OPTIONS $file
36          done
37      fi
38  fi
39  exit $RC
$ []
```

Figure 8.I.1

J. A LAST EXAMPLE

This section defines a problem, and shows and explains its solution as programmed using the Bourne Shell. Those parts of the solution shown here are complete, but not all parts of the solution are given. You are encouraged to

414

enter the shell procedures shown and to program those portions not shown. Remember that your solutions should be consistent with the partial solutions given here, with respect to the treatment of errors, command values, and files. Especially remember that your solution must solve the problem as defined in the paragraphs that follow.

The problem to be solved is to build a user-friendly system, called STORES, that helps you record and manage your department store catalogue orders. The set of operations needed is:

● ORDERING - You can order an item from any store catalogue, e.g., Sears, Penney's, or Wards. Further, you can order several items, including items previously ordered but not received. Each complete order should be kept separately from other orders, as a store typically fills one order at a time. The information needed for ordering each item from a store is the stock number, the quantity, a brief description (duplicate orders need not have identical descriptions), the unit cost, and the ordering catalogue's page number. You should be allowed to edit a complete order to fix any typographical errors. Further, a master list of all items not received should be maintained. This list must include the date ordered and the store ordered from. Soon, home computers will be able to transfer the order electronically to the store. Until then, orders must be printed on the line printer and carried there.

● RECEIVING - The store, stock number, and quantity received become the key into the system. When you have picked up the items you've ordered from the store, you need to post receipt of an order. The system adjusts the list of items not yet received as appropriate. Remember that the same item may be ordered several times before any items are received. Finally, the system should also maintain a master list of all items received, along with the date received and the store name.

● ITEMS NOT RECEIVED - You may need a listing of items not received, either listing all items or listing items for a specific store. The system should display an item, and then let the you decide whether to continue listing items or stop.

● ITEMS RECEIVED - This function should use the items received master list, and should operate the same as the ITEMS NOT RECEIVED function.

● ITEM QUERY - You may need to know when an item was received and its cost. This type of information may be needed for insurance purposes, for example. The system should provide a function that lets you look through the items received master list, either one item at a time or by supplying some part of the description. The system should also let you decide whether to continue or stop after each item is listed.

● HELP - The system should provide a separate help function that tells you how to use the system. In addition, each function must help you when you supply illegal information.

The STORES system should have only a single interface point so that you need enter only one command. STORES requires the information listed below.

FIELD	DEFINITION
NAME	The user's name.
ADDRESS	The user's street address.
CITY	The user's city.
STATE	The user's state and zip code.
ORDERDIR	A directory where orders are saved.
RECEIVED	A file used to store the received master list.
NRECEIVED	A file used to store the not received master list.
EDITOR	The user's favorite editor.

As recommended in Chapter 5, this information must not be requested each time STORES is run. Instead, it should be stored as user-defined variables, using the names given above, in a file named *.stores*. This file should be located in the user's home directory.

STORES should check that all files do exist and that they have the appropriate file permissions. STORES should create any missing files and establish permissions as necessary.

STORES should prompt for a function and should accept all reasonable alternatives. The user should be allowed to leave STORES at any time by entering DELETE or RUBOUT through the keyboard, by hanging up the telephone, or by sending STORES the software termination signal. Finally, STORES should guard those parts of the system that are sensitive to interruption. Figure 8.J.1 shows all shell procedures and the flow of files through STORES.

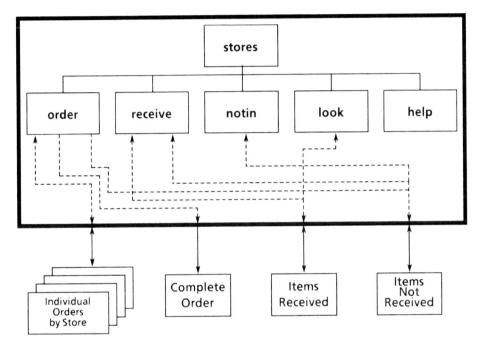

Figure 8.J.1

J.1 The stores Command

The main program in the STORES system is the **stores** program, and it is shown in figure 8.J.2.

```
$ number stores
 1  ###############################
 2  #   ORDER SYSTEM
 3  #   Order items from store catalogues
 4  #   Main order system command
 5  ###############################
 6  #   Command defaults
 7  ###############################
 8  OFILE=".stores"
 9  BB=/dev/null
10  ###############################
11  #   Pick up variables for this user
12  ###############################
13  if [ ! -r $HOME/$OFILE ]
14  then
15      echo No "$OFILE" file in your HOME directory
16      echo Please answer the following questions and I will build one for you.
17      while true
18      do
19          echo "Your name: \c"
20          read NAME
21          if [ $? = 1 -o -z "$NAME" ]
22          then
23              echo Invalid name - enter again
24          else
25              break
26          fi
27      done
28      while true
29      do
30          echo "Your mailing street address: \c"
31          read ADDRESS
32          if [ $? = 1 -o -z "$ADDRESS" ]
33          then
34              echo Invalid street address - enter again
35          else
36              break
37          fi
38      done
39      while true
40      do
41          echo "The city you live in: \c"
42          read TOWN
43          if [ $? = 1 -o -z "$TOWN" ]
44          then
45              echo Invalid city - enter again
46          else
47              break
48          fi
49      done
50      while true
51      do
```

418

```
52        echo "The state you live in, with zip code: \c"
53        read STATE
54        if [ $? = 1 -o -z "$STATE" ]
55        then
56              echo Invalid state/zip - enter again
57        else
58            break
59        fi
60    done
61    echo "A directory where orders can be saved ($HOME/orders): \c"
62    read ORDERDIR
63    if [ -z "$ORDERDIR" ]
64    then
65        ORDERDIR=$HOME/orders
66    fi
67    echo "A file where a list of received items is stored (received): \c"
68    read RECEIVED
69    if [ -z "$RECEIVED" ]
70    then
71        RECEIVED=received
72    fi
73    echo "A file where a list of items not received is stored (nreceived): \c"
74    read NRECEIVED
75    if [ -z "$NRECEIVED" ]
76    then
77        NRECEIVED=nreceived
78    fi
79    echo "Your favorite editor (vi): \c"
80    read EDITOR
81    if [ -z "$EDITOR" ]
82    then
83        EDITOR=vi
84    fi
85    echo NAME="\"$NAME\"" > $HOME/$OFILE
86    echo ADDRESS="\"$ADDRESS\"" >> $HOME/$OFILE
87    echo TOWN="\"$TOWN\"" >> $HOME/$OFILE
88    echo STATE="\"$STATE\"" >> $HOME/$OFILE
89    echo ORDERDIR="\"$ORDERDIR\"" >> $HOME/$OFILE
90    echo RECEIVED="\"$RECEIVED\"" >> $HOME/$OFILE
91    echo NRECEIVED="\"$NRECEIVED\"" >> $HOME/$OFILE
92    echo EDITOR="\"$EDITOR\"" >> $HOME/$OFILE
93 else
94    . $HOME/$OFILE
95 fi
96 RC=0
97 if [ ! -d "$ORDERDIR" ]
98 then
99    if mkdir "$ORDERDIR" > $BB 2> $BB
100   then
101       chmod u=rwx "$ORDERDIR"
102   else
103       echo "Cannot make $ORDERDIR" directory 1>&2
104       RC=1
```

419

```
105      fi
106 fi
107 if [ ! -r "$ORDERDIR" ]
108 then
109      echo "$ORDERDIR" not readable 1>&2
110      RC = 1
111 fi
112 cd "$ORDERDIR"
113 if [ ! -f "$RECEIVED" ]
114 then
115      if cp $BB "$RECEIVED" 2> $BB
116      then
117          chmod u=rw "$RECEIVED"
118      else
119          echo Cannot create "$RECEIVED" 1>&2
120          RC = 1
121      fi
122 fi
123 if [ ! -r "$RECEIVED" ]
124 then
125      echo "$RECEIVED" not readable 1>&2
126      RC = 1
127 fi
128 if [ ! -f "$NRECEIVED" ]
129 then
130      if cp $BB "$NRECEIVED" 2> $BB
131      then
132          chmod u=rw "$NRECEIVED"
133      else
134          echo Cannot create "$NRECEIVED" 1>&2
135          RC = 1
136      fi
137 fi
138 if [ ! -r "$NRECEIVED" ]
139 then
140      echo "$NRECEIVED" not readable 1>&2
141      RC = 1
142 fi
143 if [ $RC -eq 0 ]
144 then
145      export NAME ADDRESS CITY STATE ORDERDIR
146      export RECEIVED NRECEIVED EDITOR
147      while true
148      do
149          echo "Choose one of the following"
150          echo "(Type word or first letter in either case)"
151          echo " help         Help on this program"
152          echo " order        Place an order"
153          echo " receive      Print items ordered and received"
154          echo " notin        Print items ordered but not received"
155          echo " look         Locate a particular item received"
156          echo " quit      Quit this program"
157          echo ": \c"
```

420

```
158        read FUNCTION
159        if [ -z "$FUNCTION" ]
160        then
161             break
162        fi
163        case $FUNCTION in
164        o*|O*)
165             order;;
166        r*|R*)
167             receive;;
168        n*|N*)
169             notin;;
170        l*|L*)
171             look;;
172        h*|H*)
173             help;;
174        q*|Q*)
175             break;;
176        *)
177             echo "$FUNCTION" unknown - Try help 1>&2 ;;
178        esac
179    done
180 fi
181 exit $RC
$ ▢
```

Figure 8.J.2

The **stores** program controls the execution of all other programs in the STORES system. It begins by trying to read the *.stores* file. If the *.stores* file does not exist or cannot be read, **stores** tells its user what the problem is and then prompts for the information. **stores** stores this information in the *.stores* file for future uses of **stores**.

The *.stores* is read next. Its contents are executed by using a dot built-in command in line 94. Lines 97 through 142 then check all files for existence and appropriate permissions. **stores** creates files where possible and sets their permissions.

If **stores** discovers file errors during this checking procedure, it does not stop. Instead, it continues to look for more errors. A user shouldn't have to invoke **stores** more than once to find all file errors. Error messages are again written to standard error.

If **stores** finds no file errors, it prepares to prompt the user for a command request. All appropriate shell variables are exported in lines 145 and 146. All programs executed by **stores** can then use these shell variables because they are placed in their environment.

stores next prompts for a command request. A newline or end-of-file means that the user wants to stop, and the **break** in line 161 ends both the **while** loop and the **stores** program.

stores accepts a large vocabulary of command requests names since the first letter of each command request is unique. Upper and lower case are considered identical by the **case** statement beginning in line 163.

stores passes control to the appropriate shell script based on the information entered. Unknown command requests names produce a message on standard error that tells the user how to find which command requests are recognized and what they mean.

stores continues prompting for command requests names until the user wants to stop. **stores** returns true when finished.

J.2 The order Command

stores calls **order**, shown below, to build and print a complete order to be placed with the store specified. **order** also adds to the items not received master list.

```
$ number order
 1 ##############################
 2 #   ORDER SYSTEM
 3 #   Build an order
 4 ##############################
 5 #   Define constants
 6 ##############################
 7 TMP = /tmp/$$
 8 BB = /dev/null
 9 cd $ORDERDIR
10 ##############################
11 #   Get store name
12 ##############################
13 echo "Enter store name: \c"
14 read STORE
15 if [ -z "$STORE" ]
16 then
17      echo No order made
18      exit 0
19 fi
20 STORE = "'echo \"$STORE\" | tr \"[A-Z]\" \"[a-z]\"'"
21 ##############################
22 #   Get file name for order
23 ##############################
24 if [ -r $ORDERDIR/$|STORE|000 ]
25 then
26      SEQ = 'ls | tail -1 | sed "s/$STORE//"'
27      SEQ = 'expr $SEQ + 1'
28 else
```

```
29      SEQ=0
30 fi
31 if [ "$SEQ" -lt 10 ]
32 then
33      SEQ=00$SEQ
34 elif [ "$SEQ" -lt 100 ]
35 then
36      SEQ=0$SEQ
37 fi
38 FILE=$ORDERDIR/$STORE$SEQ
39 trap "rm -f $TMP $FILE; trap 0; exit 1" 1 2 3 15
40 trap "rm -f $TMP; exit 0" 0
41 touch $FILE
42 DATE=`date`
43 ###############################
44 #   Prompt for and read
45 #   requests for input
46 ###############################
47 while true
48 do
49      echo "Stock Number: \c"
50      read STOCK
51      if [ -z "$STOCK" ]
52      then
53          break
54      elif grep "^$STORE $STOCK      " $NRECEIVED > $BB
55      then
56          echo "$STOCK already ordered.  Do you want to order more?: \c"
57          read RESP
58          if [ `expr "$RESP" : "^[yY]"` -ne "1" ]
59          then
60              continue
61          fi
62      fi
63      while true
64      do
65          echo "Quantity: \c"
66          read QUANTITY
67          if expr "$QUANTITY" : "^[0-9][0-9]*\$" >$BB 2>$BB
68          then
69              break
70          else
71              echo Quantity \("$QUANTITY"\) not all numbers 1>&2
72          fi
73      done
74      while true
75      do
76          echo "Description: \c"
77          read DESCRIPTION
78          if [ -n "$DESCRIPTION" ]
79          then
80              DESCRIPTION=`echo $DESCRIPTION`
81              break
```

423

```
82        else
83            echo Item must have description 1>&2
84        fi
85    done
86    while true
87    do
88        echo "Unit cost: \c"
89        read COST
90        if expr "$COST" : "^[0-9][0-9]*\.[0-9][0-9]\$" >$BB 2>$BB
91        then
92            break
93        elif expr "$COST" : "^[0-9][0-9]*\$" >$BB 2>$BB
94        then
95            COST=${COST}.00
96            break
97        else
98            echo Cost \("$COST"\) not in correct format 1>&2
99            echo Allowable formats are: 99 and 99.99 1>&2
100       fi
101   done
102   while true
103   do
104       echo "Catalogue page number: \c"
105       read PAGE
106       if expr "$PAGE" : "^[0-9][0-9]*\$" >$BB 2>$BB
107       then
108           break
109       else
110           echo Page number \("$PAGE"\) not all numbers 1>&2
111       fi
112   done
113   echo "Ordering the following item:"
114   echo " Stock Number:  $STOCK"
115   echo " Quantity:      $QUANTITY"
116   echo " Description:$DESCRIPTION"
117   echo " Unit Cost:    $COST"
118   echo " Catalogue Page:    $PAGE"
119   echo "$STOCK\t$QUANTITY\t$DESCRIPTION\t$COST\t$PAGE\t$DATE" >> $TMP
120 done
121 ###############################
122 #   Allow editing
123 ###############################
124 echo "Would you like to edit this file?: \c"
125 read RESP
126 if expr "$RESP" : "^[yY]" > $BB 2> $BB
127 then
128     echo "I'll start $EDITOR for you"
129     eval "$EDITOR" "$TMP"
130 fi
131 ###############################
132 #   Move temporary file
133 #   to order file
134 ###############################
```

424

```
135 trap "" 1 2 3 15
136 mv $TMP $FILE
137 ###############################
138 #   Save in not received
139 #   file
140 ###############################
141 echo "Printing the order...\c"
142 sed "s/^/$STORE   /" < $FILE >> $NRECEIVED
143 (
144     echo "Please send to:"
145     echo "  $NAME"
146     echo "  $ADDRESS"
147     echo "  $CITY"
148     echo "  $STATE"
149     echo
150     IFS=" "
151     while read STOCK QUANTITY DESCRIPTION COST PAGE DATE
152     do
153         echo "Stock Number:    $STOCK"
154         echo "Quantity: $QUANTITY"
155         echo "Description: $DESCRIPTION"
156         echo "Unit Cost:    $COST"
157         echo "Catalogue Page: $PAGE"
158         echo
159     done < $FILE
160 ) | pr -h "Items Ordered from $STORE on $DATE" | lpr
161 echo Done
162 exit 0
$ ▯
```

Figure 8.J.3

order begins by requesting a store name. If you do not give a store name, **order** ends immediately and returns true. If you do give a store name , that name is first converted to all lower case letters. You need not worry how you entered the store name Sears the last time an order was made, for example.

order then generates a new file name for the order by adding a three digit number onto the store name. This number is computed by adding one to the number used for the last order made for that store. Numbering begins at 000.

When the order file name has been created, traps are set to intercept the hangup, interrupt, quit, and software termination signals and the special procedure exit signal. The **touch** program in line 41 creates the order file with a length of zero. The current date is also recorded and is used when adding to the items not received master list.

The main ordering loop begins with the while statement on line 47. **order** first prompts for a stock number, and newline or end-of-file ends the ordering process.

425

order next checks the items not received master list for an outstanding order of the same item from the same store. If the item is on order, you are asked if you would like to order more. **order** accepts any answer beginning with upper or lower case y as an affirmative response, and continues the ordering process.

order then prompts for the quantity, description, unit cost, and catalogue page number. Each is validated as lines 63 through 112 show. Notice that you are given as many tries as needed to enter correct information, and that **order** explains why an entry is incorrect.

order summarizes the item just entered and then stores the order in a temporary file. The format of this file is six fields separated by tabs. To insure that the description field contains no tabs, description is reassigned to the DESCRIPTION variable on line 80.

When an order is complete, you are asked if you would like to edit the order file. Again, all reasonable forms of yes are accepted. **order** starts the text editor you select, giving the order file as the argument.

The rest of the **order** shell procedure is sensitive to interruption, so the hangup, interrupt, and software termination signals are ignored. The temporary file is moved to the order file, and the order file is appended to the items not received master list. The store name is added to each item ordered as the item is put into the master list.

Lines 142 through 160 format and paginate the order, and print it on the line printer. The shell interprets the parentheses to mean that the standard output of all enclosed commands, which are run in a sub-shell, is piped to the **pr** program. The IFS variable is defined to be only tab. This tells the shell how to partition each line in the order file into words when **read** is executed on line 151. When a completed order is printed, **order** exits and returns true.

J.3 The notin Command

The last program given in the partial solution to the STORES system is the **notin** program, figure 8.J.4. **notin** prints a list of items not received.

```
$ number notin
 1   ################################
 2   #   ORDER SYSTEM
 3   #   Print list of items not
 4   #   received
 5   ################################
 6   BB = / dev / null
 7   IFS = " "
 8   echo "Would you like to see orders for a specific store? \c"
 9   read RESP
10   if expr "$RESP" : "ˆ[yY]" > $BB 2> $BB
11   then
12       echo "Which store? \c"
13       read STR
14       if [ -z "$STR" ]
15       then
16           echo "All orders will be listed"
17           STR = "[a-z]"
18       else
19           STR = "ˋecho \"$STR\" | tr \"[A-Z]\" \"[a-z]\"ˋ"
20       fi
21   else
22       STR = "[a-z]"
23   fi
24   grep "ˆ$STR" < $NRECEIVED | \
25   while read STORE STOCK QUANTITY DESCRIPTION COST PAGE DATE
26   do
27       echo Order from "$STORE"
28       echo " Stock Number:  $STOCK"
29       echo " Quantity:     $QUANTITY"
30       echo " Description:$DESCRIPTION"
31       echo " Cost:         $COST"
32       echo " Catalogue Page:     $PAGE"
33       echo " Ordered on:$DATE"
34       echo "Continue?: \c"
35       RESP = ˋ(read RESP; echo "$RESP") < / dev / ttyˋ
36       if expr "$RESP" : "ˆ[yY]" > $BB 2> $BB
37       then
38           continue
39       else
40           break
41       fi
42   done
43   exit 0
$ □
```

Figure 8.J.4

notin begins by asking if the list of items to be printed should be restricted to a single store. A positive response causes **notin** to ask for a store name. Store names are translated to lower case letters to match the way items are saved by **order** in the items not received master list. If no store name is given or if all stores are to be listed, the STR variable is set to a value that selects all items from the master list.

grep selects items from the master list and pipes its selections to the while loop beginning on line 25. IFS has again been changed to define how input lines are broken into words.

After each item is listed, **notin** asks if you would like to see more items. The parenthetical notation in line 35, along with the redirection operator on the same line, forces the response to be read from the terminal. If the **read** in line 35 were not redirected as shown, it would read the next line selected by the **grep** program in line 24. Remember that standard input for all commands in the while loop has been redefined to be the output of the **grep** program. An affirmative response causes the next item not received to be listed. **notin** ends when you want to stop or when all items selected by **grep** have been processed. **notin** exits and returns true.

Figure 8.J.5 shows these three shell procedures in operation.

```
$ stores
No .stores file in your HOME directory
Please answer the following questions and I will build one for you.
Your name: Lawrence R. Rogers
Your mailing street address: 232 Edinburg Road
The city you live in: Mercerville
The state you live in, with zip code: NJ 08619
A directory where orders can be saved (/usr/lrr/orders):
A file where a list of received items is stored (received):
A file where a list of items not received is stored (nreceived):
Your favorite editor (vi): ex
Choose one of the following
(Type word or first letter in either case)
        help        Help on this program
        order       Place an order
        receive      Print items ordered and received
        notin       Print items ordered but not received
        look        Locate a particular item received
        quit        Quit this program
: o
Enter store name: sears
Stock Number: B132-JK
Quantity: 10
Description: Grass Trimmer Cord
Unit cost: 1.89 each
Cost (1.89 each) not in correct format
Allowable formats are: 99 and 99.99
Unit cost: 1.89
Catalogue page number: 237
```

```
Ordering the following item:
      Stock Number:  B132-JK
      Quantity:      10
      Description:   Grass Trimmer Cord
      Unit Cost:     1.89
      Catalogue Page: 237
Stock Number:
Would you like to edit this file?: Y
I'll start ex for you
"/tmp/199" 1 line, 68 characters
:.
B132-JK  Grass Trimmer Cord  1.89     237 Mon May  7 09:06:05 EDT 1984
:q
Printing the order...Done
Choose one of the following
(Type word or first letter in either case)
      help          Help on this program
      order         Place an order
      receive       Print items ordered and received
      notin         Print items ordered but not received
      look          Locate a particular item received
      quit          Quit this program
: n
Would you like to see orders for a specific store? y
Which store? sears
Order from sears
      Stock Number:  B132-JK
      Quantity:      10
      Description:   Grass Trimmer Cord
      Cost:          1.89
      Catalogue Page: 237
      Ordered on:    Mon May  7 09:06:05 EDT 1984
Continue?:
Choose one of the following
(Type word or first letter in either case)
      help          Help on this program
      order         Place an order
      receive       Print items ordered and received
      notin         Print items ordered but not received
      look          Locate a particular item received
      quit          Quit this program
: q
$ □
```

Figure 8.J.5

The shell procedures shown here combine many features of the Bourne Shell to solve the STORES system defined at the beginning of this section. When you solve problems using the UNIX system, concentrate on understanding the problem before you select a language and design data structures for use in the problem's solution. Use the Bourne Shell to help you better understand a problem because it lets you build and debug prototype solutions quickly and easily.

When you've completed a prototype problem solution using the Bourne Shell, don't abandon it in favor of another version written in a conventional programming language. If the prototype solution meets the needs of its intended users, there is little reason to rewrite it. Many software tools in the UNIX system are shell procedures that could be rewritten as C language programs. They remain shell procedures because they solve the problem as defined.

CHAPTER 9
THE BERKELEY C SHELL

A. INTRODUCTION

Shells in the UNIX system are not part of the operating system kernel but instead are powerful application programs that provide many of the capabilities of the UNIX system through a command language. One shell already described in this book is the Bourne Shell, a shell common to all UNIX systems. The Berkeley C Shell, originally developed by Bill Joy at the University of California at Berkeley, is another popular shell so named because its programming language constructs are patterned after those of the C language. This chapter describes both the interactive features of the C Shell and the batch, or programming, features. Examples used here are taken from examples in Chapters 3 and 8 that described the Bourne Shell so that you can see the differences between the two shells.

It is difficult to say which shell is better. Each has superior qualities, so the selection of a shell depends on the general application area. For interactive use, the C Shell has more features that aid its user than does the Bourne Shell. The C Shell therefore is the preferred shell for interactive use.

For batch, or programming, use, the selection is not so easy, as each shell has features needed to build problem solutions. This chapter draws no definitive conclusion but instead rewrites examples developed for the Bourne Shell and comments on the ease of solution development. As a problem solver and programmer, you must decide which shell is appropriate for an application.

The rest of this chapter concentrates on the interactive and batch use of the Berkeley C Shell. Similarities between the concepts presented here and in the chapters on the Bourne Shell are intentional to allow you to compare both shells solving exactly the same problems. As a UNIX system user, you should be fluent in each shell to be able to solve problems in either as requirements dictate.

B. COMMAND EXECUTION

The C Shell executes commands typed at your terminal and commands read from files. Every command names a program that the C Shell must run, and commands optionally specify flags, flag arguments, file names, and C Shell directives. Examples of C Shell directives are redefinitions of the standard input, output, and error files. This section defines the C Shell's basic command structure and how it executes commands.

B.1 What is a Command?

A C Shell command is a sequence of words separated by any combination of spaces and tabs. The first word of a command names a program to be run by the C Shell. Programs must be either executable files located somewhere in the file system or functions built into the C Shell. All remaining words in a command, except for those words that have special meaning to the C Shell, are passed to the named program as arguments.

A word is usually a sequence of non-space, non-tab characters; but there are exceptions. The C Shell treats single instances of the characters &, |, ;, <, >, (, and) as separate words, meaning that the command:

% **who>/tmp/whos__on**

Figure 9.B.1

contains three words: who, >, and /tmp/whos__on. Notice that although this command contains three words, neither spaces nor tabs are used as word separators. The C Shell also recognizes four two-character sequences, namely &&, ||, <<, and >>, as words.

You can use quote characters, ", ' and ', to change the C Shell's interpretation of words. For example, the command:

% **"who am I"**

Figure 9.B.2

contains one word – "who am I" – which the C Shell interprets as the name of a program to be executed. Because of the quote characters, the C Shell recognizes the enclosed text as a single word. Furthermore, the C Shell does not recognize the special characters and character sequences listed above as individual words when quoted.

B.2 How the C Shell Locates a Program

When the C Shell reads a command from your terminal or a file, it first breaks the command into words. The first word names a program to be executed by the shell. The C Shell checks to see if this named program is a function built into the C Shell. If it is, the C Shell executes that function, handling the arguments appropriate to that function.

If the named program is not a builtin function, the C Shell next examines the program name to see if it uses either relative or absolute file name addressing, specified by combinations of the . (dot) and / path name characters. Program names containing these characters are not searched for in the file system, as the C Shell assumes you know where the program file is located and have told it so.

All other program names force the C Shell to find an executable file in the file system with the same name as the program named in the command. You can tell the C Shell where in the file system to look for file names as program by setting the path variable to a list of directories. For example, the command:

% **set path**=**(. /bin /usr/bin /usr/local/bin /usr/rogers/bin)**

Figure 9.B.3

names five directories in the file system where the C Shell must look when searching for executable files. Directory order is important, because the C Shell begins its search at the first directory listed and continues until the appropriate executable file is found or the directory list is exhausted. If the program named in a command cannot be found in the directories listed in path, the C Shell displays the message

program: Command not found.

on your terminal.

When an instance of the C Shell is started, that is, when you login to the UNIX system, when you execute a C Shell procedure, or when you add a directory to the path directory list, the C Shell looks in each directory listed in the path variable to find all executable files. Each executable file found is recorded by the C Shell in an internal table that relates the executable file name to the directory where the file resides. When the C Shell reads a command and must find the program named in the command, it uses this internal table to locate the corresponding executable file in the file system. Once found, the C Shell starts the program, passing to it the arguments given as part of the command.

The C Shell does not use its internal table to load entries or to search for entries when processing the current directory, named dot, in the path directory list. The C Shell treats this directory specially by always looking through it when searching for an executable file.

The C Shell's file locating mechanism has both advantages and disadvantages. The advantages are that programs named in commands can be found rapidly. Commands are located quickly and the C Shell uses searches a minimum of directories.

The disadvantages are that when a new program is installed in a directory listed in the path variable, you must tell the C Shell to reconstruct its internal table with the **rehash** builtin function. **rehash** is so named because the internal table maintained by the C Shell uses a hashing technique for storing and retrieving entries. It's a good idea to execute the **rehash** function if you've been logged in to the UNIX system for a long time or whenever you install a new program or shell script to add newly installed commands to the internal table of your login shell.

B.3 How the C Shell Executes Commands

The C Shell executes programs named in commands the same way that the Bourne Shell does. For a non-builtin function, the C Shell first creates a new process consisting of a copy of itself. This "clone" child process then assumes that the file found by searching its internal table is a binary executable file and attempts to run it with an **exec**() system call as described in Chapter 7. If successful, the command executes at your mercy or until it finishes.

If the executable file cannot be run using the **exec**() system call, the C Shell child process then assumes that the file is a C Shell procedure and prepares to read and execute the commands in the file. Part of this preparation involves executing a file named .cshrc located in your login directory. The .cshrc file is useful if, for example, you want to set certain shell variables. After reading and executing .cshrc, the C Shell child process then reads the file found through the hash table search and executes the commands in that file. Remember that a C Shell procedure file must have read and execute permission to be executed.

When the C Shell is started as your login shell, it also reads and executes commands found in the .login file, again located in your login directory. The .login file lets you customize the UNIX system to your needs in much the same way that the .profile file does for the Bourne Shell.

Once the C Shell has executed the commands in .cshrc and optionally in .login, it is then available to execute commands entered at the terminal or read from a file. The next five sections describe how you can exploit the basic command structure described in this section. These sections describe the C Shell's history mechanism, its aliasing facility, file name substitutions, shell variables, and input/output redirection. It is these features that make the C Shell the shell of choice for the interactive use of the UNIX system.

C. HISTORY SUBSTITUTIONS

The C Shell provides a powerful history substitution feature that allows you to re-execute commands you've just entered. The C Shell maintains a list of commands entered so that you can easily reference them again as is or with modifications. You can adjust the number of commands that the C Shell's remembers by setting the C Shell variable history to the number of events you want the C Shell to remember. For example, the command:

% **set history=20**

Figure 9.C.1

tells the C Shell to remember the last twenty commands entered at the terminal.

This section describes the C Shell's history substitution features and shows how to use them. It is important to understand history substitutions since they are also used in aliases as described in section D.

C.1 Event Specifiers

In the figure below, *file1.c* is created with the **ex** text editor and then compiled using the C compiler. The number before the % prompt is the event number assigned by the C Shell and optionally printed based on your definition of the prompt shell variable. See Section F of this chapter for a complete discussion of shell variables.

```
1% ex file1.c
"file1.c" [New file]
:a
#include        <stdio.h>

main()
{
        printf("Hello, world\n);
        exit(0);
}
.
:w
"file1.c" [New file] 7 lines, 68 characters
:q
2% cc -O file1.c -o hello
"file1.c", line 5: newline in string or char constant
"file1.c", line 6: syntax error
3% ex file1.c
"file1.c" 7 lines, 68 characters
:5
        printf("Hello, world\n);
:s/)/")/p
        printf("Hello, world\n");
:w
"file1.c" 7 lines, 69 characters
:q
4% cc -O file1.c -o hello
5% hello
Hello, world
6% □
```

Figure 9.C.2

Because of errors in *file1.c*, the file must be re-edited and then compiled again. This time, compilation is successful, so the executable file *hello* is run and it prints a message on the terminal.

For the type of interaction shown in figure 9.C.2, the C Shell's history substitution mechanism is useful because it lets you reference and rerun previously executed commands, called *EVENTS*, without having to type the entire command line again.

In figure 9.C.3, history substitutions are applied to the previous example.

436

```
1% ex file1.c
"file1.c" [New file]
...
:q
2% cc -O file1.c -o hello
"file1.c", line 5: newline in string or char constant
"file1.c", line 6: syntax error
3% !e
ex file1.c
"file1.c" 7 lines, 68 characters
...
:q
4% !c
cc -O file1.c -o hello
5% hello
Hello, world
6% ☐
```

Figure 9.C.3

In event 3, a reference is made to a previous event by using the special history character !. This reference tells the C Shell to execute the most recent command that started with the letter e. The C Shell searches the history list backwards from the most recent event to the least recent event. It responds with the text of the event it selected and then executes that command. Event 4 shows another similar reference, this time to the most recent command that started with the letter c. While these history references use only one character to select an event, more characters can be used as needed to identify the required event. For example, you could have said !cc to reference the last command that started with the letters cc.

Another way to reference events in the C Shell is by an event number as discussed previously. To see what event numbers have been assigned to commands, use the **history** built-in C Shell function as figure 9.C.4 shows.

```
1% ex file1.c
"file1.c" [New file]
...
:q
2% cc -O file1.c -o hello
"file1.c", line 5: newline in string or char constant
"file1.c", line 6: syntax error
3% history
    1  ex file1.c
    2  cc -O file1.c -o hello
    3  history
4% !1
ex file1.c
"file1.c" 7 lines, 68 characters
 ...
:q
5% !2
cc -O file1.c -o hello
6% hello
Hello, world
7% ☐
```

Figure 9.C.4

In this figure, **history** shows that the C Shell has assigned 1 to the **ex** command and 2 to the **cc** command. To re-execute the **ex** command, you need only provide the C Shell with its event number as is done in event 4. Again the C Shell responds with the text of the command and then executes it. Event 5 shows another example.

Event numbers can also be given to the C Shell as a number relative to the current event number. Events 3 and 4 in figure 9.C.5 below show references to the next to the last command entered.

```
1% ex file1.c
"file1.c" [New file]
...
:q
2% cc -O file1.c -o hello
"file1.c", line 5: newline in string or char constant
"file1.c", line 6: syntax error
3% !-2
ex file1.c
"file1.c" 7 lines, 68 characters
...
:q
4% !-2
cc -O file1.c -o hello
5% hello
Hello, world
6% □
```

Figure 9.C.5

Finally, events can be selected by giving the C Shell an imprecise specification of a command. Figure 9.C.6 shows a reference to the last event containing the string hello.

```
1% ex file1.c
"file1.c" [New file]
...
:q
2% cc -O file1.c -o hello
"file1.c", line 5: newline in string or char constant
"file1.c", line 6: syntax error
3% !-2
ex file1.c
"file1.c" 7 lines, 68 characters
...
:q
4% !?hello
cc -O file1.c -o hello
5% hello
Hello, world
6%□
```

Figure 9.C.6

Imprecise specifications are literal strings, meaning that regular expression patterns are not recognized when specifying an event substring.

C.2 Word Specifiers

The C Shell also lets you select arguments from previous commands. Figure 9.C.7 shows an example.

440

```
1% ex file1.c
"file1.c" [New file]
...
:q
2% cc -O !$ -o hello          # also !^
cc -O file1.c -o hello
"file1.c", line 5: newline in string or char constant
"file1.c", line 6: syntax error
3% !e
ex file1.c
"file1.c" 7 lines, 68 characters
...
:q
4% !c
cc -O file1.c -o hello
5% hello
Hello, world
6% □
```

Figure 9.C.7

Event 2 refers to the last word from the last command entered, namely !$ which the C Shell replaces with *file1.c*. The comment in event 2 states that !^, which selects the first argument word, could also have been used to select the *file1.c* argument, as the command in event 1 only has one argument.

The next example shows several different types of word specifiers and begins with event 1 executing the **echo** command with eight arguments.

1% **echo this is an example of history word selectors**
this is an example of history word selectors
2% **echo !:0 !:ˆ !ˆ !:$!$**
echo echo this this selectors selectors
echo this this selectors selectors
3% **echo !1:1-4**
echo this is an example
this is an example
4% **!1:-4**
echo this is an example
this is an example
5% **echo !:***
echo this is an example
this is an example
6% **echo !***
echo this is an example
this is an example
7% **echo !ˆ too !:2-4**
echo this too is an example
this too is an example
8% **echo !-2:ˆ too !-2:2***
echo this too is an example
this too is an example
9% **!:0- elephant**
echo this too is an elephant
this too is an elephant
10% ☐

Figure 9.C.8

Event 1   This event defines 8 words used in the remaining events in this example.

Event 2   This event introduces the colon metacharacter to the history substitution vocabulary. Colons separate event specifiers from word specifiers, and sometimes are optional. In this example, !:ˆ and !ˆ both select the first argument from the specified event and !:$ and !$ both select the last argument. The word specifier !:0 selects the zeroth word, the program named by the command. When no explicit event is referenced by the event specifier, that is, when the colon immediately follows the history reference character, the last event entered is selected.

442

Event 3   This event selects arguments one through four inclusive from event 1.

Event 4   This event selects words zero through four inclusive from the first event, event 1. After the history substitution is made, the C Shell divides the resulting command into words and executes the program named by the first word of the command, here **echo.**

Event 5   This event selects all argument words from the last event.

Event 6   This event shows that the colon separator is also optional when it prefaces the * word specifier metacharacter.

Event 7   This event juxtaposes the word too between the first and the second through the fourth argument words of event 6.

Event 8   This example duplicates the job done by event 7, but uses a different syntax. The notation $n*$ is an abbreviation for the range n-$.

Event 9   Finally, this event selects words zero through the next to the last word from event 8, then adds the word elephant onto the end of the event.

C.3 Word Modifiers

So far, the history substitutions shown have only selected events and words to be used "as is" in a command. This section describes the history substitution syntax for modifying words selected from events.

For the first example, imagine two source files, *main.c* and *subs.c*, that incorrectly reference the include file for the Standard I/O library. Each reference must be corrected by removing the string sys/ and each file recompiled. Figure 9.C.9 shows one way to fix the errors using event and word specifiers and word modifiers.

```
1% ex main.c
"main.c" 7 lines, 72 characters
:/sys
#include        <sys/stdio.h>
:s/sys./
#include        <stdio.h>
:w
"main.c" 7 lines, 68 characters
:q
2% cc -c !$ -o !$:s/.c/
cc -c main.c -o main
3% !e:s/main/subs
ex subs.c
"subs.c" 22 lines, 216 characters
:/sys
#include        <sys/stdio.h>
:s/sys./
#include        <stdio.h>
:w
"subs.c" 22 lines, 215 characters
:q
4% !c:gs/main/subs
cc subs.c -o subs
5% □
```

Figure 9.C.9

Event 2 twice selects the last argument word, main.c, from the last event, the second time removing the suffix. Word modifiers are separated from event and word specifiers by colons. The next line shows the command formed by applying the substitutions and modifications.

Event 3 shows another example that uses an event selection and a word modification. After selecting the last command that begins with the letter e, the string subs is substituted for the first instance of the string main. Unlike with the **ex** and **vi** text editors, the search string, main, is assumed to be a literal string and not a regular expression containing metacharacters. In contrast, notice that the last / string delimiter is optional, just as it is for **ex** and **ed**.

Finally, event 4 shows a global substitution applied to an event. Unfortunately, the syntax for this type of substitution is also slightly different from global substitutions in the editors.

444

Figure 9.C.10 shows another solution to the editing and recompilation problem solved in the last figure, with one difference.

```
1% ex main.c
"main.c" 7 lines, 72 characters
:/sys
#include        <sys/stdio.h>
:s/sys./
#include        <stdio.h>
:w
"main.c" 7 lines, 68 characters
:q
2% cc -c !$ -o !$:r
cc -c main.c -o main
3% !e:s/main/subs
ex subs.c
"subs.c" 22 lines, 216 characters
:/sys
#include        <sys/stdio.h>
:s/sys./
#include        <stdio.h>
:w
"subs.c" 22 lines, 215 characters
:q
4% !c:gs/main/subs
cc subs.c -o subs
5% ☐
```

Figure 9.C.10

Event 2 uses a different word modifier that extracts the root name from the selected word. The notation !$:r yields the string main irrespective of the suffix. Similarly, the modifier :e, not shown in the figure, removes all but the suffix or extension, again irrespective of the extension.

The next example shows two more word modifiers that also use key letters.

```
1% ls -l /etc/passwd
-r--r--r--  1 root     bin         575 May 29 17:53 /etc/passwd
2% ls -ld !$:h
ls -ld /etc
drwxrwxr-x  3 root     sys        1360 Jun 21 18:51 /etc
3% cd !$
cd /etc
4% ls -l !1:$:t
ls -l passwd
-r--r--r--  1 root     bin         575 May 29 17:53 passwd
5% □
```

Figure 9.C.11

Event 2 modifies the argument *letc/passwd* by removing the last path name component, leaving only the head, */etc*. Similarly in event 4, the notation !1:$:t removes all leading path name components, leaving only the tail, *passwd*.

Figure 9.C.12 shows another example using a key letter word modifier.

```
1% ls -l /etc/passwd /etc/group
-r--r--r--  1 root     bin         237 May 29 17:50 /etc/group
-r--r--r--  1 root     bin         575 May 29 17:53 /etc/passwd
2% ls -l !:2:s'/etc'/backuproot/etc' !:3:&
ls -l /backuproot/etc/passwd /backuproot/etc/group
-r--r--r--  1 root     bin         237 May 25 02:00 /backup/etc/group
-r--r--r--  1 root     bin         575 May 29 02:00 /backup/etc/passwd
3% □
```

Figure 9.C.12

The ampersand character, &, means to repeat the previous substitution on the selected words.

The next key letter modifier, q, can be used to tell the C Shell that no other substitutions should be applied to the words selected. In figure 9.C.13, event 1 shows five arguments to the **echo** program.

```
1% echo 5 * 7 = 35
5 main.c subs.c 7 = 35
2% echo !*:q
echo 5 * 7 = 35
5 * 7 = 35
3% ☐
```

Figure 9.C.13

Normally, the C Shell scans all words for file name expansion and shell variable replacement. The second word, *, is replaced by all file names in the current directory.

When referenced in event 2 with the q word modifier, the C Shell passes all selected words to the **echo** command with no additional replacement. While the commands executed in events 1 and 2 appear to show the same command, the output of event 2 shows that the * file name metacharacter is passed to **echo** as is.

The last word modifier explained in this section is the p modifier. p tells the C Shell to do all history substitutions and to assign an event number to the resulting command, but not to execute the command. You should use the p modifier to check the results of a complex history substitution before execution.

Figure 9.C.14 shows several history substitutions in event 2, the last of which uses the p word modifier.

```
1% echo this is an example of the history word substitutions
this is an example of the history word substitutions
2% echo !:7 !:2 !:3:s/n// !:8:p
echo history is a word
3% history
    1  echo this is an example of the history word substitutions
    2  echo history is a word
    3  history
4% !2
echo history is a word
history is a word
5% ☐
```

Figure 9.C.14

The position of p is irrelevant, as the C Shell won't execute the command if the p modifier is discovered anywhere in the command. **history** in event 3 shows that the number 2 was assigned to the command, and event 4 causes this command to be executed.

C.4 Special Abbreviations

The C Shell also provides two shorthand techniques that let you re-execute the last command entered. Figure 9.C.15 shows a command that meant to reference the *etc/passwd* file, but the final d was mistakenly left off. Event 2 re-executes the command, adding the missing *d* onto the end.

```
1% ls -l /etc/passw
/etc/passw not found
2% !!d
ls -l /etc/passwd
-r--r--r--   1 root      bin         575 May 29 17:53 /etc/passwd
3% ☐
```

Figure 9.C.15

Finally, figure 9.C.16 shows another attempt at listing the *etc/passwd* file, but again mistypes the name.

```
1% ls -l /ect/passwd
/ect/passwd not found
2% ^ct^tc^
ls -l /etc/passwd
-r--r--r--   1 root      bin         575 May 29 17:53 /etc/passwd
3% ☐
```

Figure 9.C.16

Instead of being forced to use the !:s/ct/tc history substitution, the C Shell allows simple editing using the ^ history character. Again, search strings are literal strings rather than regular expressions containing metacharacters, and the final ^ is optional. Only the first instance of a string may be replaced using the ^ history character.

The C Shell's history substitution features let you refer to previous commands and words from those commands using event and word specifiers. You can also edit commands and words using word modifiers. Several commonly used substitutions are implied by key letter word modifiers that further reduce the number of characters you must enter at the terminal. In addition, the C Shell provides two methods for referring to the last command entered, either executing the command as entered or editing it first. These features are important to you as a C Shell user because they let you concentrate on problem solving instead of spending your time re-entering commands and fixing typographical errors.

D. ALIAS SUBSTITUTIONS

The C Shell's alias substitution feature lets you execute often used command sequences without building shell procedure files, but in a different way than do history substitutions. Whereas a history substitution lets you easily re-execute a command sequence you've already entered, perhaps changing parts of these commands, an alias substitution lets you define a new command name that can consist of a sequence of commands. The C Shell also lets you reference the arguments given to the alias. This section describes aliasing and builds on the history substitution syntax explained in the last section.

An *ALIAS* relates a program name to a set of words. When the C Shell discovers that a program named by a command is an alias, it replaces the program name by the set of words defined by the **alias** built-in command. Figure 9.D.1 shows an example.

```
1% alias lsl ls -l
2% alias
lsl     (ls -l)
3% lsl
total 2
-rw-r--r--   1 rogers   writers      18 Sep 15 15:38 example.1
----------   1 rogers   writers     231 Sep 15 15:39 typescript
4% lsl /etc/passwd
-r--r--r--   1 root     bin         575 May 29 17:53 /etc/passwd
5% □
```

Figure 9.D.1

Event 1 defines the alias lsl and event 2 lists all aliases known to this instance of the C Shell. When the lsl command is entered as event 3, the C Shell replaces lsl with the command ls -l and then executes it. In event 4, lsl is also replaced by ls -l, and the C Shell preserves the *etc/passwd* argument as part of the command line. The C Shell then executes the command ls -l /etc/passwd.

When the C Shell completes the replacement operation, it checks to see if the program named by the new command is the same as the program named by the old command. If both program names are the same, the C Shell assumes there are no more aliases and executes the new command, otherwise it looks for more aliases. This means that a program may be aliased to itself, letting you define an alias that specifies the same program but enables some options, for example. Figure 9.D.2 shows such an alias.

```
1% alias rm rm -i
2% alias
rm      (rm -i)
3% rm chap.9
rm: remove chap.9? n
4% ls -l chap.9
-r--r--r--  1 rogers   writers   100395 May 29 17:53 chap.9
5% ▢
```

Figure 9.D.2

ls is an alias to ls -l, meaning that all invocations of ls will always produce a long listing of the files given as arguments.

Recall the standard command format defined in Chapter 5. If a software tool recognizes flags, flag arguments, and file names given in the standard command format, then alias substitutions referencing that software tool also recognize these arguments. The tool's alias can reference the tool, and can also specify some flags. Invocations of the alias can also specify flags, as the standard command format allows for several flags given as separate arguments. For example, the **rm** program defined in the alias shown above recognizes the standard command format, so you can specify any combination of flags, flag arguments, and file name arguments to the alias. In contrast, the **od** program shown in Chapter 8 recognizes flags only as the first argument; so aliases referencing **od** are restricted. A shell procedure like the one built in that chapter must be written to deal with arguments given in the standard command format.

You can can rearrange arguments given to an alias by using history substitutions. The C Shell treats the command line using an alias as the last event entered, so the alias definition can use history substitutions to access the arguments.

For example, figure 9.D.3 shows the definition of the ec alias.

```
1% alias ec 'ex \!ˆ; echo cc -O \!ˆ -o \!ˆ:r; cc -O \!ˆ -o \!ˆ:r'
2% alias
ec        ex !ˆ; echo cc -O !ˆ -o !ˆ:r; cc -O !ˆ -o !ˆ:r
3% ec main.c
"main.c" [New file]
:a
#include        <stdio.h>

main()
{
        printf("Hello, world\n");
        exit(0);
}
.
:1,.p
#include        <stdio.h>

main()
{
    printf("Hello, world\n");
    exit(0);
}
:w
"main.c" [New file] 7 lines, 68 characters
:q
cc -O main.c -o main
4% main
Hello, world
5% □
```

Figure 9.D.3

ec puts its invoker into the **ex** text editor to edit the file given as the first argument, and then compiles the program. The set of words related to ec is quoted to remove the special meaning of the ; characters. Further, the history reference character ! is prefaced by a backslash to postpone its history substitution until ec is referenced as a command. If the backslash characters were left out, the C Shell would apply history substitutions to the alias definition instead of the alias reference. The rest of the figure shows **ec** in action.

unalias does the opposite of **alias** by breaking the relationship between its argument and the set of words defined in an **alias**. **unalias** understands file

451

name metacharacters in its argument and expands the argument according to the aliases it knows. The command unalias * therefore breaks all aliases known by the shell. Figure 9.D.4 shows an example.

1% **alias ls ls -l**
2% **alias me who am i**
3% **alias**
ls   (ls -l)
me   (who am i)
4% **unalias [lm]?**
5% **alias**
6% ☐

Figure 9.D.4

Aliases provide an easy way to define new commands as a sequence of existing commands. For simple command sequences, aliases also eliminate the need to build shell procedure files. Further, command sequences defined as aliases are more efficient than commands stored in shell procedure files because the shell executes commands defined in an alias without first creating a new copy of the C Shell.

E. FILE NAME SUBSTITUTION

The C Shell also provides a file name substitution facility similar to that of the Bourne Shell, but with two extensions. Figure 9.E.1 shows examples of file name generation reminiscent of the Bourne Shell as explained in Chapter 3.

```
1% ls
02
03
abc
acc
adc
2% ls ??
02
03
3% ls *
02
03
abc
acc
adc
4% ls a??
abc
acc
adc
5% ls a[bc]c
abc
acc
6% □
```

Figure 9.E.1

The metacharacters shown in this figure, ?, *, and [ ], operate identically in both shells. Refer to Chapter 3 for a complete explanation.

The C Shell file name substitution facilities extend beyond those of the Bourne Shell in two ways. The first is shown in the figure below.

```
1% echo *
02 03 abc acc adc
2% echo a?c
abc acc adc
3% echo a[cbd]c
abc acc adc
4% echo a{c,b,d,e}c
acc abc adc aec
5% □
```

Figure 9.E.2

When you give the C Shell a file name expression that uses braces, as does the expression in event 4, the shell replaces the expression by a non-sorted list made from each alternative contained in the list. In the example shown, the C Shell replaces the file name expression a{c,b,d,e}c with four words: acc, abc, adc, and aec. Notice that in the output of event 1, aec is not a file in the current directory, yet the C Shell still expands the file name expression as though it were. The key is that a file name expression using braces is not expanded using file names in a directory, but instead is treated like an abbreviation, often used in place of a file name list. Because of this difference, you must be careful when you use a file name expression with braces.

The second file name substitution facility uses the tilde character, ˜. When used alone, tilde references the directory named by the home shell variable, usually set to the name of your login directory. When tilde precedes a name made from letters, digits, and the underscore character (_), the C Shell attempts to locate the user named by this name in the password file, substituting that user's login directory for the ˜name abbreviation. Names that cannot be found in the password file cause the C Shell to print

Unknown user: *user*

Figure 9.E.3 shows an example of both uses of tilde.

```
1% ls -ld ˜
drwx------  35 rogers   writers    1056 Sep 15 14:06 /usr/rogers
2% ls -ld ˜bob
drwxr-xr-x  12 bob      fathers     448 Sep  7 00:57 /usr/bob
3% □
```

Figure 9.E.3

The tilde character has special meaning only when it appears as the first character of a file name. All other uses are not expanded by the shell.

File name substitutions provide another way to reduce the number of characters you must enter at the terminal. The C Shell offers you the same substitutions that the Bourne Shell does, along with two additional powerful and useful substitutions.

F. SHELL VARIABLES

Shell variables in the C Shell let you store, retrieve, and manipulate strings by name. They also let you further customize the C Shell to your needs. This section describes the C Shell's shell variable syntax and shows how to use shell variables when interacting with the C Shell.

In the C Shell, you assign values to shell variables with the **set** built-in command. The general form for assigning values to variables is

$$\text{set } name = value$$

Variable names may be up to 20 characters long, where the first character must be a letter and all others may be either letters or numbers. Spaces and tabs may surround the = operator, and *value* is either a word or a list of words enclosed in parenthesis.

Figure 9.F.1 shows four shell variable assignments.

```
1% set A = "this is a test"
2% set B = 'this is a test'
3% set C = this\ is\ a\ test
4% set D = (this is a test)
5% echo $A, $B, $C, $D.
this is a test, this is a test, this is a test, this is a test.
6% ☐
```

Figure 9.F.1

The first three use different methods for assigning the same word to the variables A, B, and C, and the last assigns a list of words to the variable D. Event 5 displays the value of these shell variables.

You can think of a C Shell variable as an array because you can initialize the array with a list of words, you can reference an element by an index, and you can dynamically determine the array's size. Figure 9.F.2 shows an example of each operation.

455

```
1% set A=(this is an example of multiple words in a shell variable)
2% echo $A
this is an example of multiple words in a shell variable
3% echo $#A
11
4% echo $A[6] $A[10] $A[7]
multiple shell words
5% echo $A[-2] $A[3-5] $A[7-]
this is an example of words in a shell variable
6% echo $A[12]
Subscript out of range.
7% ☐
```

Figure 9.F.2

In event 1, the shell variable A is set to a list of words, and in event 3 the number of words in the list is displayed with the $# shell variable prefix. Event 4 references elements 6, 10, and 7 from the array using a notation similar to that of the C language. The index of the first word in a shell variable array is 1, and an index can also be a shell variable. Event 5 shows how to use a range index, where the words selected extend from the first number, or 1 if not given, to the last number, or $# if not given. The special index * selects all words in the array. Event 6 shows that references beyond $# produce an error message.

The rest of this section explains the five types of shell variables in the C Shell. See Chapter 8 for a discussion of the Bourne Shell equivalents of these shell variable types.

F.1 User-definable Shell Variables

User-definable shell variables are variables to which you can assign a value. Shell variable A in figure 9.F.2 is an example of a user-definable shell variable. Further, the C Shell recognizes nine user-definable shell variables as special in that their values cause the shell to change its actions. These user-definable shell variables are explained below.

cdpath   The cdpath shell variable contains a list of directories that the C Shell uses when executing a **cd** built-in command. cdpath is to **cd** the way path is to program execution. Figure 9.F.3 shows an example.

```
1% set cdpath=(. ~ /usr)
2% echo $cdpath
. /usr/rogers /usr
3% ls $cdpath
.:
02
03
abc
acc
adc

/usr:
adm
bin
dict
games
include
lib
man
pub
rogers
spool
sys
tmp
tsh.help

/usr/rogers:
.login
.profile
.stores
bin
chap.4
chap.5
chap.6
chap.7
chap.8
chap.9
orders
4% cd bin
5% pwd
/usr/rogers/bin
6% ls $cdpath[1]
help
7% cd include
8% pwd
/usr/include
9% ls $cdpath[1]/a*
./a.out.h
./ar.h
./assert.h
10% cd sys
11% pwd
```

```
/ usr / include / sys
12% ls $cdpath[1]/a*
./acct.h
13% cd bin
14% pwd
/ usr / rogers / bin
15% ☐
```

Figure 9.F.3

The cdpath shell variable is assigned a list of three directories in event 1, and each directory's contents are shown by the **ls** command in event 3. When given the **cd** command in event 4, the C Shell searches in order each directory listed in cdpath for the named directory, finding a *bin* directory in the ˜ or home directory. The next **ls** command shows the files in that directory, and the example continues, showing the files in each directory after the **cd** command is executed.

histchars   Only the first two characters of the histchars shell variable have meaning to the C Shell. The first, which defaults to !, defines the history substitution character and the second, which defaults to ˆ, defines the character used when editing the previous command. Figure 9.F.4 shows an example of redefining the value of histchars.

```
1% date
Fri Sep 16 14:13:27 EDT 1983
2% !!
date
Fri Sep 16 14:13:28 EDT 1983
3% ˆdateˆwho am I
who am I
rogers   tty02   Sep 16 14:13
4% set histchars=,/
!% ,d
date
Fri Sep 16 14:13:55 EDT 1983
!% /date/who am I
who am I
rogers   tty02   Sep 16 14:13
!% ☐
```

Figure 9.F.4

458

history   The value of history, which must be a number, defines how many commands the C Shell saves for history substitutions. Irrespective of history's value, the last executed command is always saved. There is no predefined maximum number of commands that may be saved. Instead, the limit varies based on the amount of memory that the C Shell can allocate for maintaining the history list. The size of the history list should be big enough to hold a moderate amount of command lines (somewhere between 20 and 30) but small enough to fit on a display screen when printing the history list. Figure 9.F.5 shows an example that assigns different values to history.

```
1% history
    1  history
2% echo $history
15
3% set history=1
4% date
Fri Sep 16 14:16:00 EDT 1983
5% date
Fri Sep 16 14:16:01 EDT 1983
6% date
Fri Sep 16 14:16:03 EDT 1983
7% history
    6  date
    7  history
8% set history=2
9% date
Fri Sep 16 14:16:18 EDT 1983
10% date
Fri Sep 16 14:16:19 EDT 1983
11% date
Fri Sep 16 14:16:20 EDT 1983
12% history
   10  date
   11  date
   12  history
13% ☐
```

Figure 9.F.5

home   The home shell variable names a directory to where the shell changes when you execute a **cd** command with no argument. The C

459

Shell also uses this directory when you use the ~ abbreviation as explained in the section on file name substitutions.

mail   The mail variable defines a list of files checked by the C Shell for receipt of mail. If the first word in the list, $mail[1], is a number, then the C Shell checks all files in the list every $mail[1] seconds for mail. The default time interval is 600 seconds (10 minutes). Receipt of mail in a file means that the file has been modified since the shell last checked and the file has a non-zero length. Figure 9.F.6 shows an example of setting the mail variable to a time interval and two file names.

```
1% set mail=(1 /usr/spool/mail/rogers /tmp/rogers)
2% mail rogers
testing testing testing
.
New mail in /usr/spool/mail/rogers.
3% mail
From rogers Fri Sep 16 14:23:28 1983
testing testing testing

? d
4% cp /etc/passwd /tmp/rogers
New mail in /tmp/rogers.
5% ls -l /tmp/rogers /etc/passwd
-rw-r--r--   1 rogers   writers     575 Sep 16 14:23 /tmp/rogers
-r--r--r--   1 root     bin         575 May 29 17:53 /etc/passwd
6% ☐
```

Figure 9.F.6

When you name more than one file in the mail variable, the C Shell identifies the file where mail has been received.

path   The path variable defines a list of directories where the C Shell looks for executable files when searching for programs named by commands. Section B explains how the C Shell uses these directories when executing commands.

prompt   When the C Shell prompts you for a command, it first prints the prompt shell variable. prompt defaults to % followed by a space for ordinary users and # followed by a space for the super-user. The C Shell replaces all instances of ! in prompt with the next event number. Remember to force a ! character into the prompt string by prefacing it with a back slash to prevent the C Shell from attempting a history substitution. Figure 9.F.7 shows redefinitions of the prompt shell variable. Event 6 sets prompt to the value used in the examples in this chapter.

```
1% set prompt="rogers-> "
rogers-> date
Fri Sep 16 14:33:18 EDT 1983
rogers-> set prompt="\! - "
4 - date
Fri Sep 16 14:33:36 EDT 1983
5 - !4
date
Fri Sep 16 14:33:39 EDT 1983
6 - set prompt="\!% "
7% date
Fri Sep 16 14:33:52 EDT 1983
8% □
```

Figure 9.F.7

shell   The program named by the shell shell variable defines the command language interpreter used to execute shell procedures. shell defaults to the executable file name of the C Shell, meaning that from within the C Shell, only C Shell shell procedures can be executed.

Your system may contain an additional feature in the UNIX system kernel that lets you select which command language interpreter to use to interpret a shell procedure. This directive must be the first line in the shell procedure and has the following syntax:

       #! *fully_qualified_name_of_interpreter*

The #! string, which must be the first two characters of the file, has special meaning to the UNIX system and causes it to interpret the rest of the first line as the name of the command interpreter to be applied to the file. The UNIX system starts the named command interpreter instead of the program named by shell. The UNIX system also passes to the interpreter the name of the executable file given as the program name in the original command. For example, if the executable file **printit** contains the following:

```
1%  number printit
1   #!/bin/sh
2   ################################
3   #   printit
4   #   print file arguments on
5   #   the line printer
6   ################################
7   for file
8   do
9       pr $file | lpr
10  done
11  exit 0
12  □
```

Figure 9.F.8

The UNIX system starts the program **/bin/sh** and passes the file name printit as the first argument, followed by the rest of the arguments to the original **printit** command. In other words, the UNIX system transforms

    printit filea fileb

into

    /bin/sh printit filea fileb

time   If set, the C Shell displays the user, system, and real times, and a percentage that represents the ratio of user and system time to real time for all commands that take more than time CPU seconds. Setting the time shell variable reduces the need to use the **time** program and is also more efficient, as the C Shell does the timing instead of having timing done by a separate process. Figure 9.F.9 shows an example in which time is set to zero, forcing the C Shell to report timings for all commands. Rounding errors make the numbers appear to be erroneous.

```
1%  set time = 0
2%  who am I
rogers  tty04   Sep 16 14:51
0.0u 0.2s 0:02 10%
3%  □
```

Figure 9.F.9

F.2 Positional

The C Shell recognizes the same notation for positional parameters that the Bourne Shell does, namely $1 through $n, where n is the number of arguments passed to the shell. The C Shell also lets you refer to positional parameters by using the argv shell variable. Recall that argv is the recommended name of the arguments string vector passed to a C language program from the UNIX system kernel. When using argv, $argv[1] is the same as $1; and $#argv, analogous to argc in a C language program, tells how many arguments are in argv. Figure 9.F.10 shows an interactive session using argv.

```
1% set argv=(-atesting -bthis -c feature)
2% echo $argv
-atesting -bthis -c feature
3% set argv='scf abc ab $argv'
4% echo $argv
-a testing -b this -c -- feature
5% echo $#argv
7
6% echo $7
feature
7% shift
8% echo $argv
testing -b this -c -- feature
9% echo $#argv
6
10% ☐
```

Figure 9.F.10

After setting argv, **scf**, explained and used in Chapter 8, next rearranges the argv shell variable into the standard command format as defined in Chapter 5. The rearranged arguments are then displayed along with a count of the number of words in argv. The **shift** operator renames $argv[2] to $argv[1], $argv[3] to $argv[2], and so on, reducing the number of words in argv by 1. This interactive session shows how to process arguments to shell procedures and will be used again in programming examples later in this chapter.

F.3 Predefined

The C Shell also contains predefined shell variables as does the Bourne Shell, but of two different types. The C Shell supports both string valued predefined shell variables and set valued shell variables, while the Bourne Shell, as you will remember, supports only string valued predefined shell variables. String valued variables are those whose value is established by the C Shell and set valued variables are those whose values are irrelevant but their status of being set is important. Each type is explained in the next two sections.

F.3.a String valued The C Shell sets four variables to strings based on specific operations. The first shell variable, named cwd, is set by the C Shell to either the argument given to a **cd** built-in command or $home, if no argument is given. Figure 9.F.11 shows an example where cwd's value is used to build the prompt string.

```
1% alias cd 'cd \!$;set prompt="$cwd-> "'
2% cd /
/-> cd ~
/usr/rogers-> cd /usr/include/sys
/usr/include/sys-> □
```

Figure 9.F.11

The cd alias in event 1 defines the **cd** built-in command so that the prompt string can be redefined each time **cd** is executed. The last three events show examples of the cd alias.

Next is the status shell variable. The C Shell assigns the value returned by the last command executed to status. status is the C Shell equivalent of the ? predefined shell variable in the Bourne Shell. Recall from Chapter 8 that a return value of zero means that a command executed successfully and non-zero means that a command was unsuccessful. Figure 9.F.12 shows how status changes based on **grep**'s success in finding the search string in the password file.

```
1% grep root /etc/passwd
root:fV5M2Ms0Wz5kk:0:10:The root of all evil:/:/bin/csh
2% echo $status
0
3% grep ROOT /etc/passwd
4% echo $status
1
5% □
```

Figure 9.F.12

The $ shell variable always contains the process identification number of the shell that is currently executing commands, that is either the login shell or the shell started to execute a shell procedure. Usage of $ in the C Shell is the same as $ in the Bourne Shell.

Finally, the < predefined shell variable contains the next line read from the standard input file. Recall that a C Shell shell variable can be thought of as an array of words, so each word in the line read from the standard input can be accessed using the array element reference notation, $name[index]. Figure 9.F.13 shows an example.

```
1% set LINE=$<
this is a test of the $< shell variable
2% set INPUT=($LINE)
3% echo $#INPUT
9
4% echo $INPUT[1] $INPUT[$#INPUT]
this variable
5% set LINE=$<

6% set INPUT=($LINE)
7% echo $#INPUT
0
8% set LINE=$<
^D
9% set INPUT=($LINE)
10% echo $#INPUT
0
11% 
```

Figure 9.F.13

The C Shell assigns one line from standard input to LINE in event 1. **set** in event 2 then causes LINE to be assigned to INPUT to make each word individually available. **echo** in event 3 displays the number of words read and **echo** in event 4 displays the first and last word. Next, event 5 causes the C Shell to read another line from standard input and to assign it to LINE. This time the line contains no words, as the **echo** program in event 7 shows. Finally, events 8 through 10 repeat the command sequence, but here end-of-file is typed. **echo** in event 10 again shows no words read. Unlike the Bourne Shell's **read** built-in command, which also causes one line to be read from standard input and assigned to a variable, the C Shell does not distinguish between end-of-file and a line with no words. When this distinction is important, the Bourne Shell must be used.

F.3.b Set valued Set valued predefined shell variables are C Shell variables whose values are irrelevant but their state of being set or unset is significant. Set valued shell variables cause the C Shell to change its behavior. All set valued variables known to the C Shell are described here, although only two are set based on the flags given to an instance of the C Shell.

Set valued shell variables are set with the **set** built-in command and unset with the **unset** built-in command. Because their values are not important, the =*value* part of a **set** statement is usually omitted.

All set valued predefined variables are defined below.

echo   echo causes the C Shell to display each command as it will be executed after first doing all required substitutions. echo is also set by specifying the -x flag to an instance of the C Shell. Figure 9.F.14 shows an example.

1% **set X=argument**
2% **echo $X**
argument
3% **set echo**
4% **echo $X**
echo argument
argument
5% ☐

Figure 9.F.14

ignoreeof   ignoreeof forces the C Shell to disregard all end-of-file characters that would otherwise cause the login shell to end. The C Shell responds to these eof characters with the message

Use "logout" to logout.

telling you that the only way to log off the system is with the **logout** built-in command.

noclobber   noclobber tells the C Shell to abandon all commands using output redirection that would either destroy an existing file or append onto the end of a non-existing file. Section G shows examples of noclobber.

noglob   noglob forces the C Shell to ignore the file name expansion phase of command execution. All file name arguments containing metacharacters are passed to the specified command unchanged. Figure 9.F.15 shows an example.

```
1% echo *
02 03 abc acc adc
2% set noglob
3% echo *
*
4% ☐
```

Figure 9.F.15

nonomatch   nonomatch causes the C Shell to pass all unexpandable file name arguments containing metacharacters to the program named in a command. The C Shell normally complains that a file name argument cannot be expanded and does not start the named program. Figure 9.F.16 shows an example of setting nonomatch.

```
1% ls
02
03
abc
acc
adc
2% ls A*
No match.
3% set nonomatch
4% ls a*
a* not found
5% ☐
```

Figure 9.F.16

verbose   verbose causes the C Shell to display commands as entered after doing all history substitutions. verbose can also be set with the -v flag. Figure 9.F.17 shows an example of verbose and echo. When used together, verbose and echo let you see which commands are executed before and after all shell variable and file name substitutions respectively.

467

```
1% set X=argument
2% set verbose
3% echo $X
echo $X
argument
4% set echo
set echo
5% echo $X
echo $X
echo argument
argument
6% !e
echo $X
echo argument
argument
7% □
```

Figure 9.F.17

F.3.c Command substitution Command substitution in the C Shell works the same way that command substitution does in the Bourne Shell. Both use grave accents, also called back quotes, as the way to delimit a command sequence whose standard output replaces the back quoted string. Each newline in the replacement string is changed into a space before substitution. Figure 9.F.18 shows an example of command substitution.

```
1% set date='date'
2% echo $date
Fri Sep 16 15:47:27 EDT 1983
3% echo $#date
6
4% set date="'date'"
5% echo $date
Fri Sep 16 15:47:47 EDT 1983
6% echo $#date
1
7% □
```

Figure 9.F.18

In event 1, the output of the **date** program – 6 words – is assigned to the date shell variable. Event 3 displays the number of words in the date shell variable. In event 4, the output of the **date** program is combined into a single word with double quote, and event 6 shows that there is only one word in date.

F.3.d Parameter substitution The C Shell supports only two types of parameter substitution and both use the $? prefix. When applied to a shell variable name, $?name has the value 1 if name is set, and 0 otherwise. Figure 9.F.19 shows an example.

```
1% echo $?a
0
2% set a="this is a test"
3% echo $?a
1
4% ☐
```

Figure 9.F.19

When applied to the shell variable 0, $?0 has the value 1 if the C Shell knows the name of the file used as input to the shell, and 0 otherwise. If $?0 has the value 1, then $0 contains the shell's input file name.

G. RE-DIRECTING INPUT AND OUTPUT

The C Shell also provides input and output file direction facilities that use directives similar to those in the Bourne Shell. However, the C Shell goes beyond the Bourne Shell in one sense by letting you guard against those redirections that destroy file contents. The next two sections describe the C Shell's file redirecting and pipelining capabilities.

G.1 Redirection with Standard Files

Recall from Chapter 3 that every process has three files already opened by the UNIX system and available for use. These are standard input, standard output, and standard error. Programs that receive their input data from the standard input file, send their output data to the standard output file, and send their error data to the standard error file are called filters.

The C Shell lets you redefine the identity of these standard files with special directives given as part of a command line. These directives are interpreted by the C Shell and cause it to reconnect the referenced standard files to the files identified by the directives. As is true for the Bourne Shell, the C Shell reconnects these standard files before the program named in a command line becomes a process.

The C Shell provides the same directives for standard input, standard output, and standard output append redirection that the Bourne Shell does, namely <, >, and ≫. However, files named by these directives are subject to variable, command, and file name expansion by the C Shell. The Bourne Shell does not expand files named by redirection directives. Figure 9.G.1 shows examples.

```
1% ls -l * /etc/passwd
-r--r--r--   1 root     bin          575 May 29 17:53 /etc/passwd
-rw-r--r--   1 rogers   writers        1 Oct 10 14:58 aa
-rw-r--r--   1 rogers   writers        2 Oct 10 14:58 bb
-rw-r--r--   1 rogers   writers        4 Oct 10 14:58 cc
-rw-r--r--   1 rogers   writers        8 Oct 10 14:58 dd
2% cat < /etc/passwd > a*
3% ls -l
-rw-r--r--   1 rogers   writers      575 Oct 10 14:59 aa
-rw-r--r--   1 rogers   writers        2 Oct 10 14:58 bb
-rw-r--r--   1 rogers   writers        4 Oct 10 14:58 cc
-rw-r--r--   1 rogers   writers        8 Oct 10 14:58 dd
4% cat [abc]? ≫ d*
5% ls -l
-rw-r--r--   1 rogers   writers      575 Oct 10 14:59 aa
-rw-r--r--   1 rogers   writers        2 Oct 10 14:58 bb
-rw-r--r--   1 rogers   writers        4 Oct 10 14:58 cc
-rw-r--r--   1 rogers   writers      581 Oct 10 14:59 dd
6% ☐
```

Figure 9.G.1

The C Shell also provides the >& directive for changing the destination of the standard error file. Unfortunately, the C Shell does not distinguish between the standard output and standard error files, redirecting both to the file named by >&. It is therefore difficult, though possible, to save the standard output of process in one file and the standard error of the same process in a different file. Figure 9.G.2 shows how to do this.

```
1% number standard.c
 1   /*
 2    *    standard
 3    *        write capital letters to standard output
 4    *        and all else to standard error
 5    */
 6
 7   #include    <stdio.h>
 8   #include    <ctype.h>
 9
10   main(argc, argv)
11   int argc;
12   char *argv[];
13   {
14       register int c;
15
16       while ((c = getchar()) != EOF ) {
17           if (isupper(c)) {
18               putc(c, stdout);
19           } else {
20               putc(c, stderr);
21           }
22       }
23       exit(0);
24   }
2% cc -o standard standard.c
3% standard >& ELSE > UPPER
Ambiguous output redirect.
4% (standard > UPPER) >& ELSE)
This is a test of the Upper and Lower Program.
^D
5%  cat UPPER
TULP6%  cat ELSE
his is a test of the pper and ower rogram.
7% □
```

Figure 9.G.2

In event 3, the standard output and standard error files of **standard** are redirected to a file named *ELSE* and then the standard output file is redirected to *UPPER*, with the intent of first reconnecting both standard input and error to one file and then reconnecting only standard error to another. Unfortunately, the C Shell complains about the duplicate redirections. In event 4 then, **standard** is run in a subshell using the parenthesis notation. In that subshell, the standard output of **standard** is redirected to *UPPER*. This means that the standard output file of the subshell will be empty because it has been redirected. Only the information in the standard error file remains, and it is routed to *ELSE*.

471

The & modifier can also be applied to the ≫ standard output append directive. This causes the C Shell to append both the standard output and standard error files of a process onto the file named by ≫&.

The C Shell provides another redirection modifier to be used with the noclobber set valued shell variable. If noclobber is set, the C Shell abandons any command that would destroy the contents of a file named by either the > or >& directives and displays the message:

file: File exists.

on your terminal. To suppress this check and force overwriting of an existing file by the C Shell, add an exclamation mark, !, modifier onto the > or >& directive. For example, the command sequence:

```
1% unset noclobber
2% cat /tmp/npasswd > /etc/passwd
```

Figure 9.G.3

is the same as:

```
1% set noclobber
2% cat /tmp/npasswd >! /etc/passwd
```

Figure 9.G.4

assuming the */etc/passwd* file exists when the C Shell attempts standard output redirection.

Finally, ! can be applied to the append directives ≫ and ≫&. However, its meaning is different from >! and >&! in that if noclobber is set, the C Shell abandons any command that uses ≫ or ≫& and names a file that does not exist. The ! modifier suppresses this check so that ≫! and ≫&! can redirect standard output and standard output and error respectively to a new file.

G.2 Pipelining

The C Shell also supports pipelining between processes, where the standard output of one process is connected to the standard input of another process. The vertical bar, |, directs the C Shell to make the connection between the two programs named on either side of the |. Normally, the C Shell connects only the standard output to standard input, but it will also add the contents of the standard error to standard output with the |& directive.

472

The C Shell features described in the last five sections are most often used with an interactive C Shell, the login shell for example. In contrast, the next five sections describe the C Shell features most often used in C Shell shell procedures. These sections describe conditional tests, structured looping, builtin shell commands, debugging C Shell procedures, and the STORES system originally explained in Section J of Chapter 8. Examples used in these sections are taken from the related sections in Chapter 8, again for comparison.

H. CONDITIONAL TESTS

The C Shell supports the Bourne Shell's notion of a command being true or false based on the command's return value. Furthermore, the C Shell uses the Bourne Shell's true and false convention, in which a zero return value from a command means true and all other return values mean false. As with the Bourne Shell, conditional tests in the C Shell let shell procedures execute commands based on a command returning true or false. However, conditional tests in the C Shell do not rely on the return value of commands as the only way to control command execution. c ommand execution is only one of several primary types that can be evaluated to control which commands are to be executed. The C Shell provides an extensive expression evaluation mechanism that extends beyond command evaluation to include arithmetic operations, local operations, string operations, and file typing. This section first describes C Shell expressions and then the C Shell's if statement.

H.1 Expressions

C Shell expressions consist of primary types – numbers, strings, and file names – optionally related to other primary types by operators – arithmetic and relational – based on the primary types. Expressions are used in the C Shell's if and while statements to control command execution. Expressions are also used in shell variable assignment statements the same way that variables are assigned expression values in the C language. This section concentrates on the values returned by expressions being assigned to shell variables and leaves the if and while statements for later sections.

Expression values are assigned to shell variables with the @ built-in command. The form of the assignment is:

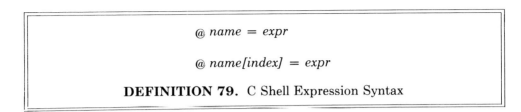

$$@\ name\ =\ expr$$

$$@\ name[index]\ =\ expr$$

DEFINITION 79. C Shell Expression Syntax

where *index* must be less than or equal to the number of elements in *name*. Furthermore, all *op=* assignment operators available in the C language are also available with @, as are the ++ and -- postfix operators.

Figure 9.H.2 shows a simple shell procedure, named **wordcounter**, that uses expression value assignments.

```
1% number wordcounter
1    ###############################
2    #   wordcounter
3    #   count words on two lines
4    #   and total
5    ###############################
6    @ LINENO = 0
7    echo Enter some words followed by a newline.
8    set LINE=$<
9    @ TOTAL = $#LINE
10   @ LINENO++
11   echo You entered $#LINE words in line $LINENO.  Thanks.
12   echo ""
13   echo Now enter some more words followed by a newline.
14   set LINE=$<
15   @ TOTAL += $#LINE
16   @ LINENO++
17   echo You entered $#LINE words in line $LINENO.  Thanks again.
18   echo ""
19   echo You entered a total of $TOTAL words on $LINENO lines.
20   exit 0
2% □
```

Figure 9.H.1

When run, **wordcounter** works as shown below.

```
1% wordcounter
Enter some words followed by a newline.
This is a test of the wordcounter program.
You entered 8 words in line 1. Thanks.

Now enter some more words followed by a newline.
This is another test of wordcounter, but this line has more words.
You entered 12 words in line 2. Thanks again.

You entered a total of 20 words on 2 lines.
2% ☐
```

Figure 9.H.2

The C Shell recognizes four primary types: command execution, numeric values, string values, and file attributes. The sections that follow describe each primary type and the operators that operate on them.

H.1.a Command execution A command execution primary type consists of a command enclosed in braces. If the command returns true, then the command execution primary has the value 1. If the command returns false, then the command execution primary has the value 0. Command execution primaries can be related to numeric primaries using arithmetic operators or to string values using string operators.

Recall from Chapter 8 that every software tool you forge must clearly define true and false, and that the appropriate value must be returned to the invoking process. When a software tool returns true or false consistent with the success or lack of success of an operation, the tool can be used in an expression as a command execution primary type.

Figure 9.H.3 shows the **inpass0** shell procedure that uses a command execution primary type.

```
1%  number inpass0
 1  ##############################
 2  #   inpass
 3  #   check password file for
 4  #   login - version 0
 5  ##############################
 6  set NAME = root
 7  if ($#argv) set NAME = $1
 8  @ INPASS = { grep $NAME /etc/passwd > /dev/null }
 9  echo $NAME is in password file only if $INPASS equals 1.
10  exit 0
2% []
```

Figure 9.H.3

H.1.b Numeric values C Shell expressions support the following operators from the C language:

OPERATOR	MEANING
+, -, /, *,%	Plus, minus, division, multiplication, and remainder on division (modulo) operators.
&, |, ^, ~	Bit-wise and, or, exclusive or, and one's complement operators.
≪, ≫	Left and right shift operators.
==, !=	Equal and not equal operators.
<, >	Strictly less than and strictly greater than operators.
<=, >=	Less than or equal and greater than or equal operators.
&&, ||, !	Logical and, or, and not operators.

The C Shell also recognizes the relative binding strength of operators and evaluates expressions according to the following precedence table, ranging from tightest to loosest.

476

OPERATOR	BINDING
~	tightest
!	
+, -, /, *, %	
≪, ≫	
<=, >=, <, >	
==, !=	
&	
^	
|	
&&	
||	loosest

When the operator evaluation order does not meet your needs, use parentheses to change the order. Subexpressions delimited by parentheses are always evaluated first based on the precedence table and then combined with other primary types and subexpressions according to the operators selected. Also, no two primary types of an expression can appear in the same word, meaning that the expression:

    7+3

is incorrect and must be rewritten as:

    7 + 3

Finally, any subexpression that contains <, >, |, or & must appear inside a set of parentheses so that the shell does not mistake these characters as file redirection directives and command separators.

Figure 9.H.4 shows the **newmath** shell procedure that uses numeric values in expressions.

```
1% number newmath
 1   ################################
 2   #   newmath
 3   #   exercise the C Shell's
 4   #   mathematics functions
 5   ################################
 6   echo -n "Enter a number: "
 7   set X = $<
 8   echo -n "Enter another number: "
 9   set Y = $<
10   @ Z = $X + $Y
11   echo "$X + $Y = $Z"
12   @ Z = $X - $Y
13   echo "$X - $Y = $Z"
14   @ Z = ($X & $Y)
15   echo "$X & $Y = $Z"
16   @ Z = ($X ^ $Y)
17   echo "$X ^ $Y = $Z"
18   @ Z = ($X << $Y)
19   echo "$X << $Y = $Z"
20   @ Z = $X == $Y
21   echo "$X == $Y = $Z"
22   @ Z = ($X < $Y)
23   echo "$X < $Y = $Z"
24   @ Z = ($X && $Y)
25   echo "$X && $Y = $Z"
26   exit 0
2%□
```

Figure 9.H.4

Figure 9.H.5 shows **newmath** in use.

478

```
1% newmath
Enter a number: 31
Enter another number: 2
31 + 2 = 33
31 - 2 = 29
31 & 2 = 2
31 ^ 2 = 29
31 << 2 = 124
31 == 2 = 0
31 < 2 = 0
31 && 2 = 1
2%
```

Figure 9.H.5

H.1.c String values The C Shell also supports operations that use string valued primary types. The operators are == and !=, to compare two strings for equality and inequality. The C Shell also supports the =~ and !~, operators to compare a string with a pattern that uses the *, ?, and [...] file name metacharacters for equality and inequality. Because this facility is built into the shell, C Shell procedures don't have to use the **expr** command to do string comparisons.

Figure 9.H.6 shows an example:

```
1% number stringcheck
1  ##############################
2  #   stringcheck
3  #   compare strings
4  ##############################
5  echo -n "Enter a string: "
6  set STRING = $<
7  @ EQUAL = $STRING == "HELP"
8  echo If $EQUAL equals 1, then $STRING matches HELP.
9  @ EQUAL = $STRING =~ [hH]*
10 echo If $EQUAL equals 1, then $STRING starts with h or H.
11 exit 0
2%
```

Figure 9.H.6

and figure 9.H.7 shows **stringcheck** when executed.

1% **stringcheck**
Enter a string: **HELP**
If 1 equals 1, then HELP matches HELP.
If 1 equals 1, then help starts with h or H.
2% **stringcheck**
Enter a string: **fred**
If 0 equals 1, then fred matches HELP.
If 0 equals 1, then fred starts with h or H.
3% ☐

Figure 9.H.7

H.1.d File attributes Finally, the C Shell also supports primary types that provide information about files. The general form is

-*attribute file__name*

where attributes are:

ATTRIBUTE	MEANING
r	readable
w	writable
x	executable, or searchable if the file is a directory
e	exists
o	owned by you
z	zero length
f	an ordinary file
d	a directory file

If the named file has the specified attribute, then the primary type has the value 1. If the named file does not have the specified attribute, if the file does not exist, or if the file cannot be accessed, the primary type has the value 0. Because the shell contains file attribute primary types, C Shell procedures don't have to use the **test** command to ask about files.

Figure 9.H.8 shows a shell procedure using file attribute types and includes an example of its execution.

```
1% number filetype
1   ###############################
2   #   filetype
3   #   check file attributes
4   ###############################
5   echo Enter a file name
6   set FILE = $<
7   @ EXIST = -e $FILE
8   @ DIRECTORY = -d $FILE
9   @ READABLE = -r $FILE
10  echo If $EXIST equals 1, then $FILE exists.
11  echo If $DIRECTORY equals 1, then $FILE is a directory.
12  echo If $READABLE equals 1, then $FILE is readable.
13  exit 0
2% filetype
Enter a file name
/dev/null
If 1 equals 1, then /dev/null exists.
If 0 equals 1, then /dev/null is a directory.
If 1 equals 1, then /dev/null is readable.
3% filetype
Enter a file name
/usr
If 1 equals 1, then /usr exists.
If 1 equals 1, then /usr is a directory.
If 1 equals 1, then /usr is readable.
4% □
```

Figure 9.H.8

H.2 Simple Conditional - if

C Shell expressions are of limited benefit when used only in shell variable assignment statements. The C Shell's if statement also uses expressions to decide which commands to execute. This section describes the C Shell's if statement and uses the examples rewritten from Section D in Chapter 8.

The C Shell's if statement has the form:

---

if (*expr*) *command*

DEFINITION 80. Basic C Shell if Statement - Version 1

---

where *expr* is an expression as described previously and *command* is a simple command that does not use a pipeline, a command list where commands are separated by ;, ||, &&, or &, or a parenthesized command list. Only if the value of *expr* is non-zero is *command* executed. Both if and *command* must be entirely on the same line, and if must be the first word.

Figure 9.H.9 shows the **inpass1a** shell procedure that uses the if statement.

```
1% number inpass1a
1    ##############################
2    #   inpass
3    #   check password file for
4    #   login - version 1a
5    ##############################
6    set NAME = root
7    if ($#argv) set NAME = $1
8    if ( | set VAR='grep $NAME /etc/passwd' | ) echo $NAME is in password file
9    exit 0
2% □
```

Figure 9.H.9

Notice that the command execution primary type in line 7 tests the success of the **set** built-in command that uses the **grep** command instead of **grep** alone. **set** must be used as shown when the command in a command execution primary type generates an unneeded data on its standard output file because redirection in the expression portion of an if statement does not work correctly.

When a more complex command or a sequence of commands is to be executed conditionally using an if statement, use the if statement form shown below.

---

if (*expr*) then
　　　　commands
endif

DEFINITION 81. Basic C Shell if Statement - Version 2

---

if and endif must appear as the first words on their respective lines and then must be on the same line as if. The form of *commands* is unrestricted.

Figure 9.H.10 shows another version of **inpass** that uses this form of the if statement.

1% **number inpass1b**
```
 1   ##############################
 2   #   inpass
 3   #   check password file for
 4   #   login - version 1b
 5   ##############################
 6   set NAME=root
 7   if ($#argv) set NAME=$1
 8   if ( | set VAR='grep $NAME /etc/passwd' | ) then
 9       echo $NAME is in password file
10   endif
11   exit 0
```
2% ☐

Figure 9.H.10

---

if statements in the C Shell may also use an else clause that defines a set of commands to be executed when *expr* evaluates to zero. This if statement has the form:

---

if (*expr*) then
　　　　commands__1
else
　　　　commands__2
endif

DEFINITION 82. Advanced C Shell if Statement

---

where *commands__1* are executed only if *expr* has a non-zero value when evaluated and *commands__2* are executed otherwise. Figure 9.H.11 shows version 2 of **inpass**.

```
1%  number inpass2
1   #############################
2   #   inpass
3   #   check password file for
4   #   login - version 2
5   #############################
6   set NAME=root
7   if ($#argv) set NAME=$1
8   if ( { set VAR='grep $NAME /etc/passwd' } ) then
9       echo $NAME is in password file
10  else
11      echo $NAME is not in password file
12  endif
13  exit 0
2%  ☐
```

Figure 9.H.11

Finally, an else statement may introduce another if statement with the form:

if (*expr__1*) then
        commands__1
else if (*expr__2*) then
        commands__2
else if (*expr__3*) then
        commands__3
        .
        .
        .
else
        commands__n
endif

DEFINITION 83. Complete C Shell if Statement

In this form, the if keyword does not have to be the first word on a line when the line begins with else. Figure 9.H.12 shows **inpass** version 3 that uses this if statement form.

```
1% number inpass3
 1  #############################
 2  #   inpass
 3  #   checks password file
 4  #   for login, and failing
 5  #   that, checks group file
 6  #   version 3
 7  #############################
 8  set NAME=root
 9  if ($#argv) set NAME=$1
10  if ( | set VAR='grep $NAME /etc/passwd' | ) then
11      echo $NAME is in password file
12  else if ( | set VAR='grep $NAME /etc/group' | ) then
13      echo $NAME is in group file
14  else
15      echo $NAME is not in either
16      echo password or group file
17  endif
18  exit 0
2% □
```

Figure 9.H.12

The next four examples show the C Shell versions of the procedures originally written for Bourne Shell in Chapter 8. These show numeric value (figure 9.H.13), string value (figure 9.H.14), and file attribute primary types (figure 9.H.15).

```
1% number postage
1    ##############################
2    #    postage
3    #    compute third class postage rate
4    ##############################
5    if ($#argv != 1 || "$1" < 1 || "$1" > 16) then
6         echo usage: $0 weight
7         set RC=1
8    else
9         if ($1 <= 1) then
10            set cost=.20
11        else if ($1 > 1 && $1 <= 2) then
12            set cost=.37
13        else if ($1 > 2 && $1 <= 3) then
14            set cost=.54
15        else if ($1 > 3 && $1 <= 4) then
16            set cost=.71
17        else if ($1 > 4 && $1 <= 6) then
18            set cost=.85
19        else if ($1 > 6 && $1 <= 8) then
20            set cost=.95
21        else if ($1 > 8 && $1 <= 10) then
22            set cost=1.05
23        else if ($1 > 10 && $1 <= 12) then
24            set cost=1.15
25        else if ($1 > 12 && $1 <= 14) then
26            set cost=1.25
27        else if ($1 > 14 && $1 <= 16) then
28            set cost=1.35
29        endif
30        echo The cost of a $1 ounce, third class item is \$cost.
31        set RC=0
32   endif
33   exit $RC
2% postage
usage: postage weight
3% echo $status
1
4% postage 5
The cost of a 5 ounce, third class item is $.85.
5% □
```

Figure 9.H.13

```
1% number namer
1   ###############################
2   #  namer
3   #  makes comments on the first
4   #  argument, assumed to be
5   #  a name
6   ###############################
7   if ($#argv != 1 || "$1" == "") then
8       echo usage: $0 non__zero__string
9       set RC=1
10  else
11      echo -n "The name you have selected is"
12      if ("$1" =~ [bB]ob) then
13          echo " $1."
14      else if ("$1" !~ [tT]om) then
15          echo "n't tom or Tom, it's $1."
16      else
17          echo " $1."
18      endif
19      set RC=0
20  endif
21  exit $RC
2% namer
usage: namer non__zero__string
3% echo $status
1
4% namer tom
The name you have selected is tom.
5% namer Tom
The name you have selected is Tom.
6% namer fred
The name you have selected isn't tom or Tom, it's fred.
7% ▯
```

Figure 9.H.14

```
1% number filet
1  ##############################
2  #   filet
3  #   comment on a file
4  ##############################
5  if ($#argv != 1 || "$1" == "") then
6      set FILE=.
7  else
8      set FILE="$1"
9  endif
10 echo $FILE is:
11 if (-r "$FILE") then
12     echo " readable, "
13 endif
14 if (-w "$FILE") then
15     echo " writable, "
16 endif
17 if (-x "$FILE") then
18     if (-d "$FILE")   then
19         echo " searchable, "
20     else
21         echo " executable, "
22     endif
23 endif
24 if (-f "$FILE") then
25     echo " a regular file, "
26 endif
27 if (-d "$FILE") then
28     echo " a directory, "
29 endif
30 if ( -z "$FILE" ) then
31     echo " and has more than zero bytes."
32 else
33     echo " and is zero bytes long."
34 exit 0
2% filet
. is:
 readable,
 writable,
 searchable,
 a directory,
 and has more than zero bytes.
3% filet /bin/ls
/bin/ls is:
 executable,
 a regular file,
 and has more than zero bytes.
4% □
```

Figure 9.H.15

I. STRUCTURED LOOPING

The C Shell provides the same structured looping statements that the Bourne Shell does, but the C Shell uses a different statement syntax and different keywords. True to its name, the C Shell's structured looping statements closely resemble the structured looping statements in the C language. This section describes the C Shell's while and foreach structured looping statements, loop control with break and continue, unstructured looping using gotos, labels, and **exit**, and multi-way branching. Examples in this section are taken from Section E in Chapter 8.

I.1 The while Loop

The C Shell's while loop has the form:

---

while (*expr*)
> *commands*
end

DEFINITION 84. The C Shell while Statement

---

where *commands* are executed as long as *expr* is non-zero when evaluated. Both the while and end keywords must appear alone on their input lines. Because of this, you cannot write a one-line while loop like you can with the Bourne Shell.

Figure 9.I.1 shows an example of another version of the **inpass** shell procedure that uses the while statement,

```
1% number inpass7
 1  ###############################
 2  #   inpass
 3  #   check password file for
 4  #   login - version 7
 5  ###############################
 6  echo -n "Name: "
 7  set NAME=$<
 8  while ("$NAME" != "")
 9      if ( | set VAR='grep "$NAME" /etc/passwd' | ) then
10          echo "$NAME" is in password file
11      else
12          echo "$NAME" is not in password file
13      endif
14      echo -n "Name: "
15      set NAME=$<
16  end
17  echo ""
18  exit 0
2% □
```

Figure 9.I.1

and figure 9.I.2 shows an example of execution.

```
1% inpass7
Name: root
root is in password file
Name: rogers
rogers is in password file
Name: fred
fred is not in password file
Name:
2% □
```

Figure 9.I.2

Unlike the Bourne Shell, the C Shell does not contain an until structured looping statement, but the C Shell does contain a unary negation operator, !, used to reverse the logical sense of an expression. An until loop can be written as:

> while (!(*expr*))
>> *commands*
>
> end

in the C Shell and figure 9.I.3 shows an example of this construction.

```
1% number parg
1   ###############################
2   #   parg
3   #   print arguments to a
4   #   shell file
5   ###############################
6   @ NUMBER=0
7   while (!($#argv == 0))
8       @ NUMBER++
9       echo Argument $NUMBER is $1
10      shift
11  end
12  exit 0
2% parg arg1 arg2 arg3
Argument 1 is arg1
Argument 2 is arg2
Argument 3 is arg3
3% ☐
```

Figure 9.I.3

Finally, you can enter a while loop interactively with the C Shell. The shell will prompt you for each line with a ? until a line with just the end keyword is read. Recall from Chapter 8 that the Bourne Shell also lets you give a while loop to an interactive shell, but it prompts with the string stored in the PS2 shell variable. There is no C Shell equivalent to the Bourne Shell's PS2 shell variable. Figure 9.I.4 shows an example of a while loop given to the C Shell.

```
1% @ X = 1
2% while ($X < 5)
?       echo help
?       @ X++
? end
help
help
help
help
3% history
    1  @ X = 1
    2  while ( $X < 5 )
    3  history
4% @ X = 1
5% !w
while ( $X < 5 )
?       echo help
?       @ X++
? end
help
help
help
help
6% ☐
```

Figure 9.I.4

Notice that the C Shell saves only the first line of the while loop in the history list. If you need to re-execute this while loop, you must re-enter the commands in the loop and the end keyword.

I.2 The foreach Loop'

The foreach loop is the C Shell's equivalent of the Bourne Shell's for loop and has the form:

> foreach *name* (*wordlist*)
> *commands*
> end
>
> **DEFINITION 85.** The C Shell foreach Statement

name is a shell variable that is assigned each successive word in *wordlist*, and *commands* are executed once per word in *wordlist*. Again, foreach and end must appear on separate lines, meaning that you cannot write a one-line foreach loop. Figure 9.I.5 shows an example.

```
1% number inpass8
 1  ###############################
 2  #   inpass
 3  #   check password file for
 4  #   login - version 8
 5  ###############################
 6  foreach NAME ($argv)
 7      if ( | set VAR = 'grep "$NAME" /etc/passwd' | ) then
 8          echo "$NAME" is in password file
 9      else
10          echo "$NAME" is not in password file
11      endif
12  end
13  exit 0
2% inpass8 root rogers fred
root is in password file
rogers is in password file
fred is not in password file
3% 
```

Figure 9.I.5

As a last example of the foreach loop, recall the **OD** shell procedure from Chapter 8. **OD** was written to provide a standard command format interface for the **od** command because **od** does not recognize the standard command format. Figure 9.I.6 shows version 1 of **OD** written as a C Shell shell procedure.

```
1% number OD1
1   ###############################
2   #   OD
3   #   general interface to
4   #   the od(1) command
5   #   version 1
6   ###############################
7   set OPTIONS NAMES PREFIX
8   foreach arg ($argv)
9       if ("$arg" =~ -*) then
10          set OPTIONS=$OPTIONS'echo $arg | sed s/.//'
11          set PREFIX=-
12      else
13          set NAMES="$NAMES$arg "
14      endif
15  end
16  if ("$NAMES" == "") then
17      od $PREFIX$OPTIONS
18  else
19      foreach file ($NAMES)
20          echo "=====$file"
21          od $PREFIX$OPTIONS $file
22      end
23  endif
24  exit 0
2% echo this is a test > testfile
3% OD1 -c -b testfile
=====testfile
0000000   t   h   i   s       i   s       a       t   e   s   t  \n
          164 150 151 163 040 151 163 040 141 040 164 145 163 164 012
0000017
4%
```

Figure 9.I.6

I.3 Loop Control

The break and continue loop control statements in the C Shell operate identically to those in the C language. break exits the enclosing while or foreach loop and continue resumes the next iteration for the same types of loops. Figure 9.I.7 shows an example.

```
1%  number getnum
 1  #############################
 2  #   getnum
 3  #   prompts, reads, and
 4  #   validates a number from
 5  #   standard input
 6  #############################
 7  set TTY = /dev/tty
 8  while (1)
 9      echo -n "Enter a number: " > $TTY
10      set NUMBER=$<
11      if ("$NUMBER" != "") then
12          set NUMBER=$1
13      endif
14      if ( | set VAR='expr  "$NUMBER" : '`[0-9][0-9]*$'' | )then
15          break
16      else
17          echo "Number ($NUMBER) not all digits" > $TTY
18      endif
19  end
20  echo $NUMBER
21  exit 0
2% □
```

Figure 9.I.7

When the C Shell reads and executes a break or continue statement, it continues to read and execute the rest of the commands on the input line before transferring control to the appropriate command. By coding more than one break or continue on one line, you can continue to redefine where the C Shell transfers control. Because of this, you can produce a multi-level break or continue analogous to the break n and continue n in the Bourne Shell.

I.4 Unstructured Looping

Unlike the Bourne Shell, the C Shell supports the dreaded goto statement and labels. goto names a label that must be of the form *label:* and must be on a separate line. A goto can either forward reference or backward reference a label, and the C Shell stops execution of a shell procedure when a goto names a label that cannot be found. Figure 9.I.8 shows an example.

495

```
1% number parg
1  ###############################
2  #   parg
3  #   print arguments to a
4  #   shell file
5  ###############################
6  @ NUMBER = 0
7  loop:
8  if ($#argv == 0) then
9      goto alldone
10 else
11     @ NUMBER++
12     echo Argument $NUMBER is $1
13     shift
14     goto loop
15 endif
16 alldone:
17 exit 0
2% parg arg1 arg2 arg3
Argument 1 is arg1
Argument 2 is arg2
Argument 3 is arg3
3% parg
4% □
```

Figure 9.I.8

The C Shell also provides **exit** as a way to end a shell procedure anywhere in the procedure. Its use is recommended only at the physical end of the procedure, and only one **exit** should be coded per procedure. The structured programming philosophy that recommends only one entry and exit per module of code written in a conventional programming language also applies to Bourne Shell and C Shell shell procedures.

I.5 Multi-way Branching - The switch Statement

The C Shell also has a switch statement similar in execution to the case statement in the Bourne Shell. The switch statement has the form:

```
                     switch (string)
                     case pattern_1:
                            commands_1
                            breaksw
                     case pattern_2:
                            commands_2
                            breaksw
                                 .

                                 .

                                 .

                default:
                            commands_default
                            breaksw
                endsw
```

DEFINITION 86. The C Shell switch Statement

The expression *pattern_i* is a regular expression that uses the special characters defined for file name generation, namely *, ?, and []. *pattern_i* can also be a shell variable. switch and endsw must appear alone on input lines, and each case keyword and the default keyword must appear at the beginning of a line.

The C Shell executes a switch statement the same way that the Bourne Shell executes a case statement. The C Shell compares *string* with each successive *pattern_i* until either *string* matches *pattern_i* or the shell finds the keyword endsw. All strings match default, which should be the last case in a switch statement. The shell then executes the commands associated with the matching pattern.

If the shell executes a breaksw while executing *commands_i*, the shell transfers control to the first command after endsw. If the shell does not execute a breaksw nor any other transfer statement (i.e., break, continue, goto, or exit), the shell continues to execute commands, even if these commands appear in the next case. In other words, a case in the C Shell can "fall through" to another case like it can in the C language.

Finally, you can define several patterns for a case by coding:

```
switch (string)
        case pattern__1__a:
        case pattern__1__b:
        .

        .

        .

        case pattern__1__n:
                commands__1
                breaksw

        .

        .

        .

endsw
```

If *string* matches any of *pattern__i__j*, the shell executes *commands__i*.

Figure 9.I.9 shows version 2 of **OD**. This version uses the switch statement for pattern matching instead of the if statement used in version 1. Since pattern matching in both versions 1 and 2 is done internally by the shell, both versions run at the same rate.

```
1% number OD2
1   ###############################
2   #   OD
3   #   general interface to
4   #   the od(1) command
5   #   version 2
6   ###############################
7   set OPTIONS PREFIX NAMES
8   foreach arg ($argv)
9       switch ($arg)
10      case -*:
11          set OPTIONS=$OPTIONS'echo $arg | sed s/.//`
12          set PREFIX=-
13          breaksw
14      default:
15          set NAMES="$NAMES$arg "
16          breaksw
17      endsw
18  end
19  if ("$NAMES" == "") then
20      od $PREFIX$OPTIONS
21  else
22      foreach file ($NAMES)
23          echo "=====$file"
24          od $PREFIX$OPTIONS $file
25      end
26  endif
27  exit 0
2% ▢
```

Figure 9.I.9

Finally, figure 9.I.10 shows version 3 of **OD**. Version 3 uses **scf** as explained in Chapters 5 and 8 to rearrange the arguments according to the standard command format. This version operates identically to its Bourne Shell counterpart.

499

```
1% number OD3
 1   ##############################
 2   #   OD
 3   #   general interface to
 4   #   the od(1) command
 5   #   version 3, using scf
 6   ##############################
 7   set argv='scf bcdox "" $argv'
 8   if ($status != 0) then
 9       echo "usage: $0 -bcdox [file ...]"
10       set RC=1
11   else
12       set OPTIONS PREFIX
13       set RC=0
14       foreach arg ($argv)
15           switch ($arg)
16           case --:
17               shift
18               break
19           case -[bcdox]:
20               set OPTIONS=$OPTIONS'echo $arg | sed s/.//'
21               set PREFIX=-
22               shift
23               breaksw
24           endsw
25       end
26       if ($#argv == 0) then
27           od $PREFIX$OPTIONS
28       else
29           foreach file ($argv)
30               echo "=====$file"
31               od $PREFIX$OPTIONS $file
32           end
33       endif
34   endif
35   exit $RC
2% echo this is a test > testfile
3% echo this is also a test > testfile2
4% OD3 -c -b testfile testfile2
=====testfile
0000000   t   h   i   s       i   s       a       t   e   s   t  \n  \0
        164 150 151 163 040 151 163 040 141 040 164 145 163 164 012 000
0000017
=====testfile2
0000000   t   h   i   s       i   s       a   l   s   o       a       t
        164 150 151 163 040 151 163 040 141 154 163 157 040 141 040 164
0000020   e   s   t  \n
        145 163 164 012
0000024
5% ▢
```

Figure 9.I.10

500

J. BUILT-IN SHELL COMMANDS

The C Shell contains several built-in commands that are useful both with interactive shells and in shell procedures. Many commonly used functions are built into the C Shell, making the C Shell more efficient than the Bourne Shell. This section describes the C Shell built-in commands and shows examples of their use.

J.1 alias and unalias

alias with more than one argument causes the C Shell to relate a program name given as the first argument to the set of words given as the remaining arguments. When the C Shell encounters a command in which the program named in the command is an alias, it replaces the program name with the related set of words according to the rules described in Section D. **alias** with no arguments causes the shell to display all the aliases it knows, and **alias** with one argument causes the shell to display the set of words related to the program name argument.

unalias does the opposite of **alias** by breaking the relationship between its argument and the set of words defined in a previous **alias. unalias** understands file name metacharacters in its argument and expands the argument according to the aliases it knows. The command unalias * therefore breaks all aliases known by the shell.

J.2 cd and chdir

cd and **chdir** cause the C Shell to change to the directory named as the argument. If no argument is given, the shell changes to the directory named by the home shell variable. The C Shell always sets the cwd shell variable to the fully qualified name of the directory to where the shell has changed.

The shell uses the cdpath variable as a list of directories to search when looking for the directory given as the argument. The shell uses cdpath only when the argument doesn't begin with the / or dot pathname separator characters. Figure 9.J.1 shows an example of **cd** and **chdir**.

```
1% echo $cdpath
. / usr / rogers
2% cd /
3% cd work
~ / work
4% echo $cwd
/ usr / rogers / work
5% cd bin
~ / bin
6% echo $cwd
/ usr / rogers / bin
7% cd /usr
8% cd lib
9% pwd
/ usr / lib
10% chdir
11% pwd
/ usr / rogers
12% echo $cwd
/ usr / rogers
13% ☐
```

Figure 9.J.1

J.3 pushd, popd, and dirs

The C Shell lets you remember the names of the directories you've visited so that you can return to them at some future time. Directory names are saved using a stack mechanism, where the top element of the stack names the current directory and all other elements of the stack name directories that you've saved.

To save the current directory on the directory stack, use the **pushd** built-in command and specify a directory as the argument. **pushd** saves the current directory on the directory stack, causes the shell to change to the directory named as the argument, and displays the contents of the directory stack. To return to the last directory saved, use the **popd** built-in command. **popd** removes the top directory name from the stack, changes to the directory named by the new top of stack, and again displays the contents of the directory stack.

You can also exchange the top two directory names on the stack with a **pushd** command with no arguments. Should you loose track of the directory stack contents, use the **dirs** built-in command to display the directory stack. Figure

9.J.2 shows an example.

```
1% cd
2% dirs
~
3% pushd /usr/bin
/usr/bin ~
4% dirs
/usr/bin ~
5% popd
~
6% dirs
~
7% pushd /usr/bin
/usr/bin ~
8% pushd
~ /usr/bin
9% dirs
~ /usr/bin
10% pwd
/usr/rogers
11% ☐
```

Figure 9.J.2

J.4 echo

echo displays its arguments on the standard output file, separating each argument in the standard output by a single space. **echo** also displays a newline at the end of the arguments, unless you specify the -n option as the first argument. Figure 9.J.3 shows an example.

```
1% echo this is a test
this is a test
2% echo -n this line has no newline
this line has no newline3% echo this one does, though
this one does, though
4% ☐
```

Figure 9.J.3

J.5 eval and exec

eval and **exec** operate the same in the C Shell as they do in the Bourne Shell. For examples of their use, see Section H of Chapter 8.

J.6 exit

exit causes a shell procedure or an interactive shell to end. If the interactive shell is your login shell, you are also logged off the system.

exit accepts an expression as an argument and returns the value of the expression to the command that started the shell procedure or interactive shell. If no argument is given, **exit** returns the value of the status predefined shell variable, which reflects the value returned by the last command executed.

J.7 glob

glob accepts a list of words as an argument, expands each word in the list according to the files in the named directories, and writes one line on the standard output file that contains the expanded file names. File names written on standard output are separated by null characters, ASCII 0, and the line ends with a single null character. Figure 9.J.4 shows an example of **glob**, where **glob**'s output is displayed as characters using the **od** program.

```
1% cd /usr/bin
2% echo e*
enable ex
3% glob e*
enableex4% glob e* | od -c
0000000 e  n  a  b  l  e  \0  e  x  \0
0000011
5% ☐
```

Figure 9.J.4

J.8 hashstat, rehash, and unhash

When the C Shell is given a command to execute, it first does all history substitutions specified in the command, and then breaks the command into words. The shell next does all alias substitutions based on the first word in each command produced after each alias substitution. Variable substitutions are next, followed by all command and file name substitutions. When all substitutions are complete, the C Shell has a set of words that define the command to be executed.

The first word in this set of words names the program to be executed. The C Shell then looks to see if the program names a built-in command, executing that command line if it is built-in. If the program is not built into the shell, the shell must find a file with that name in a directories listed by the path variable.

To reduce directory searching time, the C Shell maintains a hash table that it uses to find files in the file system named as programs in commands. The C Shell provides three built-in commands that let you operate on this hash table.

hashstat tells you how effective the hash table is by keeping track of the number of successful and unsuccessful **exec**() system calls. A successful **exec**() system call means that when the shell executed **exec**(), the **exec**() was able to start the command you gave to the shell. An unsuccessful **exec**() system call means that the **exec**() was not able to start your command because the program named in the command was not in the directory where the shell thought it was.

In general, the hash table names the correct directory where the program resides. However, when you name the current directory (dot) in path, the shell blindly executes an **exec**() to try to start the command you've entered. To improve the effectiveness of the hash table, put the current directory at the end of the list of directories in the path variable. Figure 9.J.5 shows an example.

```
1% set path=(/bin /usr/bin ~/bin .)
2% hashstat
3% cd ~/bin
4% hashstat
5% echo who am I > me
6% hashstat
7% chmod u=rwx,go=rx me
8% hashstat
1 hits, 0 misses, 100%
9% cd
10% hashstat
1 hits, 0 misses, 100%
11% me
me: Command not found.
12% hashstat
1 hits, 1 misses, 50%
13% rehash
14% hashstat
1 hits, 1 misses, 50%
15% me
rogers   tty04   Oct 11 18:27
16% hashstat
```

```
2 hits, 1 misses, 66%
17% date
Tue Oct 11 18:28:02 EDT 1983
18% hashstat
3 hits, 1 misses, 75%
19% ls -l /usr/bin/fgrep
-rwxr-xr-x  1 root    root       9216 Jul  9 1981 /usr/bin/fgrep
20% hashstat
4 hits, 1 misses, 80%
21% fgrep root /etc/passwd
root:G4S2TGIOLCtlg:0:10:The root of all evil:/:/bin/csh
22% hashstat
5 hits, 1 misses, 83%
23% unhash
24% fgrep root /etc/passwd
root:G4S2TGIOLCtlg:0:10:The root of all evil:/:/bin/csh
25% hashstat
6 hits, 2 misses, 75%
26% □
```

Figure 9.J.5

Event 1 in the example defines the directories to be used by the shell when searching for program files. When path is changed with the **set** command, the C Shell reconstructs its hash table. Notice that the current directory is the last directory in path.

hashstat in events 2, 4, and 6 gives no hash table statistics because the commands in events 1, 3, and 5 are built into the shell, so the hash table wasn't needed to find them. However, **chmod** in event 7 is not a built-in command, so the shell must find a file named *chmod* in the file system. **hashstat** in event 8 shows that only one **exec**() system call was needed to start **chmod** successfully.

The **me** command executed in event 11 was added to the ~/*bin* directory, but the shell could not find it even though ~/*bin* is in path. When you add a new command to a directories listed in your path variable, you must tell the C Shell to reconstruct its hash table by executing the **rehash** built-in command as event 13 shows. When the **me** command is executed in event 15, the shell finds it in its hash table and is able to start the **me** command.

When the shell was unable to find **me** in its hash table, the shell then guessed that **me** was in the current directory. The shell looked in the hash table first because of the order of directories listed in path. The shell tried to start the **me** command by executing an **exec**() system call using the files in the current directory. This **exec**() was unsuccessful because of the **cd** in event 9, and the shell said that it couldn't find **me**. **hashstat** showed the unsuccessful **exec**() as a miss and recomputed the hash table effectiveness.

Finally, **unhash** in event 23 disables the shell's use of the hash table, forcing the shell to try an **exec**() of each program named in a command, using each directory listed in path. To see what the shell does when the hash table is disabled, notice that output of the **ls** program, event 19, shows that **fgrep** is located in the */usr/bin* directory and that */usr/bin* is the second directory listed in path. When **fgrep** is executed in event 24, the shell first tries to execute */bin/fgrep*, and, failing that, tries to execute */usr/bin/fgrep*. **hashstat** in event 25 shows one more miss and one more hit, reflecting the unsuccessful **exec**() of */bin/fgrep* followed by the successful **exec**() of */usr/bin/fgrep*.

J.9 kill

kill sends the signal given as the first argument to the processes given as the remaining arguments. Signals can be given as numbers or as names, where the names are taken from the manifest constants defined in */usr/include/signal.h*, after first removing the SIG prefix. Figure 9.J.6 shows an example in which process number 5699 is sent the hang-up signal.

```
1% sleep 60 &
5699
2% kill -HUP 5699
Hangup
3% ▯
```

Figure 9.J.6

J.10 login and logout

The **login** built-in command ends your login shell and starts the login process all over again. **logout** ends your login shell, and also gives control to the **getty** program that re-establishes your terminal characteristics.

When you log off the system with **logout**, **exit**, or ˆD, the C Shell executes the *.logout* shell procedure located in your home directory. The *.logout* shell procedure is useful if you want to save your history command list to remind you when you log back in to the UNIX system what you were doing before you logged off, for example. Figure 9.J.7 shows an example of a *.logout* shell procedure.

```
1% number .logout
1   #################################
2   #   .logout
3   #   save essential data for
4   #   the next login session
5   #################################
6   history > ~/.lastcommands
7   clear
2% □
```

Figure 9.J.7

J.11 nice

The **nice** command lets you decrease the priority of a command so that it will run slower and have less impact on others working on your UNIX system. **nice** is recommended when you run a command in the background that you want to finish, but you don't care when.

nice's syntax is:

> nice *command*
> nice +*number command*

The first form runs *command* at a nice value of 4, and the second form runs *command* at a nice value of *number*. Commands started by the **nice** built-in command run slower as the nice value gets larger.

J.12 nohup and onintr

The C Shell also lets you control signals in a shell procedure with **nohup** and **onintr**. **nohup** without an argument tells a shell procedure to ignore all hang-up signals sent to that procedure. Hang-up signals are sent to all of your background processes when you log off the UNIX system.

When you give a command as an argument to **nohup**, that command is run with hang-up signals ignored. This feature lets you start a command in the background and then log off the system. Because the command ignores the hang-up signal sent when you log off, the command will run until it finishes.

onintr tells the shell how to handle interrupts. With no arguments, **onintr** tells the shell to reset all interrupts to their default values, meaning that interrupts will be caught and the shell procedure will end. With a '-' argument, **onintr** tells the shell to ignore all interrupts. Both forms should be used to bracket critical, non-interruptible sections in a shell procedure as the figure below shows.

508

```
onintr -                        # turn off all interrupts
...                                    # critical section
onintr                          # turn interrupts back on
```

Figure 9.J.8

The final form of **onintr** takes a label argument that tells the shell where to transfer control when an interrupt occurs. This form is useful when a shell procedure must remove the temporary files it creates when interrupted.

Recall from Section G in Chapter 8 that the interrupt catching mechanism must be started before a temporary file is created. This insures that the file will be removed when an interrupt occurs. Figure 9.J.9 shows a shell procedure skeleton that correctly handles interrupts and removes a temporary file.

```
1       set TMP = /tmp/$$
2       set INTERRUPTS = 1
3       onintr gohome
4       cat /dev/null > $TMP
5       ...
6       onintr -
7       set INTERRUPTS = 0
8       gohome:
9       rm -f $TMP
10      exit $INTERRUPTS
```

Figure 9.J.9

This skeleton also correctly reflects the shell procedure's interrupt status back to the process that called it through the procedure's return value.

Figure 9.J.10 shows the **catcher** shell procedure that catches interrupts and exists with the proper return value. DELETE means that the DELETE, DEL, or RUBOUT key was entered from the keyboard.

```
1% number catcher
 1  ##############################
 2  #   catcher
 3  #   catches an interrupt
 4  ##############################
 5  set INTERRUPTS = 1
 6  onintr gotone
 7  @ COUNT = 0
 8  while ($COUNT < 10)
 9      echo Nothing yet
10      @ COUNT++
11  end
12  onintr -
13  set INTERRUPTS = 0
14  gotone:
15  if ($INTERRUPTS == 1) then
16      echo ""
17  endif
18  exit $INTERRUPTS
2% catcher
Nothing yet
Nothing yet
Nothing yet
Nothing yet
Nothing yet
Nothing yet
Nothing yet
Nothing yet
Nothing yet
Nothing yet
3% echo $status
0
4% catcher
Nothing yet
Nothing yet
Nothing yet
Nothing yet
Nothing yet
<DELETE>
5% echo $status
1
6% ☐
```

Figure 9.J.10

J.13 repeat

repeat causes the command given as the second argument to be repeated first argument times. Figure 9.J.11 shows an example.

510

```
1% repeat 3 echo help
help
help
help
2%□
```

Figure 9.J.11

J.14 set, unset, setenv, and unsetenv

set is used to assign values to shell variables and **unset** is used to remove shell variables from the shell's internal list of set variables. **unset** accepts a pattern as an argument.

Most variables whose values are established with **set** are not placed in the environment of the child processes. The exceptions are user, term, and To place a variable in the environment of a child process, use the **setenv** command, the C Shell equivalent of the Bourne Shell's **export** command. **setenv** has syntax:

   setenv *name value*

where the form of *name* and *value* are the same as the form of *name* and *value* for the **set** built-in command.

unsetenv removes variables given by the pattern argument from the environment. **unsetenv** is the import function missing from the Bourne Shell.

Figure 9.J.12 shows an example in which variables are set and then unset, and variables are placed into the environment and then removed from the environment. The example uses another instance of the C Shell as the child process to show what variables are in the environment. To distinguish the login shell from the new instance, the login shell's prompt is changed to $.

```
1% set prompt="$ "
$ set
argv    ()
history 15
home    /usr/rogers
ignoreeof
path    (. /bin /usr/bin /usr/rogers/bin)
prompt  $
shell   /bin/csh
status  0
term    concept
$ printenv
HOME=/usr/rogers
PATH=.:/bin:/usr/bin:/usr/rogers/bin
EXINIT=set ai sm sw=4 ts=4
TERM=concept
$ set path=($home/bin /bin /usr/bin .)
$ set
argv    ()
history 15
home    /usr/rogers
ignoreeof
path    (/usr/rogers/bin /bin /usr/bin .)
prompt  $
shell   /bin/csh
status  0
term    concept
$ printenv
HOME=/usr/rogers
PATH=/usr/rogers/bin:/bin:/usr/bin:
EXINIT=set ai sm sw=4 ts=4
TERM=concept
$ set X=argument
$ echo $X
argument
$ unset X
$ echo $X
X: Undefined variable.
$ setenv MYNAME rogers
$ csh
% printenv
HOME=/usr/rogers
PATH=/usr/rogers/bin:/bin:/usr/bin:
EXINIT=set ai sm sw=4 ts=4
TERM=concept
MYNAME=rogers
% ^D
$ unsetenv MYNAME
$ csh
% printenv
HOME=/usr/rogers
SHELL=/bin/csh
```

512

```
PATH=.:/usr/rogers/bin:/usr/local/bin:/bin:/usr/bin
TERM=concept
USER=rogers
CDPATH=. /usr/rogers
% ^D
$ ☐
```

Figure 9.J.12

J.15 shift

shift with no arguments simulates execution of the following shell procedure segment.

```
1     if ($#argv == 0) then
2             echo shift: No more words.
3     else
4             @ X = 2
5             while ($X <= $#argv)
6                     @ Y = $X - 1
7                     set argv[$Y] = "$argv[$X]"
8                     @ X++
9             end
10    endif
```

Figure 9.J.13

and also reduces $#argv by 1. **shift** with a shell variable argument does the same operations on that shell variable. Figure 9.J.14 shows an example.

```
1% set argv=(arg1 arg2 arg3 arg4 arg5)
2% echo $argv
arg1 arg2 arg3 arg4 arg5
3% echo $#argv
5
4% shift
5% echo $argv
arg2 arg3 arg4 arg5
6% echo $#argv
4
7% set X=(1 2 3 4 5 6 7 8)
8% echo $X
1 2 3 4 5 6 7 8
9% echo $#X
8
10% shift X
11% echo $#X
7
12% ☐
```

Figure 9.J.14

J.16 source

source is the C Shell equivalent of the dot command in the Bourne Shell. **source** reads commands from the file named as the argument and executes them as though they were entered in place of the **source** command. **source** is useful when you change your *.login* and *.cshrc* files and you want the changes to effect your login shell without logging out and logging back in. Figure 9.J.15 shows an example.

```
1% echo $X
X: Undefined variable.
2% echo set X=argument > file
3% source file
4% echo $X
argument
5% ☐
```

Figure 9.J.15

514

J.17 time

time tells you the amount of user, system, and elapsed time used by the login shell and all programs run by that login shell since the time you logged in. With a command argument, **time** gives the same information, but only for that command. Figure 9.J.16 shows an example of **time**.

1% **time**
0.3u 0.7s 0:30 3%
2% **time date**
Wed Oct 12 10:44:31 EDT 1983
0.0u 0.0s 0:00 5%
3% **time who am I**
rogers   tty04   Oct 12 10:44
0.1u 0.1s 0:01 20%
4% ☐

Figure 9.J.16

J.18 umask

umask in the C Shell defines a mask of permissions you wish to exclude from files created by the shell. By default, files are created with mode 666, meaning files are readable and writable by you, your group, and others. The value given as the argument to **umask** stays with the login shell and all processes started by that shell, and is used by commands that create files. Figure 9.J.17 shows examples of **umask**.

1% **umask**
22
2% **cat /etc/passwd > tpasswd**
3% **ls -l tpasswd**
-rw-r--r-- 1 rogers   writers   575 Oct 12 17:53 tpasswd
4% **umask 26**
5% **rm tpasswd**
6% **cat /etc/passwd > tpasswd**
8% **ls -l tpasswd**
-rw-r----- 1 rogers   writers   575 Oct 12 17:53 tpasswd
8% ☐

Figure 9.J.17

J.19 wait

wait causes the shell to wait for all commands running in the background and works the same as **wait** in the Bourne Shell. Figure 9.J.18 shows an example of the **wait** command that waits until **sleep** finishes.

1% **date; sleep 10& wait; date**
8017
Wed Oct 12 10:48:16 EDT 1983
Wed Oct 12 10:48:26 EDT 1983
2% ☐

Figure 9.J.18

This is the same as:

1% **date; sleep 10; date**
8017
Wed Oct 12 10:48:52 EDT 1983
Wed Oct 12 10:49:12 EDT 1983
2% ☐

Figure 9.J.19

K. DEBUGGING SHELL PROCEDURES

The C Shell offers better shell procedure debugging options than does the Bourne Shell. These options let you isolate and correct syntax and logic errors more quickly and accurately than do the Bourne Shell options. This section describes how to debug C Shell procedures.

The example shell procedure used to show debugging techniques in the C Shell is the same shell procedure used in Chapter 8. Figure 9.K.1 shows version 4 of **OD**.

```
1% number OD4
 1  ################################
 2  #   OD
 3  #   general interface to
 4  #   the od(1) command
 5  #   version 4
 6  ################################
 7  set OPTIONS PREFIX NAMES
 8  set RC=0
 9  foreach arg ($argv)
10      switch ($arg)
11      case --:
12          shift
13          break
14      case -*:
15          shift
16          echo $arg is not a legal flag
17          set RC=1
18          breaksw
19      case -[bcdox]:
20          shift
21          set OPTIONS=$OPTIONS'echo $arg | sed s/.//'
22          set PREFIX=-
23          breaksw
24      default:
25          break
26      endsw
27  end
28  if ( $RC == 1 ) then
29      echo "usage: $0 [-bcdox] [file ...]"
30  else if ( $#argv == 0 ) then
31      od $PREFIX$OPTIONS
32  else
33      foreach file ($argv)
34          echo "=====$file"
35          od $PREFIX$OPTIONS $file
36      end
37  endif
38  exit $RC
2% □
```

Figure 9.K.1

Figure 9.K.2 shows how **OD4** reacts when run with options that it should recognize.

```
1% echo testing | OD4 -c -b
-c is not a legal flag
-b is not a legal flag
usage: OD4 [-bcdox] [file ...]
2% □
```

Figure 9.K.2

Before debugging any C Shell procedure, it's a good idea to run the file through the C Shell syntax checker. This helps you eliminate all syntax errors before you start intensive debugging. To check a C Shell procedure for correct syntax, specify the -n option to the shell as figure 9.K.3 shows.

```
1% csh -n OD4
2% □
```

Figure 9.K.3

The C Shell will tell you what syntax errors it finds. You should then correct them and check the file again until you fix all errors.

The first technique to use when debugging a shell procedure is to invoke explicitly the C Shell with the echo and verbose options turned on. These options cause the shell to display all commands just after all history substitutions are made and just before the commands are executed. Figure 9.K.4 shows this technique applied to the **OD4** shell procedure.

```
1% echo testing | csh -x -v OD4 -c -b >& /tmp/output
2% number /tmp/output
 1
 2
 3
 4
 5
 6
 7  set OPTIONS PREFIX NAMES
 8  set OPTIONS PREFIX NAMES
 9  set RC=0
10  set RC=0
11  foreach arg ( $argv )
12  foreach arg ( -c -b )
13  switch ( $arg )
14  switch ( -c )
15  shift
16  shift
17  echo $arg is not a legal flag
18  echo -c is not a legal flag
19  -c is not a legal flag
20  set RC=1
21  set RC=1
22  breaksw
23  breaksw
24  end
25  end
26  switch ( $arg )
27  switch ( -b )
28  shift
29  shift
30  echo $arg is not a legal flag
31  echo -b is not a legal flag
32  -b is not a legal flag
33  set RC=1
34  set RC=1
35  breaksw
36  breaksw
37  end
38  end
39  if ( $RC == 1 ) then
40  if ( 1 == 1 ) then
41  echo "usage: $0 [-bcdox] [file ...]"
42  echo usage: OD [-bcdox] [file ...]
43  usage: OD [-bcdox] [file ...]
44  else if ( $#argv == 0 ) then
45  else if ( 0 == 0 ) then
46  exit $RC
47  exit 1
3% □
```

Figure 9.K.4

Lines 1 through 6 are blank because the first six lines of **OD4** are comments. Each command executed by the shell is shown twice: once because echo mode is enabled and once because verbose mode is enabled.

The debugging output shows that both the -c and -b arguments match the -* case, so the shell executes the commands on lines 15 through 18 in figure 9.K.1. Why does the shell execute these commands instead of the commands on lines 20 through 23 in figure 9.K.1? That is, why do -c and -b match -* and not -[bcdox]?

The problem is that the C Shell looks at cases in a **switch** statement in the order written. The shell finds -* before it finds -[bcdox] and since -c and -b match — *, the shell executes the associated commands. The debugged version is shown below, along with a sample of execution.

```
1% number OD4a
1   ###############################
2   #   OD
3   #   general interface to
4   #   the od(1) command
5   #   version 4a
6   ###############################
7   set OPTIONS PREFIX NAMES
8   set RC=0
9   foreach arg ($argv)
10      switch ($arg)
11      case --:
12          shift
13          break
14      case -[bcdox]:
15          shift
16          set OPTIONS=$OPTIONS'echo $arg | sed s/.//'
17          set PREFIX=-
18          breaksw
19      case -*:
20          shift
21          echo $arg is not a legal flag
22          set RC=1
23          breaksw
24      default:
25          break
26      endsw
27  end
28  if ( $RC == 1 ) then
29      echo "usage: $0 [-bcdox] [file ...]"
30  else if ( $#argv == 0 ) then
31      od $PREFIX$OPTIONS
32  else
33      foreach file ($argv)
34          echo "=====$file"
35          od $PREFIX$OPTIONS $file
36      end
37  endif
38  exit $RC
2% echo testing | OD4a -c -b
0000000   t   e   s   t   i   n   g  \n
        164 145 163 164 151 156 147 012
0000010
3% □
```

Figure 9.K.5

Another way to enable echo and verbose modes is with the **set** built-in function. Remember that echo and verbose are set valued predefined shell variables, so their values are irrelevant. Use **unset** to disable echo and

521

verbose.

In long shell procedures, you can be swamped by debugging information produced by the C Shell when echo and verbose modes are enabled for the entire shell procedure. You can reduce debugging output by bracketing the section of code in question with set echo verbose/unset echo verbose. This technique lets you concentrate your efforts on the place or places where you suspect the problem is in a shell procedure.

The second technique parallels a technique used in debugging Bourne Shell procedures. When debugging a C Shell procedure, add **echo** statements to display additional information and to show the flow of control through a procedure. **OD4b** as modified by **echo** statements is shown below.

```
1% number OD4b
 1  ###############################
 2  #   OD
 3  #   general interface to
 4  #   the od(1) command
 5  #   version 4b
 6  ###############################
 7  set OPTIONS PREFIX NAMES
 8  set RC=0
 9  foreach arg ($argv)
10      switch ($arg)
11      case --:
12          echo "=====$arg matches --"
13          shift
14          break
15      case -*:
16          echo "=====$arg matches -*"
17          shift
18          echo $arg is not a legal flag
19          set RC=1
20          breaksw
21      case -[bcdox]:
22          echo "=====$arg matches -[bcdox]"
23          shift
24          set OPTIONS=$OPTIONS`echo $arg | sed s/.//`
25          set PREFIX=-
26          breaksw
27      default:
28          break
29      endsw
30  end
31  if ( $RC == 1 ) then
32      echo "usage: $0 [-bcdox] [file ...]"
33  else if ( $#argv == 0 ) then
34      od $PREFIX$OPTIONS
35  else
36      foreach file ($argv)
37          echo "=====$file"
38          od $PREFIX$OPTIONS $file
39      end
40  endif
41  exit $RC
2% □
```

Figure 9.K.6

When executed, **OD4b** displays:

```
1% echo testing | OD4b -c -b
= = = = = -c matches -*
-c is not a legal flag
= = = = = -b matches -*
-b is not a legal flag
usage: OD4b [-bcdox] [file ...]
2%
```

Figure 9.K.7

Again, the output shows that -c and -b match a different pattern than intended, meaning that cases are in the wrong order. When rewritten, **OD** produces the expected result as shown previously.

L. THE STORES SYSTEM - C SHELL STYLE

As a final example of shell procedures, consider the C Shell versions of the STORES System explained in Section J of Chapter 8. Recall that Section J emphasizes that solutions to the STORES System must solve the problem as defined. To this requirement, add the notion that the C Shell version should operate identically to the Bourne Shell version shown in Chapter 8. You are again encouraged to enter the shell procedures shown in this section and to program those portions not shown. You are further encouraged to mix Bourne Shell procedures with C Shell procedures to be certain that interprocedure interfaces are correct and that the C Shell versions solve the problem the same way that the Bourne Shell versions do.

By rewriting the **stores, order,** and **notin** Bourne Shell shell procedures, some differences between the two shells come to light. The first difference is that the C Shell redirection operators cannot be used to force output to go to the standard error file as required by the STORES System problem description. One solution to this problem is the **toerr** program shown below.

```
1% number toerr.c
1   /*
2    *   toerr
3    *       write standard input on standard error
4    */
5
6   #include    <stdio.h>
7
8   main()
9   {
10      register int c;
11
12      while ((c = getchar()) != EOF) {
13          putc(c, stderr);
14      }
15      exit(0);
16  }
2%□
```

Figure 9.L.1

toerr is used when these shell procedures must write messages on the standard error file.

The second difference appears in both the **order** and **notin** shell procedures. The problem is that the C Shell does not allow a redefinition of the standard input of each command in a structured loop as does the Bourne Shell. To solve this problem in **order**, **prorder**, figure 9.L.2 is used to print an order.

```
$ number prorder
 1  ###############################
 2  #   ORDER SYSTEM
 3  #   Print an order
 4  ###############################
 5  echo "Please send to:"
 6  echo "  $1"
 7  echo "  $2"
 8  echo "  $3"
 9  echo "  $4"
10  echo
11  IFS=" "
12  while read STOCK QUANTITY DESCRIPTION COST PAGE DATE
13  do
14      echo "Stock Number:    $STOCK"
15      echo "Quantity: $QUANTITY"
16      echo "Description:  $DESCRIPTION"
17      echo "Unit Cost:    $COST"
18      echo "Catalogue Page: $PAGE"
19      echo
20  done
21  exit 0
2% □
```

Figure 9.L.2

notin's also requires a special purpose program because its description says that "... the system should display an item, and then let the customer decide whether to continue listing items or to stop." notin uses prnotin, figure 9.L.3.

526

```
1%  number prnotin
1   ################################
2   #   ORDER SYSTEM
3   #   Print list of items not
4   #   received
5   ################################
6   BB = / dev / null
7   IFS =" "
8   while read STORE STOCK QUANTITY DESCRIPTION COST PAGE DATE
9   do
10      echo Order from "$STORE"
11      echo " Stock Number: $STOCK"
12      echo " Quantity:    $QUANTITY"
13      echo " Description:$DESCRIPTION"
14      echo " Cost:        $COST"
15      echo " Catalogue Page:    $PAGE"
16      echo " Ordered on:$DATE"
17      echo "Continue?: \c"
18      RESP = '(read RESP; echo "$RESP") < /dev/tty'
19      if expr "$RESP" : "^[yY]" > $BB 2> $BB
20      then
21          continue
22      else
23          break
24      fi
25  done
26  exit 0
2% □
```

Figure 9.L.3

L.1 The stores Command

The C Shell version of the **stores** command operates identically to the Bourne Shell version. Notice especially that the C Shell version redefines interrupts to handle correctly those interrupts generated by the customer who ends the **notin** command by typing RUBOUT or DELETE.

```
1% number stores
 1 ###############################
 2 #   ORDER SYSTEM
 3 #   Order items from store catalogues
 4 #   Main order system command
 5 ###############################
 6 #   Command defaults
 7 ###############################
 8 set OFILE=".stores.csh"
 9 set BB=/dev/null
10 ###############################
11 #   Pick up variables for this user
12 ###############################
13 if (! -r ~/$OFILE) then
14     echo No "$OFILE" file in your HOME directory
15     echo Please answer the following questions and I will build one for you.
16     while (1)
17         echo -n "Your name: "
18         set NAME=$<
19         if ("$NAME" == "") then
20             echo Invalid name - enter again
21         else
22             break
23         endif
24     end
25     while (1)
26         echo -n "Your mailing street address: "
27         set ADDRESS=$<
28         if ("$ADDRESS" == "") then
29             echo Invalid street address - enter again
30         else
31             break
32         endif
33     end
34     while (1)
35         echo -n "The city you live in: "
36         set TOWN=$<
37         if ("$TOWN" == "") then
38             echo Invalid city - enter again
39         else
40             break
41         endif
42     end
43     while (1)
44         echo -n "The state you live in, with zip code: "
45         set STATE=$<
46         if ("$STATE" == "") then
47             echo Invalid state/zip - enter again
48         else
49             break
50         endif
51     end
```

528

```
52     echo -n "A directory where orders can be saved ($HOME/orders): "
53     set ORDERDIR=$<
54     if ("$ORDERDIR" == "") then
55         set ORDERDIR=$HOME/orders
56     endif
57     echo -n "A file where a list of received items is stored (received): "
58     set RECEIVED=$<
59     if ("$RECEIVED" == "") then
60         set RECEIVED=received
61     endif
62     echo -n "A file where a list of items not received is stored (nreceived): "
63     set NRECEIVED=$<
64     if ("$NRECEIVED" == "") then
65         set NRECEIVED=nreceived
66     endif
67     echo -n "Your favorite editor (vi): "
68     set EDITOR=$<
69     if ("$EDITOR" == "") then
70         set EDITOR=vi
71     endif
72     echo set NAME=\($NAME\) > $HOME/$OFILE
73     echo set ADDRESS=\($ADDRESS\) >> $HOME/$OFILE
74     echo set TOWN=\($TOWN\) >> $HOME/$OFILE
75     echo set STATE=\($STATE\) >> $HOME/$OFILE
76     echo set ORDERDIR=\($ORDERDIR\) >> $HOME/$OFILE
77     echo set RECEIVED=\($RECEIVED\) >> $HOME/$OFILE
78     echo set NRECEIVED=\($NRECEIVED\) >> $HOME/$OFILE
79     echo set EDITOR=\($EDITOR\) >> $HOME/$OFILE
80 endif
81 set RC=0
82 source ~/$OFILE
83 if ( ! -d "$ORDERDIR" ) then
84     if ( { mkdir "$ORDERDIR" >& $BB } ) then
85         chmod u=rwx "$ORDERDIR"
86     else
87         echo "Cannot make $ORDERDIR directory" | toerr
88         set RC=1
89     endif
90 endif
91 if (! -w "$ORDERDIR" || ! -r "$ORDERDIR") then
92     echo "$ORDERDIR" not readable/writable | toerr
93     set RC=1
94 endif
95 cd "$ORDERDIR"
96 if (! -f "$RECEIVED") then
97     if ( { cp $BB "$RECEIVED" >& $BB } ) then
98         chmod u=rw "$RECEIVED"
99     else
100        echo Cannot create "$RECEIVED" | toerr
101        set RC=1
102    endif
103 endif
104 if (! -w "$RECEIVED" || ! -r "$RECEIVED") then
```

```
105     echo "$RECEIVED" not readable/writable | toerr
106     set RC=1
107 endif
108 if (! -f "$NRECEIVED") then
109     if ( | cp $BB "$NRECEIVED" >& $BB | ) then
110         chmod u=rw "$NRECEIVED"
111     else
112         echo Cannot create "$NRECEIVED" | toerr
113         set RC=1
114     endif
115 endif
116 if (! -w "$NRECEIVED" || ! -r "$NRECEIVED") then
117     echo "$NRECEIVED" not readable/writable | toerr
118     set RC=1
119 endif
120 if ($RC == 0) then
121     setenv NAME "$NAME"
122     setenv ADDRESS "$ADDRESS"
123     setenv TOWN "$TOWN"
124     setenv STATE "$STATE"
125     setenv ORDERDIR "$ORDERDIR"
126     setenv RECEIVED "$RECEIVED"
127     setenv NRECEIVED "$NRECEIVED"
128     setenv EDITOR "$EDITOR"
129 quit:
130     while (1)
131         onintr leave
132         echo "Choose one of the following"
133         echo "(Type word or first letter in either case)"
134         echo " help          Help on this program"
135         echo " order         Place an order"
136         echo " receive       Print items ordered and received"
137         echo " notin         Print items ordered but not received"
138         echo " look          Locate a particular item received"
139         echo " quit          Quit this program"
140         echo -n ": "
141         set FUNCTION=$<
142         if ("$FUNCTION" == "") break
143         onintr quit
144         switch ($FUNCTION)
145         case o*:
146         case O*:
147             order
148             breaksw
149         case r*:
150         case R*:
151             receive
152             breaksw
153         case n*:
154         case N*:
155             notin
156             breaksw
157         case l*:
```

```
158        case L*:
159            look
160            breaksw
161        case h*:
162        case H*:
163            help
164            breaksw
165        case q*:
166        case Q*:
167            break
168            breaksw
169        default:
170            echo "$FUNCTION" unknown | toerr
171            echo Try help | toerr
172            breaksw
173        endsw
174    end
175 endif
176 leave:
177 exit $RC
2% ☐
```

Figure 9.L.4

L.2 The order Command

The **order** command also operates identically to its Bourne Shell counterpart. The only difference is that **prorder** is used to format the order before printing. Because **prorder** is written as a Bourne Shell procedure, lines 120 and 123 change and restore the shell to be used, respectively.

```
1% number order
 1  ################################
 2  #   ORDER SYSTEM
 3  #   Build an order
 4  ################################
 5  #   Define constants
 6  ################################
 7  set INTERRUPTS = 1
 8  onintr leave
 9  set TMP = /tmp/$$
10  set BB = /dev/null
11  cd $ORDERDIR
12  ################################
13  #   Get store name
14  ################################
15  echo -n "Enter store name: "
16  set STORE=$<
17  if ("$STORE" == "") then
18      echo No order made
19      exit 0
20  endif
21  set STORE='echo "$STORE" | tr "[A-Z]" "[a-z]"'
22  ################################
23  #   Get file name for order
24  ################################
25  if ( -e $ORDERDIR/$|STORE|000 ) then
26      set VAR=$|STORE|*
27      set SEQ=$#VAR
28  else
29      set SEQ=0
30  endif
31  if ("$SEQ" < 10) then
32      set SEQ=00$SEQ
33  else if ("$SEQ" < 100) then
34      set SEQ=0$SEQ
35  endif
36  set FILE=$ORDERDIR/$STORE$SEQ
37  onintr removefiles
38  touch $FILE
39  set DATE='date'
40  ################################
41  #   Prompt for and read
42  #   requests for input
43  ################################
44  while (1)
45      echo -n "Stock Number: "
46      set STOCK=$<
47      if ("$STOCK" == "") break
48      if ({ grep -s "^$STORE  $STOCK      " $NRECEIVED >& $BB }) then
49          echo -n "$STOCK already ordered. Do you want to order more?: "
50          set RESP=$<
51          if ( "$RESP" !~ [yY]* ) continue
```

532

```
52      endif
53      while (1)
54          echo -n "Quantity: "
55          set QUANTITY=$<
56          if ( { set VAR=`expr "$QUANTITY" : '^[0-9][0-9]*$'` } ) then
57              break
58          endif >& $BB
59          echo Quantity \("$QUANTITY"\) not all numbers | toerr
60      end
61      while (1)
62          echo -n "Description: "
63          set DESCRIPTION=$<
64          if ("$DESCRIPTION" != "") then
65              set DESCRIPTION=`echo $DESCRIPTION`
66              break
67          endif
68          echo Item must have description | toerr
69      end
70      while (1)
71          echo -n "Unit cost: "
72          set COST=$<
73          if ( { set VAR=`expr "$COST" : '^[0-9][0-9]*.[0-9][0-9]$'` } ) then
74              break
75          endif
76          if ( { set VAR=`expr "$COST" : '^[0-9][0-9]*$'` } ) then
77              set COST=${COST}.00
78              break
79          endif
80          echo Cost \("$COST"\) not in correct format | toerr
81          echo Allowable formats are: 99 and 99.99 | toerr
82      end
83      while (1)
84          echo -n "Catalogue page number: "
85          set PAGE=$<
86          if ( { set VAR=`expr "$PAGE" : '[0-9][0-9]*'` } ) then
87              break
88          endif
89          echo Page number \("$PAGE"\) not all numbers | toerr
90      end
91      echo "Ordering the following item:"
92      echo " Stock Number: $STOCK"
93      echo " Quantity:     $QUANTITY"
94      echo " Description:$DESCRIPTION"
95      echo " Unit Cost:   $COST"
96      echo " Catalogue Page:   $PAGE"
97      echo "$STOCK $QUANTITY $DESCRIPTION $COST $PAGE$DATE" >> $TMP
98 end
99 ###############################
100 #   Allow editing
101 ###############################
102 echo -n "Would you like to edit this file?: "
103 set RESP=$<
104 if ( "$RESP" =~ [yY]* ) then
```

```
105     echo "I'll start $EDITOR for you"
106     eval $EDITOR "$TMP"
107 endif
108 ################################
109 #   Move temporary file
110 #   to order file
111 ################################
112 onintr -
113 mv $TMP $FILE
114 ################################
115 #   Save in not received
116 #   file
117 ################################
118 sed "s/^/$STORE   /" < $FILE >> $NRECEIVED
119 echo -n "Printing the order..."
120 set shell = /bin/sh
121 prorder "$NAME" "$ADDRESS" "$TOWN" "STATE" < $FILE | \
122     pr -h "Items Ordered from $STORE on $DATE" | lpr
123 set shell = /bin/csh
124 echo "Done"
125 ################################
126 #   Remove files, also for
127 #   interrupts
128 ################################
129 set INTERRUPTS=0
130 removefiles:
131 onintr -
132 if ($INTERRUPTS == 1) then
133     rm -f $FILE
134     echo ""
135 endif
136 rm -f $TMP
137 leave:
138 exit $INTERRUPTS
2% □
```

Figure 9.L.5

L.3 The notin Command

notin operates identically to the Bourne Shell version. Again, lines 20 and 22 change and restore the shell to be used.

534

```
1% number notin
1   ##############################
2   #   ORDER SYSTEM
3   #   Print list of items not
4   #   received
5   ##############################
6   echo -n "Would you like to see orders for a specific store? "
7   set RESP=$<
8   if ( "$RESP" =~ [yY]* ) then
9       echo -n "Which store? "
10      set STR=($<)
11      if ("$STR" == "") then
12          echo "All orders will be listed"
13          set STR="[a-z]"
14      else
15          set STR=`echo "$STR" | tr "[A-Z]" "[a-z]"`
16      endif
17  else
18      set STR="[a-z]"
19  endif
20  set shell=/bin/sh
21  grep "^$STR" < $NRECEIVED | prnotin
22  set shell=/bin/csh
23  exit 0
2%
```

Figure 9.L.6

Figure 9.L.7 shows a sample of execution.

```
1% stores
No .stores.csh file in your HOME directory
Please answer the following questions and I will build one for you.
Your name: Lawrence R. Rogers
Your mailing street address: 232 Edinburg Road
The city you live in: Mercerville
The state you live in, with zip code: NJ 08619
A directory where orders can be saved (/usr/lrr/orders):
A file where a list of received items is stored (received):
A file where a list of items not received is stored (nreceived):
Your favorite editor (vi): ex
Choose one of the following
(Type word or first letter in either case)
        help        Help on this program
        order       Place an order
        receive     Print items ordered and received
        notin       Print items ordered but not received
        look        Locate a particular item received
        quit        Quit this program
    : o
Enter store name: sears
Stock Number: B132-JK
B132-JK already ordered.  Do you want to order more?: y
Quantity: 5
Description: Grass Trimmer Cord
Unit cost: 1.89 each
Cost (1.89 each) not in correct format
Allowable formats are: 99 and 99.99
Unit cost: 1.89
Catalogue page number: 237
Ordering the following item:
        Stock Number:   B132-JK
        Quantity:       5
        Description:    Grass Trimmer Cord
        Unit Cost:      1.89
        Catalogue Page: 237
Stock Number:
Would you like to edit this file?: y
I'll start ex for you
"/tmp/1555: 1 line, 66 characters
:p
B132-JK 5       Grass Trimmer Cord      1.89    237     Tue May  8 07:44:57 EDT 1984
:q
Printing the order...Done
Choose one of the following
(Type word or first letter in either case)
        help        Help on this program
        order       Place an order
        receive     Print items ordered and received
        notin       Print items ordered but not received
        look        Locate a particular item received
        quit        Quit this program
```

536

```
: n
Would you like to see orders for a specific store? y
Which store? sears
Order from sears
        Stock Number:   B132-JK
        Quantity:       10
        Description:    Grass Trimmer Cord
        Unit Cost:      1.89
        Catalogue Page: 237
        Ordered on:     Mon May  7 09:06:05 EDT 1984
Continue?: y
Order from sears
        Stock Number:   B132-JK
        Quantity:       5
        Description:    Grass Trimmer Cord
        Unit Cost:      1.89
        Catalogue Page: 237
        Ordered on:     Mon May  8 07:44:57 EDT 1984
Continue?:
Choose one of the following
(Type word or first letter in either case)
        help          Help on this program
        order         Place an order
        receive       Print items ordered and received
        notin         Print items ordered but not received
        look          Locate a particular item received
        quit          Quit this program
: q
2%
```

Figure 9.L.7

EPILOGUE

The UNIX system is a system built on software tools that provides a substantial base for building software tools. It is not only an excellent software development system, but it is also an excellent model for building software based systems. The software tools philosophy – where a software tool solves a general problem and is so easy to use that others use it in preference to building their own – is the cornerstone of software development in the UNIX system. It has been used in developing the software tools distributed with the UNIX system.

A Programmer's Guide to UNIX System V describes and shows examples of many of the program development software tools available with the UNIX system. Among the software tools described are the Bourne Shell and the C Shell, the **ex** and **vi** text editors, the C compiler, the **ar** and **ranlib** archive utilities, and the **make** utility. These tools are the main tools used when writing programs with the UNIX system.

A Programmer's Guide to UNIX System V also describes and shows examples of the more important and useful subroutines and system calls available with the UNIX system. Among the subroutines described are the subroutines in the Standard I/O library, subroutines for manipulating strings, converting characters, manipulating time, managing storage, and accessing variables in the environment. Among the system calls described are system calls for manipulating the file structure and controlling processes. Subroutines and system calls make up most of the internals of the software tools built with the UNIX system.

Finally, **A Programmer's Guide to UNIX System V** describes and shows examples of the UNIX system software tools development philosophy. This philosophy is fundamentally important to building quality software tools using the program development tools and the subroutines and system calls available in the UNIX system. The software tools development philosophy explains how to combine subroutines and system calls to build software tools that are easy to use, consistent in invocation syntax with other software tools, and portable to other versions of the UNIX system.

As a programmer, you must be aware of the software revolution now happening in the software industry. Gone are the days when it was common practice to write programs that only the writer understood and that were insensitive to the user. In those days, portability was not even a topic of discussion.

Instead, today's software industry is more aware of the end user. This awareness will continue as personal computers decline in price, thereby allowing more people to purchase them. With the rapid introduction of new and more powerful CPUs and the ever increasing cost of software development, portability is often a requirement of a software system. Structured software design and development methodologies use the walkthrough technique as the way to encourage the writing of readable code.

The UNIX system caters to this software revolution by providing the software tools that let you concentrate on solving a problem instead of on the steps required to build the problem solution. **A Programmer's Guide to UNIX System V** was written to explain these tools and to explain a programming philosophy that defines how these tools should be combined to build your own software tools. The rest is up to you.

APPENDIX A
KEYWORDS

ABSOLUTE PATH NAME - a file name qualified from the root of the file structure, e.g. */usr/rogers/.login*.

ALIAS - a named reference to a given file, established with the **link**() system call and broken with the **unlink**() system call. Also a relation between a program name and a set of words made with the C Shell **alias** builtin function.

ALIASING - the process of making an alias.

APPLICATION - a program that helps you solve a problem that is not directly computer related.

ARGUMENTS - all words in a command line, except the command name and those words that are special to a shell.

BACKGROUND - a command no longer attached to a terminal.

BOOT BLOCK - a block at the beginning of a file system that usually contains a program that reads the kernel image file into the computer's memory and executes it.

CHANNEL - a connection between a process and a file that appears to the process as an unformatted stream of bytes.

CHILD PROCESS - the process created as the result of a successful **fork**() system call.

COMMAND - the unit of conversation used with the shell.

COMMAND FILE - a file containing a sequence of shell commands.

COMPILERS - programs that translate programming language source files into working programs.

CONTEXT - the mode in which the process is running, either user mode or kernel mode.

CONTEXT SWITCH - a change from user mode to kernel mode or a change from kernel mode to user mode.

CRITICAL REGION - a set of operations on a data structure shared by more than one process that must exclude one another in time.

CURRENT WORKING DIRECTORY - the name of the directory in the file system where a process is working. This directory is considered part of the process state.

DAEMON PROCESS - a process that services the requests of other processes. Some daemon processes are started when the UNIX system is started; others are started on demand.

DATA BLOCKS - the part of the file system that follows the i-list and contains the data for all files in the file system and all blocks not yet allocated to files.

DEPENDENCY - a relationship between files in a makefile.

DEVICE DRIVER - a part of the kernel that controls a device to do those jobs required by other parts of the kernel and by user processes.

DIRECTORY - a file containing a list of file names and i-numbers that is used by the kernel to locate files in the file structure.

DIRECTORY FILES - a file with a predefined format that ties the file structure together.

EFFECTIVE IDs - the pair of owner and group IDs that defines who owns a process for the duration of that process.

ENVIRONMENT - an array of strings made available by the **exec**() family of system calls.

EVENTS - previously executed commands.

FIFO FILE - a type of file that automatically provides synchronization between writer processes and a reader process, and guarantees that the number of bytes specified by a writing process' **write**() system call will be placed at the end of the fifo file and will not be mixed with the information written by another writing process.

FILE DESCRIPTOR - a small, non-negative integer that identifies the channel for I/O between a process and a file in the file structure.

FILE POINTER - a long integer maintained by the kernel and used to keep track of the next byte to read or write in a file.

FILE SYSTEM - a subtree in the file structure that can be grafted to the file structure tree and ungrafted as necessary.

FILTER - a software tool that reads its input data from the standard input file, writes its output data to the standard output file, and writes error messages to the standard error file.

I-LIST - an array of i-nodes that follows the super block in a file system.

I-NODES - a data structure that defines all the specifics of a file except its name and its contents.

I-NUMBER - a short integer that names an i-node in the i-list.

INIT PROCESS - the process that gives rise to all processes except the kernel.

KERNEL - the central operating system program that coordinates the execution of all user programs and controls all physical resources.

KERNEL MODE - an unrestricted context where only the kernel process runs.

KEYS - the long integer name of a message queue, a semaphore set, or a shared memory region.

LINK - an i-number that names an i-node.

LOGIN SHELL - the program named in the password file and started by **login** that lets you execute commands once you've logged in to the UNIX system.

MAKEFILE - the file that defines the relationships between files in a program and the method for transforming those files into an executable program.

MANIFEST CONSTANTS - constants whose uses are obvious from their names.

MESSAGE - a variable sized unit of information with no predefined format.

METACHARACTERS - special characters in words in a command line.

ORDINARY FILES - files of information in no particular format.

PIPELINE - the connection between two process.

PRIORITY A measure of the importance of a process which is typically used by the scheduler to select which process is to be allocated the CPU.

PROCESS - a running program.

PROCESS ID A positive integer that uniquely identifies each process.

PROCESS SWITCH - a change from one process executing in kernel mode to the kernel process, or from the kernel process to another process executing in kernel mode.

PROCESS TABLE - a table maintained by the kernel that describes all processes in the system at any point in time.

RANDOM ACCESS - a capability of the UNIX system that allows reading and writing anywhere in a file.

REAL IDs - the pair of owner and group IDs that defines who the real owner of a process.

REDIRECT - to change the source of standard input, or the destination of standard output or standard error in a command.

REDIRECTION OPERATORS - shell directives that redirect standard input, output, and error files in a command.

RELATIVE PATH NAME - a file name given in relation to the current working directory.

RETURN CODE - the value returned by a command.

RULES - the commands that define how to transform the dependency files into the target file in a makefile.

RUNTIME ENVIRONMENT - the basic interface to the operating system, which includes file handling and I/O.

SEMAPHORE - a data structure shared by several processes. It is used by those processes to synchronize their operations on a resource so that those operations do not interfere with each other.

SHARED MEMORY - main computer memory shared by one or more processes.

SHELL - a program that interprets commands and executes programs.

SHELL PROCEDURE - a command file.

SHELL VARIABLES - string-valued data structures used in a shell.

SIGNALS - software interrupts sent to a process when a pre-defined condition happens.

SOFTWARE TOOL - a program that solves a general problem and not a special case, and is so easy to use that people will use it instead of building their own tool.

SPECIAL FILE - a file that represents a physical device.

STANDARD COMMAND FORMAT - the recommended order for options, option arguments, and file names in a command.

STANDARD ERROR - the source of error output for a software tool, which is usually connected to the terminal's screen.

STANDARD INPUT - the source of input for a software tool, which is usually connected to the terminal's keyboard.

STANDARD OUTPUT - the source of output for a software tool, which is usually connected to the terminal's screen.

STRING - an array of characters that ends with a NULL character.

STRING VECTOR - a data structure consisting of a pointer to an array of pointers to character strings.

SUPER BLOCK - a block in a file system located directly after the boot block that describes the file system.

SWAPPING - the process of moving processes between main memory and a secondary storage device.

SYSTEM CALL - a subroutine call that causes the kernel to do some operation for a process.

SYSTEM CALL INTERFACE - the interface from a process to the kernel.

TEXT - the instructions that the CPU will execute once the process created from the program runs.

TOKENIZING - the process of removing all white space from a programming language file and logically grouping all remaining characters into tokens.

TOPOLOGICAL ORDER - the correct order for object files in an older style archive, as determined by **tsort** and **lorder**.

TRAP - a mechanism used to catch a signal in a Bourne Shell procedure.

USER MODE - a restricted context in which all processes except the kernel process run.

UTILITY - a program that does an auxiliary job, such as linking programs, converting files from one format to another, and editing files.

WHITE SPACE - any combination of spaces, tabs, and newline characters.

WORDS - the constituent parts of a command.

APPENDIX B
DEFINITIONS

1. Bourne Shell Functions – Page 47

function_name() *command*

function_name() {
command_list
}

2. Suggested C Compiler Command Line – Page 74

cc [*-option...*] *source_and_object_files* [*-llibrary...*]

3. Preprocessor include Statement – Page 75

#include *filename*

4. Preprocessor define Statement – Page 76

#define *identifier token-string*

5. Preprocessor undef Statement – Page 77

#undef *identifier*

6. Preprocessor if Statement – Page 78

#if *constant_expression*
source_code_true
#else
source_code_false
#endif

7. Preprocessor ifdef Statement – Page 78

#ifdef *identifier*
source_code_true
#else
source_code_false
#endif

8. Create Archive Command Line – Page 92

ar rv *archive_file object_files*

9. Extract From Archive Command Line – Page 93

ar xv *archive_file* [*object_file ...*]

10. Add To/Replace Archive Commands – Page 93

ar rv *archive_file object_files*

SCF	→	program [options] [separator] [files]
program	→	*2-9 lower case letters and digits*
options	→	-option white_space options*
option	→	noarg_options* arg_option | noarg_options+
noarg_option	→	letter
arg_option	→	letter white_space string
string	→	character+
letter	→	*lower or upper case letter*
character	→	*ASCII character*
white_space	→	*blanks and tabs*
separator	→	--
files	→	file white_space files
file	→	- | name
name	→	*any valid UNIX file name*

```
FILE *
fopen(file_name, option_string)
char *file_name;
char *option_string;


FILE *
freopen(file_name, option_string, stream)
char *file_name;
char *option_string;
FILE *stream;
```

```
int
fclose(stream)
FILE *stream;
```

```
int
fflush(stream)
FILE *stream;
```

17. Line Oriented I/O Subroutines – Page 154

```
char *
gets(string);
char *string;

int
puts(string);
char *string;

char *
fgets(string, count, stream);
char *string;
int   count;
FILE *stream;

int
fputs(string, stream);
char *string;
FILE *stream;
```

18. Character I/O Subroutines — Page 157

Function	Operation	Type	File	Syntax
getchar	READ	Macro	Standard input	int c; c = getchar();
putchar	WRITE	Macro	Standard output	char c; int x; x = putchar(c);
getc	READ	Macro	Any	FILE *stream; int c; c = getc(stream);
putc	WRITE	Macro	Any	FILE *stream; char c; int x; x = putc(c, stream);
fgetc	READ	Function	Any	FILE *stream; int c; c = fgetc(stream);
fputc	WRITE	Function	Any	FILE *stream; char c; int x; x = fputc(c, stream);

19. Object Oriented I/O Subroutines – Page 160

```
int
fread((char *)ptr, sizeof(type), nitems, stream)
type ptr;
int nitems;
FILE *stream;
```

```
int
fwrite((char *)ptr, sizeof(type), nitems, stream)
type ptr;
int nitems;
FILE *stream;
```

20. File Status Subroutines – Page 162

```
int
feof(stream)
FILE  *stream;
```

```
int
ferror(stream)
FILE *stream;
```

21. The printf Subroutine Family – Page 165

```
int
printf(format [ , arg ] ... );
char *format;
```

```
int
fprintf(stream, format [ , arg ] ... );
FILE *stream;
char *format;
```

```
int
sprintf(s, format [ , arg ] ... );
char *s, *format;
```

22. Field Width and Precision – Page 170

%[flags][field__width][.precision][l]format__specifier

23. The scanf Subroutine Family – Page 175

```
int
scanf(format [ , pointer ] ... );
char *format;


int
fscanf(stream, format [ , pointer ] ... )
FILE *stream;
char *format;


int
sscanf(s, format [ , pointer ] ... )
char *s, *format;
```

24. Direct Access Subroutines – Page 182

```
int
fseek(stream, offset, mode)
FILE *stream;
long offset;
int mode;


long
ftell(stream)
FILE *stream;


rewind(stream)
FILE *stream;
```

25. The system Subroutine – Page 188

```
int
system(command)
char *command;
```

26. The Pipe Subroutines – Page 191

```
FILE *
popen(command, operation);
char *command, *operation;


int
pclose(stream);
FILE *stream;
```

27. C Language Character String – Page 194

```
char    string[length];
```

28. String Manipulation Subroutines – Page 195

SUBROUTINE	DESCRIPTION
char * strcpy(*string1*, *string2*) char *string1*, *string2*;	Copies *string2*, including the NULL terminator, to the area in memory pointed to by *string1* and returns the value of *string1*.
int strcmp(*string1*, *string2*) char *string1*, *string2*;	Compares *string1* and *string2* and returns less than zero, zero, or greater than zero if *string1* is lexicographically less than, equal to, or greater than *string2*.
char * strcat(*string1*, *string2*) char *string1*, *string2*;	Adds a copy of *string2* onto the end of *string1* and returns the value of *string1*.
int strlen(*string*) char *string*;	Returns the length of *string* excluding the NULL terminator.
char * strchr(*string*, *character*) char *string*, *character*;	Returns a pointer to the first occurrence of *character* in *string*, or NULL if *character* does not appear in *string*.
char * strrchr(*string*, *character*) char *string*, *character*;	Returns a pointer to the last occurrence of *character* in *string*, or NULL if *character* does not appear in *string*.
char * strncpy(*string1*, *string2*, *n*) char *string1*, *string2*; int *n*; strncmp(*string1*, *string2*, *n*) char *string1*, *string2*; int *n*; char * strncat(*string1*, *string2*, *n*) char *string1*, *string2*; int *n*;	These subroutines all use a third argument, *n*, that defines the size of the area in memory to be copied, compared, or added onto.
char * strpbrk(*string1* *string2*) char *string1*, *string2*;	Returns a pointer to the first occurrence of any character in *string2* in *string1*, or NULL if there are no characters from *string2* in *string1*.

29. Memory Manipulation Subroutines – Page 198

SUBROUTINE	DESCRIPTION
char * memcpy(*mem1*, *mem2*, *n*) char *mem1, *mem2; int *n*;	Copies *n* characters from the area in memory pointed to by *mem2* to the area in memory pointed to by *mem1* and returns the value of *mem1*.
char * memccpy(*mem1*, *mem2*, *c*, *n*) char *mem1, *mem2; int *c*, *n*;	Copies characters from the area in memory pointed to by *mem2* to the area in memory pointed to by *mem1* and returns the value of *mem1*. The copy operation stops when either *n* characters have been copied or the *c* character has been copied.
int memcmp(*mem1*, *mem2*, *n*) char *mem1, *mem2; int *n*;	Compares the first *n* characters of *mem1* and *mem2* and returns less than zero, zero, or greater than zero if *mem1* is lexicographically less than, equal to, or greater than *mem2*.
char * memchr(*mem*, *character*, *n*) char *mem; int *character*, *n*;	Returns a pointer to the first occurrence of *character* in the first *n* characters of *mem*, or NULL if *character* does not appear in *mem*.
char * memset(*mem*, *c*, *n*) char *mem; int *c*, *n*;	Sets the first *n* characters in the area pointed to by *mem* to the character *c* and returns the value of *mem*.

30. Character Classification and Conversion Subroutines – Page 199

MACRO	OPERATION
isalnum(c)	returns true if c is an upper or lower case letter or a digit
isalpha(c)	returns true if c is an upper or lower case letter
isascii(c)	returns true if c is in the range from 0 to decimal 127 (octal 177)
iscntrl(c)	returns true if c is in the range 0 from to decimal 31 (octal 37) or is 127 (octal 177)
isdigit(c)	returns true if c is a digit
isxdigit(c)	returns true if c is a decimal digit or a hexadecimal digit in the range from 0 to 9, A to F, or a to f
islower(c)	returns true if c is a lower case letter
isupper(c)	returns true if c is an upper case letter
isprint(c)	returns true if c is an ASCII character but is not a control character
ispunct(c)	returns true if c is an ASCII character but is not a control character nor an alphanumeric character
isspace(c)	returns true if c is a horizontal or tab, a linefeed, a formfeed, a carriage return, or a space
tolower(c)	returns the lower case equivalent of c, where c is an upper case letter
toupper(c)	returns the upper case equivalent of c, where c is a lower case letter

31. Time Subroutines – Page 203

SUBROUTINE	DESCRIPTION
char * ctime(*time*) long *time*;	Converts its argument into a 26-character string, and returns a pointer to that string.
struct tm * localtime(*time*) long *time*;	Converts its argument to local time and then breaks that value into seconds, minutes, hours, day of the month, month of the year, day of the week, day of the year, and a logical value that shows if daylight savings time is in effect. These values are stored in a structure of type tm as defined in */usr/include/tm.h.* **localtime**() returns a pointer to this structure.
struct tm * gmtime(*time*) long *time*;	Breaks its time argument, assumed to be in Greenwich Mean Time, into seconds, minutes, hours, day of the month, month of the year, day of the week, day of the year, and a logical value that shows if daylight savings time is in effect. These values are also stored in a structure of type tm and **gmtime**() returns a pointer to this structure.
char * asctime(*tm*) struct tm *tm*;	Converts its argument, assumed to be from either **localtime**() or **gmtime**(), into a 26-character string and returns a pointer to that string.
extern long timezone;	timezone contains the difference in seconds between Greenwich Mean Time and local time.
extern int daylight;	daylight contains non-zero if daylight savings time is in effect, according to the U.S.A. conventions.
extern char *tzname[2]; void tzset()	The environment variable TZ describes the time zone according to the format XXXYZZZ, where XXX is the standard local time zone abbreviation (e.g. EST), Y is the difference in hours from Greenwich Mean Time, and ZZZ is the dalight savings local time zone abbreviation (e.g. EDT). The **tzset**() subroutine extracts the value of TZ from the environment and sets tzname[0] to the local time zone abbrevation and tzname[1] to the daylight savings local time zone abbrevation.

32. Memory Management Subroutines – Page 206

```
char *
malloc(area__size)
unsigned area__size;

char *
calloc(num__elements, element__size)
unsigned num__elements, element__size;

char *
realloc(area__pointer, new__size)
char *area__pointer;
unsigned new__size;

free(area__pointer)
char *area__pointer;
```

33. The getenv Subroutine – Page 212

```
char *
getenv(name)
char *name;
```

34. The perror Subroutine – Page 219

```
void
perror(s)
char *s;
```

35. The creat System Call – Page 222

```
int
creat(file__name, mode)
char *file__name;
int mode;
```

36. The open System Call – Page 223

```
#include <fcntl.h>

int
open(file__name, option__flags [ , mode ])
char *file__name;
int option__flags, mode;
```

37. The close System Call – Page 224

```
int
close(file__descriptor)
int file__descriptor;
```

43. The stat and fstat System Calls – Page 245

```
#include        <sys/types.h>
#include        <sys/stat.h>

int
stat(file__name, stat__buf)
char *file__name;
struct stat *stat__buf;

int
fstat(file__descriptor, stat__buf)
int file__descriptor;
struct stat *stat__buf;
```

44. The access System Call – Page 251

```
int
access(file__name, access__mode)
char *file__name;
int access__mode;
```

45. The chmod System Call – Page 254

```
int
chmod(file__name, mode)
char *file__name;
int mode;
```

46. The chown System Call – Page 256

```
int
chown(file__name, owner, group)
char *file__name;
int owner, group;
```

47. The umask System Call – Page 259

```
int
umask(cmask)
int cmask;
```

48. The ioctl System Call – Page 261

```
#include        <termio.h>

int
ioctl(file__descriptor, request, arg__pointer)
int file__descriptor;
int request;
struct termio *arg__pointer;
```

49. The exec Family System Calls – Page 265

```
int
execl(file__name, arg0 [ , arg1, ..., argn ] , 0)
char *file__name, *arg0, *arg1, ..., *argn;
```

```
int
execv(file__name, argv)
char *file__name, *argv[];
```

```
int
execle(file__name, arg0 [ , arg1, ..., argn ] , 0, envp)
char *file__name, *arg0, *arg1, ..., *argn, *envp[];
```

```
int
execve(file__name, argv, envp)
char *file__name, *argv[], *envp[];
```

```
int
execlp(file__name, arg0 [ , arg1, ..., argn ] , 0)
char *file__name, *arg0, *arg1, ..., *argn;
```

```
int
execvp(file__name, argv)
char *file__name, *argv[];
```

50. The getuid, geteuid, getgid, getegid System Calls – Page 268

```
int
getuid()
```

```
int
geteuid()
```

```
int
getgid()
```

```
int
getegid()
```

51. The fork System Call – Page 270

```
int
fork()
```

52. The getpid **and** getppid **System Calls – Page 272**
> int
> getpid()
>
> int
> getppid()

53. The wait **System Call – Page 272**
> int
> wait(*status*)
> int *status*;

54. The exit **System Call – Page 274**
> void
> exit(*status*);
> int *status*;

55. The signal **System Call – Page 277**

> int (*
> signal(*signal__name, function*))
> int *signal__name*;
> int (**function*)();

56. The kill **System Call – Page 283**
> int
> kill(*process__id, signal__name*)
> int *process__id, signal__name*;

57. The alarm **System Call – Page 286**
> unsigned
> alarm(*seconds*)
> unsigned *seconds*;

58. The setjmp **and** longjmp **Subroutines – Page 289**
> #include   <setjmp.h>
>
> int
> setjmp(*state*)
> jmp__buf *state*;
>
> void
> longjmp(*state, value*)
> jmp__buf *state*;
> int   *value*;

59. The chdir **System Call – Page 291**

```
int
chdir(directory__name)
char *directory__name;
```

60. The pipe **System Call – Page 295**

```
int
pipe(file__descriptors)
int file__descriptors[2];
```

61. The msgget **System Call – Page 301**

```
#include   <sys/types.h>
#include   <sys/ipc.h>
#include   <sys/msg.h>


int
msgget(key, flag)
key__t key;
int   flag;
```

62. The msgsnd **and** msgrcv **System Calls – Page 307**

```
#include   <sys/types.h>
#include   <sys/ipc.h>
#include   <sys/msg.h>


int
msgsnd(id, message, size, flag)
int id, size, flag;
struct msgbuf *message;


int
msgrcv(id, message, size, type, flag)
int id, size, flag;
long type;
struct msgbuf *message;
```

63. The msgctl **System Call – Page 314**

```
#include   <sys/types.h>
#include   <sys/ipc.h>
#include   <sys/msg.h>


int
msgctl(id, command, buffer)
int id, command;
struct msqid__ds *buffer;
```

64. The semget System Call – Page 318

```
#include    <sys/types.h>
#include    <sys/ipc.h>
#include    <sys/sem.h>


int
semget(key, number, flag)
key_t key;
int number, flag;
```

65. The semop System Call – Page 319

```
#include    <sys/types.h>
#include    <sys/ipc.h>
#include    <sys/sem.h>


int
semop(id, operations, number)
int id;
struct sembuf (*operations)[];
int number;
```

66. The shmget System Call – Page 337

```
#include    <sys/types.h>
#include    <sys/ipc.h>
#include    <sys/shm.h>


int
shmget(key, size, flag)
key_t key;
int size, flag;
```

67. The shmat and shmdt System Calls – Page 338

```
#include    <sys/types.h>
#include    <sys/ipc.h>
#include    <sys/shm.h>


char *
shmat(id, at_address, flag)
int id;
char *at_address;
int flag;


int
shmdt(dt_address)
char *dt_address;
```

74. Single Line Bourne Shell while **Statement – Page 385**

while *condition*; do *command__1; command__2; ...;* done

75. The Bourne Shell for **Statement – Page 385**

for *name* [in *word* ...]
do
       commands
done

76. Single Line Bourne Shell for **Statement – Page 386**

for *name* [in *word* ...]; do *command; command; ...;* done

77. The Bourne Shell case **Statement – Page 391**

case *word* in
pattern__1)
      commands__1
      ;;
pattern__2)
      commands__2
      ;;

    .
    .
    .

esac

78. The Bourne Shell trap **Command – Page 404**

trap *commands signals*

79. C Shell Expression Syntax – Page 474

@ *name* = *expr*

@ *name[index]* = *expr*

80. Basic C Shell if **Statement - Version 1 – Page 482**

if (*expr*) *command*

81. Basic C Shell if **Statement - Version 2 – Page 483**

if (*expr*) then
      commands
endif

82. Advanced C Shell if **Statement – Page 483**

if (*expr*) then
      commands__1
else
      commands__2
endif

83. Complete C Shell if Statement – Page 483

```
if (expr__1) then
        commands__1
else if (expr__2) then
        commands__2
else if (expr__3) then
        commands__3
        .
        .
        .

else
        commands__n
endif
```

84. The C Shell while Statement – Page 489

```
while (expr)
        commands
end
```

85. The C Shell foreach Statement – Page 493

```
foreach name (wordlist)
        commands
end
```

86. The C Shell switch Statement – Page 497

```
switch (string)
case pattern__1:
        commands__1
        breaksw
case pattern__2:
        commands__2
        breaksw
        .
        .
        .

default:
        commands__default
        breaksw
endsw
```

INDEX